BURIED

ALIVE

BURIED
ALIVE

The Startling Truth about Neanderthal Man

Jack Cuozzo

Master Books

First printing: November 1998
Second printing: August 1999
Third printing: October 1999

ISBN: 0-89051-238-8
Library of Congress Number: 98-66310

Cover by Janell Robertson.

All Scripture verses are from the New American Standard Bible unless otherwise noted.

Cover photo and figure 13 are reprinted from Hundret Jahre Neanderthaler/ Neanderthal Centenary, G.H.R. Von Koenigswald, ed., Drukkerij en Uitgerversmaatschappij v/h Kernink en Zoon, N.V., Utrech, Netherlands, 1958, by permission of the Wenner-Gren Foundation for Anthropological Research, Inc., New York, NY.

Back cover photo: Inside La Chapelle-aux-Saints' burial cave, La Chapelle, France.

Printed in the United States of America.

Please visit our website for other great titles:
www.masterbooks.net

To my wife, Diane

Acknowledgments

I would like to thank the following museums for the use of their ancient craniofacial remains and other artifacts in my research: Musée de l'Homme, Paris, France; Museum für Vor-und Frühgeschichte, Berlin, Germany; Institut de Paléontologie University of Liège, Liège, Belgium; British Museum, London, England; Israel Department of Antiquities and Museums, Jerusalem, Israel; Saint Germain-en-Laye Musée des Antiquitiés Nationales, Paris, France; Peabody Museum, Harvard University, Cambridge, MA; Smithsonian Institution, Washington, DC; The Armed Forces Institute of Pathology, Walter Reed Hospital, Washington, DC.

I would also like to thank the following paleoanthropologists for the use of the precious remains entrusted to their care and/or for the addition of valuable information to my research: Dr. Yves Coppens, Dr. Chris Stringer, Dr. Robert Kruszynski, Dr. Theya Molleson, Dr. Ubaghs, Dr. Joseph Zias, Dr. W. Menghin, Dr. David Pilbeam, Dr. P. Sledzik, Dr. Alison Wilcox, the late Dr. J. Lawrence Angel, Dr. D.H. Ubelaker, and Dr. Alan Walker. I would like to thank Dr. Rolf Behrents for his valuable help in this project.

I would like to thank my wife, Diane, for her love and care for me and our family during this long and difficult project.

I would like to thank the following people for their support in various ways at different times throughout the years of our research. There has been hope but also some periods of discouragement in the past 20 years. It was the amazing grace of God provided so often through the assistance and sometimes the prayers of these mentioned below that buoyed us up. For that I am very grateful.

Theresa Cuozzo and the late Dr. P.J. Cuozzo, my mother and father; the late Margaret and Frank Dostalek, my wife's mother and father; Dr. John Cuozzo Jr. and Dr. Lilia Cuozzo; Dr. Brian and Margie Garner; Francis Cuozzo; Lt. Daniel and Alison Cuozzo; Joshua Cuozzo and the future Christine Cuozzo; Dr. Gary and Peggy Cuozzo; Dr. John and Patricia McCue;, Frank Dostalek; John Dostalek; Joe Dostalek; Rose Cuozzo; Dr. Patrick Cuozzo; Dr. Michael Scagnelli; Dave and Peggy D'Amico; Roberta Fine; the late Rev. Robert Fine; the late Dr. Francis Schaeffer; the late Dr. Wilton M. Krogman; Dr. Wayne and Betty Frair; Dean Kevin Rhodes; Dr. Don and Betty Duffy; Dr. Henry Morris; Dr. John Morris; Dr.

Duane Gish; Bob Walsh; Dr. Andrew Snelling; Gordon Franz; Coach Ron Brown; Udo Middleman; Ken Swain; Joseph Maffongelli Jr., Esq.; Dr. George Kuryllo; Dr. Maria Tammi; Dr. Edward Baker; Dr. Pearly Hayes; Dr. Steve and Dr. Leila Koepp; Dr. Austin Robbins; Dr. James Maguire; Dr. Brad and Marilyn Mellon; Dr. Norm and Dorothy Gunn; the late Dr. Curt Hester; the late Dr. J. Allister Weir; Dr. Thomas Kotch; Dr. Don Moeller; Mary Deatheridge; Frank DeMiro; Vito Locasio; Russ Bixler; Dr. Lloyd Zbar; Dr. Roger Nettune; Dr. Jack Altomonte; Dr. David Solomon; Dr. Ed Gold; Dr. Pier Mancusi-Ungaro; William Curtis; James Sundquist; Dr. Robert Foster; Rev. Gerald Cleffi; Mark Emma; Billy Nelson; Wight Martindale; Tom Basile; Bill Williams; Jamie Hutzel; Elaine Pasquale; Dominick and Marie D'Amico; Israel and Lilia Gonzalez; Will and Janean Garner; Robert Dilworth, Esq., and Faith Dilworth; Richard and Marie Amoroso; Otis Birdsong; Buck Williams; Mike O'Koren; Darryl Dawkins; Walt Singletary; Jeff Rogers; the late Rev. Douglas Gleeson; Diane Gleeson; Rev. Dewey Friedel; Rev. Bruce Koczman; Four Winds Fellowship; Jim Davies ; Rev. Ed Banghart; Montclair Community Church; the Newall's prayer group; the "Called Aside" Women's Group; Gwen Robinson; Rev. Kyle Atkins; Rev. Jim Rose; Dr. Robert and Lynn Hultquist; George and Mary Van Dyke; the late Rev. J. O'Hara; the late Michael Meola; and Rod Dixon.

For their very special help with the multitude of reference articles so crucial to the book, I would like to thank the Mountainside Hospital librarians, Patricia Regenberg and Valarie Manuel. They filled all my requests for information when I'm sure they had many other duties to accomplish.

I am grateful to Rocky Mountain Data Systems of Calabasas, California, for their analysis of my cephalometric radiographs. I appreciated the care of my x-ray machine donated by the General Electric Corporation, now Gendex, of Des Plaines, Illinois. Also, I am indebted to the Wehmer Corporation of Addison, Illinois, for the x-ray cassettes and x-ray film.

I would also like to thank Jim Fletcher, my editor, for the skill and care given this book. I would also like to thank Dianna Fletcher, Tim Smith, Judy Lewis, and Janell Robertson for their superior work on this project. A special thanks to my publisher, Tim Dudley, for having confidence in me and my research so that this material is no longer "Buried Alive."

CONTENTS

INTRODUCTION

As a young man and a product of two university graduate educational programs and one on an undergraduate level, I was completely convinced that the Bible could not be taken as a scientific or historically accurate book. The early chapters of Genesis, therefore, were not to be taken seriously as the explanation for the true origin of mankind. As a matter of fact, in college I thought anyone who believed that Adam and Eve were real people who spoke to a snake were definitely not biology majors and probably belonged to a "flat earth society" or worse. This belief was common among most of my university friends.

As a result of this widespread attitude in our higher institutions of learning, we have raised a generation in America who do not believe the Bible speaks the truth about anything. Therefore, what may be beautiful writing, poetry, and exciting stories are just that — religious tales, myths, and allegory, but certainly not truth. The marginilization of the Bible is one of the tragic stories of our time.

If we want truth, we are told, we must look to science. Modern science has the answers and the great museums of the world hold the keys to our past. In those great temples of learning, all the prehistoric "relatives" of mankind have been assembled for our education and supposed edification. Large multi-national corporations have often sponsored expensive high-tech, multi-media exhibits to pursue these ends in a dramatic fashion. The effects of this collaboration have been enormous.

Millions of children visit these citadels each year on school field trips to view their animal relatives. They are immersed in a sea of naturalism while being indoctrinated in the official position of the establishment. But is this official position correct? Are there opposing points of view? And the sixty-four thousand dollar question is: Do the museums contain any fossils, artifacts, or information that would contradict the doctrine of evolution?

I invite you to take a trip with me through the past by exploring the great museums of the world in the storage rooms and laboratories reserved only for access to scientists. I am not going to take you through the exhibit halls where all the tourists go, but into the dark recesses of the paleontological world where you would not be allowed. You are going to see things that you never thought existed, and look at skulls and jaws through the eyes of an orthodontist. All the bones you will see are the actual ones. This is original work done on the real fossils. You will also visit real caves that were frequented by ancient man.

There are scientific sections in this book necessary for those interested in the facts of the research, but everything is wrapped up in the story of our personal family adventure, because we did everything as a team. My research assistants were my children, all of whom are now adults.

Another facet of this book is the reaction of the scientific world to my findings. I think that you may be incredulous at first by the perceived breach of security and the threat that a questioning orthodontist and his family posed to such gigantic institutions. It was a shock to us all. I did not lie to anyone at any time. I merely stated that I was an orthodontist who was interested in the growth and development of early man, and particularly in the teeth and the jaws. Some of the scientists were open-minded and some were not. I am certainly not condemning all paleoanthropologists. To be perfectly candid, I did not expect to find what I did. However, I had no idea that the specimens I examined had not been allowed to display the truth within themselves.

The process of writing this book took close to five years. It is my hope that it will reach many people in all walks of life. I think perhaps that even parts of it could be used in academic settings. As the real-life story unfolds, it will become evident that the evolutionists were right about one thing, and that is "change." All living forms are changing. Their only problem is that they had the direction wrong. The theme that flows throughout this entire book and shares the spotlight with that of burying the truth is "devolution." It is a process by which all of life is degenerating — just as the Bible describes.

Therefore, what began as a curiosity about the past ends with a secure belief about the future. Come along with us as we explore the world of ancient men, the Neanderthals. Let us take a close look at our ancestors, whose real history has for so long, been buried alive.

Part 1
A Search for Truth

Chapter 1

The Chase

It was about 10 p.m. on August 18, a warm, dark Saturday night in 1979. We slammed the van doors behind us, running full speed to the entrance of the basement hallway in an apartment complex in Les Ulis, outside of Paris. This 30 to 40-foot hallway had energy-saver light switches on one end and a tiny elevator at the far end. We flew down the hallway like hunted foxes and squeezed into the tiny elevator meant only to carry a few people.

We were two adults and five children. The lights that I switched on as we came in blinked out a few seconds before the elevator door creaked shut. It seemed like forever before it finally closed. We were dripping with anxious sweat from the run. This was the culmination of about an hour-long high-speed car chase through the streets of Paris and out into the suburbs. As the elevator jerked and strained upward towards the floor of our borrowed apartment, I held our three year old in my arms. My wife and I just looked at each other, speechless for a moment, as the events of the last 48 hours gelled in our minds.

Never did it occur to us while we were making plans for this trip over the past six months that anything like this might happen. Who would have guessed that my research would produce such a violent reaction. We had been followed by at least one, and sometimes two, small sports cars. At first the pursuit was slow and secretive but as events escalated during the last five or six hours, they became more visible and threatening.

We had a slow, white Volkswagen van that obviously stood out from the rest of the traffic. Our adversaries had a couple of fast sport cars; one dark blue, one yellow. In the pursuit from the restaurant, the yellow one had sideswiped a parked car and failed to stop after the collision on a one-way street. That's when I realized they were dead serious about this chasing business. We were both going the wrong way. I had headed down that street in the wrong direction hoping to lose them at the next corner. My hope was that a car would come into that street going in the proper direction after I exited and thereby get between us. It happened just that way and we gained a slight advantage. I made a dash for the Arc of Triumph, the memorial that the American troops marched through after liberating Paris from the Nazis. There was the usual traffic jam around the huge monument as cars and other vehicles swirled around the circle. We became enmeshed in the bunch and thought for a moment we had shaken them. The kids thought this was a great adventure and were hanging over the seats looking out the back window. John, our oldest, was 13. He had helped me conduct the research in the museum. Margie, our daughter and Mom's helper, was 11 and a bit tearful at this point. Frank, 10, and Daniel, 8, thought this was just like "the movies." Joshua, though only 3, still remembers this harrowing event. It made an indelible impression on all of us.

From the Arc, I floored the gas pedal down along a large tree-lined boulevard, hoping to be stopped by a police car. We went through all the red lights but still did not attract a single gendarme. At the edge of Paris we came to a large wooded park where I jumped a curb, making sure there were no pedestrians in sight, and drove headlong into the bushes and trees. I was hoping and praying that I wouldn't smack into a tree or put a large branch through the windshield. After driving into this camouflage for about 50 or 75 feet, I shut off the engine. We all sat in enforced silence for about 15 minutes breathing a temporary sigh of relief. We didn't think we could be seen from the road that twisted through the park. We were counting on them just whizzing by while we laid low in our hiding place. When we thought we were safe, I backed out of the woods with twigs and leaves stuck in various places. Leaving a trail of dirt, sticks and foliage in the road with some attached leaves still flapping in the wind, we made a beeline for the highway to Les Ulis. To my horror, as I glanced at the fuel gauge, I saw the needle on empty. How could we stop for gas now? There didn't seem to be any choice. Either get gas or get stuck, and then maybe a foot race along the highway with five children, and me carrying one of them.

There was no sign of them anywhere when we pulled into the highway gas station. In what seemed like the longest time in history it ever took to fill a quarter of a tank of gas, seven pairs of eyes scanned the terrain for any kind of sports car. The racing car teams at Indy had nothing on us. Still nothing in sight, as we sped away into the night with about ten more miles until home. After only a few miles, one of the boys said with a terrified voice that he spotted them and I floored it again. Only the Lord knows how we made it this time. I purposefully got off the highway a few exits early and zigzagged down streets until we found our way back to the apartment. Now we're at the place where you began to read about this adventure, as we jumped out of the van and ran into the hallway.

As the elevator door slid open with a cranking noise, we were only a few steps from the apartment. It had a double-door entrance. My hands shook as I opened the first door, which had a border of wood with a full-length glass pane in the center. I didn't think that this would be much of an obstacle for them, but there also was another, stronger door. There was a small foyer between the two doors. In it we had stored our valuable research x-ray machine, before and after our work at the Musée de l'Homme in Paris. There was only one other x-ray machine in the world like it. This one had been loaned to me by a doctor from a midwestern university. We quickly passed through the foyer and slammed the second door behind us. The second door, thankfully, was made of solid wood.

After closing the second door behind us and making sure it was double-locked, we felt *somewhat* relieved, because we had no idea what their next move would be. "Quickly," I said, "get every piece of furniture that can be moved and put it up against this door, in case they try to force their way in." We placed everything we could up against that door. There was a big bureau, backed up by a couch and some large living room chairs and a few other things I can't quite remember. It was a formidable barricade. Years later, while seeing the Broadway production of "Les Miserables," I was reminded of this humble barricade in our own French revolution of 1979.

What kind of revolt had I led that provoked this situation? I had been to France a number of times before I was married, serving aboard the USS *Enterprise* (CVAN) 65. I was a U.S. Navy dental officer on this huge aircraft carrier and had participated in two Mediterranean cruises in 18 months. Whenever our crew of 4,000-plus men would descend upon a coastal city there would be justifiable anxiety by the townspeople and no lack of trouble. However, our MPs usually took charge of each brawl or escapade by drunken sailors and eventually peace was restored. But this was different. We were being pursued by some sort of French authority, almost like a CIA or FBI type of operation. What were they after? What kind of a threat could an American family pose to the French national interests?

Chapter 2

The Catalyst

It all began when I started to question the evolutionary record of fossils in 1976.[1] However, in practical terms the catalyst for this first trip to France was my association with my good friend and mentor, the late Wilton M. Krogman, Ph.D. He was my anthropology professor at the University of Pennsylvania during the time I attended dental school in the early sixties. I met up with him again in the seventies in Amish country at the Lancaster Cleft Palate Clinic on Lime Street in Lancaster, Pennsylvania. He and I developed a close relationship through correspondence and personal conversations over the years. I took several of his courses at the clinic, one of which was entitled "Forensic Medicine." This course was concerned with identification of dead persons by means of teeth and bones and their legal aspects.

Dr. Krogman had identified the remains of Adolf Hitler and his consort, Eva Braun, in their bunker in Berlin, where they were entombed in rubble by the allied bombardment at the end of WW II . All that was left were bones and teeth. The bodies had been burned either intentionally or by explosive fire. He showed us the lantern slides that he had made of the dental remains and radiographs of the fuhrer.[2] Our soldiers had found the radiographs.

Lantern slides were made of glass and were much larger than modern day Kodachrome slides. The film was sandwiched between two glass pieces and glued together somehow. The old projectors used to project these images had a sliding carriage which would only take one slide on either side of the projector at a time.

Most of the dictator's vital data were recorded by Dr. Krogman using this type of visual record. After a forensic identification had been made from photographs and the dental records, and it had been verified that this was the fuhrer, Dr. Krogman then left for the evening, as he recalled to me. When he returned the next morning, he found that Adolf Hitler's remains were gone. American soldiers who stood watch over the burnt bodies that night told him of a high-ranking

Russian officer who barged in with some Russian soldiers and just picked up Hitler's skeletal parts and departed. Apparently it was well-marked and probably in some sort of a container. He told me over lunch one day in a Lancaster restaurant that he believed the remains were sent to Russia, probably to prove to the Soviet strongman Stalin that Hitler was really dead. He said that he had tried to protest this thievery but the American authorities took no action.

Dr. Krogman and I had numerous discussions about human fossils, which had become a growing interest of mine. I saw him in May of 1979 at a children's growth course. He encouraged me to seek out the real fossils in the countries of origin and do firsthand research on these bones. He explained that most of the ancient human fossils in the USA are merely copies of the originals.[3] When I asked him how this seemingly impossible task could be accomplished, he volunteered to write a letter of introduction to a fellow anthropologist, a human paleontologist, in France. He wrote that letter on June 18, 1979, and sent a copy to me. It was addressed to Professor Doctor Denise Ferembach at the Centre Nationale de la Recherche Scientifique, Ecole Pratique des Hautes Etudes, Paris, France. The following are excerpts from that letter:

"In August a good friend of mine will visit Paris and would like to study the original Neanderthal skeletal material housed in several Museums of Paris. His name and address follow:" Then he gave Dr. Ferembach my address. He followed by saying, " Since my retirement from the University of Pennsylvania in 1971, I have, as it were, been removed from the mainstream of Physical Anthropology, and especially Human Paleontology. You are, in very truth, the one person I may turn to in this matter." Then he made this appeal on my behalf: "I think it would be a good idea for you and Dr. Cuozzo to correspond prior to his coming to Paris, so that his aims in coming may be made more explicit. I shall write for him a letter of introduction which he can present to you upon his arrival in Paris. (Please write him the specific address where he might contact you.)" He signed it:

Cordially yours,
Wilton Marion Krogman, Ph.D.

Weeks passed and I never heard one word from Professor Doctor Ferembach. There was total silence from France. As far as I can remember, she never wrote back to Dr. Krogman, either.

Chapter 3

Valuable Equipment and the Apartment

E very winter in the month of February, the annual meeting of the Chicago Dental Society takes place in downtown Chicago. My wife was raised in Countryside, Illinois, a suburb of Chicago, and her parents were still living there in the 1970s. We found it convenient to visit Grandma and Grandpa while I did some catching up on the latest developments in dentistry at the meeting.

It was in February of 1979 that I first met Dr. Brown[1] while wandering down an aisle of commercial exhibits at the Chicago Mid-Winter meeting. Dr. Brown was displaying portable dental equipment that could be used to treat patients in rural and inaccessible areas. My interest was heightened when I saw a small portable x-ray machine. I immediately thought of the possibility of obtaining a large x-ray machine similar to the one I had in my office for use in fossil research overseas. Dr. Brown told me that he had created just such a machine with the General Electric Corporation. In 1978 he had taken it into the jungles of South America to x-ray the heads of the natives.

It was an interesting experience since he had to give away a lot of glass bead necklaces and wrist bands to obtain their cooperation. He received some feather head pieces, darts, and a blow-gun in return. He explained this was a rough bunch. One false move and he could have had a blow dart in his back. Happily, he made it through that project to be able to be present at this dental convention in 1979, the year I wanted to go to France.

The beauty of this portable machine was that it would not only produce a powerful x-ray beam but an accurate image as well. There are two important points to consider when x-raying a living person's head or a fossil skull. The first is that a powerful beam is needed. The second is that you can't make any measurements from a radiograph if the head or skull is tilted or rotated in any way. Then the image would be distorted because of its position, and therefore not measurable. The mid-plane of the subject's head has to be at a right angle to the central beam of the x-ray to achieve this objective. He convinced me that his apparatus would hold any head or skull in this uniform fixed position and that it could be done any time, any place, as long as all the various parts were locked together in the proper manner. The big job was to be able to assemble the parts exactly in the proper position each time. This maneuver took quite a bit of practice. A large transformer was also needed to convert the powerful European 220 volt current to 110 volts for usage by the machine if taken to France. Two hundred and twenty volts would blow the guts right out of this beautiful apparatus. He explained that all the parts of the machine, except the transformer, could be safely stored in two large metal containers that had a combined weight of about 350 pounds. These could then be subjected to rigorous jolting and jostling around on any freight handler's dock and still be unharmed. The only other portable cephalometric unit that existed in the world at that time was created by Arne Bjork in the 1940s and it was in Sweden. Dr. Brown had this one, which was more modern. But would I be able to use it?[2]

After our long conversation in the aisle of the commercial exhibits, he seemed partially convinced about my purpose and asked that I send him a letter outlining my plans and goals. I did this as soon as I returned home. In his response to my request, he gave me permission to take the machine to France.

I flew to Chicago with my two oldest boys on July 17, 1979. We picked up the x-ray machine after a complete briefing on its use, shipped it back home via air freight, and flew back to Newark Airport the next day. A big piece of the research trip puzzle had fallen into place.

There was a slight problem that arose after we had left Dr. Brown that wouldn't leave my conscience. One of the things he showed us on the day of the demonstration was a number of big Red Cross emblems pasted on the sides of both boxes. He had told me that he put these large red and white seals on the boxes. I had asked him if he was associated with the Red Cross or whether it was really official Red Cross equipment. He said that he wasn't associated with the Red Cross, but this ploy helped to get the boxes across international borders easily. This labeling was used to facilitate the customs inspection in each country. If the boxes weren't labeled as such, one would need a document called an "ATA carnet." This document obviated the necessity of paying duty on the machine when entering or leaving a country. I didn't want to continue with this Red Cross charade because it seemed to be illegal.

Therefore, I purchased an ATA carnet from the U.S. Council of International Chamber of Commerce Inc. in New York City before we embarked for France. It involved a lot of procedures, red tape, and the purchase of a large bond equivalent to the machine cost. The carnet covered taxes if the equipment was sold in that particular foreign country. But it was all legal and the Red Cross stickers would have caused untold problems if we were caught.

With the equipment problem solved, we still didn't have a place to stay. Hotels were out of the question. Three weeks in France could be an astronomical expense. We were seven people and needed at least two hotel rooms. Most of all, if we couldn't cook for ourselves, eating out every day and night would literally "eat up" our budget.

In 1978 another amazing thing happened which some would call coincidence and some, like us, would call God's provision. One day, a lovely French family walked into my office.[3] They were seeking orthodontic treatment for their daughter. They were living temporarily in New Jersey and had been referred to me by a friend. During the course of treatment for this little girl, the family mentioned that they were only in the USA for a year or so on business and that they actually lived outside of Paris. Wheels started turning in my mind when I heard that, and especially when we started to make plans for our trip in 1979. It wasn't until May that I approached them on this subject. They believed that the best way to find an apartment for us was to have one of their relatives in Paris do some searching around. However, when July of 1979 arrived, not only had no word come from Dr. Ferembach but no apartment could be found for us either.

We went over to the French family's house one night near the end of July to discuss the distressing situation. We were going to depart on the 29th, which was getting close. After describing their fruitless search, we were shocked when they said that we could use their own empty apartment at no cost for three weeks and handed us the keys. Needless to say, we drove home that night very grateful for God's provision.

Chapter 4

The Vietnamese Connection to the Unholy of Unholies

My father had been a practicing dentist in Glen Ridge, New Jersey, for 47 years when he died in 1978. He had been a great influence on my life for which I am very grateful. He also had a big heart for people in trouble and turmoil. It was during the exodus of masses of boat people from Vietnam that he took on a whole family of refugees as patients and charged them no fee. They had found their way to New Jersey from the west coast and were struggling to make ends meet. Dad asked me to treat one of the little children who needed braces also for no fee, as a charity case. I agreed and in the years of 1977-79, we made a special acquaintance with the Bach Nguyen family. They invited our whole family to dinner at their apartment in June of 1979. We brought all the kids and were treated to a special Vietnamese meal. During dinner our conversation turned to the subject of our trip to France, whereupon Bach related a story about how he was separated from his aged mother and his sister in their escape from Vietnam. He told us that he and his wife and children were allowed to immigrate to the USA while his mother and sister could only go to France. He thought it would be a great thing for us to give them a call when we were in Paris since they lived nearby. He would write to them and let them know of our travel plans. We promised to do that and he gave me their telephone number. Later I gave him the telephone number of the apartment that we would be borrowing in Les Ulis to send to his sister.

Once in Paris and embarked upon this project, I found this was a hard promise to keep because of our tight schedule. We had a big problem with the machine the first time we tried to start it up, which will be described a bit later. However, one day while working in the laboratory my conscience started to bother me about my pledge to Bach. Also, I was more than a little concerned that my French wouldn't be good enough to converse with his relatives. Diane had no French in nursing school and only one of the children had touched this subject in school. I knew that the secretary in the lab office spoke English. So, I asked her to call Bach's sister for me and explain how busy we were, and that I would call her later in the week when things calmed down. She said that no one answered the first time she called, so I left the telephone number with her and went back to work.

Giving away this number to her, and eventually the museum people, was to prove to be a disastrous mistake. The secretary copied this number down for future reference and gave it back to me. To this day, I have no idea what I did with that piece of paper. It's not written in my little daily reminder book or in any of my folders. The significance of this telephone number is vital to an understanding of the events that led up to us barricading ourselves in the borrowed apartment.

I had been very careful not to reveal our place of residence to any of the museum people because of a general ominous feeling that I had when first setting foot in the museum. It seemed like we were entering a great temple of Baal worship similar to those described in the Old Testament. All these creatures from which we were supposed to have evolved were set up in display cases almost like idols to worship. If, in truth, they were our ancestors, then a certain amount of reverence appeared due them. Ancestor worship is not uncommon in many parts of the world today. Departed spirits and such are treated like gods.

It's not that I hadn't been in museums like this before in the USA. I had, but this was very different. It was a foreign country, there were real Neanderthal fossils, and we were about to penetrate the "inner sanctum" or "the unholy of unholies." The high priests of Baal worship, in this case, were the paleontologists. They were responsible for placing the animals on these pedestals. It was a temple of naturalism.

Somehow, Dr. Krogman seemed different to me. I had been able to share my faith with him on numerous occasions and he was open and responsive. He gave his heart to the Lord.[1] He sympathized with the goals of my research.

In the Musée de l'Homme, I was beginning to have very uneasy feelings about my present condition, especially when I found out that some of the actual Neanderthal fossils did not look like they did in the textbooks. I was continually seeking God's wisdom each step of the way. Some days we were really walking on eggs. My agreement with the museum authorities was to hand in one copy of each of my radiographs upon completion of my project. What if the radiographs clashed with the textbook descriptions of these fossils? I saw that some of them would and I was genuinely scared. All they had to identify and track us in France was Bach's sister's telephone number.

Chapter 5

The Prehistory Business

We had arrived in France at the Charles De Gaulle Airport on July 30, 1979. After settling into the apartment in Les Ulis, we discovered that there was no hot water in the complex due to basically unknown causes. Unknown, because the superintendent explained everything to me in rapid-fire French and all I caught was "five or six days." We wanted to see the prehistoric region of southern France, so we decided that this was the best time to visit the Perigord for five or six days.

Les Eyzies, in the ancient province of Perigord, is known as the "Capital of Prehistory" of France. This area is generally referred to as "the Dordogne" in honor of the Dordogne River valley which traverses its countryside. We had reservations at a hotel in the nearby city of Perigueux, but our focal point was Les Eyzies.

When we first drove into Perigueux on the night of August 2 we passed a large castle on the main road between Angoulême and Perigueux, Le Chateau Saint-Vincent. Within a short time we realized that we had made reservations at what turned out to be a creaky old fire-trap of a hotel in Perigueux. Quickly backing out the front door, we excused ourselves and backtracked to the castle. It was only a guess whether there would be any vacancies in the ancient edifice. To our surprise there were two rooms available. We quickly settled in for the night after carrying our bags up a dimly lit, spiral, stone staircase. Staying in this 14th century medieval structure was a memorable experience for my whole family. This was recorded in my son John's diary the next morning with these words: "Friday — August 3 — This morning I woke up in a castle!"

Just a short drive from Perigueux, high on a limestone cliff above the town of Les Eyzies and the Vézère River, stands a statue of a prehistoric man. He is a rather strongly built, brutish character, supposedly the typical stone age man. A museum stands off to the side of this statue and is built into the side of an even higher cliff. This is the National Museum of Prehistory in the Castle of Tayac. The celebrated Cro-Magnon[1] man cave is nearby and within a short drive are some of the most famous Neanderthal sites in the world. Fossils such as Le Moustier in Le Moustier, Peyzac, La Ferrassie in Savignac du Bugue, and Pech de l'Azé in Carsac have put this area on the map of paleoanthropology.[2] Decorated caves and rock shelters are major tourist attractions which draw thousands of visitors each year.[3] The focus of all these localities seemed to concentrate on one big theme: the Evolution of Man. It became increasingly evident that a major part of the French tourist industry is firmly cemented into Evolution with a capital *E*.

People are curious about where they came from. They are seeking answers to the deep feelings within them. Evolution provides an answer, both in history and science. It is that men and women are nothing more than animals, too. This is the source of all men's problems; an animal heritage. Humanistic answers are very popular in modern Europe, where great cathedrals are mere tourist attractions themselves. The religion of the new age is evolution. Therefore, many francs are made in the prehistory business.

Everywhere we went the parking spaces in Les Eyzies were filled with cars, and the hotels and restaurants were overflowing with people. From Perigueux, the gate-way to the Perigord, to the many small towns in the surrounding countryside, the "cave man" culture had created an economic boom. Cafes with sidewalk tables and umbrellas were filled with sightseers. Platters of cheeses were carried back and forth, French wines flowed freely, and goose paté was consumed with gusto. This was southern France, it was August, and this was a prehistoric amusement park. I had never seen anything like this in the USA.

Amidst all the gaiety and vacation atmosphere, an ominous thought occurred to me. If anyone was able to cast a shadow on the evidence which supports this flourishing trade, they would probably find themselves in a heap of trouble. It seemed very much like Paul telling the Ephesians around A.D. 52 that Artemis was not a god.

The words of Demetrius, a silversmith from the ancient city in Asia minor, who made the silver shrines of Artemis came back to me, "Men, you know that our prosperity depends on this business. . . . this Paul has persuaded and turned away a considerable number of people, saying that gods made with hands are no gods at all" (Acts 19:25-26). Whether it be in Paul's journey in the first century or in 1979, the threat by Christians to the idol business remains the same, even though the names of the idols change. Demetrius stirred up the people of Ephesus by saying, "Not only is there danger that this trade of ours fall into disrepute, but also that the temple of the great goddess Artemis be regarded as worthless," and a riot ensued (Acts 19:27-29).

Chapter 6

Amicus Plato, Sed Magis Amica Veritas

D ear is Plato, but dearer still is truth" was spoken by Aristotle, the re-
nowned philosopher of ancient Greece.[1] This statement was made in
reference to his conflict with Plato over the fundamental principles of
philosophy. Plato was his beloved teacher, but Aristotle held firm beliefs quite
contrary to those of his master. Aristotle's search for truth had led him into this
dilemma, but instead of shrinking from the battle, he embraced it, even if it meant
contradicting the man to whom he owed so much.

This same type of dilemma has been presented to me, by the evolutionists.
I have been accused of biting the hand that fed me. During a lecture at Penn State
University on March 15, 1990, at the Hetzel Union Student Center, in the "fish
bowl" in front of an audience of approximately 500, I was confronted by an anthropology professor in the front row. Before I even began he asked who was
paying me for this lecture. The lecture was sponsored by the Penn State Chapter
of Campus Crusade for Christ, to which two of my children, Margie and Daniel,
belonged at the time. I told him that I wouldn't accept any payment for this lecture, and I didn't. The professor, surrounded by his students, kept interrupting me
throughout the lecture. I wanted to introduce some preliminary thoughts and background material for my research, while he insisted that I show the Neanderthal
radiographs and photographs. He wouldn't let up on me. During the talk some
nasty remarks came from the middle rows.

A few days before, a large advertisement in the campus paper had announced
that I would present original Neanderthal research. This advance notice was enough
to fuel the flames of intolerance and anti-creationist feeling so much that by the
time I arrived on campus, the inferno had peaked. I walked into a booby-trap. I

found myself in the midst of my own Ephesian-like idol worship controversy with Demetrius in the front row.

The Spirit of Demetrius

I succumbed to his pressure as well as the snide remarks from many of his students. I stopped in the middle of my introductory material and asked the projectionist to change the carousels on the projector. I proceeded to show the Neanderthal slides, much to the amazement of the angry professor. Seeing that I really had goods to deliver and that this wasn't some sort of flim-flam show, he listened intently until I came to some conclusions with which he vehemently disagreed. I was so nervous that I dropped some of my preliminary overheads and made an error, too.

Super-confidently, he asked how could I try to disprove the fossil evidence which I was so graciously allowed to see. After all, he explained, they didn't have to let me into their museum. I said that I was grateful but believed the search for truth surpassed all else. This probably sounded a little cold, but then consider what Jesus has said about leading little ones astray. False museum displays and textbook diagrams do lead children astray. While never having an Aristotle-Plato relationship with the museum people, I still must insist that "dearer still is truth." In fact, I always thought that this was what all scientists were supposed to believe. That was before I saw what was in their museums.

What followed thereafter was nearly a riot. After an interrogation by this man about what I really knew, he proceeded to take the microphone out of my hand and started to address the crowd. He tried to persuade them that I had made no case at all for biblical truth. To him, evolutionary doctrine was the only thing that made any sense to the intellectuals. After some loud remarks from the crowd, a large group rushed forward at me and surrounded the podium. Everyone was shouting at once. Demetrius had done his job well. These kids were furious. In the midst of all the confusion while I was trying to make a quick exit and not leave anything behind, a student to my right side started to ask me a question. Someone grabbed him from behind with a choke-hold on his neck and told him not to ask me anything because, "He's just a preacher anyway." We backed out of some doors amidst a near riot. I'll never forget that night. Margie, Daniel, and my nephew, Jack Dostalek, also a Penn State student, were as upset as Diane and I.

Chapter 7

The Golden Scepter

We arrived back in Les Ulis on Sunday, August 5, and early the next day went to Paris to acquaint ourselves with the city and to find the Musée de l'Homme. Before we left, I had tried to reach Dr. Ferembach by phone, but to no avail. She wasn't listed in the phone book. At this point, I began to realize that I had come to France with my young family, all my highly technical equipment and no permission or assurance that I would be allowed to even see a real Neanderthal fossil.

All seven of us were driving together in the white van into Paris when the Eiffel Tower came into view. We had come in through the Porte de St. Cloud around a curve to a large road that led right down along the River Seine. This was the Avenue de Versailles which turned into the Avenue du President Kennedy. We were heading north and slightly east on this expansive avenue and it wasn't long before the huge Eiffel Tower dominated the scene on our right. Immediately to the left was a massive semi-circular edifice constructed of white granite and marble. It was divided in half by a large decorated stone plaza with two sets of steps on either side that converged upon a long reflecting pool. The Pont D'Iéna, a bridge across the Seine, appeared to connect the Eiffel Tower to this impressive divided building. This was our destination point, the famous Palais de Chaillot, home of the Musée de l'Homme or Museum of Man. The Palais sat high above the river and looked cold and impenetrable. However, cheerfully on both sides of a beautiful reflecting pool, the Trocadero gardens were resplendent with trees and walkways. They filled the semicircular expanse with verdant hues and adorned the ornate palace in regal grandeur. After driving once around this majestic but formidable scene, my hands shook on the steering wheel as I thought about the prospect of walking into the Palais uninvited.

I felt like Queen Esther when she went into see King Ahasuerus uninvited in order to save her people. Esther was his newly chosen queen. Jews in 127 provinces from India to Ethiopia were going to be destroyed according to the evil plan of a man named Haman. He convinced the king that the Jews were different and did not observe the king's laws, mainly because of his hatred of Esther's uncle Mordecai.

Mordecai persuaded Esther that it was her duty to go into the king's chambers and plead with the king to rescind this order. Esther was finally convinced. She knew, however, that if she went in to see the king uninvited, she risked death. It was a law of the kingdom that anyone who went into the king's inner court who had not been specifically summoned would be put to death unless the king extended to that person the golden scepter. This act alone would save her life (Esther 3-4). We can find examples of this hatred today.

The Hamans of this world have spoken in our generation. Preston Cloud, professor emeritus of biogeology and environmental studies at the University of California, Santa Barbara, in speaking about the issues involved in creation vs. evolution debate has said, "The other [issue] is whether an extremist group of religious bigots shall be permitted to abridge the constitutionally guaranteed separation of church and state."[1] Cloud seems to be saying that these people are different and they don't want to observe the laws of the state.

Words exactly like Haman's are heard lashing out thousands of years later at God's people. Over 100 years ago, Thomas Huxley argued in the same way against the fundamentalist Christian view that men were not descended from apes by stating, "Could not a sensible child confute, by obvious arguments, the shallow rhetoricians who would force this conclusion upon us?"[2] As a young man Huxley had his naturalist experiences aboard a ship appropriately named the HMS *Rattlesnake*.

MUSÉE DE L'HOMME

As we pulled up to this mighty edifice of the evolutionary kingdom on Monday, August 6, 1979, I knew in my heart that I had to go into the inner court of the head of this kingdom uninvited and unannounced. Of course some of the kids wanted to go in with me, and this helped break some of the tension, but we all agreed that I must go in alone.

As the elevator rose to an upper floor, I could feel the adrenaline rising. To my surprise, I was ushered into the office of the under-director of the museum and not the director. I was informed that the director was away on vacation.

Dr. Yves Coppens looked up at me standing in front of his desk as I handed him the introductory letter from Dr. Krogman to Dr. Ferembach. He stared at it with a strange look, wondering what this had to do with him. I nervously explained to him my inability to contact Dr. Ferembach and that in a last effort to gain approval for my research, I had come in desperation to him for his consideration of this project. He was a very stern and intelligent man. I didn't know whether he would believe me or not and I was banking on Krogman's letter. He said he knew of Dr. Krogman's research in anthropology but did not know the man himself. He was adamant about not letting me in the museum labs with the famous skulls.

We spoke of Dr. Krogman's work during WW II and that must have hit a responsive note in his memory. As I turned to leave and was about ready give up the whole thing, he told me that his father and mother had been captured by Nazis during the occupation of France. Their lives had somehow been saved by American soldiers in the liberation campaign after the invasion on June 6, 1944. The Nazis had threatened their lives, but some American GIs rescued them and returned them to their home. For this reason he was very grateful and said that he owed the Americans a favor. He said he had never paid us Americans back for what we did for his parents. Therefore, it was because of this act by some courageous soldiers during WW II that he would allow me to do my research project on the Neanderthal fossils in the Musée de l'Homme.

I was stunned. He had extended to me the golden scepter and told me to come back at 2 p.m. to meet the lab workers. With my mind reeling, I sincerely thanked him and floated down on the elevator and out to the van where an expectant group of people awaited my arrival and the verdict.

I thought I would need smelling salts to revive everyone but we all agreed that the goodness of God is beyond all we may expect or think. It was 1 p.m. and I had to report back in an hour, so we went across the street to a sidewalk cafe to celebrate on ham and Swiss cheese sandwiches made with that delicious French bread.

I reported back at the appointed time and met some of the lab assistants and saw where the famous fossils were stored. Dr. Coppens was to leave for vacation the next day so, basically, I was to be only superficially supervised.

That night my two oldest boys, John and Frank, helped me squeeze the 350 pounds of x-ray equipment and all the other necessary things into the van to be ready to go the next morning.

Chapter 8

The General Electric Miracle

My oldest son John and I were up early on Tuesday, August 7, and raring to go. He was to be my research assistant at the age of 13 and a half. I must add that he was far more advanced than other 13 year olds. He was to go on to be valedictorian of his graduating class in high school out of over 350 seniors. My trust was well-placed. He kept a good eye over the project the entire time. I had assigned him the task of memorizing the entire breakdown and setup of all the machinery, which was no small job. This incredible machine was separated into many parts and neatly packed in the two metal containers with nuts and bolts and great wads of foam strategically placed to prevent damage during transit.

We were met at the back entrance of the museum by some men who assisted us in hauling everything up to the lab on the third floor. With all the delays of morning rush-hour traffic, finding the back entrance, unloading and setting up the machine, it was around 12:30 p.m. when we first realized something was drastically wrong. The machine wouldn't work. We turned it on after setting it up perfectly with the 220 volt transformer connected but it wouldn't give us that characteristic "hum" when the button was pressed. It didn't produce any x-rays. There was no response, no matter what we did. I couldn't believe that so many doors were opened for this project only to have the whole thing go "down the drain" because of faulty equipment.

Before we had left the States I had spoken by phone with Dr. Brown about just such a circumstance. He had assured me that because of the construction of this machine and the packing around it, very little could go wrong. Besides that, he said he anticipated all possible problems and had made allowances for them by including extra parts. This was all well and good if we knew anything about the inner workings of the apparatus and how to replace those parts. It was all we could do just to put it together in proper alignment so as to take standardized cephalometric (skull held in exact, measurable position) radiographs. There was a "little" knowledge gap here which would have to be bridged quickly if we wanted to accomplish anything of value.

Once again, I appealed to the English-speaking secretary and requested that she find the closest General Electric X-ray Service office in Paris to see if a serviceman could come and fix the machine. Well, to those of you who have called servicemen to your home because of dishwasher, washing machine, or other appliance problems, this will sound very familiar. The answer was simply that it would take a week or two for someone to come and look at the machine and they couldn't be sure about that because a large number of these men were going on vacation very soon and it might even be a month. Nevertheless, if we could bring the apparatus over to their office today before 5:00 p.m. they might have someone look at it, but no promises could be made.

When I inquired about the location of this office, the secretary said that it was on the east side of Paris and that it would take about an hour to get there, especially if we hit the rush-hour traffic. We lost little time in taking everything apart and putting each piece back in its pre-determined place. All the parts were disassembled, screwed down, and covered with foam as we locked the lids into place about 45 minutes later. Transporting the two boxes on the large flatbed carts down the hallway to the freight elevator and finally to the loading dock and into the van took up more precious time. By approximately 2:30 p.m. we were on our way to the G.E. office. The name of the section of Paris where the office was located is unclear in my memory so I won't hazard a guess, but suffice it to say that it took us about an hour to get there. With a map in John's hand and me at the driver's wheel, we managed to maneuver through the bustling streets of Paris to arrive at our destination at approximately 3:45. We found a parking space close to the front of a small office building in which the G.E. Service Center was located on the first floor. We both went in and explained the entire problem to a receptionist behind a window in a large waiting area. I couldn't help but notice that there were at least six or seven uniformed repairmen sitting on the seats that lined the walls of this waiting room. I had no idea what they were doing there. The receptionist instructed us to bring the boxes inside and she would have someone look at the machine.

John and I carried the metal containers through the front door, through a second set of swinging doors, into a workshop, and placed them on the floor. Almost immediately, a few of the repairmen followed us through the second door into the work area. They lifted the control box onto a large metal table. Their curiosity was aroused and they started speaking quickly to one another in French, none of which we understood. It was as if we had dragged a flying saucer into a university physics lab and the students were flocking around it to see how it worked. Poking and probing around, three sets of hands began investigating our dilemma. It wasn't more than 15 minutes until we heard some French equivalents of "Aha! Aha!" and one of the men pointed to a battery of fuses in one section of the control box. I was gazing over their shoulders when the same man started securing all the fuses more tightly in their sockets and replacing one or two others. After this procedure, the unit was turned on and the push buttons lit up for the first time since we left New Jersey. When the switch button on the end of the cord was pressed, x-rays flowed out of the head accompanied by a beautiful and familiar "hum." One of the repairmen explained to us in part-English and part-French that it was only a few fuses that were the source of the difficulty.

It was only a few minutes later that the receptionist burst into the workroom with the good news that all the paychecks had come in by courier and that the men could now have them and be on their way to their respective vacations. Stunned by this news, John and I realized that if the paychecks had made their appearance prior to our arrival, there wouldn't have been any repairmen in the shop at all. Or, if they came while they were working on the thing, their interest might have rapidly faded. Good news for them would have been bad news for us. Once again we saw God's hand move on our behalf and we were struck with awe, wonder, and praise.

Chapter 9

Neanderthal Skulls Put to an Orthodontic Test

W hat is the big deal about this special kind of x-ray test for the Neanderthal[1] skulls? This type of x-ray was going to allow measurements to be made accurately inside the skulls while at the same time seeing the true outside dimensions. It was also going to be able to see the places where the bones were glued together with a kind of plastic material. It might then be possible to discover if the reconstruction was done properly or if some artistic license was involved.

After the General Electric miracle of August 7, we returned to our apartment with the newly restored equipment. On the eighth of August, 1979, the first cephalometric x-rays of Neanderthals in history were taken in the Museé de l'Homme laboratory. Why had it taken so long for the two disciplines to cross? I do not know, but on that day, Neanderthal human paleontology and orthodontic science were joined together.

The machine was humming nicely all day and we had the key to the French Neanderthal kingdom which was contained in a small cabinet in the lab. I did not take this responsibility lightly. These were national treasures which we were allowed to handle, and I must emphasize that we treated them with utmost respect. I was told by Dr. Krogman that these were the fossils sought after so earnestly by Hitler's men in their attempt to find more evidence to support his Darwinian claim of "survival of the fittest." It was, and still is, an important teaching in the evolutionary process that natural selection eliminates those creatures that are weak while the strong ones move on. For Hitler, these fossils could have been a way of validating a thought process intent on destroying those whom he designated as weak, and building up those whom he had designated as strong, (i.e., the Aryan race). These, then, were the fossils that were kept out of harm's way by the wisdom of the

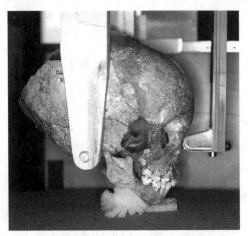

Figure 1. Pech de l'Azé child in x-ray head-holder.

French paleontologists. I found this difficult to believe with the Nazis occupying the whole country.

It is no wonder that my hands shook when I first picked Pech de l'Azé, the little Neanderthal child's skull, out of the drawer. My son John kept cautioning me, "Dad, be careful!" I was trying as hard as I could. We had large piles of sponges that we gently placed under each skull when we set it in the head-holder, so as to support it from underneath. Please refer to the Research Notes for the scientific details of this and other Neanderthal children's studies, and figure 1 for a picture of the Pech child in the head-holder.[2]

One thing you must understand is that at this point in my research career, my reference material was not very plentiful. I had a copy of the *Catalogue of Fossil Hominids*[3] and, most importantly, a book called *Neanderthal Centenary,*[4] given to me before the trip by Dr. Krogman. This was his personal copy since 1958, a gift of the Wenner-Gren Foundation, and he signed it for me on the inside cover:

> *To John Cuozzo, D.D.S., in friendship with all good wishes*
> *Wilton Krogman Ph.D. June 1979.*

This book was remarkable because of what it contained. It was on page 270 that I saw something that just about shocked me to the foundations of my being. There on that page in black and white was an article about the little Neanderthal child that was sitting on the lab bench right in front of me. This was no coincidence. It was totally in French and written by E. Patte of Poitiers, France. On the next page there was an illustration of this skull, with what appeared to be its lower jaw out of joint. This was not a photograph, it was only a drawing. Nevertheless, it was supposed to represent the real relationship of the lower jaw to the upper jaw and the skull. So, why did this upset me so much?[5]

I picked up the Pech de l'Azé skull in my hands and carefully placed the lower teeth against the upper teeth in what we orthodontists call centric occlusion (normal, central position of upper and lower teeth with maximum contact of all the cusps). I did this over and over three, four, five times, and each time the jaw condyles (ends) fit perfectly together in the sockets when the teeth were in this maximum centric occlusion position. It didn't look like the drawing at all!! *Well, I thought, maybe there is a good reason for this.* I checked what Patte had to say

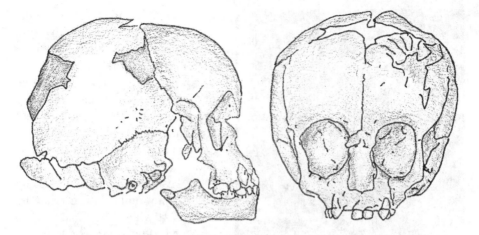

Figure 2. Patte's diagram of Pech de l'Azé skull with lower jaw out of joint.

in his description in the text of the article. I did take three years of high school French and two years in college, and I was thankful that I could at least read French even though I couldn't speak it very well.

He said, "Lorsque les dents sont mises en contact, le condyle ne s'articule pas avec le crane." Translation: When the teeth are placed in occlusion or contact, the condyle does not fit properly (articulate) with the socket in the cranium or skull.

But it really *did fit* with the teeth in the normal occlusion, normal contact position. See figure 2 for Patte's reconstruction of Pech de l'Azé.

With great trepidation, I first checked the real photos of Pech in the illustrations in the back of the *Neanderthal Centenary* book. They matched exactly, only it didn't show the lower and the upper jaw together with the teeth in contact. Besides that, the name Pech de l'Azé was written on the right side of the skull that I held in my hands. There was no mistaking it, this actually was the Pech child.

However, this was a new non-ape-like position of the lower jaw. For a moment my mind was unable to entirely comprehend what I was really observing. I thought back to my agreement with Dr. Coppens concerning the handing in of the duplicate x-rays when the project was complete. I knew that if I placed the lower jaw where it should be, that this would be a major clash with E. Patte's reconstruction and evolutionary theory. If I took my radiographs in this new and correct position, because the teeth fit together perfectly, this would be a shock for everyone in the department of human paleontology, in France, and eventually in the world. See figure 2A.

I did what I had to do. I took all the pictures and radiographs in the new, anatomically correct, real position. I was unaware of it then but Francis Ivanhoe had written an article in *Nature* magazine in 1970 defining the teeth as "grossly maloccluded with numerous enamel and crown anomalies."[6] This was also wrong.

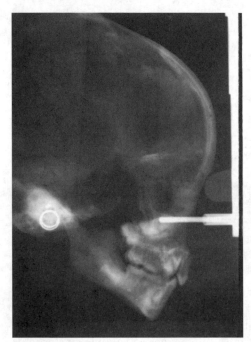

Figure 2a. Lateral ceph x-ray of Pech de l'Azé.

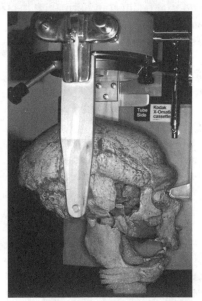

Figure 3. La Chapelle-aux-Saints in x-ray head-holder.

Grossly maloccluded means that the teeth didn't fit together in good occlusion (bite). I had been an orthodontist at the time of this discovery for 13 years and at the time of this writing for 31 years. If there's one thing that I know, it's how teeth are supposed to fit together by their cusps and wear patterns and what is and what isn't a normal occlusion (bite). I can't imagine Ivanhoe seeing what I saw and writing what he wrote. It wasn't grossly mal-occluded. He was grossly wrong.

The exact same thing happened with the famous La Chapelle-aux-Saints skull and jaws (see figure 3). When I saw that the wear pattern on the only whole tooth in the lower jaw matched exactly the wear pattern of the only opposing tooth in the upper jaw, I put these two jaws together in a new position and took x-rays and photos in this position. This was also a new non-ape-like position for the lower jaw. I did not have Day's book with me in France but I had seen some pictures of this fossil before. I must admit I did not realize at the time the magnitude of this new position with the two teeth in correct occlusion.

The photo illustrations in the first edition of Michael Day's *Guide to Fossil Man*[7] had the lower jaw in a forward ape-like position. It was corrected later in the 4th edition to match the wear patterns on the teeth, but only in one view, the frontal view of the skull where it is not so noticeable. It was not corrected in the lateral view where the skull faces right instead of left (the side of the only teeth) and the teeth have been *blacked out*.[8] Tell me this is not hiding facts!

This partial correction was done because of an article that came out in 1985, six years after our research in 1979. This work was cited by Day when he said, "A reappraisal of the dentition has suggested that he may have had intact upper and lower incisors, canine and premolar teeth on the left side and similar teeth in the maxilla of the right side. This would have been sufficient to allow mastication."[9] This was accomplished by an American, N.C. Tappen of Milwaukee.[10] What Day really said was that the teeth probably allowed this old man to chew his food, because he most likely had other teeth in his jaws where there were empty sockets. These tooth sockets would have filled in with bone if he lost the teeth when alive. Obviously! What Tappen did was to rearrange the jaw position without admitting the fact that someone failed to recognize this or did not want to recognize the perfectly fitting wear patterns on those two teeth originally. Figure 4 shows the occlusion of the two bicuspids in 1979 as I found them. My reappraisal in 1979 was never recognized except unofficially in the form of a hot pursuit.

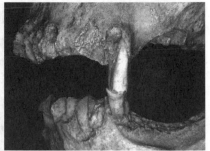

Figure 4. La Chapelle-aux-Saints' two whole remaining opposing teeth. A perfect fit.

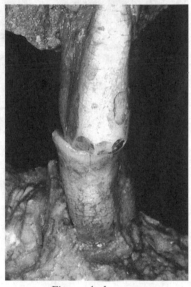

Figure 4 close-up.

A CRO-MAGNON DENTIST?

Figure 5 also exhibits a very interesting piece of dental work on the upper tooth. Unless La Chapelle had visited the local Cro-Magnon dentist, it appears as if he attempted to sharpen his own upper tooth. This is an upper bicuspid tooth, which is named because it usually has two cusps or pointed elevations. Having lost these cusps, it is plain to see that either he or someone else tried to carve a more incisive (sharper) anatomy on the crown. Notice the three neatly filed facets on the edge of the crown. Keep in mind that this is a classic Neanderthal whom most paleontologists claimed was unable to draw on cave walls because of his strong but clumsy hands. It looks like they were capable of much more precise movements than had ever been previously reported.

EVOLUTION AFTER DEATH

One other incident I must mention concerns the La Quina V skull on the cover of this book. One of the remaining paleontologists who didn't go on vacation in August was working on the famous La Quina adult female jaws, La Quina V. He

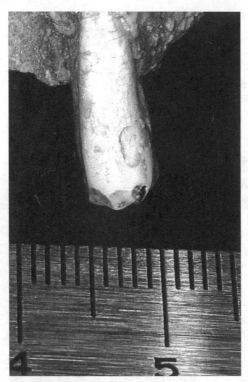

Figure 5. La Chapelle-aux-Saints' hand-carved upper bicuspid.

was placing all the teeth in the lower jaw into new positions in a plastic substance. He also was reshaping the chin. As the cover shows, the lower jaw had a pretty fair-sized chin on it when it was first discovered. This human paleoanthropologist brought the jaw over to me when he finished setting up the lower teeth and asked me "how they looked." Not much I could say but, "Fine! Can I take a photo of that set-up?" Actually, the chin had started to disappear in *The Neanderthal Centenary* photograph in 1956, in the two illustrations by L. Pales.[11] Plate V, our cover, shows a chin in the original block of stone originally excavated in 1911 by H. Martin. So between 1911 and 1956 La Quina V lost part of its chin. The remaining amount disappeared in the summer of 1979 while I was in that museum. Whoever that person was, he had removed the rest of the chin and used a plastic-like material so that no real chin appeared anymore. This could truly be called evolution after death. Figure 6 shows this new reconstruction. Pretty imaginative, wouldn't you say?

This is how presuppositions of an ape heritage actually block out all other interpretations and the reconstructions. Apes have no chins either. With presuppositions and reconstructions like this, evolutionists have nothing to fear from the evidence.

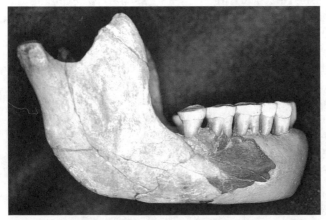

Figure 6. La Quina V in 1979 without a chin. Compare to cover photo with chin in 1911.

Chapter 10

The Curtain Comes Down in the Museum

We worked from Wednesday, August 8, through Friday, August 10. We completed everything in the waning hours of Friday afternoon. We had succeeded in our goal of obtaining the first Neanderthal cephalometric radiographs in history with the jaws in their correct positions. We set out on Monday morning, the 13th, to break down the equipment and move out of the museum. This was the day that I handed in the duplicate set of radiographs to the English-speaking secretary and said our final goodbyes to the museum people, who had been very helpful.

On the 14th we had a picnic in a park, rode an elevator to the top of the Eiffel tower, and had the x-ray machine stowed away back at the apartment. We were *extremely naive* about two things. First of all, that August 15 was a national holiday in France. Secondly, that there would be no repercussions from our research results.

The holiday schedule of the 15th closed the customs office at the Charles De Gaulle Aeroport, so it took a lot of time for Pan Am cargo to get the boxes approved for transit back to the USA; pretty much all day! We dropped them off and went back a few hours later, when I believe *an angel* in a customs uniform, knowing what was to transpire in the next few days, authorized the transaction. This relieved us of this heavy, bulky burden in the car when the machine passed inspection and had wings to Kennedy Airport. I imagine it didn't have to be an angel, but if you're an American and you can get a French customs official to inspect and certify your cargo on a national holiday please let me know and I will say it wasn't an angel.

SOME STRANGE TELEPHONE CALLS

We were in the borrowed apartment on Thursday, August 16, and had just finished breakfast when the telephone rang. Certainly, the call couldn't be for us, right? Wrong! I picked up the phone with some hesitation knowing that my French wouldn't get me too far. "Bon jour," the female voice with a very distinct French accent said on the other end, "this is Bach Nguyen's sister. I am calling to ask you to come to dinner at our home on Saturday night, the 18th." *Funny*, I thought. *Bach said that his sister didn't speak English too well.* "We can come and pick you up," she continued before I could say very much.

"No," I said. "I'm very sorry but we may not be in Paris on Saturday. We are leaving today for Normandy to see the invasion beaches from World War II."

"Okay," she replied, "but when can you come?"

I thought about it for a few seconds and responded that I was not sure when we could come, but that we did want to visit them and that I would call them back as soon as we returned on Saturday or Sunday. I also told her that I had lost her number, so she gave it to me and I never recognized it as being different from the one Bach had given me. After I hung up, I began to wonder how she got our number, but I remembered that I gave it to Bach before we left home.

Pick us up, I thought. *Isn't that nice?* I didn't have the slightest doubt that I was talking to Bach's sister. Why should I? Not until the day before we left France did I know anything different.

We were so busy packing and the kids were so exited about seeing the invasion beaches in Normandy, that I gave only a little more thought to this telephone call and put it out of my mind. I put the slip of paper with her number in my wallet and off we went in our white van.

Before we left, I had made a reservation at the Novotel on the north side of Caen, France, which is very close to the Normandy beaches. We reached our destination in the afternoon of the 16th and it was getting late, so we checked into the motel and just drove around a bit until dark. We took no special precautions of any kind because we never had any idea that we were being followed wherever we went. After dinner, we all went to bed but I had to go out to the car a few times for various things. I still was oblivious to any lurking trouble.

The next morning, August 17, as we walked through the lobby past the registration desk, one of the attendants behind the counter stopped me to ask a question. He asked if I was Mr. McCue. I said no. I had no idea who he was talking about. He explained that someone had just called and was looking for this Mr. McCue, who the caller had said was an American. He continued by saying that we were the only Americans in the Novotel at that time. I explained that I did not know this man but my brother-in-law was named McCue. Obviously, this wasn't anyone calling for him since he was back in the USA. So we went on our way.

After a full day exploring the invasion beaches, we found an inviting restaurant on the coast near Arromanches on a fearful night. As we sat there in the warm atmosphere of the small French restaurant with its windows completely steamed over from the luscious aromas of the soup and omelets inside and the cool ocean spray outside, I pondered who this Mr. McCue might be. We left between eight and nine o'clock. Into the dark of the night, against the background of the choppy waves of the English Channel, and with the billowing mist drifting across the sand dunes dampening our faces, we hurried to the van.

I took the roads that I thought led back to the Novotel in Caen, but it was soon readily apparent that we were lost. *Strange*, I thought, *there is another pair of lights behind us that seems to be just as lost as we are*. I didn't say anything immediately, partly because I wasn't sure, partly because everyone was getting drowsy, and partly because I was getting scared. Up and down deserted dark coastal roads with this car behind us at about 60 yards. Wrong turn, wrong road, same pair of lights! Finally I mentioned it to my wife, and with that notice, some of the children perked up. It was only by the grace of God that I found the correct road back to our hotel at a speed that was increasing by the minute. The trailing vehicle pulled away as we drove into the parking lot and for the first time we realized something was wrong. No one said much as we headed for the rooms. I wasn't sure yet what this really meant.

Chapter 11

Do You Know What That
Painting Is About?

W e awoke early on Saturday, August 18, to a brighter day, and packed up
as quickly as a family of seven is able, checked out, and headed for
Paris. I had promised to take everyone to the famous tourist attraction
in Paris, the Louvre. Featuring the famous *Mona Lisa* by Leonardo da Vinci, the
palace and museum contain some of the most beautiful works of art in existence.
Though my family was young, they were not uneducated and the children's ex-
citement grew as we sped eastward on the highway towards Paris. I noticed nothing unusual during the drive. After a couple of stops, we arrived in Paris in front
of the Louvre in the early afternoon.

It is a physical impossibility to see the entire Louvre Museum in one day,
much less one short afternoon. However, just getting a taste of its masterpieces,
antiquities, and sculpture would be more than satisfying for us. We hurried in and
found the courtyard entrance swarming with people. Visitors from every land
crowded into the open doors. It was a bustling place with enormous salons of art.
People stood three and four deep in front of the more illustrious works of art.
Many different languages were overheard as we tried to steer a course with our
map in hand. Each one of us was holding tightly to another hand as our small
family chain wound its way with open mouths around these cherished pieces.
Some of the paintings took up an entire wall, some shared a wall. We didn't stop
too long in front of anything because we kept being driven by the thought of what
might be in the next room. I think back now and wish we had tarried a little
longer at various places. It was kind of like looking out the window of a speeding
train.

Everything went by pretty quickly, until we were standing in front of the huge piece, the *Coronation of Napoleon*. Allow me to describe this setting for you. We were bunched up in a large group of people all intently gazing at this expensive masterpiece created by J.L. David in 1807. In the painting, Napoleon stands on the altar of Notre Dame Cathedral with both hands holding a crown high in front of himself. The empress is kneeling down in front of him on the steps of the altar. Napoleon appears as if he is about to crown Josephine and not himself. We stopped by this painting longer than usual because it aroused our curiosity.

As we stood there, an American voice behind us rang in our ears and shattered our supposed anonymity. He was a middle-aged, black man, dressed casually like us. He asked me this question: "Do you know what that painting is about?" I turned around to see who this voice belonged to and replied that I didn't know anything about it. Immediately, a tall, serious-looking white man in a suit and tie, behind the black man, answered the question rather authoritatively. His answer was short, to the point, in English, and with a distinct American accent. I got a good look at his face, and somewhere, I thought, I had seen this man before. Was this Mr. McCue from the Novotel in Caen?

After this brief episode in front of Napoleon and Josephine, we decided to visit the sculpture gallery in a distant part of the Louvre on the ground floor. We had to hurry because it was near closing time and it was a long walk. The crowds were thinning out as we approached the room where Michelangelo's two statues were kept. As we entered, we realized that we could let go of each other's hands because there were so few people in the gallery. We found the two unfinished stone carvings by Michelangelo. The first one, *The Dying Slave*, is portrayed in all his agony and the second, *Rebellious Slave*, is also in a tortured pose. A heavy atmosphere of gloom seemed to permeate the room, especially when one of the kids said to me, "Daddy, isn't that the same man who was standing behind us near the Napoleon picture?" It was, and there were only a handful of people in the entire room. Putting two and two together very quickly, we made a beeline for the exit, hands held tightly at a brisk pace, but not really running so as to betray our anxiety.

Once outside, we ran out of the Louvre grounds, into the van, and off to Notre Dame Cathedral. I was determined that I wasn't going to let this series of events spoil our day.

The great Cathedral of Notre Dame stands on an island called the Ile de la Cité in the Seine river. The Ile de la Cité is only a few blocks down the river from the Louvre. The sun hadn't gone down yet and I wanted to take some pictures of the magnificent flying buttresses of this cathedral to use in my research on the human head. I had a brilliant professor in graduate school at Loyola of Chicago by the name of Harry Sicher. He wrote extensively on bones and had compared some of the bones in the human head to these flying buttresses. He said that they supported the heavy roof so large stained-glass windows could be built into cathedral walls. He lectured to us on the buttresses of the skull that protect the eye in the same manner.

THE PIZZERIA CRISIS

By this time, it was getting late and there wasn't one of us not hungry. We traveled several blocks into the now darkened streets of Paris, with their quaint street lights glimmering in the soft summer evening. Spotting the glow of a small corner restaurant which had a "Pizza" sign in its window, we were able to find a parking space on a nearby cobblestone side street. The cars were not parked entirely on the street as in other areas of town, since this was a small residential area. It reminded me of the Georgetown section of Washington, D.C., where I had gone to college. Only there was something different here. Cars in Georgetown didn't park with two wheels up on the sidewalk as they did here. Apparently these streets were never designed for automobiles in the first place. So when they are parked on both sides of the street, the roadway became much too narrow. Therefore, cars are allowed to jump the curb and place both right or left wheels on the brick sidewalk, depending upon which side of the street they are on.

Please try to picture this scene. It was a cobblestone one-way side street with brick sidewalks, quaint little streetlights, and houses. It ran into another small street which had at the end of the block a warm, glowing Italian restaurant with a garlic-like aroma wafting from its portals. What a romantic setting! But not with five tired kids.

Spurred on by the prospect of hot pizza, we proceeded to enter and find seats at a long table about 25 feet from the bar. Decorative vegetables hung in bunches from various places around the inside. Strands of red peppers also dangled in array around the red-checkered, table-clothed tables. Lighted candles centered on each table seemed to invite us to an evening of dining and relaxing pleasure. As we plopped down into our seats, I took the one at the end of the table facing the bar.

After ordering, I excused myself and went to the wall telephone that was situated on the right side of the bar near the entrance. It was my intention to try to get in touch with Bach's sister, since I had promised that I would call her when we arrived back in Paris after our trip to Normandy. I pulled the number out of my wallet and tried to put the call through. On the other end of the line there was no answer, it just rang and rang and rang. *Strange,* I thought, *Saturday night, no answer.* This was the night she had asked us to come to dinner. I wondered if this was the right number. I dialed it a few times but still to no avail. It was the one she gave me herself, when she had called before we left for the trip. My mind didn't start putting facts together until sometime later, because the pace of this adventure was picking up so quickly. I went back to the table. "Couldn't reach Bach's sister," I said sitting down just as the hot pizzas were being served. We said the blessing, as each of us bowed our heads giving thanks for the food and also thanking God for His protection.

Everyone dug in, with the tomato sauce, pepperoni, and drippy hot mozzarella cheese extending from plates to mouths while I glanced around with a slice hanging in my mouth and still chewing. I guess you could say I was a bit paranoid at this point. Diane sat to my left as I looked behind me and to the right. The pizza nearly stuck in my throat when I saw a man whom I immediately recognized as the one who answered the question in front of Napoleon's painting and had followed us into Michelangelo's exhibits. I couldn't get another bite down and didn't want to alarm anyone or start any kind of fracas in the bar.

If I confronted this man, all of our lives were in jeopardy. If we stayed and ate, he had longer to call in other forces. If I said anything at the table it was a sure bet that everyone would turn around and create an embarrassing set of circumstances. What were my chances against this guy in a fight?

I had no weapons except those from Ephesians 6:10-18. These were not physical but spiritual weapons. I knew we had the "helmet of salvation, the shield of faith, the breastplate of righteousness, the sword of the Spirit, we were girded with truth, and our feet shod with the preparation of the gospel of peace." I knew that they worked through "prayer and petition," and we were to be "strong in the Lord, and in the strength of His might."

BACK TO THE APARTMENT

The decision to get up from the table in the pizzeria was preceded by a note written on a napkin that I asked to be quietly passed around to each one in the family. Well, with little kids it's hard not to get excited about what the note said. It said this: "Please don't stare at him now, but the same man from the museum is sitting behind us. We're being followed." I whispered that we're going to get up slowly and leave after I pay the bill. I also said that after I paid the bill, we would walk to the door and from that point we would run to the car. I would carry Joshua. As soon as the note reached each pair of little hands our trust remained but some of our quietness disappeared. " Please, please," Mommy and I said, "be quiet." Otherwise he'll know that we know! I didn't want to give him the advantage of paying his bill early so he could follow us closely out the door. If he even paid his bill.

We did exactly as we planned and as I was going out the door behind everyone, I saw our "friend" get up to leave. We ran down the brick sidewalk, I fumbled for the keys, opened the van, everybody piled in, and we were off. Our friend jumped in a dark blue sports car that looked very familiar and was joined by the yellow one described in chapter one. The chase proceeded as detailed earlier and eventually we found ourselves behind the barricade in the apartment in Les Ulis praying in "quietness and trust."

What do we do now? I told everyone not to turn on any lights and this order was carried out. However, I also said for them not to look out of any of the windows and this was harder to do. While I was checking the barricade, two or three of the boys gently lifted one of the blinds and in hushed but frightened voices declared that our pursuers left their cars and ran into the wooded area across the street. Hearing this, I had to see for myself. Sure enough, they were right. We were really in trouble. Some hours later they emerged from their hiding places and took up positions in the parking lot leaning on the hoods of their sports cars and smoking. We had to pray and make a plan. This we did, and our plan was to lay low for the night hoping that they didn't try to break into the apartment. I was glad we weren't on the first floor. In order to get in they had to climb a ladder or break down the front door. We also thought that they might not know which apartment we were in. If these men were part of a secret French police force, society, or museum employees, they probably wouldn't want to create too much of a public disturbance. After all, what could they say they were doing following an American family who broke no laws (except after we were chased).

Our plan was simple. In the morning, if they were gone — and this was a big if — we would drive southeast and escape through Switzerland where we had been in 1977 when I studied with Francis Schaeffer. In 1977 we had rented a chalet in Villars sur Ollon, near L'Abri, which was in Huemoz in the Swiss Alps.

However, we had three problems with this course of action. The first was that we had plane reservations to leave from Charles De Gaulle airport on Tuesday, August 21, but I thought I could change them in Geneva since it was a Pan Am flight. We had flown to Paris on Air France but were thankful we were going back on a U.S. airline.

The second problem was more important than the first. As soon as I said to my wife that we had to leave right away the next morning, she protested that we couldn't leave the apartment dirty after our stay.

"Oh great," I replied, "seven corpses in a clean apartment, that'll really fool the authorities. They'll spend years trying to figure this one out." My wife wanted to dust and vacuum, wash the sheets and pillowcases, and everything else to make the place look like the first day we arrived. We decided with some sort of conditioned reflex that came from deep within our genetic past that we should clean up.

The third problem was that Joshua, the youngest, had developed a high fever during the night and was coming down with some illness.

We waited out the night, half-sleeping, half-awake, and every once in a while lifting up one of the blinds very slightly to see if they were still there. The kids were up early and announced that they were gone. I really don't know when they left but it was some time after midnight.

We had put the whole situation in the Lord's hands. If Josh was well enough to make the long trip to Switzerland, then we would go after we cleaned. If his fever was still high, we would stay one more night in the apartment. This was pretty risky, and it meant giving those pursuers another shot at us in the same place.

Morning dawned early and I went right in and stuck a thermometer into Joshua's mouth. I paced back and forth wondering what tale the mercury would tell. At the stroke of three minutes I gently withdrew the glass thermometer from his mouth and read the verdict. The silver column reached up to the 102-1/2° level, which sealed our fate. We were to stay another day, clean up the apartment, and barricade the door for one more night. I had brought some ampicillin powder with me for just such times as these.

Josh had not been too healthy from the moment he was born. In 1975, at four weeks of age, it was discovered that the reason why he was not growing well was that he had a missing liver enzyme and pyloric stenosis (small benign muscle tumor) at the base of his stomach. These were genetic (recessive) disorders that my wife and I carried in us without manifesting any outward signs. He had to have surgery after eight days at Columbia Presbyterian Hospital in New York City. The chief pediatric surgeon told us that his chances of living were not good if the liver enzyme didn't regenerate. After surgery on the stomach and a small section being taken from his liver, the enzyme miraculously started to come back. The surgeon greeted me in the hall and said, "Somebody up there likes you."

Walking around with Joshua in my arms that morning in France, my thoughts went back to his earliest days. His little life was a miracle and now it was a sign for us not to flee to Switzerland. This day passed uneventfully with no sign of any danger anywhere. Our plane was to leave on Tuesday morning, the 21st, but we really thought we'd better evacuate the apartment on Monday morning, the 20th, and find accommodations close to the airport. We wished to make a quick departure on Tuesday morning.

The barricade went up again on Sunday night after prayer and singing of some familiar hymns. The apartment sparkled. The darkness brought more anxious thoughts, but reading Philippians 4:4 helped push them away.

Chapter 12

Bathroom Doors to the Rescue

I did not take a chance and call ahead for a room reservation for Monday night, thinking that perhaps our line in the apartment had been tapped. We loaded all our belongings into the van and drove away to an unknown destination near the Charles De Gaulle Airport. Diane had been checking out a novotel brochure while we traveled down the highway towards Paris. One place seemed to stand out in the brochure and on the map as being strategically located near the airport and in a fairly busy location. We were definitely not looking for a remote little hideaway for obvious reasons. We settled on a novotel called Paris Aulnay-sous-bois on Rn. 370. It looked less than 10 km from the airport and right off a large road. After check-in, we found our rooms were on the second floor. Diane, Dan, Joshua, and I shared one room while John, Frank, and Margie had a room across the hall. Our room overlooked a rooftop.

At dinnertime I spotted a familiar face seated on a couch in the lobby. I couldn't be sure but I thought it was one of the pursuers. He was looking at a newspaper as we walked by him to get to the dining room, and I got a chill down the middle of my spine. We proceeded to eat our dinner in haste (by this time, I was getting used to it). We were about ready to make our exodus from the dining room when I noticed that this individual was gone. I then decided to try to call Bach's sister one more time. This time, though, I asked the girl behind the front desk to call for me. I gave her the number that I had obtained from "Bach's sister" on the phone. As I said before, I had given this number originally to the secretary at the museum and couldn't find it after that. Bach had given me that first number. I requested that the front desk person double-check this number because I was starting to wonder why there *never was any answer.*

"Monsieur," she said, "this phone is not a private one, it is a phone booth in St. Germain-en-laye." At this point I felt like my heart stopped pumping blood to my brain and I felt a little faint. St. Germain-en-laye! I was pretty sure that Bach's sister didn't live there. Why would she give me a number of a phone booth? That couldn't have been *her* on the phone. Who was it? They were going to pick us up and take us to dinner at their house. How did they ever get the number to the apartment? I had been very careful not to let anyone have it. Right then, I knew that we had to make survival plans for that night.

As I unlocked the door to our room, I nervously went over every detail. What could prevent them from forcing the door open? The lock didn't appear to be very strong. I think I could have pried it open with a credit card or some sort of flat piece of metal from the hallway. There was a small safety device, but I was unimpressed by its strength as well. As I gazed about, something caught my attention and then my imagination. *What if,* I thought, *what if we removed the bathroom door and wedged it up against the doorknob of the hallway door.* "Guys," I said, "let's start taking the pins out of the bathroom door hinges." I had brought a small tool kit for emergencies and found a screwdriver and small hammer. This was just enough to get the pins up and out of the hinges. We took the door off and turned it sideways with its vertical height now horizontal so that we could wedge it against the doorknob of the hallway door and the clothes closet that protruded out from the wall just far enough away to form a solid resistance to the other end of the door. This closet was like a built-in wardrobe attached very firmly to the right wall as you walked into the room. At the proper angle this thing was immovable. It jammed the door perfectly. They'd have to go at it with a battering ram in order to get in and by that time half the hotel guests on the floor would be awake and in the hallway. I was convinced that this would do it. But . . . could the boys do the same thing across the hall without me? They had to, because once the door was jammed, no one could leave the room.

We rehearsed the procedure several times with John, Frank, and Margie in their room. Now came the test. With the bathroom door off in their room, I closed the door and waited until they said it was ready to be tested from the outside. They unlocked their door but left the bathroom door jammed in the proper place at the proper angle. I twisted their doorknob from the outside and tried to open their door. I was met by a considerable force of the bathroom door wedged against their wardrobe closet. I couldn't budge it no matter how hard I pushed. The only problem was that I had to do the same thing in our room with only my wife, Dan (age 9), and Josh (age 3).

We struggled with the door as best we could. The easiest thing was to get the pins out. After that, maneuvering it into position was a lot tougher. Finally, after banging around the walls a bit and almost smashing a finger and my wife's hand in the process, we were able to fit the door in the jammed position without getting anybody stuck behind it. This was a real accomplishment and we all sat down on the beds and admired our grand protective device.

We all went to bed around 10 p.m. Sleep came quickly. However, I awoke at around 1 a.m. because our air conditioner seemed to have gone off and it was very warm in the room. Everyone was still asleep when I went over to the window and opened it for some air. I walked back to the bathroom. Just as I got into the bathroom, I heard voices outside speaking in French in a startled tone. "Fenêtre ouvert, Fenêtre ouvert." "The window is open," they were saying to each other. I quickly ran over to the window and slammed it tight, locking it in the process. I immediately thought of someone climbing onto that roof and trying to get in the window. Diane woke up in the meantime, but Dan and Josh kept sleeping. Our eyes went right to the doorjamb and the doorknob. The knob started to turn. There were hands on the other side of our door trying to get in. There seemed to be more than one of them, because there was more than one voice. They appeared to have unlocked the door and were pushing against it with some force. Our fate now was in the hands of the Lord, His protective angels, and the stability of our bathroom door against the closet.

The door didn't budge an inch. They started to make more noise in the hall, pushing and yelling at each other.

Our pursuers, with all their efforts, were not able to get into our room on this hot night in France. Within the 5 or 6 minutes that seemed like an hour, there were lots of irate French people in their nightclothes opening their doors on our hallway to see what all the ruckus was about. They were yelling, too. Only they were yelling for the peace and quiet for which they had paid. Our attackers had no taste for public awareness of their tactics and in very quick order disappeared into the night. I don't know how much we slept after that, but by the grace of God we had escaped once again. What happened across the hall in the other room? How long would this night-time attack strategy go on? We could not tell, but it seemed that God wanted this information to get out in the open, and we were being protected.

The deeds of darkness had to be exposed. Paul had emphasized this in his letter to the Ephesians. "And do not participate in the unfruitful deeds of darkness, but instead even expose them" (Eph. 5:11). It began to look like this was our mission.

Chapter 13

Going Home

The next morning, we were relieved to find out that the kids across the hall had escaped without an attempt being made to get into their room.

I had many thoughts about preserving the valuable radiographs that I was to transport to the USA that morning of Tuesday, August 21. After much discussion, we finally settled on one plan. Before we packed any of our clothes I made sure that the real Neanderthal radiographs were hidden inside some French Donald Duck comic books. These I placed in a small, orange child's briefcase that we had purchased at a supermarket for one of the kids. However, I made up another package. This was a fake radiograph package wrapped in brown paper and tied up with string, which said, "Neanderthal Cephalometric Radiographs" right on the front surface. I was going to hand over the fake package to the customs authorities in the airport when we checked through their counter.

When we checked out of the motel, the clerk said nothing about the previous night's adventure, so we said nothing. We drove to the airport with eyes searching everywhere. We turned the van in and went into the airport in a phalanx-shaped group, prepared for anything. I carried the fake package, one of the children carried the real thing. As we went through customs, I threw the fake package out first.

To our amazement, the customs officials wouldn't take the package. Evidently, our pursuers were not connected to the airport customs team. So we boarded the plane and sat down with a sigh of relief. It was good to be on an American plane (Pan Am), even though we weren't actually home yet. The flight was uneventful and as the hours passed, so did many of our anxieties. We had made it at least this far.

I'm sure Kennedy Airport and Long Island do not look very pretty to someone returning from an exotic foreign country, but they certainly were a pleasant sight to us. As soon as I arrived at our home I made a call to the Glen Ridge Police Department where I had a friend, Ken Swain, a detective on the squad. He was a strong Christian and I knew that I could trust him with my discoveries from France. He responded at once by meeting me at the station, and taking my valuable package of radiographs and putting it into his safe or "lock box." I related our adventures to him and he assured me of the protection of the Glen Ridge police at my office, if I were to find myself in similar circumstances.

Chapter 14

Some Chilling News

I flew to Boston on the 18th of September to take a course on computerized measurements of cephalometric radiographs given by Rocky Mountain Data Systems, formerly of Encino, California. This was an important step for me. I was interested in obtaining more information on standardized computer models of modern children so that they might be used to make meaningful comparisons in relation to my Neanderthals. In other words, how did the Neanderthal child from Pech de l'Azé compare to modern children of the same age? The big question was: How old was this Neanderthal? What age modern child do we compare it to?

After consulting with the lecturer, I decided that I would send copies of the radiographs to them if they were willing to test them against all the necessary ages. They agreed and when I returned home I purchased an x-ray film copier, took the radiographs from Ken, made a number of copies, and sent some to California.

The next thing I did was to call Bach to tell him about our trials and tribulations in France. He was very upset with me, much to my surprise. He then said, "Why did you make a date to go to my sister's house for dinner and then not show up?"

"Bach," I said, "what in the world are you talking about? We made no date with your sister for dinner. I only told her that we would call her when we arrived back from Normandy. I tried several times and I never got any answer. Then, I had the number checked and it turned out to be a phone booth."

"A phone booth?" he said. "I gave you her number before you left for France. She said that you called her and told her you would come to dinner on Friday night, the 24th. They all stayed home from work that day to prepare a big Vietnamese meal for you and you never showed up! They were very upset and so am I," he said in a very sharp and obviously hurt tone of voice.

I couldn't say a word as my mind raced to figure out what had happened. "Bach," I explained as calmly as I could, "we flew home from Paris on the 21st, Tuesday morning. Why in the world would I tell your sister that we were coming to dinner on the 24th, three days after we were to leave France?" He was incredulous. I then told him the whole story of what happened.

Two big questions remained when I hung up the phone. Number one, who called Bach's sister and set up the phony date? The only one that had her number was the secretary in the museum. Number two, who called us? Whoever it was wanted to come and pick us up. A kidnapping? Arranging a date would have kept Bach's real sister from calling us.

Dr. Brown Found Dead

A week or so later I was alone at my office after the dental assistants had left for the night. It was about 5:45 p.m. when there was a sharp rap on the front door. I'm in a medical building on the upper floor so it's open until around 6:00 on most evenings. The door was locked. A man with a foreign sounding voice demanded to come in to use the telephone. I told him that I was closed for the day and that there was a public telephone across the street in the hospital. He didn't accept that and kept knocking. I instantly picked up the phone and dialed the Glen Ridge police, who had been forewarned about just such a possibility. Speaking loudly so as to be heard by the intruder, I told the police to come over as quickly as possible because I was having an attempted break-in. With that the intruder must have run off because when the police arrived only moments later he was gone. They escorted me to my car and I went home.

I shipped the x-ray equipment back to Dr. Brown shortly after returning from France. I had called him to let him know that the machinery was on its way. I didn't go into a lot of detail about what had happened with the French. I just mentioned that we were able to get everything done that I had set out to do, and that my results would be quite startling to all those involved. I told him that his machinery was never in any danger, and about the mis-firing fuses that GE had cleared up at no charge. I never thought for one instant his life could be jeopardized by my research.

All during the fall I was busy in the office with my private practice of orthodontics and I spent every available hour trying to decipher what the Rocky Mountain x-ray data, which I had received by this time, meant.

Shortly after New Year's Day, I called Dr. Brown's home in the midwestern city where he lived and there was no answer. I tried to call several times, but each one produced the same results. I finally called the school of dentistry with which he was associated. I spoke to the secretary at the main switchboard of the school and she said, "Haven't you heard?"

"Heard what?" I replied.

"Dr. Brown was found dead in his home a few days ago." These words pierced through my heart like a sword. *Oh dear God*, I thought, *what had hap-*

pened? After a heart-stopping pause, I inquired as to the cause of death, and she said it was some type of asphyxiation due to an explosion of a gas tank in his basement, but she was also very unsure about this explanation. I hung up the phone and just stared in disbelief. Right away, I thought of his name, address, and all the Red Cross emblems being on both metal boxes sitting on the lab floor in the museum, exposed the entire time I was there. He had wanted this identification on the boxes as sort of an advertisement for his young corporation. He made other portable medical and dental equipment and was in the process of selling them when we first met in the aisle of the Chicago Mid-Winter Dental Meeting. I called his widow and asked her what happened. Her explanation was also unclear, so I told her that we'd come to see her the week of February, 16-23, 1980. Did the people who pursued us in France get back at him or was it something else?

His widow explained to us in February that it appeared to be an overdose of sleeping pills coupled with heart failure. I was not really that satisfied with her explanation. Quite a few years later, after I had related to her some of the problems concerning our safety, she told us what really happened. They had been away together and he came home first, alone. When she returned, the house was locked and she couldn't get in. The police broke open the door. They found Dr. Brown, and his naked body was covered with needle marks, hundreds of them. In his system, the coroner found cocaine and xylocaine (dental anesthetic). Was it a murder or was it suicide and drug experimentation? No one knows for sure. His widow, Barbara, still does not know what to think. She thinks it probably was an accidental suicide. All the mirrors in the apartment were covered with white sheets. The medical examiner thought it was a murder. If it really was, then it was a horrible form of torture. The case was closed because no further evidence could be found and there was no sign of entry. I still don't know how a person could insert a needle into his own hands, feet, limbs, and trunk hundreds of times.

I was stunned and scared by what this might mean for me and my family. However, I was determined that my research be seen by the scientific world.

THAT THEY SHOULD KNOW

My scientific world started with the American Association of Orthodontists, where I was a dues-paying member since 1967. My hopes and dreams were to see these new discoveries be revealed to my organization first. I was supernaive in thinking that this would be possible. I never for a minute thought there would be any resistance to my findings. This was original research, wasn't it? These men and women of my association were open-minded scientists and practitioners, weren't they? I was approached by a local orthodontist, Curt Hester, to present my research at our regional meeting in October of 1980. I agreed.

In May of 1980 I received a letter from the co-chairman of the Committee on Continuing Education of the Middle Atlantic Society of Orthodontists. It went as follows:

May 1, 1980

Dear Jack,

I received your kind acceptance to present your Neanderthal research at the Middle Atlantic Society of Orthodontists meeting to be held in Baltimore, 1980.

I have sent a copy of your letter to Dr. Larry Holt* in Washington, who is this year's general arrangements chairman, so that he can make the proper allocations of space and time with you.

You have advanced our knowledge and that is the purpose of continuing education via research. We all thank you.

Sincerely,

Fred H. Martin*

*Fictitious Names

Please, dear reader, note well the compliments and gratefulness of this man on behalf of the entire organization. This pleasant attitude toward my work did not last very long. Within a few weeks I was asked to send in a summary or abstract of the paper that I would present. It must have sent them reeling, because in it I discussed what I had uncovered in France.

The scientific presentations of the October meeting were to last from Saturday, October 25, to Tuesday, October 28. After the summary was read and digested by the committee, I was placed last on the program on the last day, Tuesday afternoon, October 28 at 5:00 p.m. The cocktail hour also started at five p.m.

The North Ballroom of the Baltimore Hilton hotel was occupied by at least 250 orthodontists and wives, assistants etc., all day, from the first presentation on Tuesday at 8:30 a.m. There were seven speakers and a business meeting in the North Ballroom before I came on. Each speaker had a sign made for him by the Association and placed on an easel at the doorway to the large ballroom. When five o'clock came there was no sign for my talk on the easel. Many men and wives had congregated in the hallway right outside the ballroom, where cocktails were being served, while my wife and I were setting up the carousels to show my slides.

In a room that could seat at least 300 people, there were a total of 7, including my wife. I was supposed to be finished by 5:30 but went a bit over. A few of the six men who heard this for the first time in a public forum seemed as if they were amazed at the results. A couple were quite old and looked as if they just couldn't get up from the last few speakers. One of them was even sleeping. The noise from the hallway revelries was drifting into the room and distracting me, too. I tried very hard not to be too emotional both in my talk and afterward going up to our room, but I was brokenhearted. Little did I know that this was just the beginning. I kept going over it in my mind; last on the program on the last day and during the cocktail hour with no sign at the door. Why would anybody want to come into that room? It appeared as if my work was going to be *buried alive* by the scientific community.

Chapter 15

Windsor Chapel to Windsor Castle

t was a relief to be invited by an old friend, Wight Martindale, to speak at his church, the Windsor Chapel, right next to Princeton, New Jersey, and that great university. On Sunday, November 16, 1980, I gave the Sunday morning message on the faithfulness of God with some excerpts from the France trip. Little did I know how prophetic this event was to be. In less than one year, I would pay a visit to the land of Windsor Castle, Great Britain, in order to study the human fossils in the British Museum of Natural History.

In December, work went on in deciphering the Neanderthal data that had recently been generated by the Rocky Mountain Data Corp. from the French material. It also marked the beginning of my quest to publish this information. It was beginning to be very obvious that the Neanderthals were different than us in the shape and size of their face and head. These differences had been attributed to lots of different factors and the Neanderthals were also well-known for their muscular strength. They even had a muscle in their shoulder that was more developed and attached to the side of the shoulder blade in a stronger position.[1] It is in a deeper position rather than attached close to the outer edge. It was called the Teres minor muscle and it helped give them more precise arm control in the throwing motion.

Because of this reputed strength, I thought of a possible comparison to another group of strong individuals for the sake of muscle influence only. All scholars agree that you cannot make genetic references between two separate people groups in space and time, but you can examine them for muscular evidences, since they both used their teeth for tools.

In July and August of 1980 I had been allowed to examine Eskimo remains in the Smithsonian Institution in Washington, D.C., for the first time . I was very curious to know whether the peculiar Neanderthal face and jaw structure had anything to do with heavy chewing forces. You couldn't find any heavier chewers than the Eskimos that lived before modern civilized food came to the northlands. This material is covered in chapter 28, under the title "Opening Up A Rusty Gas Can."

During 1980 I had been in correspondence with Chris Stringer, Ph.D., primary researcher of the Department of Paleontology, British Museum, London, England. I have letters from him dated January 8, 1980; April 29, 1980; February 11, 1981; and June 3, 1981. I believe Chris is one of the real experts on Neanderthal fossils in the whole world. He has written scores of articles and recently coauthored a few books. One is entitled *The Human Revolution.* [2] My letters to him consisted of comparing data from the French Neanderthals. I knew that he had spent time with the originals as did I, and I respected his judgment.

On January 21, 1981, I also inquired about doing research on the Neanderthal fossils that his department held in their vaults. My first reply (February 11, 1981) was a negative, because Theya Molleson, a colleague in the department, had said that the radiographs of their fossils were "technically excellent," and they didn't see any need for me to duplicate their efforts. I quickly replied, in a few days, that mine was a special type of x-ray machine that took cephalometric radiographs which are measurable because of the stringent conditions and standardized methods with which they were taken. I also related how internal dimensions of the skulls and jaws would be easily calculated in contrast to the sometimes inaccurate physical measuring devices that were currently used. Besides all of that, I felt that the cross-over between two disciplines like paleoanthropology and orthodontics was a healthy thing. I still think that is true.

It took them until April 29, 1981, to decide to let me into their museum. A Mr. J. G. Francis, the museum Radiological Safety Officer, was one of the authorities to oversee our work. It seems that they were very concerned about the radiation given off by our machine. Just a humorous note about this detail is now in order.

When we unloaded the equipment in early August, we were ushered deep into the basement where the walls between the rooms were at least two feet thick and made of reinforced concrete. We learned from Mr. Francis that these were the rooms that the British Cabinet was to occupy if its regular above-ground meeting places were bombed during an air-raid in WWII.

Chris Stringer et al. had decided that this was the safest place to keep us from exposing museum employees to harmful radiation. We were led into one of these bomb shelters. Mr. Francis had us set up the x-ray machine and aim it directly at the wall of an adjoining storage room. Actually the room that we were in was also a storage room. He set up a radiation detector in the next room and then we blasted away at the two-foot wall with our roentgen rays. He could not pick up a trace of radiation. I think those walls could have withstood a bazooka.

We tried again at the hallway wall and again everything was right, prim, and proper — no penetration at all. We were safe, isolated underground, and ready to go.

Before I go any further, I must tell you about an encouraging note from my friend, Dr. Wilton Krogman, that I received before we left for England. I had just taken the forensic anthropology course given by him in Lancaster, Pennsylvania, on the 20th of June, mentioned earlier. I can't say enough good things about this man, because he was an inspiration to me. On June 21, 1981, he wrote a short note at the bottom of a copy of the dedication page from a newly written orthodontic textbook.[3] The book was dedicated to him for his many contributions to the understanding of craniofacial growth and development, his many accolades and awards, the Viking Award in Anthropology, and for being the "father of forensic anthropology." It reads:

Dear Jack,   Sun. 6/21/81

It was heartwarming to see you again. Your friendship is an inspiration to me. I send my love and all good wishes to you and your family. (I share with you my happiness and pride — this recognition by my former colleagues.)

Cordially,
Bill

The reception of a note like that from such a brilliant man was a great send-off for our next trip.

The British Museum of Natural History is an awesome place. This was our second overseas research trip. We arrived at London's Heathrow Airport on Monday, July 27, 1981. We first stayed at the home of Robert and Belva Foster. Bob, an M.D., was the International Director of Africa Evangelical Fellowship and a close friend of Bob and Roberta Fine, also missionaries in AEF. After a few days at Bob's home and a trip to the north for a few days, we were finally able to settle into a home reserved for traveling missionaries on Appleby End, in Tilehurst, Reading. Bob had made all the arrangements for the house and the van, so necessary for the equipment and large family. We were very grateful. This was the summer of the "big wedding" of Prince Charles and Lady Diana. Tourists had flocked to London and the surrounding towns for the enormous event on Wednesday, July 29, 1981.

It was a pleasant experience to work in the British Museum. We moved our equipment in on Monday, August 3. This time we had an automatic x-ray developer that we borrowed from Dr. Brown's widow. We had multitudes of problems with this system because our radiographs kept coming out dark black. We finally found a dark closet and did the developing by hand as we did in France.

Chris Stringer had assigned a most congenial assistant to work with us. His name was Bob Kruszynski. He couldn't have been more helpful. Both of my oldest sons, John and Frank, ages 15 and 12, were my attentive helpers.

A LOCK OUT

Before I tell you about discoveries, allow me to relate a story that happened in this grand old repository of ancient bones and archeological artifacts.

My two "scientist" boys, John and Frank, were clad in long white lab coats so they would look more official. One day, after we had worked for almost a week, I sent the two of them out with a lot of trash not knowing exactly where they had to go to dispose of it. Looking for the trash bin, they went out a door that locked behind them into an open-air quadrangle with laboratories on all four sides. They dumped the trash and went back to the same door and found it locked. Not knowing how to get back in, they noticed they were surrounded by windows belonging to the various museum laboratories. The only problem was that these windows opened into English basements whose floors were below the level of the quadrangle. After knocking on windows, someone opened a window and they crawled in, onto a counter-top with glass tubes and delicate instruments. No doubt these British scientists conducting serious research just loved two American boys, dressed up to look like scientists, climbing over research equipment. As you may well imagine, this didn't go over too well in the museum and it wasn't very long until most of the people who worked in our section found out about us, which wasn't exactly what I wanted to happen. I caught a real tongue-lashing by an irate scientist who I think would have liked to turn *us* into fossils.

If you will read the notes, you will realize that fossils aren't always put together accurately. This is true concerning the lower jaw of Gibraltar II, the Neanderthal child. I will also add, for anyone who hasn't read this detailed description, that when I saw this child I knew that the person who reconstructed this lower jaw obviously wanted to make it look older than it really was.[4]

Part 2
Controversial Research

Chapter 16

My Objectives

TWO BULLET HOLES AND A DISEASE

My objectives started to become clearer in the British Museum. In France we were captivated by our presence amongst the relics of ancient history and tense because of the enormous task at hand. In England some of the fascination and tenseness started to wear off, for we knew we were doing this for a second time. We also were better organized. I began to get more ideas about what the term "Neanderthal" meant and because of this I knew more about what I was looking for in the fossils.[1] I started to get the eerie feeling that many things had been changed to show what they wanted to show. I began to see more evidence that the Bible was accurate in its description of ancient man.

We were able to photograph, x-ray, and study some of the most famous fossils from three continents: from Zambia, Africa, the Broken Hill or Rhodesian Man Skull, without a lower jaw; from the Middle East, Israel, Tabūn C-I, found in one of the Mount Carmel caves; from the Island of Gibraltar, at the mouth of the Mediterranean Sea, Gibraltar I and II, a female adult Neanderthal and a Neanderthal child. For some unknown reason, however, I was not allowed to see the Gibraltar II bones of the side of the head or the ear bones. The real shocker came, I must admit, when I was caught by surprise because of one of their prized possessions. It was the Broken Hill skull from Zambia.

At first, Bob and Chris didn't think that we could penetrate the Zambian fossil with our x-rays because it was permeated with lead and zinc. It had been found in a lead and zinc mine in 1921. It had a very strange, almost symmetrical hole in the left side of the head (temporal bone, squama) (see figure 7). It's not as if there were no holes or broken parts of the other Neanderthal skulls; there were. This hole was different. It appears on the outside of the skull and is wider than it

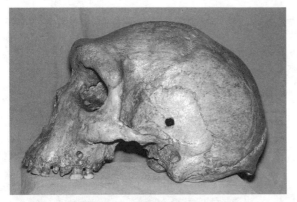

Figure 7. Broken Hill Man.

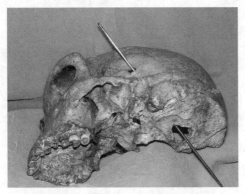

Figure 8. Rod passes through entrance and exit bullet holes in Broken Hill skull.

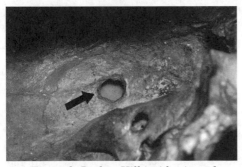

Figure 9. Broken Hill inside view of entrance wound — note bevel.

is high. However, the cephalometric radiograph revealed an almost round hole. Its measurements on the radiograph (slight distortion) were 7.7 mm wide by 8.0 mm high. Allowing 4% foreshortening because of the angulation of the temporal bone from the radiographic plate, it is very close to 8mm by 8mm round. It was very suspicious. It appeared as if it were made deliberately, but not by the old process of trephining.

Trephining is probably one of the oldest operations performed by man on the skull. It consisted of making a rectangular-shaped hole in the head and skull for various reasons, medical or superstitious, either before or after death. Sometimes a rounded hole was made. This Zambian hole is different for two reasons.

First, there is another hole in the back part of the bottom (occipital bone) of the skull, well inside the neck area where no trepanning during life is possible. This second hole is not the foramen magnum, where the spinal column enters the skull. The second hole in the bottom part is also much larger than the first hole. In figure 8 a steel rod passes between the two holes. What process could have produced these holes? It looked as if it had been made by a high velocity projectile, a bullet. Second, the first hole in the side of the head is larger inside the skull (brain side) than on the outside.[2] It also has a bevel. Figure 9 displays this feature. This fits the description of an entry point for a bullet.[3] Someone may have used it for target practice but this might have shattered a dry fossil, or the bullet could have actually killed this person. The fact that it was found 60 feet down in the mine mitigates against a "target practice" explanation.

In any event, I saw no evidence of healing of the bone around the entrance hole, which if present would mean an operation produced this defect during a lifetime, with some recovery later. The raised lip on the outer and lower surface of the entrance hole in the temporal bone has two distinct cracks (splits) which is not characteristic of healing.

Also, Oakley reports in 1958 that the cave in which this fossil was found contained no extinct species of any mammal but one, and he thought it was possible but doubtful.[4] Cooke, in 1964, reports on most of the fossils being from living species with only two of them from extinct species.[5] Because of the dubious nature of extinct fossils in the cave, my guess is that the skull is of recent origin with a bullet entry and exit holes. One other author mentions this possibility.[6]

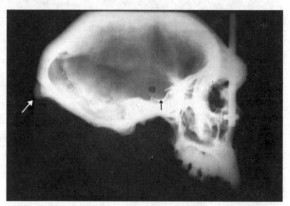

Figure 10. Lateral ceph x-ray of Broken Hill Man. Black arrow points to the former seat of the pituitary gland. White arrow is on the occipital protuberance.

What then is the explanation for the Neanderthal-like morphology (bony characteristics) of the skull? Some say that the features are like modern *Homo sapiens* in some areas.[7] Campbell, in 1964, labeled it *Homo sapiens rhodesiensis.*[8]

The lateral view radiograph (figure 10) shows an enlarged and flattened turkish saddle (sella turcica) or pituitary fossa, the site of the pituitary gland in the middle of the skull. Figure 11, a posterior-anterior view of the skull, shows many air pockets (excessive pneumatization) in the forehead (frontal) and other paranasal sinuses of the head and similar large air pocket formations in the mastoid process on the left side. Figure 12 shows that this

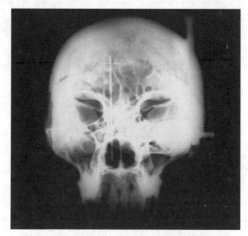

Figure 11. PA x-ray of Broken Hill. Note extensive sinus formation (empty spaces), also permeation of lead and zinc from the mine (solid white).

Figure 12. Arrow points to broken or cut mastoid process of Broken Hill. Same phenomenon as chin in La Quina V.

one remaining left mastoid process has been broken off or chopped off short of its full length.

The British museum people told me that no lower jaw was found with the skull. This seemed to be very unfortunate because the lower jaw is important in diagnosing certain diseases of the bones of the head. You must understand that this skull really cries out disease. Most of the teeth are badly decayed, and the bones of the vault of the skull are extremely thick. The base of the occipital bone is 8mm thick. Normally this area is close to 6mm or less.[9] From the lateral cephalometric radiograph we see that the upper part of the occipital bone is 13.8mm. This is far from normal.

The lateral radiograph view, figure 10, also displays the external occipital protuberance (pointed bone on the back of the skull). This pointed projection of the occipital bone appears to have been flattened even though most of the right side of the cranium has been damaged and is missing. Most of the right side has been replaced with an artificial section including part of the external occipital protuberance. Both frontal and side view x-rays show extremely thickened tables of bone which form the outline of the skull.

There are many features that testify to a diagnosis of acromegaly or excess secretion of growth hormone in adulthood, as seen in modern humans who exhibit most of these same features.[10] It seems that the Broken Hill skull from Zambia, being found without a lower jaw and having a chopped-off or broken-off mastoid process, could very well be an example of a *Homo sapiens* with acromegaly, a disease of the pituitary gland which produced all these bony changes. The lower jaw would have been a key factor in this diagnosis. If it was really long and its teeth were far in front of the teeth of the upper jaw when the jaws come together in occlusion, the bone under the lower front teeth would be very, very thin. If this had been found with the skull, it would have been a substantial piece of the Broken Hill diagnosis. The most incriminating factor is the broken-off, mastoid process on the left side. These are very elongated in acromegalic persons. This looks very suspicious.

A further observation about the lateral radiograph is in order. There was another radiographic side view of the Rhodesian (Broken Hill) man cranium published in 1958 by R. Singer of Capetown, South Africa.[11] It was interesting because it was published as a negative and not a positive print of the radiograph. Why was this done? In a negative radiograph all the white bony parts are black instead of white and all the space around the skull is white instead of black. In Singer's negative the entrance bullet hole should have been white with the surrounding bone shades of gray and black. But in Singer's negative there is no bullet hole at all. The inside of the cranial cavity is all grayish, so the bullet hole is erased.

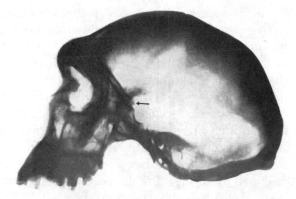

Figure 13. Arrow points to small bony projection (anterior clinoid process) in Broken Hill skull in x-ray by Singer in 1958.

More crucially, in Singer's radiograph the anterior clinoid process is very short (figure 13). In my radiograph it is clearly seen and even undercut with a space. Figure 14 shows a close-up view of the anterior clinoid process in my photograph. Could this be a new addition since Singer's radiograph was taken or is his radiograph just of poor quality? If it truly is an addition to make the sella space look smaller, this little piece of bone would extinguish any

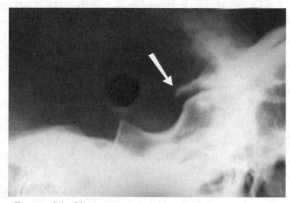

Figure 14. Close-up x-ray of larger bony projection (anterior clinoid process) in Broken Hill skull, 1981. How did it grow in a dead skull?

thoughts of a pathological pituitary gland as seen in acromegaly. This would be serious tampering with a skull. I am not accusing the present staff of the British Museum with this because it probably goes back to the late fifties and early sixties when someone knew they needed a little extra proof against pituitary disease. The amazing thing is that this skull is supposed to be 200 thousand years old.[12]

EERIE FEELINGS AND ODD STORIES

As I said in my article in BSN, "Since 1979 I have been collecting human fossil data in museums and universities, and I have noticed a definite pattern.[13] It appears as though the paleoanthropologists have made a concerted effort to adhere to a rigid uniformitarian viewpoint concerning the growth, maturation, and aging process in ancient populations no matter what the evidence showed." This eerie feeling persisted with me throughout all my expeditions into the world of evolutionary dogma.

In January of 1985, when I began to realize that the ear and head bones that I had not seen might contain some crucial evidence as to the real (chronological) age of Gib II, I wrote to Chris Stringer about a second visit to the museum.

He wrote me back on February 15, 1985, and said, "I heard some rather odd stories about your work in New York and I wonder if you could give me any more information about how your research is progressing and what your objectives are." In the first sentence he agreed to my re-visit and again at the end of the letter he closed by saying, "But, I repeat, in principle we have no objection to your visit." He really is to be commended for this attitude.

Rumors about me were flying everywhere in anthropology circles. Who was this orthodontist going from country to country x-raying Neanderthal fossils? An important link to this letter was forged in Israel.

We went to the Rockefeller Museum in Jerusalem, Israel, in August of 1983. There I worked with the director of the Paleoanthropology Department, Joe Zias, originally from Cleveland, Ohio. One day as we were working in the photographic developing room, I shared my faith in Jesus Christ with Joe. I also spoke about some of the goals of my research activity. My son Daniel was my main assistant in Israel.

Joe must have spoken to Chris in 1984 somewhere between April and September at the New York exhibit of human paleontological fossils called "Ancestors, Four Million Years of Humanity," held at the American Museum of Natural History. This occasion must have been what Chris referred to when he said he had heard "some rather odd stories" about me in New York. I know that Joe Zias came to New York and brought the "Amud" skull, because I wrote to him about coming to dinner at our house, if he could find time. He responded after he was back in Israel, saying he was too busy to accept our invitation. The British Museum did not contribute anything to the exhibition. Chris came to New York and did not exhibit anything. I heard through the grapevine that the British officials did not want to bring the Broken Hill skull to New York for fear that the country of Zambia would claim it and return it to its homeland.

On March 10, 1985, I responded to Chris with the following letter:

Dear Chris,

Sorry for not replying sooner, however I caught the flu and was sick for a week with a lot of catching up to do at the office. I must tell you about my specific objectives. I do not know what you heard from whom, but I'd love to know what anyone really knows about my research since I haven't published anything yet. I started out in 1979 with some clues from the Bible looking for signs of growth and development differences between modern and ancient children. My professor at Penn (Krogman, 1938)[14] studied prehistoric children from Tepe Hissar, Iran, and found only 3 cases of slight malocclusion among 34 crania. Today we find in the literature and in my practice about 79-95% incidence of malocclusion. The differences cannot be accounted for strictly by diet or environmental influences. I became interested in the Neanderthal population because they were prolific, widespread, left no succeeding generations that looked like themselves, and their facial characters were termed a "mystery." It appears from my studies that the Neanderthal kids were depositing bone in places that our kids are losing theirs at the same ages. The cephalometric comparisons are startling: their faces were retrognathic to their crania as compared to modern standards at the same ages. They grew and changed much slower. This kind of information could be vital to medical and dental research. Here's a real find: the adult muscles moved in response to the positional and functional requirements. Also Univ. of Michigan data reveal that the longer our children keep their primary teeth, the larger their arch becomes. Garrod saw some of this in Gib II.

Thanks for your help, interest and genuine objectivity,

Jack

Whatever I started here by these comments to Chris resulted in no answer to this letter. There was complete silence from the British Museum to me from this point on. This was highly reminiscent of the Middle Atlantic Orthodontic Society shut-down on communications in the 1980 presentation recounted earlier. As soon as my presuppositions were known for sure, then a total breakdown in communication resulted. However, there must surely have been an increased level of activity within the walls of British paleoanthropology because of my conclusions.

Some of you may think that I am flattering myself because of this last statement, but consider one fact. No person with a creationist world view, to the best of my knowledge, since Darwin's people took over science, has ever penetrated behind the evolutionist's lines to study their fossils with x-ray equipment. The fact that some paleoanthropologists consider them to be their fossils and not science's fossils, or open to experienced workers in the field, has been well-established. My communications with Richard Leakey demonstrate that very well. However, let's get back to the British response to my conclusions.

REPLYING TO A CREATIONIST WITH MORE ASSUMPTIONS

In 1986, Chris rushed into publication by the threat of my results and joined forces with T.G. Bromage from the University of Toronto and M.C. Dean from University College in London. They placed an article in the *American Journal of Physical Anthropology* in January of 1986. They had submitted it in August of 1985, just five months after my reply to his questions. There is some evidence that they had been working on this during the 1984 Ancestors meeting which I will present shortly. However, there was still no response to me directly.

I had also submitted a manuscript called "Neanderthal Outline" to Dr. Ian Tattersall, curator of the Department of Anthropology of the American Museum of Natural History in New York City, on February 28, 1985, for possible publication. This was done because of the encouragement of the late Dr. Harry Shapiro, emeritus curator of that museum. I had met with him earlier that year because of my friend and orthodontist, the late Curtis Hester, DDS. Curt was so enthusiastic about my research that he took me to see Harry at the museum. I laid out everything on his desk and Harry agreed that I was on the right track in my thoughts concerning these ancient people. He passed away some years later.

I believe that the Dean, Stringer, and Broomage article was a response to me from some of the anthropology community.[15]

In the abstract of the 1986 article the authors make a point of claiming that the dental eruption schedules of the Neanderthals were close to modern rates but a little accelerated (faster than the average modern child but at the low end of the modern scale). Of course, what did you expect them to say? They also believed that the cranial bones (bones in the head) showed a "remarkably precocious brain growth in this individual." This was close to Dorothy Garrod's description of it in 1928.[16] The new rule seemed to be to emphasize the precocious nature of Neanderthal children in relation to modern children.

In Garrod's description she emphasized the large head and small jaws, and she also leaned towards the teeth in those jaws as being the most accurate indicator of age.[17] She said that the ages of tooth eruption in Neanderthals were exactly the same as ours today. The belief that yesterday, today, and tomorrow are all the same is a philosophical assumption, not a scientific discovery. This was uniformitarianism in 1928 in terms of dental physiology. Uniform assumptions are found throughout science. Dental science is no exception.[18]

WILL THE JAWS AND SKULLS EVER BE ALLOWED TO SPEAK FOR THEMSELVES?

The main point of my criticism of the interpretation of the Gibraltar II child's skull and jaws is that they were never allowed to speak for themselves.[19] In outlining her main points Dorothy Garrod saw that there was much contradictory evidence present in the teeth, jaws, and head.[20] Let me enumerate them below and tell you what they say:

> A. Remarkable jaw muscle development .... old
> B. Well-worn teeth. .... old
> C. Infantile forehead .... slow
> D. Big head .... old
> E. Infantile ear bones .... slow
> F. Bulbous upper jaw .... slow
> G. Small young-looking lower jaw .... slow

So, we have a grand total of three olds and four slows which add up to a young-looking person who is old and slow developing. Remarkable evidence for a child who matured late and aged slowly. Just like the Bible said (see Genesis). But, for some evolutionists, real evidence doesn't seem to matter. It's only what they think and fabricate that counts — and speaking of counting, let's see how they count.

THE THREE REVISERS IGNORE ABOVE EVIDENCE

All of the above evidence was ignored by our modern trio of revisers. The main premise of the Dean, Stringer, and Broomage article is a tremendous uniform assumption. The assumption involves the formation of the enamel of the teeth. There is little difference between the assumptions concerning tooth eruption dates and assumptions concerning enamel formation times. These men measured grooves and elevations on a molded cast of the front or labial surface of the Gib II child's[21] unerupted permanent upper central incisor. See figure 15. They used an electron microscope to scan the surface and took photographs. No photographs are published in their article, just diagrams. I hope that this explanation will help you understand what they did and what was wrong with it and why they should have read Garrod's findings more seriously.

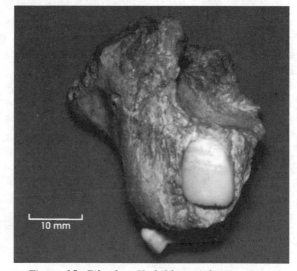

Figure 15. Gibraltar II child partial upper jaw with central incisor tooth.

You must realize right away that the stuff on the outside surface of our teeth, called enamel, is the hardest substance in the human body. It is formed on the outside of the crown (the part of the tooth that protrudes from the gum) of each tooth that you or I have, or the Neanderthals had in their mouths. Every human tooth is covered with enamel down to the gumline and even a little bit below the gumline. By weight, the enamel is approximately 96-97% mineral substance, which makes it very hard. Under the enamel is the dentin of the tooth.[22] It is softer and has less minerals. The root surface is made up of cementum. The whole root is made of dentin covered with cementum.

Now, to the rest of this particular evidence.

Chapter 17

What About This Tooth Enamel?

The mineral of the enamel is almost entirely in the form of crystals made of calcium and phosphorous. They are called "apatites." Before enamel is hardened into crystals, it starts out being made in the form of softer columns called "matrix," which is a fibrous material like that in our tendons and ligaments. The combination of hard and soft materials make up what is called the enamel "prism" or "rod." This is a long column of high complexity and orientation that runs from the surface of the dentin to the outermost boundary of the enamel of the tooth. Closely packed together, most of these prisms don't reach the surface, although variations have been reported.[1] Most of the true surface enamel is without prisms and therefore called prismless. These form sleeves, leaves, or waves of enamel on the surface, which overlap. Some remnants of prisms are found on the surface of the enamel in between the sleeves of prismless enamel and form troughs. This is where the prismless enamel is breached in a rhythmic sort of pattern. These troughs frequently are formed more or less around the whole circumference of the tooth crown. So if you can imagine a surface topography of large onion-like layers of prismless enamel and at the edge of each layer a depression, you've got it. Now each smooth band or leaf layer has this depression band, step-down, or dip showing on the surface. According to Lavelle et al., each band with its depression is called a "perikymata" or a ring around the enamel crown. According to Dean et al.[2] and Hillson[3] a perikymata is only the depression band. There are some differences here. However, the main object is to try and count the rings, whether it's only the depression or the entire wave structure, as long as one ring equals one depression.

These can only be seen accurately with a microscope. However, if the light shines from the right angle on an unworn tooth, you can see them roughly with your eye. In man today these incremental rings represent the amount of time required to form a section of the enamel. They are supposed to be like tree rings. They form in certain periods of time.

I am trying not to be too complicated, but you must know how the outside rings came to be called weekly rings, so we must look inside the enamel. Inside the enamel there are two kinds of lines that demarcate time periods. Daily lines mark sections of the prism. These are clear. These form in modern children at the rate of one every 24-hour period. They cut across the long prisms in a horizontal fashion, and show segments in the column. There are also coarser lines which flow obliquely through the entire enamel cutting across the prism columns.[4] These latter lines are supposed to represent an 8 to 10-day period of time.[5] These are the ones that connect to the depressions on the surface and form the depressions — a sort of "weekly" record of the outside waves and inside rhythm. These latter lines (stria) are brownish in color in comparison to the lighter color of the rest of the enamel and they are also clear to see, but some are wide and some are very narrow. So, to sum it up, we have two kinds of lines in the enamel, a daily line and an 8-10 day line, although it has been reported that within this "weekly" period the daily lines may vary. The "number may vary between 6 to 14 or so."[6]

Theoretically, it is possible, therefore, to count the stria which demarcate the actual numbers of these sleeves, rings, and waves. One may count these stria or perikymata on the surface of the enamel, when using a 8-10 day period (roughly a "weekly" line) as the time for each one to form, and come up with the total time it took for the crown of the tooth to form. The important thing to remember here is that it does matter what amount of time is used as the weekly period, or as you will see, the "daily period."

Dean, Stringer, and Broomage used a 7-day period — a real week.

They were not going to allow 8 to 10 days. This would have lengthened the time it took for the Gib II child's tooth crown to form. They also had to add 6 months of enamel that is formed in the cusp tip region for which you can see no perikymata. This is the biting edge of the tooth and it is called "dome" enamel. They also said "some time must be added to this crown formation time to account for the short interval between birth and the onset of incisor calcification and also for the very minimal root formation (less than 1mm)"[7] They counted 119 perikymata. They calculated a "new age" of death for Gib II which was 3.1 years. This is a "new age" in more ways than one.

Before we proceed one step further, did you notice in that last quote the words, "very short interval between birth and the onset of incisor calcification"? Is this a big assumption or not? How do they know it was a short interval? They conclude this simply because it is a short interval today. Please understand now that this is a permanent tooth, not a baby tooth. It is not one that the child will need very quickly to chew his or her food. Does this have to be a short interval? If your answer is yes, you believe as the evolutionists do, that the Genesis account with people living longer lives and proportional childhood and adolescent years is incorrect. If your answer is no, then you believe that man's development wasn't always as fast as it is today, or perhaps a little faster to conform to the ape heritage.

NEW ASSUMPTIONS, NEW CONCLUSIONS

If you start with another set of assumptions it is possible to come up with a different set of conclusions. What if the periodicity of the perikymata was not 7-10 days in ancient man? What if the time between these rings on the enamel was 14-21 days[8] or more and the "daily" increments for each prism took 48 or 72 hours. This would be a whole new ball game. With biblical assumptions substituted for evolutionary uniformitarian assumptions, a much longer time could be calculated for 119 elevations plus more than six months under the cusp. There would be more time for the root and much more time between birth and the beginning of formation of the crown itself if they held on to their baby teeth longer. An older age at death could easily be calculated for this Gib II child.

I really hesitate to call the "absolutes" of the Bible "assumptions," but this is only done in a quest for continuity of scientific thought. What this really amounts to is faith at either end. Underlying both positions is a basic faith upon which a scientific model is built. We call this faith on either side "assumptions" to give it a technical name.

Besides the faith aspect, we must also ask penetrating questions about the evidence. It is all well and good to say you have counted 119 perikymata rings but where is the proof? These men printed no illustrations of the scanning electron microscopy photographs. No evidence was presented to back up their claims. One photograph that was supposed to support the conclusions was a montage of all the Gib II bony parts seen radiographically and arranged in the way they think that the parts fit together. All this does is reinforce their viewpoint of an ape-like protruded face which I have seen in every museum in which I have studied.

Having already seen four examples of evolutionary reconstructions based on assumptions and not physical evidence,[9] you might say I am a bit skeptical of anything that comes out of that camp. Especially, since there is nothing to prove their point.

Following this work by Dean et al., I began to learn a bit about electron microscopy from my friend Steven Koepp Ph.D. Steve is a professor in the Biology Department at Montclair State University and has been in charge of scanning electron microscopy in the department for many years.

After I took an impression with a very accurate silicone-based impression material at Harvard's Peabody Museum of a relatively unworn upper central incisor tooth from Mt. Carmel, Israel, Steve and I looked at the front surface with his equipment at Montclair State. The tooth was from the Tabun excavations at level B. We had followed the procedure as recommended by Dean and Broomage[10] and saw that the lines were not arranged in perfect rows like New York Yankee

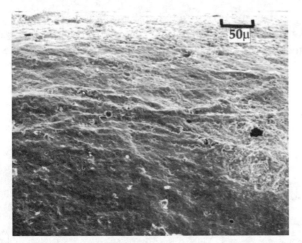

Figure 16. Electron microscope photo of a central incisor tooth found at Mt. Carmel, Israel.

pinstripes. There were many that were inter-branched and many were very faint. Some were very close and some further apart. Figure 16 shows that it was not a nicely lined-up affair that we observed but a bunch of heterogeneously mixed-up lines. I began to realize that counting these lines was like counting branches on a tree. There is a lot of subjective judgment involved so the conclusions can never be that specific as to state an exact number of lines. It probably is more like a range of lines only.

One more opposing viewpoint should be aired here. This was written to *Nature* magazine in November of 1990 by Alan Mann and his colleagues of the University of Pennsylvania, Department of Anthropology, University Museum.[11] Mann and his colleagues did another study on 12 incisors of modern man from 3000 B.C. to A.D. 800 and came up with different numbers. They found that the perikymata counts ranged from 75 to 157 (s.d. of 1-12 for individual teeth). The mean was 116. This represents a difference of 82 perikymata in their investigation.

This becomes especially significant when we find that the entire reason Stringer, Bromage, and Dean gave the Gibraltar II child a new age at death is because the number of perikymata on the exposed, unworn upper permanent incisor was 119. It is remarkable what little difference there was between the 116 of Mann et al., and the 119 of Stringer and cohorts. This means they found no difference between the number of perikymata of modern *Homo sapiens* and the Gibraltar II child.

My own feeling on this is since the Gib II upper incisor is 9.4mm (M-D) and larger than a modern average male upper incisor and if it did have less perikymata, then some of those waves of enamel would have to be pretty large. This would tend to favor either a very fast wave formation or more "daily increments" to form a wave, leaf, or sleeve. More, of course, would translate to more time. Sectioning this tooth is the only way to discover this.

THREE-PRONGED ATTACK

Even more interesting is a very quick letter to *Nature* magazine in 1985. It was entitled, "Re-evaluation of the age of death of immature fossil hominids."[12] It was essentially the same type of "assumption" logic as the January 1986 article quoted above. It was published on October 10, 1985, just six months to the day from my letter to Chris Stringer. It was received by the journal on March 7, 1985, three days prior to my letter back to Chris but less than a month after his "odd stories" letter to me. What was this?

I believe that this was the primary response to the "rather odd stories" that Chris Stringer first heard about me in New York from Joe Zias, somewhere between April and September 1984. We can't read between the lines here, but I know what I said to Joe in that developing room in Jerusalem had an impact and made part of the paleoanthropologists' world quake.

Here was a creationist who had penetrated the restricted zones of the hallowed halls of anthropology. What should they do? This could be only the beginning. There might be a whole wave of creationists hitting all the museums very quickly in the near future. Look at all the places I had been by 1983. Suppose it was an organized attack.

So there was much activity among the British group after the "meeting of the minds" in 1984 at the New York Ancestors meeting. As we have already seen, there had been frantic activity in the French organization since I handed in the duplicate x-rays. To repeat, the French had also put a certain N.C. Tappen of Milwaukee, Wisconsin, to work on the way the teeth of La Chapelle-aux-Saints came together (in occlusion) in 1984-85. Tappen's article came out in 1985 that duplicated my work but without saying that I had even been to France or done anything with La Chapelle.[13]

JOINT EFFORT

At the end of the letter to *Nature,* received March 7, 1985, Bromage and Dean give thanks to 19 people for help in working on this project. Among those acknowledged were the two Leakeys, Richard and Mary his mother, and the two governments of Tanzania and Kenya. Not one of the teeth of the skulls that they measured in their study came to the meeting in New York City in 1984.

Tanzania had sent eight fossil exhibits, none of which were the ones Bromage and Dean had worked upon in Africa. Strange, isn't it, that these key fossils were left out of the exhibit in New York City? South Africa had sent seven fossils to New York City and only one, Sts 52, was looked at by Bromage and Dean but the perikymata were not counted in the study. None of the ones used for actual age assessments went to the meeting. There is probably one reason for this strange coincidence.

Bromage and Dean were most likely in Africa taking their dental impressions of these immature fossils close to the same period of time the other "key fossils" were sent to New York City in April to September 1984. Kenya had sent no fossils at all to the meeting, so access to the Leakey KNM-ER 820[14] was easily had at the National Museums of Kenya, in Nairobi. Their microscopic scanning took place on the modeled casts in London at the Hard Tissue Unit of University College, London, probably in late 1984, so as to get the letter in to *Nature* by March 7, 1985.

I have another question. Why do you suppose that Richard, Meave, or Mary Leakey did not allow any of their original fossils to come to New York City? The foundation named after his father (L.S.B. Leakey Foundation) was one of six sponsors of the exhibit and meeting. Even if they could not be there, could they not have sent one or two? Richard's plane accident hadn't happened yet. We really have to ask for more accountability from the National Museums of Kenya, in Nairobi.

Chapter 18

Ancestors Meeting
Followed by Bullets

A nother rather unusual event took place on June 25, 1984, during the "Ancestors" exhibit. The fraternal meeting place had been going on since April. "Rather odd" stories about me were swirling through the halls of human paleontology. I had paid a visit to the American Museum in New York City to see this exhibit in May of 1984 while the stories were circulating unbeknownst to me. In June of 1984 we took three of our kids to camp in Pennsylvania.

My wife and I were driving back from taking John, Frank, and Margie to the Fellowship of Christian Athletes camps when something very unusual occurred. We were on Route 22 just outside of Easton in Wilson Borough, Pennsylvania. Diane was driving our yellow and white Volkswagen van and Joshua, Daniel, and I were seated in the back seats. As we were speeding down the highway, three shots rang out from somewhere behind us. Instantly, they hit our back window and also the back of the van and shattered the window. The window was hanging there drooping from the opening in the back door into the van. I yelled for everyone to get down as quickly as possible. Josh, Dan, and I hit the floor. Diane floored the gas pedal and drove off at the first exit. I told her to run red lights and do everything to attract police.

We tore down the small roads of Wilson Borough and found the police station before they found us. Diane pulled into the lot while we made sure there was no one following us. We all jumped out of the car and ran into the station, where we explained what had happened. They already had a report that there had been a shooting on the highway and a car had been sent out to investigate.

At 7:53 p.m. we left the police station and went home, very shocked and concerned about what more might happen to us.

The police investigation found nothing and that was the end of that. Was this just to scare us? The police believed that they were low-caliber bullets that hit us, like .22 inch type or pellets. If they wanted to kill us they said, they probably would have used a larger caliber weapon. It could even have been a coincidence; however, that possibility seemed more remote every day.

I obtained the police report from the Easton Police Department. It read: "Serial No. 848356. 6/25/84. Car No. 1744, Received by Peters, Place of Occurrence: Wilson Boro. Time Approx. 7:10 PM. Criminal or incident classification: Criminal Mischief. Founded: yes." It was signed by Lt. Davis. It ends when he wrote, "Report turned over to Wilson PD for further investigation."

Could this represent a real effort on the fraternal brotherhood of human paleontology to scare off the creationist "movement" in this field of endeavor? Up until this point in time, little or no original human paleontology research had been done by creation scientists. There had been plenty of debates, articles on reviews of the literature and lectures, but no original work on the human fossils of which I am aware.

During all these research years from 1979 up to the present, I had one man to whom I could go for advice and encouragement in creation science. His name is Wayne Frair, Ph.D, chairman of the Department of Biology at The King's College, now in Tuxedo, New York. Eventually I was appointed an adjunct professor at the college. I would give lectures to his college students concerning the developments in my work. This allowed me the give and take of scientific discussion both with biology students and with Dr. Frair. The early findings were discussed and refined through this process.

Chapter 19

Another Threat?

L et us now proceed in chronological order to the next trip to Belgium. An unusual incident took place in my office prior to our trip. In 1982 I had an advertisement in the local paper for a dental assistant/bookkeeper type position. A woman of about 30 years of age answered the ad as did a number of other women. But what was so unusual about this one woman was that she had just come from France where she had been a dental assistant. The office at which she worked was very close to the Musée de l'Homme in Paris.

I hired her out of curiosity about what she knew. I won't divulge her name because I'm still not 100% sure that she was sent by the French authorities.

After a few days I called her into my private office and told her the whole story of what happened to us in France. She proceeded at this point to describe to me the French underground forces that are sort of like our CIA. I told her about the controversial nature of my work and she told me that if I pursued this work any further, "they" would kill me. I asked, "Who are they?" She told me to get a book called *J'Accuse*. It would confirm what she had said. Our conversation ended rather abruptly.

I borrowed *J'Accuse* from a college library and she was almost right. The book spoke of the French government working with underground forces and threatening people for various reasons. I didn't know if this book was fiction or what but it was another harsh fact. I had to let her go. I had no choice. This might have been just another coincidence, but once again I thought that there had been just too many coincidences.

BELGIUM TO THE CAVES OF FRANCE

Plans went quickly in 1982 for our next European adventure. There were several objectives for this trip. I will list them in order: 1. See as many caves as possible and find out who lived in them to understand the migration of people from the Tower of Babel. 2. Explore the widest region of southwest France in the time that was available and take as many pictures as we could. 3. Study the famous Neanderthal child from Belgium: the Engis II child at the University of Liége. 4. Visit some of the other prehistoric museums in these countries. 5. Integrate all this into what we had seen in the past two research trips. This was an enormous task.

There is one caution that I must give by way of introduction to this section: some of the evidence that we are about to consider comes from the centers of evolutionary information in Western Europe. These centers have a vested interest in the evolutionary process. Whatever emanates from them must be understood in those terms.

Fossils are found in the ground or on the ground, in caves or out of them, buried under a foot of earth or with no earth or deep down under layers of earth. The disciplines of paleontology and archaeology are not as objective as you might think. They are extremely subjective. The evidence can tell you what you want to hear most of the time, if you are clever enough to invent circumstances in the past that could give rise to the present conditions by which you are confronted.

There are literally thousands of studies that have been done by scientists since Lyell had written about natural forces being responsible for all the geologic strata (rock layers) that are found today.[1] No one person can be knowledgeable about all these studies. I will try to concentrate on the central ideas by special reference to the research that I have done over the past 19 years.

Confronting Uniformitarianism for the Youth

Charles Lyell's main idea was that there were no forces active in the past except those that are working today. We saw this with our discussion of tooth enamel. By this he meant yesterday was the same as today. Tomorrow will be identical. Nothing ever really changes as far as destruction and violence in nature are concerned. Gradualistic processes formed all the major geologic features of our planet in billions of years. He was equating the attributes of geology to the attributes of Jesus Christ — the same yesterday, today, and forever (Heb. 13:8). As far as I know, God is the only one that never changes — not material things or natural things.

Essentially, Lyell was eliminating any consideration of the supernatural events recorded in Genesis, i.e., creation, the Fall, and the flood. What he communicated to the generation of mankind in which he lived was the idea that there was never a time when God could look at the entire creation and call everything "very good" (Gen. 1:31). He concluded that death and destruction were always present on earth. This also was Charles Darwin's conclusion after reading Lyell's tenets and Malthus' writings on the struggle for existence of all creatures.

Darwin himself experienced the death of his mother as a young boy of 8, and at around the age of 42 the death of his daughter Annie, in 1851. It appears that these tragedies not only weighed heavily on him but also against the concept of a good God. This type of grief could have been helped with love, good counsel, reasoning from the Scriptures, and from the natural world itself. He obviously was in a state of remorse in which he blamed God for the suffering in the world.

He wrote this in his autobiography, "This very old argument from the existence of suffering against the existence of an intelligent First Cause seems to me a strong one." I don't know what kind of advice or counsel he received at this time but he couldn't hold to the authority of the Bible and he really didn't want to. He also wrote this in his autobiography, "But I had gradually come by this time, i.e., 1836-1839, to see that the Old Testament was no more to be trusted than the sacred books of the Hindoos [sic]." He made this statement in a letter to a German student in 1879: "Science has nothing to do with Christ, except insofar as the habit of scientific research makes a man cautious in admitting evidence."[2] This seems to me the way that Darwin ruled out the supernatural, by claiming to be cautious. This caution of his opened wide the door for full-blown, 20th century naturalism. His son Francis compiled this information.

I wanted to be cautious also in my understanding of the physical world, but I also wanted to be open-minded enough so as to allow evidence that pointed to God, to be able to really point to God. Therefore, we had to look at this fossil record without allowing any humanistic presuppositions to enter the equation. These would automatically rule out the supernatural.

I had a basic feeling that much contradictory evidence to the standard evolutionary material had to be there, and in order to find it we had to cover as wide an area as possible. I knew that this trip might be my last in this part of Europe because of all the problems we had previously encountered. I wanted this trip to count for the sake of the students in our schools and colleges who had been faced with the contradictions posed by uniformitarian thinking in relation to their biblical understanding. It was around this period that my heart began to feel the pain of those young people, even in some Christian colleges. It is my hope that this book gets to as many of them as possible.

We had to have grace, wisdom, and courage this time. We didn't know what to expect in the way of opposition. We flew into Luxembourg via Iceland on Icelandic Airlines on July 26, 1982. I made a last-minute decision not to take the heavy x-ray equipment because I felt it would have been too cumbersome. We didn't know if we might have to make a quick escape in the middle of the night, and the huge metal boxes would have been too large a burden to carry along.

I had been in contact with Dr. Ubaghs at the Institut de Paléontologie, University of Liège, in Liége, Belgium, by mail. Based on my work at the British Museum, he agreed to let me study Engis II, a Neanderthal child found in Belgium. You must remember that the British Museum and I were still on good terms. They must not have said anything negative about me. This was only 1982. I hadn't been to Israel (1983) yet and told Joe my story. The events described in part of chapter 16 to chapter 18 happened in 1984-85. My son Daniel joined us at work in the lab for the first time in 1982. He showed excellent mechanical capabilities at an early age and finally became an engineer. Now, we were one dad and three expert young scientists.

I'm sure that by now some of my female readers are asking what my daughter did on these trips. She was just two years younger than John and a very smart girl. Her accurate diary provided a cross-check reference to mine and my wife's records in the writing of this book. She was a great help in the museums in Israel and Harvard, but in the beginning she was more comfortable with Mom than with dead bones.

We stayed in Liège from the 27th of July to the 30th. Engis II was the object of study. You will find in the references a detailed account of this fossil.[3] There were some outstanding features of this fossil. First, it was written in the original description of the head that it was very large. Second: the bones of the ear were very fetus-like.[4] These characteristics were obvious as I photographed and measured it. I wished I had brought the x-ray equipment by this time, but I had to be satisfied with what I had. The only teeth that were erupted were baby teeth in the little disconnected upper jaw. The head looked too large and well-developed for the small upper jaw with just the primary teeth. There were also enough loose primary and permanent teeth that I was able to put them into a simulated bite for one side of the mouth. See figure 17. The wear patterns fit exactly for every tooth except the two unerupted permanent molars.

During the process of submitting my first article on this child for publication, one fact was brought out by Dr. Andrew Snelling, editor of the *Creation Ex Nihilo Technical Journal*. He noticed the excessive amount of wear on the first primary (baby) molars as compared to the second primary (baby) molars. This suggested a more protracted time between the eruption of these teeth than found in today's children. These two baby molars usually do have unequal amounts of surface wear because of the different lengths of time in which they have been used. Today's children have their first and second primary molars erupt about 9 months to one year apart. These two teeth in the Engis child look like they

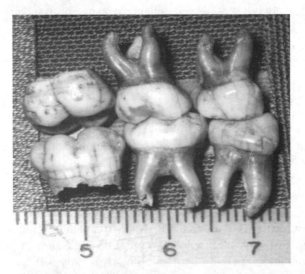

Figure 17. Two permanent and four primary (baby) molars of the Engis II child.

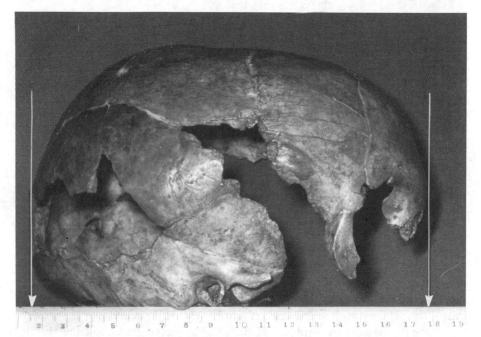

Figure 18. The Engis II child's skull. Front to back, 164mm.

were separated by a much longer time frame than that. The second baby molars appear to have come into the mouth many years after the first baby molars had been in place because of this greater wear difference. This is what protracted eruption means: more years between tooth eruption.

I also discovered that Charles Fraipont had made a huge exaggeration in his original description of the length of the head from front to back.[5] He said the skull was 188 mm long when it was only 164 mm. See figure 18. My measurement was made with the ruler resting underneath the mastoid process. I mean right under the skull! Ann Marie Tillier, a rising star in French paleontology, said in a major article in 1983 that the length of the Engis II child's skull was 176 mm.[6] She is 12 mm less than Fraipont but still 12 mm too long. She was being very diplomatic, and got it half-right. Another coincidence, I suppose, is that her article came out in 1983, one year after I had been to Belgium and measured the skull in 1982. It was getting to be like a chess match — each move I made was followed by a counter-move by them.

This must be a terrible position to be in when you come into a situation like this or in any other paleoanthropology lab and find errors in previous work. Some are probably intentional as I have shown, but some are also probably unintentional. What do you do? All of these so-called great men and women of previous years who have committed these flaws have left legacies of inaccuracies for someone to inherit.[7] Most people, I believe, just go along with the status quo and do not rock the boat. Rocking the boat requires that you believe you are doing the right thing for a greater cause.

THE BORDER CROSSING

We crossed the border from Belgium into France on Friday, July 30, on the highway from Liége towards Cambrai, without incident. We found a small village by the name of Ligny in France where we stayed our first night. We arrived in Saclay, which was southwest of Paris, on Saturday, July 31. This was our first research destination.

From Saclay on Monday morning, August 2, John and I made a very quiet and cautious trip to the Museum in St. Germain-en-laye in a suburb to the west of Paris. Remember, this is the town with the phone booth connection of 1979. This is a famous museum which contains some of the rare antiquities of prehistoric France. It is officially called Musée des Antiquités Nationales. This museum is reported to contain artifacts from the Paleolithic (Old Stone Age), 90 to 9 thousand years ago; the Mesolithic (Middle Stone Age), 9,000 to 6,500 years ago; and the Neolithic (New Stone Age), 6,500 to 1,800 years ago,[8] and perhaps the mysterious phone booth. This museum, as well as other studies, has considered the Paleolithic Age by itself and divided it into Lower, Middle, and Upper sections.

One recent work by Stringer and Gamble has placed the Middle Paleolithic, the era of the Neanderthals, as between 250 and 30 thousand years ago.[9] This period would cover as many as 10 thousand generations of people. They placed the Lower Paleolithic at least 500 thousand years ago. Implicit in all these dates, names, and numbers are assumptions of enormous proportions, not the least of which is the simple to complex assumption.

Chapter 20

More Than One Species of Man?

As soon as you say "lithic" you imply Stone Age images which pop up in comic strips, cartoons, and such. You can't help it. All of us have been permeated with evolutionary thought by all forms of media. Dinosaurs in the 1990s are the new rage. We are constantly bombarded with them from cereal boxes to toothbrushes, from cartoon characters to full-length feature films such as *Jurassic Park*. Man has supposedly never seen a living dinosaur. The flowering of mammals came many millions of years after the age of dinosaurs.

Sixty-five million years ago a great comet supposedly hit the Yucatan peninsula in present-day Mexico, and as a result of the climatic upheaval all the dinosaurs perished. Very small mammals and avian dinosaurs survived and mammalian evolution took off from there. This fact is elucidated in a movie shown to visitors on the fourth floor at the American Museum of Natural History in New York City in the Vertebrate Theater, narrated by Meryl Streep. And, since man is a larger mammal, dinosaurs and men's paths were never supposed to have crossed. There shouldn't be any pictures or carvings of dinosaurs in any caves anywhere. We will shortly see that this isn't true.

Stone Age man conjures up brutish images out of the past. Men are imagined who club women over the head and drag them by the hair into caves. Since this is not politically correct anymore, and also not true, cooperative efforts between sexes in evolution has been promoted. However, all these images also imply a lesser level of intelligence in the past. With a gradual progression of brain enlargement that went along with increased skills in manual dexterity, primitive man-like creatures slowly lumbered along the trail of evolution towards greater complexity. It is typical, therefore, for any naturalistic[1] museum to foster these images. The museum in St. Germain-en-laye portrayed naturalism magnificently, because it had many original artifacts from the caves and shelter excavations of France. Not once did I see any object of advanced artistic quality that was attributed to the European Neanderthals. Why is this? Because it is the prevailing opinion that none of the cave wall art could have been accomplished by Neanderthal men or women since they were incapable of performing on this high level of human development.[2]

PRECISION GRIP

Primarily, it has also been postulated that Western European Neanderthals were primarily hunters and therefore had little time to cultivate their latent talents for art, if they had any at all. These artistic talents were to be brought forth with Cro-Magnon man. It also has been proposed by Trinkaus and Villemeur that Neanderthals of Western Europe had a poor precision grip because of muscle length problems of the thumb.[3] This, of course, would mean that they could not hold a paint brush or carving point very well.

Obviously, this is one of the reasons now put forth to eliminate Neanderthal as one of the persons (if they even would call them that) responsible for wall murals in the caves and also what is termed "portable art." Portable art is that which is done on bones and rocks, and is usually found in caves or rock shelters but can be dug up anywhere. This type of thinking would relegate Neanderthals to a separate species or a sub-species. Both views are still held, but the separate species hypothesis is gaining ground because of recent DNA studies.[4] However, neither group had the advancements of *Homo sapiens sapiens.* Some think Neanderthals were too clumsy with their hands to produce a precision grip with their thumbs and fingers. How then could they produce any type of finely chiseled or tooled work?

This seems to harken back to the "handing a chimpanzee a grape" hypothesis. The fact is, if you give a chimp a grape to eat he cannot hold it between the tips of his thumb and first finger.[5] In other words, he has no precision grip. He must hold it further down on the two digits in a less secure position. I believe that this kind of thinking has influenced the way we consider these early men and women. If you only extrapolate finger use on the basis of assumptions in evolutionary history, you can come up with a result like this. Fingers gradually became more nimble as the brain enlarged . . . correct?

DENTAL CLUES

As mentioned in chapter 9, someone contemporaneous with La Chapelle-aux-Saints or La Chapelle himself attempted to make his one remaining tooth sharper by a sort of filing process. The neatly carved bicuspid or premolar tooth seen in the La Chapelle-aux-Saints upper jaw shows the marks of an artisan of teeth. The old man of La Chapelle must have filed, chiseled, or somehow carved these three sharp facets on the biting surface of his one remaining upper tooth. This unusual piece of dental work has never been revealed before. If it had been shown, the evolutionists would probably have said it was attributable to some abnormal form of tooth wear.

This cannot be attributed to abnormal tooth wear because it is too precise. The ridges produced could only have come from a careful attempt to intentionally sharpen his last upper tooth. No one can chew so precisely on small enough objects to create this neat pattern unintentionally.

Another pattern exists on the mesial (front) or in-between surface of the lower right first molar from the Le Moustier young adult. You can count at least eight or nine sharp scratches in the enamel in the flattened portion of the mesial surface of this tooth. The lower jaw was broken at this point so this surface was easy to examine and photograph. The flattened area appears to have been caused by the interproximal or in-between wear (attrition) on the tooth as it rubbed up against the adjacent tooth in its row. This would be the tooth immediately in front of it (more mesial to it, in dental language). Also, the tooth in front of it doesn't have the corresponding back side or distal side worn down to the same extent. This means that the primary or baby tooth, called the second primary molar, was the tooth that did most of the rubbing against the front surface of this permanent molar. This primary tooth is usually lost at or around 11 years of age. Some children hold on to them a year or so longer.

In my 30 years of practice as an orthodontist I have seen thousands of these primary molars and I can't remember one that caused this much wear on the front surface of a permanent molar.[6]

The scratches on the flattened surface is another phenomenon altogether. These were caused by a sharp instrument or an abrasive substance. If it were an abrasive substance I would expect that it would represent a very fine grain of sand or crystalline substance caught between the teeth for long periods of time. Each time it would be caught in a different place giving rise to what appears to be a roughly symmetrical pattern of scratches. This seems unlikely.

If done after death in the preparation of the fossil jaw, one would expect that whoever did this would have exceeded the limits of the wear area or attritional facet on the mesial surface. If done by Le Moustier himself, once again we need to attribute more manual dexterity to the Neanderthals and a special, very thin, pointed tool. What type of sharpened tool or instrument caused this type of mark?

Alexander Marshak wrote about bone grooves and complicated markings that he called "notations" dating from 30,000 B.C. He believed this practice was employed by the ice age hunters and "the tradition seems so widespread that the question arises as to whether its beginnings may not go back to the period of Neanderthal man."[7] He also qualified this remark by adding, "It is clear, too, that the notations we have analyzed are not yet writing as we know it." He went on to espouse the major assumption in most evolutionary thinking that, "By the Upper Paleolithic, modern *Homo sapiens* was capable of representational art and notation." Poor Neanderthal, just a partially evolved artist and writer.[8]

Philip Smith studied the Solutrean period in France from about 21,000 B.C., supposedly some 20,000 years later than the Le Moustier time frame, and found some flints with exceedingly thin cross-sections. He wondered how these tools could have been very useful in any kind of work since they were so delicate. He thought they might have been "showpieces and luxury items."[9] But could these be the instruments of Le Moustier? No Mousterian[10] piece shown thus far could have fit between the teeth and have made those marks. If a fine piece of metal was found in his cave you can be sure we'd never hear about it. If we did it would be called intrusive from higher levels.

More grooves have been reported on the Krapina Neanderthal teeth right at the juncture between the root and the crown.[11] This spot is called the cemento-enamel junction, because that is where the tooth crown overlaid with enamel meets the cementum covering of the root. The authors called these grooves artificial because of their distinct characteristics, such as their trough-like appearance, striations or stripe-like look, and the reaction of the root cementum to the grooves. They concluded that these grooves were caused by toothpicks. I doubt very seriously whether toothpicks made of wood would scratch enamel as it would the softer root cementum.

I personally have seen toothbrush abrasion grooves on the exposed cementum and root dentin (under the cementum) of people who brush their teeth sideways and cause their gums to shrink back leaving the cementum exposed. A hard-bristled toothbrush will abrade a groove right into the root itself, but leave the hard enamel crown relatively undamaged unless the enamel is undermined.

ANOTHER SPECIES?

A few more references must be mentioned before closing the subject of Neanderthal ineptitude and clumsiness. A recent report out of Arcy-sur-Cure associated a Neanderthal fossil with small personal decorative items.[12] This should have put to rest all opposition to Neanderthal dexterity, but it wasn't enough for these diehard evolutionists who concluded their abstract with, "The evidence supports the hypothesis of a long-term co-existence with techno-cultural interaction between the first modern humans and the last Neanderthals in Europe." Keep the faith, evolutionists, keep the faith. They might as well have said that modern men and women shared their knowledge and trinket-making ability with the poor dumb Neanderthals, obviously a different species. They did try to make a different species case as well, on the basis of the labyrinth of the inner ear. They used seven of the nine original Neanderthals I studied. I can't say they were too convincing, either. The article merely shows diagrams of the labyrinths. I would need to see the actual CT scans on those skulls before I could believe an article with just diagrams again. Too many tricks can be played with diagrams.

Looking at Neanderthal talents we find P. Mellars, in his book *Neanderthal Legacy*, asserting, "Certainly, no serious claim has been made for an association between typically Aurignacian[13] assemblages and anatomically Neanderthal remains in Europe."[14]

Francis Harrold was in disagreement with this concept when he wrote, "Neanderthals thus seem to have been capable of producing much (if perhaps not all) of the range of Upper Paleolithic material culture."[15] Therefore, there is some real conflict here, but the idea that continues to linger in the minds of modern men and women favors us as being the pinnacle of evolutionary progress.

Is there any real evidence of more than one species of man? Turning our attention to the Holy Land we find that on Mount Carmel in Israel, both modern man and Neanderthal were thought to co-exist for 50,000 years. They allegedly never inter-mixed because they were two different species. In *Discover* magazine, J. Shreeve writes, " Two human species, with far less in common than any two races or ethnic groups now on the planet, may have shared a small, fertile piece of land for 50,000 years, regarding each other the whole time with steady, untroubled, peaceful indifference."[16] Just like the Palestinians and Jews do now, right? As a matter of fact, if this were the case, it would probably be the beginning of the first NLO (Neanderthal Liberation Organization).[17]

Before I let this subject drop, because a joke isn't a proper explanation, and too often creationist and evolutionists use jokes as explanations, I must refer you to the later chapters on the ages of Neanderthal men and women. Study these carefully, especially figure 72, and there you will find the answer to why more modern-looking skulls have been found buried at lower levels than the more archaic-looking Neanderthals. According to evolution, the order should be the more modern skulls on top and the primitive or archaic ones on the bottom. Because they are found in reverse or too close to the same levels on Mt. Carmel, one could not have simply evolved into the other, so they were thought to co-exist.

ADVANCEMENT OR ACCUMULATED KNOWLEDGE?

Assumptions play an important role in the development of any theory which attempts to decipher the past by studying artifacts. One must place them in some sort of order. Chronologically, working from the earliest years of man's supposed evolution, the artifacts must by necessity be placed in an ascending order, from simple to complex. One must use the horse and buggy to the modern car type of analogy. What's wrong with that? In this case it is simple stone tools to more complex tools and art.

The problem here is in the faulty logic. It is like saying that Leonardo da Vinci would be incapable of understanding television or building a computer even if he were to be given all the essential information. It's not a matter of any deficiency in the brains of Renaissance men and women in relation to peoples of the 20th century or an advancement of them in relation to medieval peoples. It is simply a case of "accumulated knowledge." Accumulated knowledge is what allows men and women today, much less brilliant than da Vinci, to build computers and lasers. The trouble with evolutionary logic is that it never takes into account the factor of levels of intelligence in the same time frame or the tremendous impact of accumulated knowledge.

Alexander Marshak wrote, "At its simplest, I was assuming that early man was *not essentially a toolmaker,* that is, a creature whose ability to stand and to grasp and use things in his hands had been the primary advance leading to culture and civilization." He continued in this logic, "We therefore need to discuss, not the points and places of supposed origins and beginnings for such cultural processes, but a use of the potentially variable human capacity within a diverse range of conditions and contexts."[18]

Others, like Israeli archaeologist Ofer Bar-Yosef, have said that tools can tell you nothing except the way that the Neanderthals prepared their food. He exclaimed, "If you ask me, forget about the stone tools."[19] So you have these two extremes of thought concerning the tools of early men.

Stringer and Gamble made this truthful statement, "The concept, embodied in these definitions, of technological progress — whereby tools gradually became smaller and finer through time — has long been abandoned."[20] They referred to Boxgrove and Highlodge in England. Finer grades of tools were found than what they expected at both of these places with dates going back to 400-500 thousand years.

If we end with the assumption that man really does acquire more advanced skills as he evolves in the Pre Upper Paleolithic (PUP) and Upper Paleolithic, it is like saying that Henry Ford of Model T fame was a Neanderthal and Lee Iacocca of Chrysler fame was a Cro-Magnon because of the products they manufactured. Is evolution a fact? If it is, then all the humanistic conclusions are fact. If it isn't, then we might be able to make some sense out of the evidence with some clear and novel thinking.

SUB-HUMANS BEFORE ADAM?

Before discussing Adam and Eve and their historicity, we should consider the following questions about the Bible and evolution.

1. Why did God observe the entire creation that he had made and call it "very good," if blood, bones, dead bodies, and fossils were in the ground? (Gen. 1:31).

2. If Adam's hominid ancestors had been going back to dust for millions of years before the Fall, why did God curse him after the Fall and declare that he was going back to dust? That part wasn't much of a curse (Gen. 3:19).

3. Where in evolutionary history can you find the first *Homo sapiens*, Neanderthal, or *Homo erectus* female having no mother, and arising from the body of a *Homo sapiens,* Neanderthal, or *Homo erectus* male? (Gen. 2:21-24).

4. If death and killing existed before Genesis 1, why did God give all the animals, including carnivores, only vegetation to eat? (Gen. 1:29-30).

What happened to the carnivores' hinge jaws, razor sharp molars, and six-inch fangs? Did they use them to pounce on watermelons? How could they exist on vegetation? Don't you suppose that they ate straw like an ox and had different masticatory systems, similar to what they will have again and do again in the new creation described in Isaiah 11:7 and 65:25?

5. When God said to Cain, "The voice of your brother's blood is crying to me from the ground," why didn't Cain reply that this was not abnormal? If evolution were true, he could have said there'd been violence and blood in the ground for millions of years. *Australopithecines, Homo erectuses*, etc., and God had called that "very good." Why was his brother's blood not so good? (Gen. 4:9-10).

6. Isn't God's power in question if He chose to use the struggle of macro-evolution instead of instant creation? (Jer. 27:5).

7. If nature revealed only evolutionary change and not God's invisible attributes, His eternal power, and divine nature, wouldn't unbelievers have an excuse? (Rom. 1:18-20).

8. If you didn't understand the fall of Adam and Eve and its relationship to the phrase, "The creation was subjected to futility," wouldn't you think that God was evil or impotent by considering the world's daily news? (Rom. 8:20-22).

9. Aren't the arguments against the supernatural return of Jesus to earth based mainly on a lack of belief in the supernatural creation and flood events? (2 Pet. 3:3-6).

10. Since Joseph was not the biological father of Jesus Christ, and Mary was a virgin, where did Christ's 23 male chromosomes come from? Where did Adam's 46 chromosomes come from? (Luke 1:35).

11. Did Jesus Christ defeat physical death at His resurrection? In John 20:27 He told Thomas to feel the holes in His hands and the gash in His side. In Luke's account He ate fish in front of them to prove He wasn't a spirit (Luke 24:42-43). If death was natural and freely used by Him in macro-evolution, why did He have to defeat it by being physically resurrected? If Adam brought just spiritual death, why wasn't Christ's resurrection merely spiritual? Paul wrote, "For since by man came death, by man came also the resurrection of the dead" (1 Cor. 15:21).

12. Finally, if the devil brought physical death, why did Christ's sacrifice and physical resurrection only atone for the sins of mankind?

If you had problems answering these questions, think about the truth of no physical or spiritual death before Adam's sin and the historical accuracy of the Genesis account of creation and the Fall.

The idea of a sub-human man was never mentioned by Jesus Christ during His entire ministry on earth. He said clearly to the Pharisees, "Have you not read, that He who created them from the beginning made them male and female?" (Matt. 19:4). In the beginning we have a true male and a true female capable of thought concerning the future conditions of marriage, the "leaving of father and mother," and capable of commitment by joining together in a responsible way to become "one flesh." This is an historical recollection by Jesus of two intelligent people in space and time who were able to consider the commands of their Heavenly Father.

It wasn't a matter of lack of intelligence that caused man's moral rebellion against God, just as it is not a lack of intelligence that is causing our problems today. Education is the cry of an enlightenment-based mentality as the cure for society. Immorality is the real problem. We have lost our base for morals. Society is reeling because of it. It all began with a rebellion against God's moral character. It goes without saying that Adam and Eve were capable of complex human thought, will, and speech — otherwise this temptation wouldn't make any sense.

Therefore, what we are confronted with in the humanistic museums is a continuation of this rebellion. Each museum that portrays the works of supposedly sub-humans presents the Christian adult or child with a seemingly irreconcilable dilemma, a dichotomy. This is one of the great problems of the Western World. It fills all the naturalistic citadels of mankind with misinformation.

COME NOW, LET US REASON TOGETHER, SAYS THE LORD

It is crucial that we not start out in museum or cave explorations with humanistic assumptions. It is essential that we approach this subject from a biblical perspective: What is a biblical perspective when it concerns the study of early man?

1. Man was intelligent and possessed rational thinking and creative abilities from "the beginning" (Gen. 1-3).

2. It wasn't until after the fall of man that the processes of physical death and deterioration were introduced into history (Gen. 3).

3. Humans had extended longevity in the years before the flood, and for a short time after the flood, and children matured at later ages (Gen. 5 through 11).

4 If humans had longer lives, the other created creatures probably had longer lives (assumption).

5. There was a world-changing flood of volcanic and atmospheric origin with a complete change of climatic, stratigraphic, and topographic features of the earth (Gen. 7 through 8).

6. All of history must be divided into pre-flood and post-flood periods (Gen. 7:23).

7. Immediately after the flood the life spans of humans declined.

8. After the flood, in Genesis we find the beginning of officially sanctioned hunting of animals. God gave to Noah's family and succeeding generations "every moving thing that is alive" for food. God said, specifically, that He had previously given them the green plants but now they were allowed to kill animals for food (Gen. 9:3).

9. Pre-flood, we believe that animals also killed other animals, and humans killed humans (Gen. 6:11-13).

10. We also infer that if predatory habits began post-Fall, then the entire anatomical structures of these creatures began to reflect the vicious conditions by which they lived (assumption).

11. Not all humans have the same gifts, some are more intelligent than others, some have more talents and interests (Gen. 4:20-22).

12. The post-flood period was initiated by man spreading out into Europe,

Asia, and Africa due to language differences (Gen. 11:1-9).

13. From these original peoples, far less genetically deteriorated than us, came all the "races" of mankind (Gen. 9:7, Num. 36:1-13).

14. Many changes have taken place in the post-flood period to the earth and its inhabitants as compared to the Garden of Eden (Gen. 1-3).

15. The entire history of the earth and the heavens above (the far-flung universe and its galaxies) is a much shorter period of time than is presented in the museum displays (Exod. 20:11).

16. Apes and men were created separately as genetically unrelated kinds (Gen. 1:25).

17. Apes were created very good in the beginning. This means that they also were not subjected to the effects of the Fall yet (Gen. 1:31).

18. Apes probably were more complex at an early time in earth history, had more abilities, and might have been able to walk close to upright (assumption). They also were most likely created to compliment man in a closer manner than all of the other animals. We infer this from the account given in Genesis when it says, "There was not found a helper suitable for him" (Gen. 2:20). This most likely means that none of the creatures Adam named were close enough to him in kind to have been his partner for life. There must have been some that were closer than others, and this is where, I think, the complex apes fit in. None of these apes, which we now call *Australopithecines* or *Homo erectus* today, fit into the category of "wife," therefore God performed the first surgery on man by tissue removal to form a woman. This would have resulted in a missing rib for Adam. This would have been an acquired characteristic in Adam which could not have been inherited by succeeding generations. His succeeding generations had the original number of ribs: normally 12 pairs.[21] The one missing piece of side or rib was not passed on any more than teeth straightened by orthodontists are passed on from parents to children.

It's worthwhile here to recall the argument of Thomas Huxley as related by Trinkaus and Shipman against languages being the basis for racial separation. They mocked our understanding of history when they said, "Comparative, though sometimes laughable, naïve linguistic studies became an increasing popular means of tracing the relationships and contacts among these ancient tribal groups or races. In vain, Thomas Henry Huxley pointed out the fatal flaw in the logic: 'Physical, mental, and moral peculiarities go with blood and not with language.' In the United States the Negroes have spoken English for generations; but no one on that ground would call them Englishmen, or expect them to differ physically, mentally, or morally from other Negroes."[22]

There are two mistakes Huxley made. The first is that the Bible describes languages that "separate" people groups and cause them to migrate from each other, not join them together. They had no United Nations. A common language in the United States has caused gene flow from one race to another, not division. Physical separation, or isolation of a group of people or animals from their parent stock, is one of the main reasons for genetic separation from the original group. Secondly, if Huxley or Trinkaus and Shipman had ever considered the concept of devolution, the deterioration of the human and complex animal genomes, they could not have made a statement such as this. Noah's family of Shem, Ham, and Japheth and their wives were capable of giving rise to all of mankind because they carried the genes of us all. All that their progeny needed was physical separation, so as not to maintain a homogeneous population. The indicator needles on our tanks read empty now compared to them, and humans could not create any new races or species even with separation. We are far down the line.[23] By the time you finish this book I believe you will understand what I mean.

Chapter 21

Neanderthals Are Post-Flood People Not Square One People

M ost of the human remains that were found in caves and rock shelters in the countries that I visited appear to have been intentionally buried. At other burial sites the method of interment was not so clear. These humans were called Neanderthals because the first recognized partial skull was found in a valley near Dusseldorf, Germany, in 1856, in a valley named after the hymnwriter Joachim Neander. It was in this Neander Valley that workmen excavating a cave for construction purposes came upon this strange-looking top of someone's head (bone only) and some of his other bones. This particular one may not have been an intentional burial, but later on many others were found that bore evidence of human activity on behalf of the dead.

The first three adult Neanderthals that I studied in the Musée de l'Homme in Paris were intentional burials in caves and open rock shelters. I will go into more detail about these discoveries in subsequent chapters; however, for now I would like to establish the fact that the Neanderthals which I have studied all appear to have been post-flood people, mostly buried by relatives and friends.

Therefore, in this post-flood environment in western Europe with its hostile setting of cold, changeable climate, proximity to icy glaciers, completely new botanical conditions, and rugged terrain, mankind was probably spending a great amount of time just trying to survive. Add to this the fact that animals and humans had decreasing life spans and you have the makings of a small, very worried and nervous group of people who probably thought they should have stayed closer to the Middle East. But men and women being what they are, as we have seen all the way down through the ages, continued to strike out to the hinterlands looking for a better life. Migrating farther and farther from the mountains of

Ararat, the Zagros Mountains of present day Iraq, and the Tower of Babel area, all these poor folks could find were caves in which to shelter themselves from the increasingly inhospitable weather.

So, naturally when these people are found in caves and rock shelters, they are called "troglodytes" in French, meaning "cave dwellers." This is not "square one." The earth that their fathers had known was gone and newly created post-flood conditions prevailed. Because of this fact, uniform thinking is both inadequate and dead in this time frame of history. Once upon a time the earth was really different.

Neanderthal pre-history[1] is made to look like "square one" by all the museums, or perhaps square two or three if you take into account *Homo erectus* and all the australopithecines (Southern apes) in Africa. But that is not based on fact at all. Neanderthal history reflects man forced to live under harsh circumstances after the flood because of the wickedness on the earth before the flood.

People with Neanderthal-like features have been found as far west as the Island of Gibraltar; as far east as China, Iraq, and Uzbekistan; as far north as Belgium and Germany; and as far south as parts of South Africa.

INFLATION IS NOT A NEW PHENOMENA

We live in an age of monetary inflation. Little do we realize that we also live in an era of time inflation. The balloon of inflation extends back beyond current times and events. The Federal Reserve policy has nothing to do with this sort of inflation. It concerns numbers of stone, flint-like tools which had to be inflated to justify the total numbers of years that supposedly existed during the three Paleolithic Ages displayed at St. Germain-en-laye museum (90,000 to 9,000 B.C.), a period of approximately 80,000 years.[2]

Some would push the Middle Paleolithic back to 250,000 years before the present, and ending in the Upper Paleolithic about 40 to 30,000 years ago. This figure of close to 200,000 years would require even more tools to justify. If this time span was actually true, one would expect to find in this famous museum and others in Europe, beside millions of tools, evidence of thousands of Neanderthals or pre-sapien peoples who made these artifacts. Skeletons would abound. It has been estimated that there were 10,000 generations of ancient humans in the Middle Paleolithic Age.[3] That could amount to a lot of people.

J. Wymer's university textbook claimed that tens of thousands of stone chippings, called flakes, used for numerous tasks, and cores, have been found at the site of Baker's Hole (Northfleet, Kent, England).[4] This being true, why was there only one hominid skull discovered to correspond to the great numbers of these stone implements at Baker's Hole?[5] Very embarrassing, wouldn't you say? These implements have been divided quite appropriately into categories that sum up their common shapes and sizes.

Stringer has given us the total Neanderthal count of individuals as less than 500. He believed this number to be quite small for "200,000 years of human evolution."[6] Even this approximate number of 500 could be far off because I'll show you how they count "an individual" a little further on.

The common dates for Neanderthals in Europe are around 130,000 to 35,000 years ago.[7] Even though there are more Neanderthals as a group than have yet been found of any early people, the total number of fairly complete Neanderthal skeletons is only about a dozen.[8] Please note this carefully. One dozen complete or partially complete skeletons of Neanderthals have been found out of close to 10,000 generations of Neanderthals and early archaic humans.

ROCKS FROM LOWLY STOCK

The making of these implements by these few individuals has been termed "an industry," which is very odd. It is a borrowed term from modern manufacturing. This term carries with it the connotation of a modern Alcoa, Ford, or G.M. plant in the rough. They want you to believe that our industrial age all started with these poor little rock industries in western Europe or even earlier in Africa or Asia. Oh my, what humble beginnings, but what great progress we've made! We can take heart, dear evolutionary-minded world, that we will definitely continue this magnificent advancement into the distant future.

Thomas Huxley (1825-1895), a contemporary and close friend of Charles Darwin, expressed exactly the same sentiments when he said, "Nay, more thoughtful men, once escaped from the blinding influences of traditional prejudice, will find in the lowly stock whence man has sprung, the best evidence of the splendor of his capacities; and will discern in his long progress through the Past, a reasonable ground of faith in his attainment of a nobler future."[9] He seems to have said, "Now just be quiet and go to sleep. Have *faith* that natural selection, mother earth, will watch over you." "Traditional prejudice" means our biblical heritage. Once we got rid of that, he believed, we would be okay. Why was that true? Well, simply because the Bible describes man as a fallen creature and all of nature as fallen, and instead of a physical ascent there was and continues to be a descent from perfection. The "traditional prejudice" to which he referred is the absolute truth of the Bible. According to Huxley, it's simply a matter of taking on *the new faith* of evolution.

"That lowly stock from whence man has come" would be a politically incorrect statement to make in our generation. Animals that are on the ladder of evolution, according to leading evolutionists, are very close relatives and should be given all due respect. Those of you who read *National Geographic* magazine will know what I mean.

John Landon relates in a *National Geographic* article in 1995, "Jane Goodall brutalized me for four years." His company "uses chimpanzees to test vaccines for the National Institute of Health." "She condemned me as one of the cruelest people in the world," he said. His lab was invaded in 1986 by animal activists from True Friends, "who had broken in the lab, copied records, and made videotape of the cages."[10] According to *National Geographic,* Goodall and Landon are now on friendly terms and she was not part of the break-in.

This attitude of "lowly stock" would be repulsive to True Friends or People For Ethical Treatment of Animals. Yet this statement comes from a leading evolutionist in his time. How could this be? The only answer is that evolutionists can be very inconsistent, because to them truth is only relative to the times in which they live, and not absolute. It changes from generation to generation, depending upon only the prevailing opinions of the age.

This does not imply for one moment that man should mistreat nature or animals and that the Bible has ever given him the license to do so. In fact, it is quite the opposite. The Bible says, "A righteous man has regard for the life of his beast" (Prov. 12:10). Nature should be placed in its proper order. It means that God is to be worshiped and nature is to be cared for, not the other way around as you hear from the liberal pulpit. Nature is not to be worshiped. To the liberals, nature is god and ideas about God have to be cultivated out of humanistic presuppositions; henceforth you have limited gods and unlimited nature. Or to say it another way, eternal and infinite matter and finite god. This is modern man squared, as Dr. Francis Schaeffer has said quite often. [11]

Going back to the rock discussion, Wymer explained, "The hunting bands of the late Pleistocene period formed themselves into highly organized communities. Some were more advanced than others, some advanced hardly at all, but as a species, it is clear that advancement was progressing in one direction."[12] Stringer and Gamble showed four stages of tool technology in Europe, from simple Abbevillean and Acheulean, to more complex Mousterian and Magdalenian.[13]

Isn't it absurd to think that if God created man in His image that after two million years or so, Adam and Eve's grandchildren of 10^4 power were still struggling with rocks? If this were true, God must surely have left some brains out in the beginning. Strange, isn't it, that the American Indians of the Wisconsin area, and probably many more across America, were still making similar points, axes, arrowheads, and spears while Columbus was crossing the Atlantic with maps, compasses, sextants, and gunpowder?

WHAT COUNTS AS AN INDIVIDUAL?

From 25 sites of this so-called Middle to Late Pleistocene epoch Wymer lists 44 individuals whose remains date from 300,000 to 400,000 years before the period of time when the classic Neanderthals of western Europe made their appearance.[14] The entire Pleistocene is 1.6-2 million years. This is highly debatable because of the dating methodology involved.

Just so you understand what the human paleontologists call "an individual," Wymer lists skull fragments and lower jaws of seven individuals from a site in Monsempron, France. These are supposed to represent men and women, as I said before, from an earlier time than the Neanderthals of Mousterian industries. There's that word again. The Monsempron people are classified by Oakley et al. as *Homo neanderthalensis*, although very early ones.

In the *Catalogue of Fossil Hominids*, we find the actual parts which were discovered and designated 1 through 7 for Monsempron, France.[15] Number 7 is (ff) a very fragmentary top of the skull with no facial or basal bones. Number 6 is a single bone from one side of the skull or the other and (ff) very fragmentary. Number 5 is a single bone of the right side of the skull and (f) fragmentary. Number 4 is one upper front tooth. Number 3 is the right half of an upper jaw with six teeth in it. Number 2 is one upper left permanent molar. Number 1 is a lower jaw with three teeth.

It is my opinion that there is only evidence here for two or possibly three individuals at the most. *Numbers 2, 3, 4, 5, and 6 could all be one person. Numbers 7 and 1 could be two others.* Now, I have not examined these remains personally, but the catalogue does list them under seven separate numbers. It is important to see what kind of statistics authors can extract from the record books. In this case Wymer took the seven hominids out of the original records without critically analyzing the data, at least on paper. The catalogue attempts to prevent this by saying that a number given to each piece of the remains does not necessarily indicate one individual. Pales took this count and made four individuals out of it.[16] But Pales did his work back in 1958 before anyone really knew that they needed to fill 200 thousand or more years.

As another example, let's examine what the catalogue lists for the La Quina site in France. This is a true classical Neanderthal site with the remains of 22 separate individuals that were unearthed under the rock shelter in the Charente section of southwestern France. I was able to examine the remains of the La Quina V female adult at the Musée de l'Homme. This skull is on the cover of this book, with its lower jaw jutting forward.

Of the 22 individuals counted by Oakley et al. and 21 by Pales, 12 consisted of only one bone of the skull. Number 17 was one tooth. Number 4 was two teeth. Number 20 was four teeth. Number 1 was two ankle bones that could have belonged to any of the specimens. Number 19 was one kneecap from anybody, and Number 3 was a single bone of the spine, ditto. Number 23 was three skull bones. Ten bones were marked (f) for fragmentary. Number 5 was an almost complete cranium (skull) with jaws and associated bones, and Number 18 was a cranium (skull) of a child with an upper jaw. Of these 22 or 21 specimens, there could be grand total of 6 or 7 individuals but not 21 or 22.[17]

So, it is easy when you count like they do to arrive at large "groups" of individuals. We have to require more accountability from these paleontologists. But how, when these fossils are locked in drawers deep within museums?

GEOLOGICAL BUT ILLOGICAL

At this point we must examine Wymer's textbook, *Chart for "Principle Discoveries of Neanderthal Man" or Allied Human Types in the Late Pleistocene.* He explained that these cover the period of time between 130-40 thousand years B.P. He called the Neanderthals that were found at these sites *Homo sapiens neanderthalensis*, the sub species classification. When you count the number of sites he has listed in western Europe, including Yugoslavia but not Russia, there are 26 principle sites.[18] Twenty-six sites in 90,000 years seems like a big discrepancy in the amount of years or the amount of sites. The settlement in the USA since the early 1600s has been around 400 years. Have you ever seen the cemeteries we have here in New Jersey for only 400 years or less of occupation? Most of them are much, much less. They are super-crowded. It is so bad that many are building large concrete mausoleums to house the dead.

Recently Stringer and Gamble published another more inclusive list covering 224,000 years in Europe with only 38 sites.[19] I don't think it's because they haven't been looking for new sites. It is highly probable that there are more out there, but I sincerely doubt if it's 90,000 or 200,000 years worth of sites, or these long periods of time at all. These are the real numbers that count, so the next time you hear someone on TV talking about millions of years of hominids ask yourself, "How many sites and how many individuals?" The Federal Reserve can't even put a stop to this kind of inflation.

Wymer believes that glacier activities have so changed the topography of the land so many times that we don't have a good record anymore of the early hundreds of thousands of years of human pre-history.[20] Stringer and Gamble elaborated *on the lack of predicted* layers in the caves. They do not think that any cave contains a "complete sediment sequence through the Pleistocene." They also spoke of the sediments which eroded away or stopped accumulating altogether in these caves.[21] Remember, the Pleistocene epoch is supposed to be 1.6-2 million years in length. Think about the fact that there is no cave that contains a complete history of layers. I wonder why? The sediments stopped accumulating? Really, if a creation scientist ever made a statement like that, he would be attacked from every side.

Wymer further elaborated on this enigma. He spoke of putting archaeological sites in a relative order of time. He was very truthful when he admitted that it was the relative order in time that required explanation. "There are no rigid rules and certainly a subjective element is introduced, for the archaeologist must take each case on its own merits."[22]

If you have never heard this before I hope you always remember this statement when you read your Bible and compare it to the "latest archaeological discovery." Especially when the "latest archaeological discovery" contradicts the biblical text. Because of this kind of reasoning, the naturalistic archaeologists are able to turn around and make up almost any story about the temporal relationship of the layers of earth and debris that are found scattered around the world.

There is a chart on a rock near Les Eyzies, the pre-historic capital of France. It displays seven glaciations. The fact is that most "glacial geologists believe that ice ages occurred about once every 100,000 years."[23] The current estimate is that there were approximately 20 ice ages with 60 theories explaining those ages.[24]

An orthopedic surgeon once told me over lunch at our hospital that if there are five or six procedures that are employed by different doctors to operate on a shoulder separation, it probably means there is no single "best" one. The same thing applies to these multiple theories of glaciation which were made up in men's minds: no real answer, only a bunch of theories. However, there is no one amongst evolutionary geologists who holds to only one glaciation for which there is much evidence available.

Recent work by M. Oard presents convincing evidence for only one glaciation period. This glacier formation took place after the flood and covered most parts of the globe.[25] I refer you to his book on this subject since I am not a geologist. However, even though I am an outsider in this field, I cannot help but point out some very interesting contradictions both in theory and in practice.

Chapter 22

Blind Really Means Blind

I t is important to keep in mind the original purposes of the uniformitarian geologists since the time of Hutton and Lyell in the 1700s.[1] It was Hutton who
first stated in our scientific age that the earth had gradually evolved by uniform processes over an immense span of time and he started the idea of what is
called the "Uniformitarian" belief system.[2]

As previously stated, the present became the key to the past. Since they
believed that there were no supernatural interventions at their present moment of
time, they ruled out the supernatural in their own personal lives. Which, by the
way, is why the Bible calls the unbeliever "blind." Then, of course, since there
were no supernatural events in the past obviously none will occur in the future.
They are in for some really big surprises when the Lord returns.

WORKS OF GOD COMPRESS TIME

Jesus urged the Jews of His day to believe in the works that He was doing.
Supernatural works were actually done by Jesus Christ on this earth in space and
time. In John 10: 37-38, we find Our Lord saying, "If I do not do the works of My
Father, do not believe Me; but if I do them, though you do not believe Me, believe the works, so that you may know and understand that the Father is in Me,
and I in the Father." In John 10:25, He said, "I told you and you do not believe;
the works that I do in My Father's name, these testify of Me." He is talking about
supernatural works, plain and simple. He is not talking about mere natural things
that you or I or a trained ventriloquist can do.

He means turning ordinary water into first class wine in seconds, a process
that can normally take years. It starts with the growing of the vine and the grapes,
fermentation, and the necessary aging (John 2). He meant actions like multiplica-
tion of loaves and fishes, which also takes years of time in the ordinary course of
birth and growth of sea life. The whole business of growing, harvesting, and

milling flour for the baking of the dough is no short-term production (Matt. 14). He meant raising the dead, like the daughter of Jairus in Mark 5 or His next miracle in John 11, after admonishing the Jews in John 10. The miracle in John 11 concerned raising Lazarus from the dead. He'd been dead for four days. The longer Jesus waited, the longer the enzymatic breakdown process went on in the body cells, and the harder it became to reverse on a purely natural level. Lazarus' sister made this point very clear to our Lord.

There is also what is no small fact about a lack of oxygen in the brain causing permanent brain damage in minutes, not hours or days. This fact is known by every obstetrician who delivers babies. If babies don't start breathing quickly enough after they come out of the birth canal, if their little mouths aren't suctioned soon enough, their tiny brains suffer from anoxia (lack of oxygen) and they can be permanently brain-damaged.

I once assisted in a surgical procedure called a glossectomy (removal of part of the tongue). The patient was a 6-year-old boy who had an extremely large tongue that hung out of his mouth. I assisted the ENT surgeon (ear, nose, and throat) in the operating room. The little boy's heart stopped in the middle of the operation. The anesthesiologist ordered a large bold-face second-hand clock on the wall be started immediately and 2, 3, 4, 5, 6 seconds went by as the surgeon frantically tried to get the heart to start up again with CPR. By 7 or 8 seconds it started up and a huge sigh of relief spread across the OR. Everyone knew what it meant if the clock went past 30 seconds. In 10 seconds of hypoxic conditions (very low oxygen content) brains cells begin to die. In 3 minutes the entire brain can die if it's deprived of oxygen.[3] Lack of cerebral (brain) blood flow was occurring and permanent brain damage was possible. This is when all doctors, believers and unbelievers, say, "There, but for the grace of God, go I."

Jesus knew these scientific facts and that made Lazarus' resurrection an even greater miracle, if there is such a thing. Are there gradations of miracles? You and I are not capable of restoring stale bread. What can we say?

"By the word of the Lord the heavens were made" (Ps. 33:6), but by the word of uniformitarian scientists like Lyell, Hutton, and Darwin, no supernatural events like this ever occurred on our earth, nor will they ever occur. These men postulated a closed world system utilizing only naturalistic processes. They would say no supernatural events are taking place in the world, in your life or mine either. Why pray? What's the whole point of the Bible if God can't do works and intervene in His own creation? If this world of ours isn't an open world, open to God's intervention, and open for us to escape one day, we're done.

THAT'S THEN, WHAT ABOUT NOW?

Some might be saying, surely the scientific spiritual children of Hutton, Lyell, and Darwin can't believe the same things as the Jews of Jesus day. A Pharisaic attitude might influence their interpretation of science. Is there still spiritual blindness around in our day? This is not a rhetorical question.

I submit these current statements to show you what the modern scientists believe. From a college text, *The Earth's Dynamic Systems*, author W. Kenneth Hamblin states, "The assumptions of constancy in natural law are not unique to the interpretations of geological history; they constitute the logical essentials in deciphering recorded history as well. We observe only the present and interpret past events on inferences based on present observations. We thus conclude that books or other records of history such as fragments of pottery, cuneiform tablets, flint tools, temples, and pyramids, which were in existence prior to our arrival, have all been the works of human beings, despite the fact that postulated past activities have been outside the domain of any possible present-day observations. Having excluded supernaturalism, we draw these conclusions because humankind is the only known agent capable of producing the effects observed."[4]

The strange fact is that they would never consider these things listed above as happening by supernatural means; they would also never consider them as happening by chance either. They had to be man-made, the works of human beings. Why? Because their very nature implies workmanship, not accident. The fallacy in their theory is this: they say that even though all of the above listed artifacts were obviously planned and designed, man himself was neither designed nor planned, but that man just happened by a series of accidents over eons of time.

In another college text on evolutionary biology, Douglas Futuyma of the State University of New York has said, "By coupling undirected purposeless variation to the blind, uncaring process of natural selection, Darwin made theological or spiritual explanations of the life processes superfluous." He further elaborated, "Together with Marx's materialistic theory of history and society and Freud's attribution of human behavior to influences over which we have little control, Darwin's theory of evolution was a crucial plank in the platform of mechanism and materialism-of much of science, in short-that since has been the stage of most western thought."[5]

In his book, *Darwin on Trial*, Phillip Johnson relates how the National Academy of Sciences told the Supreme Court that the most basic characteristic of science is "reliance upon naturalistic explanations," as opposed to "supernatural means inaccessible to human understanding."[6]

A MIDDLE ROAD

There must be some middle road, you say. There must be some famous evolutionist who allows the works of God sometime, somewhere, maybe just to get things started in the beginning. Such a person exists, and he gave his testimony at a trial in Arkansas in 1981 for the plaintiffs who were attempting to have a balanced treatment law overturned by a judge in Little Rock. It was called Act 590 and was passed by the Arkansas legislature in 1981. It mandated that a form of creation science be taught in the public schools if evolution was also taught. In the proceedings of the trial on December 8 the famous professor of geology at

Harvard University, Stephen J. Gould, was called to the stand.

He was asked if evolutionary theory presupposed the absence of a creator. Gould answered, "No evolutionary theory functions either with or without a creator, so long as the creator works by natural laws." [7]

What kind of a god did Gould permit in his theory? The only kind Gould would approve is who one spells his name with a little "g" and not a big "G." This is the only kind of god that is allowed to work in Gould's universe. Obviously, this kind of god does nothing outside nature or "supernaturally." For those of you who follow trends of thought in history, there hasn't been much change of attitude since Jesus' day, or for that matter, from the days of the ancient Greek gods in Socrates', Plato's, or Aristotle's time. Those gods were not deity. They were nothing more than amplified humanity. The similarities between Zeus and Apollo and Mercury with the humanistic god of S.J. Gould are remarkable.

Other professors of science such as Frederick Grinnell place any supernatural interchange between God and man in a category that takes it out of the realm of logic. Grinnell claimed that the human mind is useless in this regard. He wrote, "Encountering the presence of God means extinguishing the human intellect to the point of no-thingness." He said, "True knowledge transcends the world of things, the world of contradictions, the world of logic." [8]

This is a splendid example of modern man's divided intellect. On one hand, the true God of the Bible cannot be approached with reason because the content of religion is too subjective. On the other hand, the world of science can be understood by the process of reasoning because it consists of objective fact.

Yet we have the Lord telling us to love Him "with all your mind" (Matt. 22:37) and in Isaiah 1:18 exhorting us to "Come now, and let us reason together." This certainly must mean that God considers that the concepts in the Bible are able to be comprehended with rational thought and that our minds are important.

This is not pure "rationalism" which elevates the human mind above the Scriptures. However, having said this, we cannot ignore the role of faith in this place. There is always the requirement of faith whatever the position may be. The aid of God himself in the person of the Holy Spirit is crucial to this process. Therefore, we cannot simply dismiss all theological thought as beyond our realm of understanding.

The human mind is an important ingredient because the Fall did not make man a "zero." He has some capability. However, man cannot build a natural theology starting from himself and the universe around him without ending in disaster. Yet man is told to consider the knowledge in the Scriptures and decide if it explains his most profound intellectual questions. If the mind was incapable of considering these options, what would be the point of God's exhortation to reason and what would be the point in the wisdom of the Book of Proverbs?

We must also recall the words of Charles Darwin in 1873 who, in a letter about his religious beliefs to a Dutch student, said, "The safest conclusion seems to me that the whole subject is beyond the scope of man's intellect but man can do his duty."[9] What he expressed here is that religion is beyond our ability to think about rationally, and that we must put it into some remote upper compartment in our minds where logic and reason do not dwell.

Darwin therefore affirmed his deepest belief: the Bible cannot be seriously studied and understood by man. A literal translation of the Bible to Darwin was a fallacy. For Darwin in his day and for Grinnell in our day, the Bible was only a personal, and therefore subjective, experiential type of philosophy, but no more. To them and many who followed in their footsteps, the Bible could be neither historically nor scientifically true. In Darwin's day the entire idea of "truth" began a headlong tumble from which it has never recovered.

PHILOSOPHY OR FACT?

What we have been hearing from these modern professors is that the theories of evolution are firmly seated on top of facts of science — such things as caves, tools, fossils, and such. Nevertheless, in the same creation/evolution trial in Arkansas in 1981, Michael Ruse, professor of philosophy, University of Guelph, Ontario, Canada, testified for the plaintiffs. Dr. Ruse said, "The theory of evolution does not extend to the source of life, that it takes life as a given." (Science has always held the source of life to be chemical evolution.)[10]

In an American Association for the Advancement of Science meeting in 1993 in Boston, he said something quite different. In his AAAS presentation Dr. Ruse stated that, "Evolution, akin to religion, involves making certain a priori or metaphysical assumptions, which at some level cannot be proven empirically." He also said he thought that for some prominent evolutionists, "evolution functioned, at a level, as a kind of religion."[11]

This rocked the modernistic scientific establishment, which has always held that evolution is science, while creationism is religion. To admit to a pre-suppositional faith based in such philosophical beliefs as the non-existence of the supernatural or impersonal supernatural is a unique expression of genuine forthrightness on Dr. Ruse's part.

Now this is a horse of a different color. It's like a religion, he said. Everything they think, say, and do with scientific facts now has to be seen through this new lens. It is a religious lens. This lens that Dr. Ruse permits us to use to look at the rock layers, and fossil and bone arguments reveals that they are all based on a belief system of *certain assumptions* about origins (metaphysical). This is really what we've known all along, but they've been very reluctant to admit. That is backed up by faith.

JUST THE EVIDENCE MA'AM ... JUST THE EVIDENCE!

Paraphrasing Sergeant Friday's line from the old "Dragnet" TV show epitomizes the cry of the evolutionist. This remains their plea in spite of their inner thought world, as revealed by Dr. Ruse. According to them, it is their evidence against our faith. This argument now can be very accurately described as our faith and evidence, against their faith and evidence.

Moreover, we are both basically working with the same facts only sometimes, because quite often, as this book contends, we are handed adulterated facts. It becomes a battle of faith versus faith, and the faith on the evolutionary side forces them to adjust certain data to meet the needs of the hour.

Because of this faith in uniformitarianism there is also some convenient pre-suppositional logic for any problem presented by the archaeological record. I quote Wymer's text again: "More important, to the archaeologist, is the interpretation of archaeological material found within stratified sediments. The simple law of stratigraphical succession[12] will always apply, but it also has to be remembered that these laws apply to the deposit and not to the objects found within it."[13]

This is really a clever way of not having to admit to finding something too recent or young in an older or earlier layer. This exception to the law of stratigraphical succession pretty much gets rid of all "too modern" pre-flood data in a "scientific" way.

The Bible says that Jubal played the lyre and pipe before the flood. In a moment of unusual veracity, it was admitted that a bone whistle had been found deep down at Haua Fteah, in Cyrenaica, Libya. Gowlett reported that this was the oldest musical instrument ever discovered. This instrument is supposed to be at least 60 thousand years old.[14] It was found far below the Mousterian (simpler) tool levels. The only bone whistles like it have been discovered in Paleolithic levels, more than 30 thousand years later. So this is a significant discrepancy in proficiency level assumptions.

The father of French paleontology, Henri Breuil, along with R. Lantier has written, "There will, of course, appear in each layer 'reshuffled objects,' but their physical state will normally enable them to be detected. It is logical that only the most recent objects in a layer will enable its age to be determined, provided they have not been introduced by some secondary process."

When all appears lost, they can always call it "cryoturbation."

They went on to say, "Hard frosts followed by spring thaws, produced in shallow shelters and cave entrances cryoturbation phenomena, bringing up to the surface buried objects. During the thaws they sank again, assuming an upright position, but reaching different depths and not going back exactly to where they were before. This process may have brought up near the surface older and more deeply buried objects, while more recent ones may fall lower than their original level; hence an intermingling of two levels in direct contact."[15] I imagine that you believed archaeological discoveries in caves and shelters were very precise.

WHAT TO DO WHEN FINDING AN OLD BONE TOO RECENT!

Let's make up some hypothetical situations to discover how much you learned from the previous discussions. Let's say you walked into a cave in Western Europe and found a piece of Neanderthal skull buried five inches beneath the surface. Suppose you didn't like this recent position and wanted to find a "reason" for its being too high in a very recent layer. First, you could figure out a way to say that other layers on top of this bone eroded away. Therefore leaving it almost exposed. Water, wind (in a cave?), and amateur diggers could all be blamed. Second, you could find a way to say that the sediments stopped accumulating on top of this bone in the cave 50 thousand years ago until the day you found it. All stone, dirt, and dust were suspended in mid-air for 50 thousand years. If you could find out how this was done — open up a cleaning service, you'll make millions. Third, you might want to call it cryoturbation and say it was forced up from the 50,000-year layers to more recent layers, but first check out the local ice age schedule to see if it coincides. If not, you can probably figure out a way that the Neanderthals delivered ice to that cave to keep their meat cold. Maybe that would get you into more problems trying to understand what they knew about meat spoilage. Pasteur hadn't been born yet. If you're really clever you can come up with an ante-Pasteur. But then you have to find some salami, provolone cheese, olives, and lettuce in an ice age when there were no Italian restaurants.

Chapter 23

La Chapelle-aux-Saints and Time

To understand this philosophy a little better we must start with a specific example in a town in Southern France called La Chapelle-aux-Saints or "the church of the saints." The name of this village, by its very nature, projects an image of holiness. The only problem is why it is famous. The important Neanderthal skeleton from La Chapelle-aux-Saints was found in 1908. Human paleontologists said La Chapelle and his fellow Neanderthals lived between 50 and 60 thousand years ago. Tattersall places him at 50 thousand years before the present.[1] This general range has been enlarged by Trinkaus and Shipman to between 100 thousand and 35 thousand years ago.[2]

This new expanded range is now thought to be the era when the Classic Neanderthals inhabited Western Europe. The 35-thousand-year figure has been obtained from excavations in 1979 at Saint-Césaire, France.[3] The skull found at this site is thought to be one of the latest Neanderthal survivors in history. This recent Saint-Césaire Neanderthal was found with higher grade stone tools (Châtelperronian) than are usually associated with a Neanderthal occupation.[4] This presented a major problem, because it was believed that Neanderthals only employed Mousterian (simpler) tools. However, St. Césaire was thought to be the exception and not the rule in Neanderthal culture, and consequently it didn't really make a huge difference in the way paleontologists viewed Neanderthal capabilities. They were still supposed to be inept and rather dull, although it has been acknowledged that Neanderthals could do some advanced planning.[5]

Even more recent then St. Césaire is the Neanderthal from Zafarraya, in the south of Spain, which is supposed to be closer to us at 27,000 years old.[6] It will be a surprise if the Zafarraya remains are actually confirmed at this date.

Figure 19. La Chapelle-aux-Saints' burial cave.

La Chapelle was found on August 3, 1908, near the village of La Chapelle-aux-Saints, 25 miles southeast of Brive-La-Gallard in the Corrèze region. According to the general consensus of authorities, the remains of this Neanderthal were buried around 50-60 thousand years ago.[7] We arrived in Brive-La-Gallard on August 3, 1982, precisely 74 years from the day of its discovery. This coincidence was not planned. We stayed in the Brive Mercure hotel in "Le Griffolet," on the Route d'Objat. This inn was our home base of operations for our excursions into the Dordogne and Corrèze regions with their rivers, caves, rock shelters, and limestone cliffs.

The cave in figure 19 where La Chapelle was found was excavated by three brothers, two of whom were Catholic priests. Their names were Amédée and Jean Bouyssonie and their brother Paul. The words "Par Les Abbés Amédée et Jean Bouyssonie et leur frére Paul" were on the large metal dedication plate embedded in the rock to the right and over the entrance to the cave. Moss was starting to creep over the plate in 1982 and the engravings were fading away. These words were also on the plate: "En Cette Bouffia Bonneval." In this Bouffia Bonneval (the name of the cave) "Fut découverte et exhume" was discovered and exhumed, "Le 3 Août 1908", August 3, 1908. "Le Squelette d'un Homme Mousterien." The sign plate was streaked with dirt and green drippings from above, and at the bottom it appeared to have a date of 1958 when erected.

This curious name, "Bouffia de la Chapelle-aux-Saints," was also written on a small apothecary can that I found in the same cabinet drawer that contained the La Chapelle skull in the Musée de l'Homme. This little canister contained a very worn upper permanent molar tooth. It was found in this cave and, in all probability, this is a molar from the La Chapelle upper jaw. This is seen in figure 61.

According to Trinkaus and Shipman, the word "bouffia" means "foxhole," while Bonneval was the name of the property owner.[8] They reported that only the two Abbés were the discoverers. Brother Paul was left out.

I have no reference marker for size in my photos and I took no measurements, however, I took a photo from the inside of the cave and my body was half bent over about midway inside. The kids went in and out and, according to my memory (I didn't measure it), the cave was approximately 18-20 feet deep and about 12 feet maximum down to 4-5 feet width in the back with a low ceiling less than six feet above the floor. I had to bend over to walk around in it.[9] "A bank of marly limestone" is the description of F.M. Bergounioux written in French. He went on to describe the grave itself contained in the cave as a "rectangular fossa of 30 centimeters deep and 1.45 meter length and 1 meter in width." Bergounioux continues to describe the position (carefully laid out) and direction of the body (head towards the west) as it was intentionally buried. Bergounioux also makes careful reference to the dimensions of the cave.[10]

There were no other people or guards around the site, so I was able to examine the inside of the cave very carefully. I dug in the loose but very stony sand and gravel with a small trowel and was amazed at how quickly I excavated 50-60 thousand years of time and sedimentation by digging down only 30 centimeters (a little less than a foot). Perhaps a few inches had accumulated between 1908 and 1982.

This is a very shallow grave. When it was discovered, there must have been earth packed into the very small opening of the cave which probably accumulated with time. Mellars exhibited a diagram of the La Chapelle cave from M. Boule's 1909 description.[11] It showed approximately three feet of soil or gravel on top of the grave rather than 12 inches. However, at the base or ground level where I was standing, just 74 years earlier, in August of 1908, La Chapelle's bones would have rested close to a foot beneath my feet, and that one foot of stony sand was intentionally piled up over the body. I may never understand how anyone can say that a skeleton can be buried in less than a foot of earth in a shallow cave and be preserved and undisturbed for 50-60,000 years.

BELLES PIÈCES DE JASPE

The contents of the grave brought up another interesting point. Bergounioux described them as follows: some quartz flakes, some long bones over the skull, the skull was surrounded with *"belles pièces de jaspe"* (beautiful jasper stones), tiny fragments of ochre, a paw or hoof and leg portion of a cow-type creature (a bovide) with its muscle meat and skin. The shank was still connected to the bones of the hoof or paw (the phalanges). The muscle, skin, and ligaments did not persist on the bones but it was surmised that they were present at burial because of the surviving joint connection.[12] He mentions these jasper stones twice so it seems that he was sure of their presence.

This ritualistic burial has also been described by Trinkaus and Shipman. There was no reference to the jasper stones in their description whatsoever.[13] I am aware of no other reference to the presence of these stones other than that of Bergounioux. Why is this so?

First, all pre-historians agree that Neanderthal man was not supposed to have made or worn any jewelry or semi-precious stones — only some shells, bones, and teeth.[14] For another species of *Homo* (man), this would have been very improbable. For real men and women anything could be possible. But since the prevailing opinion goes against the "normal man" approach, never has it been reported that a Neanderthal traded or mined jasper stones. There was supposed to be an explosion of ornaments for the body in the Upper Paleolithic in the early Aurignacian.[15] Stringer and Gamble make a strong statement concerning this type of ornament. "No ornaments or necklaces have been found with Neanderthal fossils."[16] Please note well here the negative tone of this fact. No means no. How can we as scientists and Christians continue to go along with hidden facts and change our biblical interpretation based on untruths? I am not implying that Stringer or Gamble knew about these, but what I am suggesting is that these jaspers of old La Chapelle were eliminated as soon as the early paleoanthropologists realized their implications and Stringer and Gamble didn't believe Bergounioux if they saw that report. Add to this the fact that Smith, an expert in Solutrean culture discoveries, indicated that in the Solutrean (c. 21,000 B.P.) times fine ground and brightly colored jaspers and quartz were plentiful.[17] The jaspers in La Chapelle's grave represents about a 30-thousand-year discrepancy in time.

"Jasper is a granular type of fine-grained quartz usually colored red by the inclusion of finely divided hematite (iron oxide), but may be yellow or brown by the inclusion of other iron oxides."[18] This finely colored mineral is found in many places in Europe and Asia and one cannot be sure if it was found in France or not. As far as I know, this is the only report of this particular Neanderthal burial custom in the literature. None of the more popular Neanderthal references in English have ever mentioned it. Here is an excellent example of natural selection. The jaspers have been "naturally selected" out of the reports. It is just "natural" for evolutionists to do this.

Being filled with natural presuppositions they have no room for anything that might give even a slight indication of any other form of thought.

Red Ochre and Time

One more example of a burial omission is important to our discussion. In reference to Neanderthal burials, it has been long held that the practice of using red ochre (lumps of iron oxide or types of haematite) was restricted to the Upper Paleolithic cultures.[19] Neanderthals were not supposed to have used it in their graves. Was there any evidence of red ochre found by the excavators of Neanderthal graves when they were discovered except what Bergounioux just mentioned?

In figure 20 (in color insert section) you can see the mandible (lower jaw) of La Ferrassie I is infiltrated with red ochre in many places. See figure 21 (also in color insert section), which also bears evidence of more red ochre used in burials. This time it was from a Neanderthal child's burial and the view looks out of the eye sockets and nasal opening from inside the skull of Pech de l'Azé.

Once again we see an example of time shrinkage as we did with the lack of remains in the human fossil record for a couple of hundred-thousand years, jasper stones in La Chapelle's grave and Solutrean culture, the amount of soil over La Chapelle-aux-Saints, and now red ochre before the Upper Paleolithic. Links from Neanderthals to Upper Paleolithic customs are growing. Time is being dissolved by facts.

MIDDLE EAST OCHRE

C.L. Wooley, a famed explorer of the fertile crescent area formerly Mesopotamia (land between the rivers, Tigris and Euphrates, present-day Iraq), found and recorded at a "Ubaidian" cemetery in Ur, red ochre on two bodies. This was from a period of time estimated at between 5000 and 3500 B.C. by Lloyd. He recorded the fact that, "In two graves, the upper part of the body was covered with fine red powder, and in one case there lay by the head a lump of red haematite paint. Whether the bodies had been painted it was impossible to say; but there was no doubt that the powder was the same as the paint in the lump."[20]

This demonstrates a burial practice shared in common among those in Europe in Neanderthal times and in the Middle East during an allegedly later period. Were they contemporaneous? This singular custom may point to a similar time frame in history. Why have these evidences been ignored? Evolution demands much more time to make biological and cultural transitions. It is natural. For as Paul says, "But a natural man does not accept the things of the Spirit of God, for they are foolishness to him; and he cannot understand them" (1 Cor. 2:14).

JASPER IN MESOPOTAMIA

Another connection can be made between the Neanderthal grave jaspers of La Chapelle in France, the Solutrean jaspers, and a certain custom of an ancient civilization of the Fertile Crescent in the Middle East. Later in time the Ubaidians gave way to the Sumerians and numerous settlements were established by them supposedly by 3000 to 2500 B.C. They are also known in the Bible as the people of the land of "Shinar" (Gen. 10:10).

"The Sumerians had established a number of independent city-states consisting of walled cities and surrounding countrysides. The earliest was Eridu, but Ur, Uruk, Umma, and Lagash were also well-known. To the north of the Sumerians, a Semitic-speaking people known as the Accadians had settled."[21] Uruk is the Erech of Genesis 10 and Accad is described in Genesis 10 as being built by Nimrod. Ham was the grandfather of Nimrod.

There were three periods designated by scholars that categorized this early

Sumerian civilization. The Early Dynastic Age was followed by one in which the Sumerian city-states were captured by the Accadians and Sargon (the son of Nimrod?), its leader. The Third Dynasty brought a reuniting of the city-states under Ur-Nammu of Ur, which was around 2070 to 1960 B.C. This was a "final flowering"[22] of Sumerian culture that was eventually destroyed when conquered by Hammurabi (1792-1750 B.C.) of the Amorites. These dates are not to be taken as absolute.

Ur should strike a note in your mind, because this city-state was the original home of Abraham who was called Abram. He was a descendent of the line of Shem. His grandfather was Nahor. His father was Terah, and he was born in the land of Ur (Gen. 11:31).

A certain object was found in excavations of the ancient dynasties of Sumer or Shinar. Objects such as this were used for identification and writing purposes. They were called cylinder seals. Such articles were made of hard baked clay, stone, or other mineral. Names or inscriptions were engraved on the surface of such seals and they, in turn, were impressed on soft materials, such as a clay tablet or a clay sealing of a jar. When used this way, they would leave an imprint in the softer material. The cylinder seal could be rolled over and a complete sentence could be spelled out. "The cylinder seal became a sort of Mesopotamian trade-mark, although its use penetrated Anatolia, Egypt, Cyprus, and Greece."[23]

One important inscription has been found on a cylinder from the circa 2000 B.C. period of Sumerian history. This was translated by E.A.W. Budge and quoted by Cornelius S. Hurlbut Jr. of Harvard University in his text, *Minerals and Man.* It reads as follows: "With a seal of Gug (red carnelian or jasper) a man will never be separated from the protection of his god."[24] This seemed to be more than a "good luck" charm. A person who carried one of these jasper stones almost had a little piece of heaven in his pocket. Could this be the reason the jaspers were placed around the old man from La Chapelle-aux-Saints as he was buried in his grave in the "bouffia"? There were no inscriptions on the Neanderthal jaspers but the thought could be the same. Were there any Neanderthals in Sumer? See "Big Foreheads of Shinar" in chapter 32.

My interpretation of the jasper connection is this: Jasper is part hematite. Hematite, because of its redness, has a connotation of life. Obviously, the color of blood is red. In order to prepare a body for "the afterlife" when it has lost all its color, red stones and red ochre powder became man's futile attempts to grasp immortality. The connection is clear. The Bible proclaims, "The life of the flesh is in the blood" (Lev. 17:11), but Paul warned us that "Flesh and blood cannot inherit the kingdom of God" (1 Cor. 15:50). For the mortal to put on immortality, the red blood of the Son of God had to be shed. There is power in His blood and not in the red powder.

Chapter 24

The Secret of Bernifal

There were four caves on our list that I thought were very important. They were all in the region of Les Eyzies. Les Eyzies is a village at the confluence of the Beune and Vézère Valleys. There is a river in the Vézère Valley and a creek in the Beune Valley, the Petite Beune River. The larger tortuous and twisted Vézère River eventually empties into the much larger Dordogne River. As described in chapter 5, Les Eyzies is the capital of pre-history in France.

In three of these caves we were escorted by tour guides, but when we entered the fourth we examined it closely *without any authorities present*. The first three: Rouffignac, 14 km from Les Eyzies; Combarelles, 3 km from Les Eyzies; and Font-de-Gaume, 2 km from Les Eyzies, all had fees for entrance and tours of the long, selected routes in each cave. There were many public passageways in these first three caves and many that were blocked off to the public.

The standard evolutionary cave propaganda was preached by each of the tour guides in French, whether it was a walking tour or a miniature train tour. If you were a creationist, you needed a very thick skin and a lot of anti-acid medicine for your stomach when you visited these caves. It also probably would help if you didn't understand French. Unfortunately, I understood a little, but enough to be uncomfortable on the tours.

The fourth cave or "Grotte," as the French call it, was the very dark and extraordinary Bernifal. Bernifal is 5 km from Les Eyzies and required some real searching to discover its whereabouts. There were no signs in Les Eyzies or outside of town indicating where it was located. The people we asked merely shrugged their shoulders. Some also puffed air out of their mouths, which seems to be almost a French custom when encountering a problem. Finally, we found a couple of friendly souls that were neither shruggers nor puffers and they gave us some rough directions which lead to the general vicinity.

I had previously purchased a small booklet at the Museum of Saint Germain-en-Laye which described this cave along with many others. It was a guide book which described the decorated caves "ouvertes au public" (open to the public).[1] It provided some directions which my small band of "middle and high school French scholars" poured over. The kids provided me with three different interpretations. I concurred with a little of each. There were some similarities, so we built on those and made our way down route D 47.

In another book that I had taken with us, Ann Sieveking describes the important caves of the valley of the Petite Beune River. She says, "Eleven decorated shelters have been found in the valley of the Petite Beune, distributed on either side of the river over a distance of about seven kilometers. Only one of these, Bernifal, is a cave of major importance and it is a deep cave while the majority of the lessor sites are daylit shelters. The shelters will here be described as they occur going upstream from the direction of Les Eyzies. Bernifal is, in fact, the third cave, but its importance allows it to be described first."[2] The guide book mentioned above described the cave as being approximately 5 km from Les Eyzies in the community of Meyrals very near route D 47.

Another problem arose when we looked for this very important cave in the recent Michelin map of the Périgord.[3] We had just purchased it in 1982, but it did not reveal the location of Bernifal, even though it did display all popular grottes (caves) and shelters. The little guide book from the museum was published in 1976 and Sieveking's book in 1979. Both had spoken about it in detail. It was strange that the Michelin map had completely left it out when it was of major importance. The guidebook advised bringing one's own light to see Bernifal. While it was open to the public, no light was provided for you to see the walls. I had never heard of a public cave with no lighting. It also said that the floor of the cave was very slippery and you just might fall without a "appui de la main" or cane. That, in itself, is enough to make one suspicious. Open but slippery and dark didn't sound too inviting to the average tourist.

Apparently these words and omissions fell on deaf ears and some people still came to Bernifal. By the time we arrived in the summer of 1982 a decision was made to close Bernifal to the public. It didn't make too much sense since the caves are large tourist attractions and therefore sources of revenue. Bernifal was open at least from 1976 to 1979. So, with Bernifal not on the Michelin map, it became almost invisible. All we could conclude was that something was wrong with Bernifal and that tourists were not to be allowed inside anymore. After weighing all the previous knowledge, we became more determined to find it.

Apparently someone else thought that closing the cave was a bad idea, too. Whoever this was unofficially opened it to the public once again. This time the cave was not opened by a bureaucratic government agency, but by someone using a much more rapid method called "the axe or sledge hammer" technique, to bash in the front door. That's how we found it when we finally located the entrance. However, locating it wasn't so simple. After driving around a while, we finally spotted the supposedly prominent landmark near the cave described in the guidebook. It was the château de Vieil-Mouly. At first, we had been baffled in our quest for this landmark. The château (castle) was supposed to be on the left side of the road. We went up and down the road several times before deciding that a stone-stucco house on the left side with a small tower-like structure attached to it could actually be called a castle or château. Of course we really had to stretch the definition of a castle to match what was really there. It certainly didn't match any of the other castles we had seen. However, there was a large farm field across the street from the château and we noticed a farm house adjacent to the field. This part fit the description. I parked the van on D47 at the end of the field far away from the farm house. A stream wound its way along the edge of the field flowing next to the road. It would be necessary to cross this stream in order to get to the field. Our guidebook said that one should walk across a "valley" after crossing the stream. Looking into the distance we could see the face of a small cliff on the other side of the field. We deducted that the field must be the "valley" and the Bernifal cave must be somewhere in the cliff on the other side. Our directions said it should be a ten-minute walk from the road to the cave. We also noticed that there was a large camper van also parked on the same side of the road but closer to the farm house. There were only two parked vehicles on that street.

We proceeded towards the farm house after we noticed that the only bridge across this stream was directly in front of the house. It was a small bridge which had a chain extending from one side of it to the other and a sign hanging from the middle of the chain. It read, "Passage interdite," meaning crossing was forbidden. We didn't have to get out our pocket French-English dictionary to translate that. Most of us knew what it meant, so we couldn't plead ignorance. The fact that crossing was forbidden was clearly meant to keep tourists off the property that belonged to the inhabitants of this farm house. No problem, we thought . . . we'll just go ask the farmer for permission to cross over the bridge. We were pretty bold, or naive, once again. There on a sunny day in southern France, a daddy, a mommy, and their five children knocked on the door of a farm house for permission to cross over private property when there was a sign saying that you couldn't cross over.

We knocked, and knocked and knocked but there was no farmer or no Mrs. farmer either. What to do? No one was home. Well, knowing us, by this time you should have guessed that we jumped over the chain and crossed the forbidden bridge. We then were on another adventure.

ACROSS THE BATTLEFIELD

We crossed the valley like a platoon of soldiers crossing a battlefield. Our eyes were constantly looking in every direction hunting for the dreaded farmer or some farm hand. We tried to stay low but we stood out like tall corn stalks above the vegetables and grass. There was a clear path that we followed through the vegetation that led to the base of the cliff. I didn't know how we were going to climb this cliff. As we pondered that question, someone saw another path that looked like it went up a large hill that might take us around the other side of the cliff. We started up the new path, and as we climbed higher and higher we came upon a plateau which was heavily wooded. By this time we were out of the sight of the farmhouse and, hopefully, safe. We moved along the path behind the cliff until eventually we found the entrance to a cave. It was nestled among a dense grove of trees, and approachable only by a deep gouge cut into the earth of the hillside. This dug-out lane was 4-6 feet high on either side and not very long. It led right up to the front door.

An amazing fact was the condition of the front door to the cave, as we found it on August 4, 1982. This large, wooden door to the primary entrance was split in half. I solemnly promise all my readers, and the French authorities, that we had no part in the splitting of this door. We entered into the pitch blackness of Bernifal, with great caution at 10:30 a.m. It was no shock to find that the floor was very muddy. Walking had to be done with care. We only had four flashlights, and we all tried to stay close together. It was a very frightening but exciting adventure for all of us. We set up the two oldest boys as a guard at the door to rotate every ten minutes, just so nobody could surprise us.

The temperature outside was about 80 degrees F. but inside the cave it was around 50 degrees F. In our bones, it felt more like 40 degrees F. The cave was over 200 feet deep according to our reports and we found the floor covered with one to two inches of mud (see figure 22). Water dripped down from many places in the ceiling and stalactites from the roof were forming everywhere. There were also many stalagmites rising up from the floor like spikes in various places. These could really put your knee out of joint in a hurry. Sliding in the mud and falling on one of these pointed things could ruin your whole day. I asked the kids if this could be the reason Neanderthals became extinct? How could I find time for humor in this situation? Well, with five children, almost anything can be funny.

We were all standing in the first chamber and had just seen a red outline of a mammoth on the left wall when the silence of the darkness was suddenly shattered by voices coming from the depths of the cave. We knew we couldn't run because we'd all be flat on our face in the mud or impaled on a stalagmite. There was nothing to do but wait and see who it was. Our door guards returned when they heard the noise. We waited in stunned silence.

Figure 22. Bernifal Cave.

We all relaxed when we heard the very pleasant sound of a little dog barking along with the voices.

As they approached, I recognized that they were speaking Italian. This was my grandmother and grandfather's native language. As the voices and the woofing drew nearer we saw a single small light coming at us. They greeted us in Italian. There were three people, two men and a woman. I spoke a little Italian and they spoke a little English. They were from a university in Italy, Turin, I believe. We confirmed the fact that this truly was Bernifal. They had some handwritten notes written in Italian that described the cave in detail. Someone at their university had been in this cave at an earlier date. We exchanged some information, and after this short conversation they said goodbye and exited from the broken front door of the cave. I wondered if they had permission or had done the same thing that we did. They couldn't have been the ones that split the door because there was no sign of an axe or sledge anywhere around the entrance, and they weren't carrying one. The big problem was that they were the ones that owned the camper we saw parked near the farmhouse. This was bad news for us.

As they left, they must have encountered the farmer and informed him about our presence in the cave to divert attention away from themselves. He immediately headed for the cave, intending not to go through the front door but to climb down through a secret opening in the ceiling. As the farmer headed towards the cave, armed with a thick walking stick, we went deeper into its bowels. We had no idea that any of this was going on. With some confidence, I relieved the two boys, John, age 16, and Frank, age 13, of their door guard duties so they could accompany us deeper into the cave.

We all held hands as we left chamber one and entered chamber two. It was a downhill slide at this point. Light flashed in all directions. Margie saw a red hand imprint on a wall — obviously red ochre (mixed with animal fat, it became wall paint). She held her hand next to it as I shot a picture (see figure 23 in color insert section). A huge claw-like structure appeared suddenly on our right and everyone gasped. It was only a stone formation, but very terrifying. The boys then saw a ladder going up to another level. Daniel and Frank climbed up and said it led to a ledge above one of the walls. They wanted to go further up but I said we should stick together. I had no idea what would await them at the next level up. I kept shooting flash pictures at anything and everything I thought was important. There had to be something in here, I thought, that was not supposed to be seen. Where was it? We investigated deeper and deeper, seeing less and less as we went and getting the feeling that impending doom was coming upon us. I was starting to get nervous about getting lost in this place and also a vague feeling of danger crept into my being. I thought that we had better turn around and get ready to leave. We had been in there at least 30 to 40 minutes and the damp coldness was beginning to penetrate our bones. I thought if Neanderthalers had lived in this, it's no wonder that they had arthritis.

As we walked and slid back into room one, I took flash pictures of a carved mammoth head and a very demonic-looking face while shooting the entire wall for completeness (see figure 25 in color insert section). Only small spots were illuminated on the walls with the flashlights, so entire wall patterns were difficult to see. It was just on the knife-edge of time that we exited through the broken door, because within about a minute right behind us appeared the farmer with his thick stick coming out of the same door. He yelled at us in French, saying the cave was closed (*fermé*), passage was *interdite* and we shouldn't have crossed his bridge. He caught up to us quickly while brandishing the large staff. He seemed anxious to know what we saw in the cave. He also asked if we were picking *champignons* (mushrooms). I said no, we weren't picking champignons but we were in the cave. I showed him my guidebook which stated that this cave was open (*ouvert*) to the public.

He kept insisting it wasn't open and he was getting angry. I gave a quick motion signal to my team and we all started a very fast walk down the path, knowing that he probably couldn't keep up with us. We kept going faster and faster until finally we were running as he followed closely behind. We sprinted across the field and splashed through the stream heading directly towards the van. We jumped in the van, slammed the doors, and sped away while it appeared as if he was writing down our license plate. We headed back to Brive at a normal speed so as not to call any attention to ourselves, while all the time praying that we wouldn't be reported to the police. We got back to the hotel unharmed, and miraculously, unreported.

DINOSAURS

One of the last things an evolutionist will ever admit or believe is that a Paleolithic man or woman saw a live dinosaur. This simply will not do. According to their theories, the age of man did not begin until some 2.5-3 million years ago with his predecessors in Africa, and certainly, they believe the men who decorated this cave existed within the last 200,000 years, most likely within the last 30,000 years. Dinosaurs, on the other hand died out at least 65 million years ago. This, to them, is fact.

Every cave that we visited and every decorated cave that the public is allowed to tour will "mammal" you to death. I mean all they will show you are mammals. This doesn't mean that down some other passageway reptiles can't be found. Where they take you there are no drawings or carvings of reptiles. It's as if reptiles never existed.

We know that this is not true because we still have reptiles today. Snakes, lizards, turtles, alligators, and tuataras are all part of our modern fauna, but conspicuously absent from cave drawings. The cave painters and engravers surely had reptiles in their age. Where were they? More specifically, we must make direct inquiry about cave evidence concerning the existence of those "terrible lizards" or dinosaurs. Are there dinosaurs depicted on cave walls?

SERPENT BITING A HEEL

Reptiles are not absent in the Paleolithic study of "portable art." Portable art means just that. These are artworks constructed by human hands that can be carried around from place to place as opposed to "fixed" mural art on cave walls. The term "portable art" in the prehistoric era usually refers to artwork carved on the surface of bones or pieces of stone.

Alexander Marshak of Harvard University is a specialist in this subject with many years of first-hand study of original objects. In his book entitled *The Roots of Civilization,* he shows a detailed bone carving found in La Madeleine, France (Dordogne region), that displays a clear representation of a serpent.[4] It is this site, La Madeleine, that gave its name to the Magdalenian period of human existence in France.[5] During this period Neanderthals were no longer supposed to be alive and more modern-looking, or Cro-Magnon peoples, populated Southern France.[6]

The serpent artifact found in La Madeleine was mysterious according to Marshak. The etchings were made on a long round bone with precision-type instruments.[7] This bony scene is presented by the author in its unrolled form, as if it were on a scroll. The drawing shows a man-like figure carrying a stick with twigs or leaves on it and two horse heads facing in the opposite direction. To us, the interesting part concerns the figure of an upside-down legless serpent or snake that appears poised to take a bite out of the lower-half of the man's right leg. Its mouth is not open but it is only inches away from the flesh. Of course, Marshak did not recognize in print its resemblance to the prophecy from Genesis, "He will crush your head and you will strike His heel" (Gen. 3:15).[8]

MICROSCOPIC CARVINGS

Much of Marshak's studies had to be conducted under the microscope to properly visualize the inscriptions and drawings. Did these early people carve these engravings with a magnifying glass or microscope? I'm sure that they did not. There is one big question that now arises: How could the ancient artists see with their eyes what we cannot see today without magnification?

I had spoken at ATT Bell Labs in 1995 and just touched on this subject briefly. After my talk someone asked me if I knew about the ancient use of "cow lenses." I said that I had never heard of this subject. He told me that on a tour of a cave in Europe a tour guide had said that early peoples had actually torn out the lens from a cow's eye and stuck it on their own eye so they could magnify objects. There are no limits to the stories tour guides can dream up in their heads for the sake of an evolutionary explanation. I told him that I didn't think it would work. I think that if you stick a cow lens over your eye that you had better have good vision in the other eye, because that's the only one that you will be seeing out of. Besides that, all the possible allergic reactions make the experiment seem doomed to failure.

THE CONFRONTATION

One of the amazing things that happened inside the Bernifal Cave was that in the process of shooting pictures in all directions, I took a picture of an actual dinosaur carving. This could be the very reason why Bernifal was suddenly closed to the public when the creation movement of the seventies and eighties started to gain public acceptance. No dinosaurs ever existed with man, they said; therefore, no paintings and no carvings. The other caves must be neatly cordoned off so that no unjaundiced eye ever sees a reptile figure on a wall. We were never supposed to see this. It was mainly carved into the rock with only a little dab of paint on it,

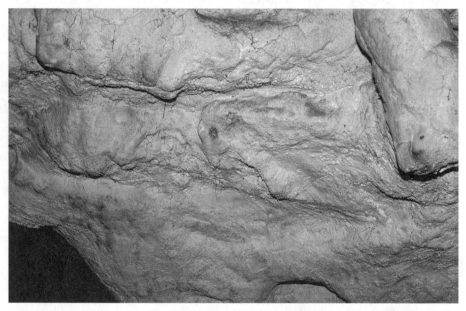

Figure 24. Dinosaur and mammoth in head-to-head confrontation, Bernifal Cave.

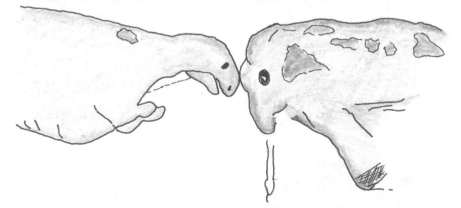

Figure 24a. Diagram of confrontation, Bernifal Cave.

therefore not easy to see, especially with flashlights.

My photograph entitled "The Confrontation" in figure 24 actually shows a dinosaur-like creature in head-to-head combat with a mammoth. This, I believe, is the first time that this carving has ever been revealed to the public. These images were carved into the walls using some of the natural configurations of the limestone as part of the anatomy. What type of dinosaur is this? The diagram of this confrontation is seen in figure 24a.

First of all it had small front limbs. It had a vertical eye slot, meaning the eye was longer in its vertical dimension than it was in its horizontal dimension. The snout in front of the eye looks to be somewhat hollowed out as if the bone in that place was concave. No large teeth protruded from either jaw but what looks like small teeth were in either the upper or lower jaw. It had a large upper jaw and a smaller lower jaw. There is a nostril opening at the front of the snout. Under the eye, the mouth line extends parallel to the top of the snout and becomes a line of muscle in the neck when it reaches a point beyond the eye, making an approximately 120-degree angle turn and travels down the short neck to the intersection between the right limb and the neck. The claws have been broken off on this right limb. Both elbows are visible. The left limb is held in the same position with a rounded paw area.

WHAT KIND IS IT?

There are two great orders of dinosaurs: the Saurischia (lizard-hipped) and the Ornithischia (bird-hipped). This division is based on the structure of the pelvis (hip). We can't see the pelvic (hip) structure in this sculpture so we have to classify it by some other means.

In the Saurischian dinosaurs the teeth of the jaws are set into the margins or only in the front. In this specimen, there are what appear to be teeth along the one side towards the front part of the snout, but not much is seen in the front of the snout. Ornithischia tended to be herbivorous while the Saurischians were carnivorous. This dinosaur is in a combative stance. Carnivores tend to be combative, but some herbivores are also combative. However, only Saurischians had a hollowed area in front of the eye. We may also infer from the short upper limbs that this was a bipedal dinosaur (walked on two hind legs).

From these features it seems possible to tentatively classify this dinosaur sculpture into the suborder Theropoda. These Saurischian creatures were almost exclusively carnivorous, bipedal, with strong hind legs and small forelimbs. They supposedly flourished during the entire Mesozoic era (230 to 62 million years ago). To go any further would be pure guesswork. To say it was a Teratosauris, Allosauris, Acrocanthosauris, or such would not be possible, given the limited data. However, to be very forthright, it must be stated that this is a dinosaur, period. How did this happen to get on the Bernifal wall?

Before we compose any theories on the dinosaur appearance, let's take a look at the mammoth. Mammoths or *Elaphas primigenius* remains have been found in the excavations in France at Cro-Magnon, La Quina, and La Roches.[9] Drawings and engravings of them have been found in numerous caves such as Rouffignac, La Baume Latrone,[10] Pech-Merle, Pair-non-Pair, Bernifal, Font-de-Gaume, and Combarelles.[11] The red outline of the mammoth or *Elaphas primigenius* seen in figure 25 (color insert section) is on the wall in the Bernifal cave below the "Confrontation." This red mammoth was noted by Ann Sieveking.[12] It corresponds well with the one carved in the "Confrontation." These mammoths had small ears in contrast to the African elephant of recent times and had a lump of fat on the top of its head, which gave it the characteristic bump-on-the-head look.

Regardless of whether this sculpture was done in the Upper or Middle Paleolithic, by either Neanderthal, Cro-Magnon, Magdelaine, or Gravettian people, it was still accomplished by a human. This human either saw a dinosaur and mammoth in battle or had a portable piece of artwork that contained this piece of information and had been handed down for several generations. Because I believe that we have rather good evidence for these caves being post-flood caves and for post-flood burials in other caves, I believe that the latter is true. It was accomplished by a person who had a piece of portable art, but a human saw it happen.

One other possibility exists and that is the post-flood existence of both dinosaurs and mammoths originating from the ark. They both could have come off together, but because of unsuitable environmental conditions the dinosaurs became extinct while the mammoth and other mammals adapted to the harsher atmospheric and terrestrial surroundings. The post-flood conditions would not favor the preservation of dinosaur skeletons or any skeletons, for that matter. Deep, rapid burial and compaction of mud flows following the flood are ideal circumstances for the making and preserving of animal bones. Consequently, we would expect that there would be very few post-flood dinosaur fossils compared to pre-flood dinosaur fossils.

RED OCHRE AGAIN

In figure 25 in the color insert section there is the red mammoth and there is also the red handprint on another wall (figure 23 in the color insert section). These undoubtedly are red ochre. Supposedly, all the cave paintings in the Upper Paleolithic made use of this material.[13] What is important is that here is this red substance again. The same kind of material used on La Ferrassie I and Pech del'Azé in their burial custom. This wall paint was probably red ochre mixed with animal fat. It seems to allow the time frame of this cave to be in a Neanderthal period.

Keeping the red ochre and the dinosaur carving in mind, we must ask how does this fit in the modern scientific view of history? It really doesn't fit at all because the dinosaur eliminates approximately 62-65 million years and makes man, dinosaur, and mammoth (a mammal) contemporaries.[14] The red ochre on the same cave walls as a dinosaur throws all the timetables off. No wonder the cave was closed.

Also, one very important question should be raised regarding the information

conveyed by this piece of Bernifal artwork. If these fossils are truly found in different layers of sedimentation, do the layers represent time or geographic separation?

I believe the cave artist of Bernifal was trying to demonstrate that these
animals were mortal enemies, that they fought, and because of this they lived in
distant ecological niches.[15] Therefore, the layers could merely represent isolated
burial sites due to the independent pre-flood habitats of these creatures, and have
nothing to do with great gaps in time.

Today, modern scientists refer to some of these habitats as eras or periods.
The Mesozoic Era is supposedly the age of reptiles which lasted approximately
120 to 165 million years with its Triassic, Jurassic, and Cretaceous periods.[16] The
early epochs of the Cenozoic Era, the age of mammals, are the Paleocene, Eocene,
Oligocene, Miocene, and Pliocene, and so on. These separate layers could very
well be only widely dispersed ecological habitats. We are now, supposedly, in the
later stages of the Cenozoic Era. There is no question that some layering of sediment takes place over time — just dig down in any historical site. However, it is
quite different to say that time is the only factor represented by sedimentation.

A few years ago in our yard at home we dug down around three feet in our
garden on the south side of the house and unearthed an early-1800 garbage pit.
There were all sorts of broken pieces of china and strange-shaped bottles, high
top rotted leather boots, an old cabinet lock which was part gold, molten glass
that had hardened on pieces of coal, plus many other broken artifacts of the 1800s.
There were dates on the bottles. Obviously, this was a pit to discard unwanted
items. Garbage pits like this are also found in restored Colonial villages like
Williamsburg, Virginia.

A question that can be posed regarding this type of discovery is this: How
does one know when digging down into so-called occupational levels of prehistoric caves that he or she is not just excavating a garbage pit?

A VERY NATURAL SELECTION

At the risk of redundancy I would like to emphasize the process of "natural
selection" when evolutionists come upon evidence such as the "Confrontation."
They naturally select only the evidence they want you to see. I offer the following
letter as evidence. It was received by me in October of 1982 after I submitted the
"Confrontation" dinosaur photo to *Science News*. I was hoping for a scientific
breakthrough, but all I received was this:

SCIENCE NEWS
1719 N. Street NW, Washington DC 20036
(202) 785-2255

Dear Dr. Cuozzo: Oct. 6, 1982

As I told you on the phone the other day, we appreciated the
opportunity to look at your photo. Unfortunately, it's not something
we can use in the magazine — while I have no doubt that the images

are there, both the editor and I don't think it would be clear when reproduced in the magazine. In addition, we need comments from an expert or two in the field who had seen it, which doesn't seem possible in this case.

I wish you the best of luck with your picture, and once again thank you for giving us the opportunity to look at it.

Sincerely,
Assistant to the Editor

If you will note carefully, the letter said that they would need comments from an expert or two in the field who has seen it. However, that was impossible. Why? First of all, the cave had probably been sealed up like a can of Campbell's soup. Secondly, without a will there is no way.

Is it because no one has seen it, no one will admit to seeing it, or no one will dare go to see it? I think the latter two reasons are the most plausible. What we are dealing with is a monolithic structure in modern science where there is absolutely no evidence which could possibly shed some doubt on the evolutionary interpretation of life. According to them, it just doesn't exist. And if it did exist, it wouldn't be scientific. Therefore, why go see it? But she did say she had no doubt that the images were there. As I write this a number of years later, I can almost guarantee that those images don't exist anymore, or at least a padlocked steel door has replaced the broken wooden one.

FONT-DE-GAUME, CLEAN CAVES, AND TIME

It seems that ever since modern men first discovered the painted caves that they have been deteriorating. Caves like Font-de-Gaume, Combarelles, and Lascaux had white walls[17] before the tourists came. These caves are not small.

We visited Font-de-Gaume officially. We stood in a long line, paid our fees, and had a guided tour. Font-de-Gaume is over 123 meters deep, with smaller sections 15, 21, and 48 meters. Most of the artwork in this cave starts at about 60 meters from the entrance. There are about 200 animals separated into about 25 tourist stops along the route through the cave. If we are to be perceptive, "wise as serpents" (Matt. 10:16), we must be careful to observe everything when going through this cave and notice the darkened walls from about just 50 years of being open to the public. They were really dark gray and made the atmosphere rather dismal.

But this fact leads to a mystery. Ann Sieveking states, "In less than half a century of public visiting the walls of Font-de-Gaume have been changed from white to deep gray by the smoke of carbide lamps but although we think its period of use in the Paleolithic covered many thousands of years it was not dirty when first rediscovered in the twentieth century; nor was Lascaux, nor Ekain in the Basque province of Guipuzcoa, both of which are caves that still have a beautiful white crystalline surface."[18] These caves, when first discovered, had white crystalline walls. Thousands of years of use and white crystalline walls, is that a contradiction or not? Please note this fact well. It really disputes thousands of years of cave use by prehistoric peoples.

Gowlett states, "Lamps were indispensable for working in dark caves, and these have been found at Lascaux and elsewhere. They were simple carved stone bowls, in which animal fats would have been burnt with a wick."[19] He forgot to add that it was probably "smokeless fat" that they were using. Notice here the beginning of a real made-up story to cover up a mystery. If this were true, we could all get rid of our exhaust fans over our stoves. I would imagine that the evolutionist would define smokeless fat as sort of like decaffeinated coffee.

Ann Sieveking admits the use of stone lamps at Lascaux but contradicts Gowlett when she states, "We know virtually nothing about the use of the deep caves, except that use hardly appears to have been made of them at all. There are no traces of big fires to light the galleries by, no blackening smoke or soot stains on the roof and almost no possessions left lying about."[20] How many times did the inhabitants or artists of these caves go in and out with their smoking torches or lamps that left no smoke marks on the walls or ceilings? How could drawings, carvings, and so forth, deep in dark, cold (50° F) tunnels under the ground be accomplished without much light?

Could they have used giant fireflies? The facts don't add up. Light for these people meant fire. This was post-flood Europe. Fire means smoke. Could these cave artworks have been accomplished without modern type light? How? Surely there were not 50 to 80 thousands of years of use of these caves. Could the artists in these caves possibly have had better eyesight than modern man? Perhaps with some an infrared type of capability?

THE ROUFFIGNAC REFRIGERATOR

Rouffignac Cave is called the cave of 100 mammoths. It is about 7 km north of Les Ezies and, according to the official guidebook, it "runs back for seven miles."[21] Engravings and drawings are found all over the cave. I wonder how dark it was at seven miles down when the artists went in many years ago. We went through this cave on a little open tourist train. It was like a kiddy ride at the amusement park. The Rouffignac train ride went along a few miles of well-lit track and was really a cold ride. It was so cold at its depths that I saw some real ice sitting on a ledge over numerous mammoth drawings. When I saw the mammoth drawings and the ice together, my first thought was that we were in an enormous "ancient meatlocker." I think mammoth meat would have stored pretty well, if not frozen in some locations in the "meatlocker." It could also have served as a refrigerator for our ancient relatives.

DANCING IN THE DARK

Recent explorations have been conducted in a cave in Bruniquel, Southern France. We didn't see this cave firsthand, but over the past six years the depths of the cave have been investigated by archaeological teams led by a number of French archeologists. They said the occupation levels of this deep cave could be 47,600 years old or much older. This is their way of saying it wasn't recent. One of the archaeologists, a François Rouzaud, said that Bruniquel cave, "shows that prehistoric men frequented the deep underground world, in total darkness, long before they began to paint on cave walls."[22] Men and women walked around in total darkness. Can you picture that? With all the stalactites hanging from the ceilings and stalagmites protruding from the floor, I can say that this is absolutely impossible without light or sonar. I know we are not related to dolphins, so there are only two choices left. Better vision in the dark or lights. That's it. The Bernifal cave would have hospitalized us all without light. I don't know which would have been worse, a stalactite in the head or a stalagmite in the knee.

Burnt bones were also found in the depths of Bruniquel, which meant whoever was in there cooked their food. However, burning fires in a cave over 300 meters from the surface would fill the cave with smoke and deplete all the available oxygen, unless it were vented. The archaeologists did not provide any evidence to prove that the cave had a source of air at these great depths. Cooked mammoth steaks, therefore, could have been brought into the dark depths of the cave for non-candlelight romantic dinners for two.

Picture this scene: Two sets of infrared human eyes stare at each other in total darkness in the depths of the Bruniquel Neanderthal Café. They suddenly realize that in the future, as their genes go silent, candlelight might have to be used to spoil the cozy atmosphere and eat up the limited oxygen in the café. A small stalactite quartet starts playing guess what? You're right, the strains of "Dancing in the Dark" come wafting out of the opening in the ground as the mammoths gather around the cave entrance swinging to the music from below, although they're not too happy about the aroma of their "charcoal-broiled" Uncle Mammu, no relation to Shamu. It was the middle stone age but no one had ever heard of "rock music." That was to come with more genetic breakdown in the so-called advanced society of the future. Now, back to reality.

Many consider these art works to have a religious significance, and if so, they have to be able to account for the coming and going of Paleolithic peoples for over thousands of years and no apparent damage to the walls except for some graffiti. There is one theory that none of the evolutionist authors will touch and that is that these cave paintings may show and tell some stories that the evolutionists are unwilling to see or listen to. Jesus asked, "Having eyes, do you not see? And having ears, do you not hear?" (Mark 8:18).

After reading about the major dating problems and controversial issues surrounding the caves of France, it is now possible to consider the biggest question raised by the previous chapters.

Part 3
Modern Implications

Chapter 25

Which Way Is Mankind Going?

This is a question that the Bible answers clearly and the evolutionists try to evade. First, if you look at the Bible in its entire context from Genesis to Revelation or to the new earth passages in Isaiah, one cannot help but be struck by the forcefulness of the message. Mankind once held a high and exalted position, and since the historic fall in Eden there has been a steady spiritual and physical deterioration. Paul says it best in his letter to the Romans:

> For the anxious longing of the creation waits eagerly for the revealing of the sons of God. For the creation was subjected to futility, not willingly, but because of Him who subjected it, in hope that the creation itself also will be set free from its slavery to corruption into the freedom of the glory of the children of God. For we know that the whole creation groans and suffers the pains of childbirth together until now (Rom. 8:19-22).

Apparently the physical cause of the deterioration of man and nature is a consequence of man's rebellion and the curse by God producing the subsequent increase of disorder in the cosmos (Gen. 3).

While visiting L'Abri, in Switzerland, I heard Dr. Francis Schaeffer say that since man was given dominion over the natural world of plants and animals, it follows that when man fell so did everything over which he had dominion. Even the earth itself was cursed by God and suffers until this day from the "slavery to corruption." It all began with the proclamation that God made following the historic immoral choice made in the Garden. To Adam God said, "Cursed is the earth because of you" (Gen. 3:17).

Perfection And Approval

There was perfection in God's creation in the beginning. Man and woman were created sinless and met God's approval. Moreover, all of creation received God's stamp of approval and commendation when the Bible says, "And God saw all that he had made, and behold, it was very good" (Gen. 1:30).

This is the basis of my judgment about the earth's original conditions. Everyone must have a basis for their thoughts and this is mine. When you project into the past or the future it is always done with faith, no matter who you are. No human can live without faith. If you are sitting in a chair reading this now, you have faith that your chair won't collapse under you, that your ceiling won't fall on your head, and the food you ate for lunch wasn't full of bacteria. Anyone that goes out for dinner to a restaurant where they have never been before has faith in the chef, waitresses, and even the dishwasher, for many reasons. When you drive your car you place your faith in a whole factory full of workers, engineers, and managers. I'm sure you can think of more examples.

Therefore, by faith, I take the proclamations of Genesis as truth. Christians and Jews need to spend more time discussing it. All things were not as they are now. This takes modern man's uniformitarian thinking and shatters it to pieces. These are infinite absolutes. Finite man with finite concepts can never create the infinite. Mathematically, finiteness can never produce an infinite absolute. [1]

Physical and Spiritual

I can vividly remember as a young boy that on every Ash Wednesday I went into a Catholic Church and received a black spot of ashes on my forehead. I wasn't supposed to wash it off until going to bed or the next day. When the priest administered the smudge upon my head he would say, "Remember man that thou art dust and unto dust thou shall return."

After many years of being a Christian I am sure that those still are powerful words, no matter who says them. Down through the ages mankind has been returning to dust because of Adam's decision.

God said to Adam, "But from the tree of the knowledge of good and evil you shall not eat, for in the day that you eat from it you shall surely die" (Gen. 2:17). They ate and it was the most expensive meal in the history of mankind. We are all still paying the bill. The curse which God pronounced upon Adam remains with us today no matter how rich or famous we may be. It does not matter to what religion we belong, men and women still have to die physically and return to dust. Death is very democratic — it treats everyone as equal. No one gets out alive unless raptured by God.[2]

Spiritual and physical death have been conquered by the death and resurrection of Jesus Christ because He really did rise from the dead in his physical body. However, for the present, this physical curse continues in us until our human bodies rise from the dead (John 5:28; 1 Thess. 4:15-17; 1 Corin. 15:51-57).

DUST TO DUST

Now, if I were Adam and God said I was going to return to dust, I would have expected to die that very hour or least by the next day. I would have been badly mistaken. The Bible says Adam didn't return to the dust until 930 years later. This meant it was to be a slow process. Adam began to die that very moment. Something happened in Adam and Eve's bodies that switched "off" the mechanisms for normal unlimited tissue renewal and God also refused them access to another regeneration system called the "tree of life" (Gen. 3:22-24). It is my opinion that the fruit of this tree could partially reset the renewal systems, even with the Curse, so that they would age and breakdown but never totally die. If God didn't deny us access to this tree, Adam, Eve, and all of us would eventually be living blobs of tissues thousands of years old incapable of functioning on a human level but still alive.

Isn't it interesting how some cultures have tried to partially counteract the curse. In Egyptian times, experts would mummify the bodies of the pharaohs and important people. In modern times, vaults and freezing methods are employed. However, all that these procedures can do is prolong the inevitable degenerative processes. Nothing has ever been found that reverses this process.

Ultimate breakdown and increase in disorder is a law. It's called the Second Law of Thermodynamics. It is my belief that this is what Paul wrote about in Romans 8 when he described the "slavery to corruption" of the whole creation. This is the same law that affects our clothes, cars, houses, boats, bikes, light bulbs, sidewalks, roads, trees — all of nature. Everything degenerates.

By definition, the Second Law, or Law of Increase of Entropy, demands that the available energy which is necessary to do work in a closed system is constantly decreasing while the amount of breakdown or degradation of matter is constantly increasing. Disorder increases in closed systems. I believe this is the key to the definition of the process before and after the fall of man. Before the Fall there was breakdown at a molecular level but there was an equal amount of renewal or reversal of that breakdown. After the Fall there is a limited amount of renewal. The more complex the biological system, it seems the more limited the renewal process even with energy input, e.g., the human body. It may be that the simpler the system, the better the renewal system works with energy input (single-celled organisms). The single-celled diatoms show little change in supposedly 3.5 billion years, although this is doubtful.

Two things can be said at this place. The first is that there are really no such things as simple creatures. Molecular biologists can tell us this when they explore the depths and complexities of yeast cells, a supposedly simple cell.[3] Secondly, there has to be some change in simple organisms, but there are no molecular studies on them from one thousand years ago to compare them with. The best that we can do now is try to reconstruct ancient proteins. When you reach the end of this book there is a short part devoted to the subject of ancient enzymes. Were they better than their modern counterparts?

All finite things break down, age, corrode, rust (oxidize), decay, degenerate, etc. Energy can be put back in those systems, but only by the expenditure of work. This is how we, as finite humans, hold off the ultimate breakdown of all our parts and those substances around us, i.e., by putting energy back into the system with work done on the system. The sun does this for the botanical world. It puts energy back into the metabolic machines so they can keep producing.

Such common things as a good diet, proper exercise, taking medicine for an ailment, and taking vitamins as a preventive measure can restore health and hinder the degenerative processes a small amount. Even chicken soup is well-known in that regard. Painting and repairing your house, car, etc., temporarily retards the ultimate fate of all material objects on earth. I look at my work as a dentist in the navy for 2 years and as an orthodontist in private practice for 31 years as a constant battle against the effects of the Second Law in the face and head of my patients. All of us, in one form or another, fight the Second Law and its effects in our jobs and our lives. Love combats the Second law (Prov. 10:12).

Another aspect of the Second Law is that the entire world economy is based on the fact that rare materials which break down least (dense or hard) and resist corrosion are the most valuable. Gold, silver, and platinum are among the most durable and most dense rare materials on earth; therefore, they are valuable and costly. Plastic and paper are among the least durable and least dense and common so they are considered cheap substances. Consider the price of oak versus pine next time that you visit a lumber yard. Hardwoods like oak, teak, and mahogany are all expensive compared to the less dense woods. Durability equates to value. Wealthy homes have stone or brick driveways and slate roofs. Castles are made of stone not wood.

Diamonds[4] and other jewels are not so dense but they are very hard, which is a different quality. The ability of one material to scratch another or wear another is called the hardness factor. Diamonds are at the top of this list.[5] Gold is not so hard but it does not shatter when hammered, making it more durable. Valuable, expensive, rare metals must have a high specific gravity and a low hardness, while valuable, expensive jewels must have a low specific gravity and a high hardness and high symmetry of its crystals. Low specific gravity and low hardness does not make a substance useless, like talc of talcum powder; however, this combination of low values renders the substance inexpensive in terms of price and value.[6]

WHAT IF THERE WAS NO SECOND LAW?

What would it be like if Adam and Eve hadn't disobeyed God? Time would go on, since time apart from sin doesn't automatically mean breakdown. It would still pass, whether Adam sinned or not. He would still accumulate years and become older in age, sin or no sin. If there were no sin, would old age necessarily mean deterioration of the tissues and general breakdown of his body parts? I believe the answer to that question is no. It may not have been the same for trees and plants.[7]

God intentionally gave them seeds to replenish themselves and multiply. Man was given seed (sperm and eggs) to multiply (Gen 1:28).

What would it have been like? I don't know, but aging and breaking down would not be synonymous. Let's begin by looking at some data on the precious minerals. The specific gravity or density, which is its weight in relation to an equal volume of water, of gold is 19.3, platinum is 21.5, silver is 10.5, iridium is 22.4.[8] These density measurements are among the highest of all the minerals. High specific gravity or density measurements mean that when comparing sizes of pieces of minerals of the same total weight, the gold, silver, platinum, or iridium would constitute a much smaller piece. In other words, a pound of aluminum ore (bauxite) with a density of 2.7 would be a much larger piece of mineral than a pound of gold. A pound of silver would be smaller in size than a pound of hematite. There are other elements such as tantalum, 16.6, whose resistance to corrosion by acids is exceptional, and tungsten, 19.3, with its high melting point.

VERY GOOD?

If there were no sin and no Second Law, would dense gold, platinum, iridium, tantalum, and silver even breakdown slightly over a period of time? The answer, most likely, is no; and perhaps that is what Moses meant when he wrote, before the fall of man, about the gold in the land of Havilah. He said, "The gold of that land is good" (Gen. 2:12). What did he mean by "good"? Was it the same thing that God meant when He looked at the creation and declared it to be "very good" on the sixth day of creation? The same Hebrew word *"tob"* is used in both places. Psalm 34:8 says. "O taste and see that the Lord is good." The same word *tob* is used here. We know God is good. This is the ultimate meaning of "good" as used in Scripture. It means whatever is described is consistent with God's character, according to his nature, "good."

Before the Fall there was no corruption on the earth, no sin or physical death of humans and animals. Therefore, can we conclude that gold did not corrode or break down in the days before the Fall? Or was God saying through Moses that the gold in that area was not "fool's gold" — iron disulfide or pyrite or chalcopyrite, a soft yellow copper material? This also could be the interpretation of "good."

Another way to interpret the concept of "good" or "very good" is that when God said in the third chapter of Genesis, "Cursed is the ground because of you," He meant everything that was in the ground — soil, sand, rocks, and all the minerals included. This could be the point in time when the degeneration of all minerals began to occur, even the radioactive ones.

In my understanding of this passage, gold was "good." This could mean lots of things, like durable, useful, beautiful, etc., but I think it meant gold wasn't subject to the law of deterioration yet. If this were true, it could also imply that all minerals were "good," even uranium-238; meaning not harmful to man. If U-238 was part of the original ground and the earth was very good in the beginning, it was also good. Then it became cursed along with everything else. The question is: Was it decaying while it was "very good," or did it start later when it was cursed?

RADIOACTIVITY IN THE CURSE

It goes without saying that radioactive materials are extremely harmful to man and animals today. Today, uranium-238 takes 4.5 billion years for one-half of its atoms to decay. Before it reaches the end stages of lead-210, Bismuth-210, polonium-210, and stable lead-206, it becomes radium-226 and radon-222. Although radium-226 has a half-life of 1,622 years, its harmful daughters can decay very rapidly. Radon-222 is a daughter with a half-life of 3.8 days. It is a gaseous product which is extremely hazardous as it leaks into basements of homes and decays into isotopes of polonium-218, lead-214, and bismuth-214. These isotopes and the radon gas are inhaled by people who live in those homes. In the USA, "An estimated 13,000 lung cancer deaths per year may be attributed to radon gas."[9]

Radon gas has been targeted as one of the main causes of myeloid leukemia and other cancers by scientists at the University of Bristol in England. They say, "The international incidence of myeloid leukemia, cancer of the kidney, melanoma, and certain childhood cancers all show significant correlation with radon exposure in the home."[10] They are not alone in their warning about radon gas. It is a well-known fact that kits can be purchased by homeowners in many countries to be able to detect this deadly decay product of radium.

A few years ago the township in which we live turned a whole area in the southwest section upside-down, after large amounts of radon were found in the soil. Large barrels of soil were removed from the yards of the affected houses and the tainted blocks were shut down for many months. Families were evacuated from their homes and traffic re-routed around their streets.

The main point of this matter is this: since the Bible says everything was created in six days, before man sinned, it must mean that all of these radioactive elements were also present in the primordial or early earth before sin. Now, you can say God created these harmful elements at a later date as some have done. However, there is no room in the Bible for progressive creations. The first words in the Bible are, "In the beginning God created the Heavens and the earth" (Gen. 1:1). Everything was completed in six days.

One of the foremost proponents of a series of creative acts throughout years of history was Swiss-born creationist Louis Agassiz (1807-1873). He was the founder of the Museum of Comparative Zoology at Harvard University.[11] Though radioactivity in the earth was yet to be discovered until after his death, Agassiz fought with Charles Darwin and his disciples for many years about the fossils. He was always on very unsteady and unbiblical ground with his "progressive creation beliefs."

VERY GOOD MEANS NOT HARMFUL

It seems to me that because everything was "very good," in the beginning, that these now-harmful radioactive elements distributed in the earth must have been shut down, i.e., not decaying in the beginning. Therefore, they could not have emitted radioactive particles to affect the human, plant, or animal world before man sinned. The major portion of these products may not have been released until the rupturing of the earth during the great flood of Noah. At that time they became even more detrimental to the biological world. The entire surface of the earth was ripped apart during this cataclysmic flow of contents from inside the planet. M. Oard has indicated that extensive volcanism during the flood is attested to by abundant layers of lava and ash, mixed with sedimentary rocks around the world.[12] I would add that billions of radioactive particles from thousands of volcanoes in the earth could also have erupted in the water, lava, and ash from the bowels of the earth, mixing with the soil and spreading contamination everywhere during the inundation of the earth. From Olsen and Fruchter we learn, "The most common magmatic volatile outgassed by volcanoes is water, often comprising 90% or more of the total volatile phase."[13] Carbon dioxide is the second largest product, followed by minor quantities of compounds such as hydrogen sulfide, sulfur dioxide, hydrogen fluoride, radon, carbon monoxide, helium, mercury, and halogenated hydrocarbons.

MOUNT ST. HELENS

From the Mount St. Helens eruption of May 18, 1980, we can learn some important lessons of volcanic activity and its biological effects on humans. In the bulk ash of this enormous mountain volcano there were deemed to be concentrations of minor proportions of the following radioactive elements: potassium-40, radium-226, and thorium-232.

Radium, as mentioned previously is dangerous because of its decay into radon gas. Radon-222 has a short half-life of 3.8 days. "It decays through a series of short-lived alpha-emitting 'daughters' to lead-210." Lead-210 has also been called radium D and it has a half-life of 22 years.[14] Lead-210 gives off dangerous gamma rays. Camiel and Thompson wrote about lead-210, "This isotope emits a √-ray of 47 kev (kiloelectron volts) which can be detected with any √-scintillation probe."[15] A kev of 47 is roughly equivalent to a 113 kilovolt x-ray beam.[16] My cephalometric x-ray machine used in this study can generate 90 kilovolts peak for a lateral head radiograph. Therefore, 47 kev is a pretty penetrating beam of radiation. The rule we learned in radiology at the University of Pennsylvania Dental School was the higher the voltage, the shorter and more penetrating the x-rays.

The first daughter of radon is polonium 218, a solid; the transition involves an alpha decay that leaves the polonium 218 atom charged for a very short time. It is during this period that the polonium has a

great affinity for any particles in the air and will ultimately attach itself to that particle. Any further decay of the polonium generally occurs while attached to the particle surface of the successive radon
daughters, Pb-214, Bi-214, Po-214, and Pb -210.

During the ashfall immediately after the May 18, 1980, eruption
of Mount St. Helens the presence of radon daughters was detected on
the ash using a Ge (Li) gamma-ray detector.[17]

At first these radon daughters were thought to be spewed out of the volcanic
plume but later studies showed that the majority attached themselves to airborne
ash. Thus, the radon was thought to be only precipitated from the natural background concentrations of the air. This was not so for the radium-226 and potas-
sium-40 and thorium-232 which are known to be associated with terrestrial matter. How did that much radon get in the air? Even though it is considered to be a
rare gas, a better question is, how did these radioactive elements, minor as they
were, become part of all terrestrial matter?

The magnitude of volcanism was displayed in 1982 when El Chichón volcano erupted in Mexico and raised up a tremendous dust veil that circled a narrow band of the earth for six months. It dispersed after that and the cloud of dust
spread over most of the Northern and part of the Southern Hemispheres.[18] One
volcano covered at least half of the earth.

Power, magnitude, and dangerous elements were displayed again on November 13, 1985, when Nevado del Ruiz, over 17,000 feet high, violently erupted
in Colombia about 90 miles west of Bogotá. The ice cap was melted, and watery
mud, ash, and stones flowed down its sides, crushing and damaging towns below
and killing more than 25,000, with thousands more injured. It is only one of a
chain of two dozen active volcanoes along the Andean Cordilla Central.[19] In Poland, a report covering the years of 1973 to 1987 was filed by three scientists in
Warsaw. They said, "Greatly increased concentrations of stable lead and radium-
226 were observed in all altitudes for several years after the Fuego volcano eruption in 1974, and also after the Nevado del Ruiz eruption in 1985."[20] The Colom-
bian connection to Poland is immense proof of the influence of these local disas-
ters on the entire planet. Radioactive material spread across the world. Hearing
about the tracking of particles from this one volcano from 1985 to the end of
testing in 1987, we can only wonder what effect Noah's thousands of volcanic
fountains of the deep must have had on the world that was. No wonder there were
no survivors except for the immediate family.

Mount St. Helens, El Chichón, and Nevado del Ruiz were only a few volcanoes with watery mud, gas, ash, and their radioactive elements. We must remember even though the proportions of radioactive elements from Mount St. Helens
were deemed minor by the experts, just multiply these volcanoes by thousands
and you will begin to see a picture of how the entire surface of the earth could
have been covered by radioactive ash particles embedded in many layers of mud,

lava, and sediment from the great flood, as the water receded. This certainly would not produce a uniform surface distribution of radioactive elements across the planet. Some places were immediately habitable post-flood and some were not. But there was no escaping the problem of radiation. Even the best of locales were still contaminated, compared to pre-flood lands. Deposits were surely varied as any modern geological map can display.

ALTAMIRA CAVE

Hints of this condition started to come in when it was first reported in 1984 that radon-222 measurements were very high in the Upper Paleolithic cave of Altamira, Spain, 30 Km. from the city of Santander.[21] The inside of this cave was supposedly painted by Cro-Magnon types (Magdalenians) and not by Neanderthals because of the beauty and delicacy of the artwork. Remember the earlier discussion of the Neanderthal thumb muscles. Also, there is a Carbon 14 date of 13,000 years B.P. for this site.[22]

However, the evidence here seems to point to increasing radioactivity as the depth of the cave increases. Poor air circulation and ventilation in the cave are probably the cause of this problem. The deeper you go, the higher the radon-222 values. Fernandez et al. state, "The concentration of radon-222 in soil capillaries several meters below the earth's surface exceeds that of ordinary outdoor air by a factor of a thousand."[23] The concentration of the soil gas at deeper levels is related to its inability to diffuse to the surface on the earth but some does diffuse into the air of the cave. They found the levels of radon-222 in Altamira Cave were from 30 to 160 pCi/l. This number represents a measuring unit called pico Curies, after the discoverers of radium, Madame Curie and her husband, Pierre. It represents pico Curies per liter of air in the cave. One pCi/l represents 2 atoms of radon disintegrating each minute in one liter of air.[24] Fernandez thinks it's probable that the higher concentration of 160 is more likely to exist most months of the year because of similar work in other caves. He therefore postulates that workers in the cave were exposed to 160 pCi/liter of air in 170 hours of work a month in 11 months, which equals 299,200 pCi-hr/liters of air. He goes on to say that this extremely high level of radiation is four times higher than the maximum level established for the protection of uranium miners. "Though the cave is now closed, reopening it to visitors may pose a problem for authorities since the cave guides would be exposed to high concentrations of radon."[25] Ordinary air is 0.2pCi/l over land[26] and over the oceans, 0.5 to 1.0 pCi/l, while air in the Colorado Plateau region of the USA has been measured at 4 to 5 pCi/l because of the uranium mining conducted there.[27] They also said soil samples within the cave were equal in radioactivity to normal soil. The big question? What is normal in a fallen world?

Did the radioactivity in Altamira Cave begin in 1980, when they did the research? No, I doubt it. It's probably been there since the great cataclysm, the worldwide flood, first created these air pockets in the earth that are called caves.

It might even have been at higher levels in ancient times.

Lest you think that this is a bit overdone, listen to what pediatricians were being told in 1989 by the American Academy of Pediatrics, Committee on Environmental Hazards. "Pediatricians should warn families living in homes with radon levels greater than 4pCi/L (0.02 working level) that they should undertake action to decrease the level of radon in the home based on EPA/CDC action timetable."[28] Remember, Altamira is 160pCi/L which is 40 times the pediatrician's recommendation for action level.

Recent work at Mystery Cave in southern Minnesota displayed high counts of lead-210 activity on the inner cave rock surfaces which were apparently daughter products of radon-222.[29] More about this later.

PLEOCHROIC HALOS

The alpha particles of the millions of free polonium-218 inclusions discovered in the form of pleochroic halos (colored rings) by Robert Gentry in primordial granite were obviously not a problem for Adam and Eve because of their early inclusion in granite (baserock of the planet). Dr. Gentry emphasized that they were "free" polonium halos because of extensive testing that he conducted to look for radioactivity in them. He found none and declared them to be extinct halos. They were not daughter products of uranium and radium.

In contrast to the Mount St. Helens polonium-218, a daughter of radium, Gentry's free Po-218 halos were innocuous because of their very short three-minute half-lives. They became extinct three minutes after creation of solid land on the third day and three days before man was created. They were frozen in time (in three minutes) in the molten rock as the granite solidified and completely cooled off; therefore pointing to a very brief cooling time for the primordial granites. Let's emphasize here that since there was U-238 in the same granites, I assume that it had other functions in a perfect world. However it was not decaying before the Fall which would have been harmful.

Therefore, it is logical to believe that after the Fall, all the harmful isotopes, rays, and gases must have been switched on when God said, "Cursed is the ground because of you" (Gen. 3:17). The restraint in the rocks was removed and the radioactive substances began to open up with a rapid burst, their harmful products possibly still at levels too deep for all of the damaging rays and gases to reach the surface. No doubt, though, some did break through and men and animals began to change immediately post-Fall.

I believe that this is how carnivorous behavior began, with a distortion or breakdown of the genetic messages in tooth and jaw formation. Some herbivorous creatures became carnivorous and were transformed similar to the caterpillar/butterfly transition. Much work needs to be done on this subject, and especially loss of genetic information. Lord willing, this will be my next effort. The radioactive elements probably made an even more disastrous debut on earth as they were spewed forth at the flood when the earth was torn asunder and "all the fountains of the great deep burst open."

By this reasoning, it would make no sense at all for God to survey His creation with an earth full of radioactive materials decaying away according to their half-life schedules, with all their injurious radiating emissions, and on the sixth day turn around and proclaim this to be very good. Unless Adam and Eve were totally resistant to radiation, which I doubt, even though they had stronger immune systems than we, the inactivity of the harmful radioactive isotopes must be postulated, "In the beginning." At the risk of redundancy it must be said that, if all was good, all was good!

What happens to the uniformitarian presuppositions if this occurred? "Good" means not destructive or harmful. All of the dating systems based on a constant rate of decay of all radioactive substances throughout history would be seriously flawed if there were a sudden burst initially coinciding with the curse of the ground. More research should be done with this, but if you'll excuse the expression, "all bets are off" if the creation was "very good" before the Fall. We must now begin to establish what "very good" meant before the Fall. Can we establish this on biologic grounds?

Chapter 26

How Long Do We Live?

odern man's average life expectancy at birth is 75 years, and the maximum longevity is 115[1] or 120 years.[2] Death, of course, can come much sooner with accidents or disease and that would have nothing to do with chronological age.

According to Moses' writings, when wickedness on earth had greatly increased, the Lord decided that man's maximum longevity should be as follows: "Nevertheless his days shall be one hundred and twenty years" (Gen. 6:3). Later on, according to David's writings in Psalm 90, man's average life expectancy at birth should be as follows: "As for the days of our life they contain seventy years, or if due to strength, eighty years" (Ps. 90:10). The words of Moses and the words of David, divinely inspired thousands of years ago suggest two things: First, God informed us of the maximum age that we are capable of attaining; and second, David revealed to us our average life expectancy at birth. Both of these facts of Scripture accord with what modern scholars have told us about these statistics.

The complete life tables of the Office of the Actuary of the USA end at the age of 119. They don't go beyond that point. It is marvelous to see how the biblical record has demonstrated its accuracy for thousands of years. Most people think we have experienced an increase in life expectancy from the mid-nineteenth century to today.[3] It is common knowledge that life expectancy at birth has doubled from 40 to close to 80 years since the early 1800s.

This is true in mathematical calculations because of one major factor. Comfort wrote, "This has been due almost entirely to a reduction in the mortality of the younger age groups — the human "specific age" and the maximum life span have not been appreciably altered."[4] What he maintained was that the increase in life expectancy from 40 to 80 is due to the fact that the deaths of many young children in the 1800s pulled the average age of death down to the level of about

40 years. With most children today surviving the early years, the average age of death has risen to the length of years revealed by David, which is about 80. Some say, that it has never really changed, but that would be missing the point. There is a change in the way most of us get to be that old and survive childhood. I think we can say it is due to modern technology that we now reach those ages, whereas in the past it was the stronger constitutions of men that enabled him to live to old ages. As man weakened through the ages science was called upon to prop him up. More about this later.

This change in the way we age, of course, is now due to modern technology. Modern medicine and immunology have decreased the death rate of infants as well as adults. Any increase that we may see in the coming years will be due to more modern medicine and technology. Comfort continued, "The large changes in the survival curve of man over the last century represent, quite simply, the removal of causes of premature death, but the age at which a man becomes old, judged by criteria of increasing infirmity and liability of death, is exactly what it was in biblical times." By biblical times, he is referring to the times of the majority of biblical peoples from Moses to King David's time through the times of Jesus Christ. He is not referring to the early peoples of Genesis.

There is, of course, the fact that "the centenarian (100+) population grew by 160% in the United States during the 1980s." And, "many demographers predict that 20 to 40 million people will be aged 85 or older in the year 2040, and 500,000 to four million will be centenarians in 2050."[5] All of this seems to say that great numbers of people surviving to a ripe old age will be increasing in the future. This seems primarily to be due to better medical care with increased emphasis on preventative medicine, maintaining good health through frequent check-ups, exercise, diet, supplements, and generally a healthy lifestyle. Raising the numbers of survivors into their nineties will most likely produce an artificially inflated average age of life expectancy at birth in the future. This will have nothing to do with evolution but everything to do with modern medical technology.

Quality of life in old age may not improve. Olshansky et al. proclaimed in 1990 that, "improved lifestyles at younger ages and medical technology will continue to strip away lethal processes that terminate life early. Left behind will be a rapidly growing elderly population that lives longer but whose additional years of life may be dominated by non-fatal but highly disabling conditions (such as arthritis, osteoporosis, sensory impairments, and Alzheimer's disease)." He continues, "In fact, we may be trading off a longer life for a prolonged period of frailty and dependency — a condition that is a potential consequence of successfully reducing or eliminating fatal degenerative diseases."[6] Hayflick added, "The majority of American centenarians are female, white, widowed, and institutionalized; were born in the United States of Western European ancestry; and have less than a ninth grade education."[7] The picture presented by modern day longevity studies isn't very rosy, is it?

As to further increases, Comfort clearly stated, "There is, in fact, a biological limit on human longevity that cannot be much transcended by conventional improvements in medicine or living conditions."[8] Thomas Perls has described the oldest person alive in the present era, Madame Jean Calment of Arles, France, who turned 120 in February 1995, making her the oldest living person in 1995 whose age has been verified. She died in 1997. Some speculate that she might have been the oldest person ever. "Most of us do not even come close to this age." He said, "Those of us with Methuselean aspirations are up against incredible odds."[9]

MADAME CALMENT — THE OLDEST PERSON EVER?

If we read the Bible as it was written, as Dr. Francis Schaeffer was fond of saying, we would have knowledge that is different than the finite knowledge of the world. We would have knowledge directly from God. We would know that the oldest person on record wasn't Jean Calment.

The oldest person in the world could have been Adam if he hadn't sinned. However, he was 930 years old when he died, just 39 years younger than Methuselah, who reached 969. Methuselah, therefore, has the record of having the oldest recorded life on earth. Beginning with Adam first, Jared was the sixth generation, and he reached 962, becoming the second oldest person to be recorded in history. Noah's life extended to 950 years, making him the third oldest person recorded. The remainder of the early patriarchs ranged from 905 (Enosh), 912 (Seth), 910 (Kenan), to a young 895 (Mahalel), and a younger still Lamech at 777.

There was, however, a way to live a longer life that was known to Adam but terminated by God once Adam and Eve had rebelled. It was called the "Tree of Life."

> The Lord God said, "Behold, the man has become like one of Us, knowing good and evil; and now, he might stretch out his hand, and take also from the tree of life, and eat, and live forever" — therefore the Lord God sent him out from the garden of Eden, to cultivate the ground from which he was taken. So He drove the man out; and at the east of the garden of Eden He stationed the cherubim and the flaming sword which turned every direction, to guard the way to the tree of life (Gen. 3:22-24).

We must be grateful for this action by God because if that tree was still available in our day, the wars waged over it would make Operation Desert Storm appear to be small in comparison. Besides that, what would we gain with a cursed body that could never die? Degenerating with time, our bodies would be practically useless but still alive. We might all look like Jobba the Hut of Star Wars fame; a big blob of protoplasm with a face and limbs.

There are other historical references to this tree. These come from the annals of the Assyrian kings as recalled by Arnett from their extant public texts of the 14th through the 7th centuries B.C. He wrote, "Each king represented the continued growth of 'the family tree' and, like Esarhaddon, prayed that Assyrian kingship could acquire the magic of the 'plant of life' (6, II, p. 248) and continue to send forth many branches (6, II, p. 253-254)."[10]

Most of my readers, I will assume at this point, will agree with the above biblical figures. However, there will be some of you, I'm sure, who, like my critic from the *American Journal of Orthodontics,* thought my reference to these biblical ages was "amusing."[11] Or, there may be some of you who think that the text is not clear about this longevity issue. May I refer you to the scene depicted in Genesis 47:7-9. "Then Joseph brought his father Jacob and presented him to Pharaoh; and Jacob blessed Pharaoh. And Pharaoh said to Jacob, "How many years have you lived?" So Jacob said to Pharaoh, the years of my sojourning are one hundred and thirty; few and unpleasant have been the years of my life, nor have they attained the years that my fathers lived during the days of their sojourning." Jacob lived 17 more years in Egypt and died at 147.

Pharaoh asked Jacob only one question. How old was he? Why do you suppose this was so? Was not the longevity of God's chosen people legendary in the world? They might have been the last of the world's population to retain genetic strength for longevity. Because of this, Pharaoh must have been very interested in obtaining some further information. "And Jacob blessed Pharaoh, and went out from his presence" (Gen. 47:10). We know that Jacob was grateful for the sanctuary Pharaoh provided for Joseph and his family but it is my opinion that Pharaoh wished to be blessed by a man of strong lineage perhaps hoping to "catch" a little of that longevity himself. It reminds us of, "O king, live forever!" said by the Chaldean magicians to Nebuchadnezzar (Dan. 2:4).

We also see from this passage that Jacob was affirming the declining nature of longevity amongst the Israelites. Also, his confession confirmed the fact that no tree of life remained to restore the body and add more years. So with this short dissertation, Jacob dispelled all Pharaoh's notions about the ongoing longevity of the line of Shem. Longevity in Pharaoh's lineage, in the line of Ham, from the tribe of Mizraim (Gen. 10:6), had probably waned by this time. Some scholars have placed Joseph's rise to power in Egypt in the 12th Dynasty (c. 1871 B.C.).[12]

Therefore, in the historical record of the Bible one finds many references to those men and even women who lived longer than Madame Calment. In Genesis 23:1 we find Moses writing that Sarah, the wife of Abraham, lived 127 years.

Are we to dismiss these ages as being exaggerated or mistaken, or are we to take them seriously? If we take them seriously our next question should be, where are all the remains of these old people? Or were they never preserved at all? Would they look like us if you found someone who lived past 200 years? It depends on what "like us" means.

Chapter 27

Age Changes in Our Head and Face

Having already seen evidence that the human race is declining in longevity, we must now explore what that longevity meant in terms of the human head and face. We begin by asking the question, "What about us?" What would happen to our head and face if we lived past 100 years as people in ancient Bible times did. We must never assume a similar rate of change in the past as in the present — that would be uniform thinking — but we can look for overall trends and make tentative predictions while "rates" will always remain in doubt.

Bishara, Treder, and Jacobsen recently wrote in the *American Journal of Orthodontics* that after the normal growth period for modern man is finished (18 to 25 years), growth still continues in the face and head.[1] They measured the same 15 men and 15 women with precision cephalometric (measurable) x-rays over a time frame of 21 years.

They started out with 175 children enrolled in the study at the University of Iowa in 1946. Measurements were taken semi-annually until age 12, annually during adolescence, once during early adulthood (25 years), and once at mid-adulthood (46 years). They ended up with only 30 adults out of those original children at the age of 46, who had been measured at age 25 — 15 males and 15 females. The comparisons were then made between the face and head of each person when he or she was 25 and when he or she was 46. The male measurements were calculated to age 25. This is called a longitudinal study.[2] This proved to be very significant indeed.

They stated in their discussion, "Overall, the present findings suggest that age-related changes in the craniofacial complex do not cease with the onset of adulthood, but continue albeit at a significantly slower rate, throughout adult life. With a few important exceptions, these changes tend to be of small magnitude, so that their clinical relevance is somewhat limited, and generally would not significantly influence orthodontic treatment planning." Therefore while playing down its importance in the plan of treatment for a patient with braces, they affirmed a real growth trend in the adult years.

Going back into history, we find numerous studies on adult growth. In fact, it is one of the most documented facts in anthropologic literature. Ales Hrdlicka of the Smithsonian Institution, said this in 1936, "There is a universal notion that when the adult stage of life has been reached, all growth except in bulkiness, has been accomplished and henceforth ceases. The very definition of an adult is that of a person grown to full size and strength. The purpose of this paper is to show that, while such a concept suffices in general, scientifically speaking the view is largely erroneous."[3]

This work goes as far back as 1836, by Parchappe in Paris, who concluded from his work that the volume of the head increased up to age 50.[4] Pfitzner, in Germany, in 1899 examined 3,400 male and female cadavers and found that their heads and faces grew into middle age, 35-45.[5] Dr. Jarcho of the Moscow University reported on age changes in the adult in 1935 to beyond 40 years.[6] He found that the heads of three groups — the Russians, the Kirghiz, and the Uzbeks — increased more in length than in breadth from ages 20-25, 26-39, and 40 years and above. An index called the "cephalic index" decreased in all groups with age.[7] In short, the heads became longer over the years and wider, too. However, the shape of the skull changed, as it gained more in length than in width.[8]

Parchappe found dramatic increases of length over width in the French study of 1836.[9] Hrdlicka also emphasized that overall the results are not entirely uniform but the general tendency is clear. He believed that adult growth of the head was a fact not to be ignored.

NOT MUCH HEIGHT INCREASE

Another facet of the adult skull growth to be considered is its height. Pfitzner's Alsatian male skull adult height figures start at 120.9 mm for age group 20-25 and finish at 121.6mm for 81 years and over.[10] This represents a mere increase of .7mm, less than 1mm of growth in head height. Female Alsatian head height actually slightly decreased from 117.1mm for the 20-25 group to 116.2 for the over 81 group. In old American white males from Hrdlicka's figures we find the male (247 skulls) height decreasing slightly from 80mm to 78.5mm between 29 and 59 years. The females showed a tiny increase between these ages (1.8mm) but nothing compared to the almost 5mm increase in length. The picture that we get here is of an aging skull which, in general terms, grows much longer, a little wider, with practically no increase in its height and sometimes a decrease. This is very important when we come to the Neanderthal growth section when the Neanderthal Le Moustier is compared to close relatives La Chapelle-aux-Saints and La Ferrassie I.

Therefore, it can be concluded that with the exception of the females of one isolated Indian tribe in the United States, all other groups of peoples studied by the aforementioned anthropologists showed the following: a skull whose proportions changed as it aged with the lengths gaining the most, the widths next, and the heights the least.[11]

T. Wingate Todd in 1924 measured 448 male skulls for thickness of the bone itself in various places. He found a sporadic thickening of the cranium (skull) during later life. He also found no evidence of real dimunition in thickness of the cranium (skull) with increasing age.[12] It has long been a myth in our society that aging was synonymous with bone loss. Here we find a top scientist early in this century contradicting that opinion. The skull gets thicker in certain places with age.

In 1966, Campbell, a radiologist, observed in his work that the cranium continues to thicken throughout life in certain places.[13]

THE FACE

Tallgren in 1957 used cephalometric x-rays of 165 women in a cross-sectional study. Her results showed that there were increases in facial height from the youngest to the oldest groupings.[14] Milo Hellman, for whom we have a coveted award given by the American Association of Orthodontists, said in 1927 that the face does keep on growing until "old age."[15] He received much criticism for this conclusion. Pfitzner also determined the increase in length of the face for his 3,400 cadavers in 1899. From the point where the nose meets the forehead to the bottom of the bony chin enlarged in height from 20-25 years to 81 years and over about 5% in men and 1.5% in women.[16] The width of the face also expanded about 2%. Hrdlicka found similar results with older Americans and concluded, "In old Americans therefore, as in the Alsatians, the face appears to enlarge appreciably during adult life, in both its height and breadth, and that up to the sixth decade."[17]

Using 10,000 Irish men, which is no small amount, Hooten and Dupertuis in 1951 expressed surprise when they found continued facial growth into the sixth decade.[18] They also documented continuous head growth. In a very crucial work, Lasker in 1953 confirmed this trend in the human head when he did his studies on Mexicans and said, "The curves for age changes reported for Mexico are essentially similar to the findings in other groups. The chief factors responsible for the age changes apparently cut across geographic and racial boundaries."[19]

Karl Sarnas wrote a Master's thesis on the growth of skulls of ancient man at the University of Rochester in 1955. He used in his study 120 skulls of ancient Indians from Indian Knoll, Kentucky, from a period supposedly 5,000 years ago. He found that the cranial length increased from the younger to the older group among males while the cranial height did not increase. The total facial height also increased in the older group even though there was wear on the teeth called "dental attrition."[20] This meant that there is a compensating mechanism to maintain the facial height and increase it in older ages. We will look into this a little further on.

In 1980, Ruff confirmed in his study of 136 ancient skulls from Indian Knoll, Kentucky, that the very same increases took place in aging and he believed that it was a phenomena that transgressed all borders of sex, race, population, genetic, mechanical, or environmental factors.[21] In other words, it was pretty much universal in character.[22]

FOLLOWING THE SAME PEOPLE FOR YEARS

With the exception of the Iowa examination, all of the above have been cross-sectional studies (different people). There are other longitudinal works of merit which we can now consider. Each of these, in contrast to cross-sectional studies, has used the same population of subjects to evaluate year after year to determine what has been happening to their heads and faces.

Buchi studied 200 Swiss adults and separated them into six age classes. He concluded in 1950 that aging resulted in gains in diameter of the head and face and also of the long bones.[23] Thompson and Kendrick in 1964 used cephalometric (measurable) x-ray analysis of 71 men aged 22-34 years. They took measurements once a year. They saw that without much attrition (wear) of the teeth the vertical dimension of the face increased significantly.[24] Kendrick and Risinger in 1967 measured the same 71 men and reported increases in head length and facial depth.[25]

Harry Israel, of the Fels Institute in Ohio, conducted and published at least 12 studies on the nature of long-term adult growth. Much of his work was criticized for lack of precision methods of x-ray technique, but some of it, like the 1977 research, has proved to be valuable and more accurate. His major accomplishment was to add a wealth of data to those who would study this subject in a serious way.[26]

At the risk of losing your interest and boring you to death with statistics, I must continue with one more longitudinal study on long term growth. Susanne in 1977 published a work done on 44 Belgian men. Susanne measured their heads twice between the ages of 25 and 60 years and found consistent increases in head length and head width, also demonstrating gains in the lengths of their faces, their noses, and their ears. He found a decrease in the size and thickness of the lips, too.[27]

Should we make this more personal? Observe a picture of yourself at a younger age if you are an older person. Observe pictures of your parents and grandparents when they were younger and older. The changes you notice are not just soft tissue changes, they are genuine bone changes. If you are over 50 try on a hat that fit you at 20. My Navy officer's cap sits on top of my head now and I have less hair than I did when I was 25.

When are the Bible-believing people going to wake up and put two and two together? If there were genuinely old people who lived in the past, don't you suppose they would have undergone the same changes in the face and head that the aforementioned studies have described? If so, where are the remains of these people? Do you think that the museums have any skulls of these very old people? Do you think the museums would ever consider this type of reasoning? The answer to the latter question is no, since the museums and secular universities are dominated by evolutionists who do not believe that the Bible has anything valuable to say in the area of science or history.

BRIAN'S SONG

My son-in-law Brian Garner is a computer expert and is married to my daughter Margie. He is a grad student very close to his Ph.D. in biomedical engineering. He composed a piece of computer work that has been like a song for what it has done for this research. It's a graphic display of the growth of the head and face of contemporary adults from middle America. I like to call it "Brian's song" after the popular TV movie. Our Brian's song was also written in the face of adversity. Knowing how most of the scientific community had ignored and despised my research, and with a very heavy graduate school schedule, Brian wrote a computer program with skillfulness based on real facts of science. For this, I am very grateful.

I had asked him to use the results obtained by Rolf G. Behrents in a study of adult aging conducted at the University of Michigan in 1984-85.[28] Dr. Behrents had been the beneficiary of a longitudinal study on a group of 113 people started at Case Western Reserve in Cleveland, Ohio, in 1928 in the Broadbent-Bolton Study. This original study started with 6,000 normal individuals who were generally of European ancestry. After narrowing down the field to those who were able to be located and would participate, and those that did not have orthodontic treatment, were in good health physically and orally, and had x-rays taken at or after the 17-year level and final x-rays after the age of 25, they settled on 113. The initial average age for the participants was 19.7 and the final average age was 46.4. This is a total of 26.7 years. This is a good range to determine what growth changes take place in the head and face. There also were 41 people at 57 years or over at their last examination.

Lateral head (cephalometric) x-rays were taken on these people and carefully digitized marking points were located on the x-rays, to be able to be reduced to mathematical data.[29] Brian extrapolated this data past the points where they ended in the 80-year range. He used only the 79 men in the study because it is believed that the amount of change that took place in the male was greater than in the female. Their ages went from 19.8 to 46.6 years. Therefore, it is assumed that while the changes were almost similar in both sexes, the male changes would be more noticeable because of the usually heavier musculature and basic nature of maleness, so we would use just the men.[30]

However, the oldest person in the study was a woman in her eighties. Figure 26 shows this adult who was 83 at the time of the second x-ray and 34 at the time

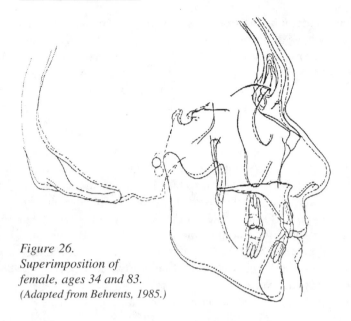

Figure 26.
Superimposition of
female, ages 34 and 83.
(Adapted from Behrents, 1985.)

of the first. The solid line is the size at 83, the broken line at 34. Starting from the forehead in figure 26, the soft tissue and bony forehead grew more at the lower half than the upper, so the brow ridges started to come forward along with the middle part above the nose. This growth was accompanied by the space called the frontal sinus growing upward and forward. The soft tissue nose became longer and the bony upper part moved forward and upward. The teeth and jaws came forward and the bony chin started to flatten a little. The cheekbones came forward, also. The eye socket moved forward and the ear hole rose. The back of the head started to develop a larger point or protuberance on the bone that is called the occipital. The lips dropped and so did the lip line. The angle of the lower jaw dropped, too. Overall, you might say the face looks as if were pulled forward.

Figure 27 is of a man when he was 45 and again at 77. All of the same changes took place to varying degrees except his nose drooped more than the old woman. Looking at the results from Brian's program of the male changes, we notice the same phenomena occurring. In figure 28, age 100 to age 500 describe what would happen to our face and head if we lived to each

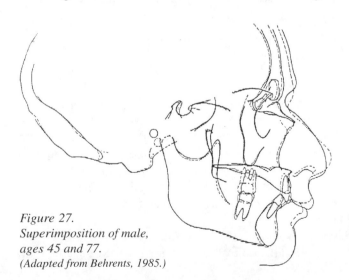

Figure 27.
Superimposition of male,
ages 45 and 77.
(Adapted from Behrents, 1985.)

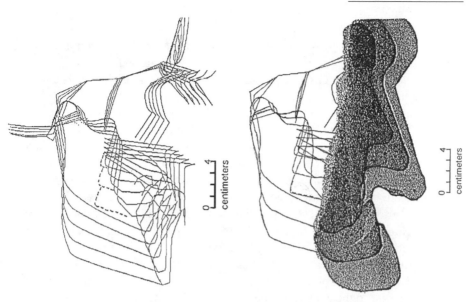

*Figure 28. Projected bony growth of a
modern male craniofacial skeleton
from 100 to 500 years of age.*

*Figure 29. Projected soft tissue growth
of a modern male craniofacial skeleton
at 100, 300, and 500 years of age.*

of the designated ages. Figure 29 adds the soft tissue of the face for better visualization.

We submitted this program in 1993 in the form of a paper to the American Association of Orthodontists (AAO) for presentation at the annual meeting in 1994 , as original scientific research. We were rejected by the AAO, but in May of 1993 we received a very encouraging letter from Dr. R. Behrents, the top researcher in the USA in this subject, about this piece of work. It reads as follows:

Dear Dr. Cuozzo,

The paper you sent me is quite interesting. It is evident that you have carefully read the monograph and understand the design and results. The extrapolation you portray is mathematically elegant and the result quite interesting. Nice job.

Sincerely,
Rolf G. Behrents, D.D.S., M.S., Ph.D.
Professor and Chairman, Dept. of Orthodontics
Univ. of Tennessee College of Dentistry[31]

THE REAL CHANGES IN FIGURES 28 AND 29

These are the changes with age when looking at the skull from the side in a true lateral view: The base of the skull moves downward and very slightly forward behind the socket of the lower jaw near the opening of the spinal column. However the angle of the base of the skull from the front of the brain to the very back seems very stable with only increases in length at either end. The point where the nose meets the forehead is moving forward at all ages. The frontal sinus — you know, the one where you get the pain when you eat ice cream too fast — just above the bridge of the nose and between the eyes, continues to develop spectacularly with age; therefore, this is coupled with forces of chewing from the teeth, and the brow ridges start to grow larger over the eyes. The brow ridges move forward faster than infilling of the chin until age 400 and 500 and then the chin area appears flatter. Behrents gave just the height measurements and no points for determining changes in the internal width of this sinus. However, the frontal sinus expansion is a wonderful indicator of continuing change in the adult head. According to Behrents, "These conformational changes are most likely due partly to the continued adaptive growth of the nasal region as the face remodels in a forward direction and the nose increases in size with age. This behavior will also be seen in general terms for the entire midface."[32]

The eye socket enlarges and moves downward and forward so as to increase the height of the orbit. It couldn't become too large for the sake of the eyeball. The base of the cheekbone also advances forward so that the midface slopes forward and gives the impression of a "muzzle." The upper jaw extends in the forward direction, so that during the adult years there is additional bone added above the upper front teeth. The upper jaw also descends as it grows forward and the back of the hard palate lowers more than the front part. The whole roof of the mouth (palate) tilts toward the rear as it descends, so that it becomes more parallel to the front base of the brain.

Examining the nose, we see the tip of the nasal bones advancing forward and elevating slightly. This is not good to dwell on if you're getting on in years.

The under-surface of the chin is an indicator of the front of the lower jaw and tells us what it is doing. This point, called "menton," another orthodontic term, is moving downward as the entire lower jaw descends. All the marks of downward and forward motion are evident for the lower jaw. The chin and lower jaw seem to be advancing forward at a faster rate than the upper jaw. This would make the lower jaw more protruding with age, unless there were to be a habit, like thumbsucking, which interfered with this growth. The angle that the lower jaw makes within itself, between the upper back part (ramus) and the lower front part (body), decreases with age. It gets squarer with time. This is important. Remember this!

The curious thing about the lower jaw is that the inside of the front border of the vertical part scoops out slightly during aging, allowing the late eruption of the third molars.[33] However, this cannot always be the case, since a large percentage of my own orthodontic patients never have enough room for their lower third molars. These teeth have caused lots of problems for many people. The joint where the lower jaw meets the skull gets wider and the knob (condyle) on the end of the ramus gets thicker. The bony projection in front of the knob (condyle), the coronoid process, elongates and then gets shorter as the muscle that attaches to it is used less and less.

Why this temporal muscle on the side of your head is used less is directly related to the forward movement of all the teeth. This is the bane of all orthodontists. No orthodontist in the world will tell you that the teeth don't shift forward with age. At least all the honest ones will admit that is a fact.

It is my belief that the muscles of mastication (chewing) shift forward as the teeth and jaws shift forward with age. However, this program could not take any muscle migration into account since it is impossible within the time span used for calculations, 26.8 years, and the fact that none of these people showed this type of change yet.[34]

If we are going to compare these computer tracings to ancient peoples who lived longer life spans, it is important to take into account that at each age the diagrams are probably larger than the actual ancient skull would have been. This is because we are using modern rates for adult growth, and ancient adult growth proceeded most likely at a slower pace. Therefore, the true 500-year-old skull will be smaller than the 500-year-old diagram tracing, and so will all the others be in their turn. Therefore, it would have taken the ancients longer to achieve these sizes.

As is visible in the 500-year-old male (figure 28), the teeth move so far forward that the chin begins to look flat. The chin is not really lost, it has only lost its prominence. Thus at 400 and 500 it looks as if it has disappeared. At 300 there is still some chin visible. This is the result of the lower front teeth tipping back and the bony housing of all the lower teeth sliding forward over the chin. The bone here fills in the hollow above the chin. All this could be altered by habits and the lower front teeth could tip forward if the tongue forces were strong enough over hundreds of years. The upper teeth move forward also, but less than the lowers. The lowers are moving through all the ages. The chin looks as if it is getting smaller because of the amount of forward movement of the teeth.

All of the lower teeth and upper teeth keep erupting throughout life (passive eruption).[35] Bone is added on the lower border of the body of the lower jaw and also to the upper margins which surround the teeth to a certain extent. Many times the bone does not quite keep up with the passive eruption and more root is exposed. This continuous or passive eruption of teeth is what compensates for the continuous wear or attrition on the biting surfaces of the teeth. This is what keeps the height of the lower face the same throughout modern man's life. If this continuous eruption process lags behind that of the surface wear on the teeth the distance between the nose and the chin decreases. If this process is equal or faster than the tooth surface wear, the distance between the nose and the chin stays the same or increases. If this process is only slightly faster over a long period of time, the distance will still increase.

The face will get longer in front or, said another way, the facial height will increase if there is very little tooth wear on the biting surfaces of the teeth. If there is more wear of the biting surfaces the overbite stays the same, or even can become an edge-to-edge bite of the front teeth. In this case, the height of the face probably stays very close to the same during aging.

The question that remains is, what happens when there is extensive wear of all the biting surfaces of the teeth and the face doesn't stay the same length but, instead, gets longer or increases in facial height? This happened in Neanderthals. Does this represent overcompensation? Would it mean a higher rate of the adult passive tooth eruption process with very rapid bone build-up on the lower border of the lower jaw in the average Neanderthal life span of 45 years[36] or 40 years?[37] Or could it be the regular process of compensation at a normal or slower rate of passive eruption with an average or slower rate of bone build-up on this border over a much longer lifetime? We will discuss this later.

Chapter 28

Le Moustier, the Baseline

JOSHUA'S GREAT CATCH

In the summer of 1991 we traveled to Berlin, Germany, to examine the Neanderthal teenager Le Moustier, discovered in 1908 by Otto Hauser in Southern France. Apparently, he sold it to the Germans. By some calculations Le Moustier was supposed to be anywhere from 16 to 18 years of age.[1] It was the hottest August that Berlin had seen in years and in the East Berlin Museum where my son Joshua and I worked on the highest floor, it was a scorcher. Josh did everything in Germany from the airport customs to the lab. He set up the machinery, took it down, and actually set up the numerous parts of the fossil skull for x-raying and photographing.

We avoided an international incident when Joshua caught a major piece of Le Moustier's skull in mid-air that had accidentally slipped off the table. The problem was that we had to wear white cotton gloves that one of the human paleontologists gave us to prevent damage to the fossils. It seemed like we would cause more damage to the fossils with those gloves. Everything slipped out of our hands. We had just set this large piece of skull up for the x-ray examination when it tumbled off the table. My heart regained its normal beat when I saw the skull in Joshua's outstretched hands, and not a crumb of bone missing. After this experience, we took the gloves off. Daniel came to Germany, too, but was only a couple of weeks out of major back surgery.

WILL THE REAL MOUSTIER STAND UP!

There are three illustrations that you ought to examine before the next discussion. The first is figure 30, the Le Moustier reproduction in the glass case of the Museum für Vor-und Frühgeschichte in the West Section of Berlin. It is very ape-like. Then look at figure 31, my radiograph of the front, top, and back of the

Figure 30. The official museum version of Le Moustier in the glass display case on the first floor of the Museum für Vor-und Frühgeschichte in Berlin, Germany.

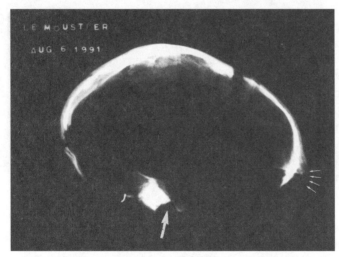

Figure 31. The top, front, and side of the skull of Le Moustier as reconstructed by x-rays.

cranium. It is not ape-like at all. Examine figure 32, the drawing of the slide purchased at the souvenir counter at the museum. The lower jaw in this slide is 30 mm (over an inch) out of the socket (TM fossa). This allowed the upper jaw to be pushed forward 30mm presenting a very ape-like appearance. This would be a dislocated lower jaw in any oral surgeon's office. How can a dislocated jaw be passed off as evidence for evolution? With everyone convinced evolution is true, anything is possible. The detailed discoveries concerning this skull and my x-ray reconstruction of it are seen in the notes.[2]

Back to the question. How in the world can I possibly call a Neanderthal teenager a baseline? A teenager still has a lot of teenage growing to do that is not classified as adult growth by any means.

Let's begin by going back a few years to my reply to Chris Stringer and my paper submitted to the American Museum of Natural History in New York. First, you'll remember what happened when I first told Chris about my theory of the immaturity of the Neanderthal child in March of 1985. A flurry of activity burst out because I had outlined my theory in the letter and also in my "Neanderthal

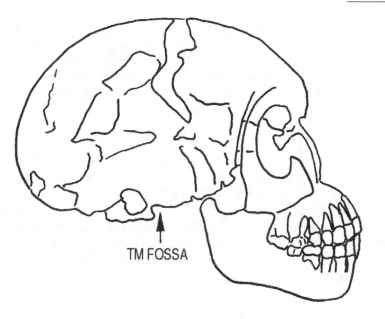

Figure 32. A drawing of the Le Moustier color slide purchased at the souvenir counter of the museum. The lower jaw is about 30 mm out of its socket (arrow), which makes the upper jaw 30 mm forward and very ape-like.

TM FOSSA

Outline." I wrote to them describing what I thought about Neanderthal maturity and old age. What I didn't tell you was that in 1986 the British made reference to a certain article from 1982 by Ann Marie Tillier, a French human paleontologist.[3]

In her article she made a case for two individuals from the Gibraltar child's remains because of the immaturity of the bones around the ear. However, Stringer and his colleagues, Bromage and Dean, would have nothing to do with the two-individual theory but this gave them a good opportunity to jump all over my claims for immaturity in Neanderthal children. They stated in their 1986 Abstract, "The results indicate that the most likely age of this individual at death was 3 years of age. This result is in agreement with an independent assessment of the age of the temporal bone of this specimen (Tillier, AM [1982] Zeitschriftuer Morphologie und Anthropologie, 73:125-148) and is concordant with dental developmental ages given for modern humans." They continued by calling on the work of two more anthropologists who believed that dental eruption schedules in Neanderthals were accelerated. Finally, they contradicted Tillier's two-child hypothesis and called the jaws normal. They believed this indicated a "remarkably precocious brain growth" and faster development in Neanderthals."[4]

CLEARLY

Tillier in 1989 said something even more revealing, "Clearly, there are many problems inherent in attempting to construct a model of skeletal growth peculiar to Middle Paleolithic hominids (including Neanderthals, other archaic *Homo sapiens,* and Proto-Cro-magnoids) on the basis of information derived from living human populations — especially in terms of growth rates. Clearly, we must beware of applying circular arguments, which apply modern standards for aging these specimens, and then employ those standards to argue for different rates of growth in the fossil specimens."[5] Clearly, we do not know who she is talking about. Did she take a shot at Dean, Stringer, and Bromage, or me? She should at least signify who it is that she is criticizing.

At this point, I would like to say, "Let me make it perfectly clear," but I don't want to sound like the late President Richard Nixon. Nevertheless, let me affirm that there is no other than yours truly in the scientific community using cephalometric x-ray standards of modern children to determine the real level of maturity of the Neanderthal children.

Is it a legitimate question to ask how these ancient children stack up against modern children? Don't the evolutionists use modern standards such as the latest tooth eruption schedules, enamel ring standards, and brain size schedules to determine growth rates? Didn't Dean, Stringer, and Bromage do exactly the same thing when they proposed the opposing argument based on known standards? The answer to the last three questions is yes.

Shouldn't we be willing to admit that perhaps our modern patterns of development might have been a bit faster if perhaps we didn't descend from the apes? One can never arrive at that (slower) hypothesis for the past generations, if one holds on to the evolutionary pre-suppositions.

RADIOGRAPH MEASUREMENTS

With this in mind, I refer to Tables A and B. These are charts that list the lower jaw angles of Neanderthal children I studied and x-rayed.[6] These tables do not include Engis II from Belgium, whose lower jaw was never found. You wonder about things like that. All the fossil ages are given in years based on modern children's tooth eruption schedules.[7] These are the ages of death of these children. The gonial or jaw angle is the bend in the lower jaw or mandible on both sides. In a cephalometric radiograph it is treated as one image.

Table A
Michigan Method (Radiograph Measurement)[8]

Specimen	Age (yrs.)	Jaw Angle (degrees)	Museum, (Location)
Pech de l'Azé	2-2.5	133	Musée de l'Homme (Paris)
Gibraltar II	3-5	127- 128 *	British Museum (London)
Le Moustier	16-18	110	Mus. für Vor-und
		23 **	Frügeschichte,(Berlin)
		(total change)	

Table B
Bolton Method (Radiograph Measurement)

Specimen	Age (yrs.)	Jaw Angle (degrees)	Museum, (Location)
Pech de l'Azé	2-2.5	135	Musée de l'Homme(Paris)
Gibraltar II	3-5	125 *	British Museum (London)
Le Moustier	16-18	<u>120</u>	Mus. für Vor-und
		15 **	Frügeschichte,(Berlin)
		(total change)	

* Represents an adjusted figure to correct the misconstruction of the original parts.

**Childhood growth is not a steady thing and I don't want to give that impression for one moment because there are "growth spurts" which mean periods of accelerated growth before one reaches sexual and skeletal maturation. For the sake of understanding overall trends in growth I am using the data as if it were smooth and not jumpy. It is like a car going fast and slow between stop lights on a highway or any road. Just because the car speeds up, slows down, and stops occasionally doesn't mean that you can't calculate an average speed for the time it took to go from your house to the ice cream parlor. Rates of jaw and facial growth speed up and slow down too, but we can figure average rates from the data.[9]

The youngest child has the large angle, the older youth a smaller one. Descending values for these jaw angles are typical of any group of children from any period in history. It's only the rate of decline that will vary from group to group. It's a function of growth of the condyle (knob at top) and remodeling of the bone by various factors, incorporated in the functional matrix theory.[10]

When calculating from Pech de l'Azé (figure 32a) to LeMoustier (figure 42), a sum of 23 degrees in (18-2) or 16 years is found using the Michigan method, and this produces an average rate of decline of 1.4 degrees per year. With the Bolton Method, which is another way to measure the same angle, the difference is 15 degrees over 16 years and an average rate of 0.94 degrees per year. I am using 16 total years here to give the evolutionists every benefit of the doubt. I could also use 16 years minus 2.5 years and have higher rates. For instance, 23 degrees in 13.5 years produces a rate of 1.7 degrees per year and 15 degrees in 13.5 years produces a rate of 1.1 degrees per year.

There must be caution here. One concealed problem is behind these numbers. The problem concerns an unstated assumption inherent in the chart which mandates the "high rate" that I found as the only possible conclusion. This assumption pertains to the ages of death of the Neanderthal children. The ages are set by the level of development of their teeth. In every case, these are modern standards or very close to modern standards that have been used to age these Neanderthal kids.

Both 1963 or 1944 tooth developmental levels are used to age children that lived hundreds or thousands of years ago.[11] How close were these children to the standards of today?[12] That is the "big question." The question hinges on what you believe about history.

Because of this question a new study was conducted by the British Museum people to remedy this situation. It claims to have measured accurately 63 remains of children from a crypt (1759-1859) in Spitalfields, London. Their ages were birth to 5.4 years as marked on their coffins or church records.[13] Theya Molleson, of that museum, was kind enough to send me a letter in which she did affirm, "Also it was frequently noted that often no teeth had erupted in 11 or 12-month children."[14] That I believe to be true, because the modern child's baby teeth in the front erupt about 6-8 months of age. These children's teeth would be later since they lived around 200 years ago. Of course they would probably chalk it up to poor nutrition. It would be very refreshing if just once this kind of work was done by people who didn't have such a commitment to the status quo.[15] Could biblical paleontologists ever be called in for a consultation on grave discoveries before all the statistics come out and the remains are re-buried? Can you imagine what that could be like. Well, I can dream, can't I?

For a comparison, look at my study of an early American child in chapter 31 and see what the Armed Forces Institute of Pathology found out.

HIGH RATES? LOW RATES?

Did man evolve from ape-like creatures? Since evolution is assumed to be correct because it is the majority opinion of the scientific community, this high rate makes the anthropologists conclude the Neanderthal children were very precocious by modern standards. They believe the Neanderthal children were at the very edge of the human range of development, on the fast side. Their pattern must have been extremely quick development since they believe that we've slowed down over the millennia and not sped up. This conclusion is produced by faster tooth development assumptions that are unstated and hidden to most readers.

What if we begin with another, just as valid, assumption called the biblical assumption? This one says that ancient children matured slower than modern children. What are we to make of the Pech to Moustier 23 degree change in 13.5 to 16 years by the Michigan method, or 15 degree change in the same amount of time by the Bolton method? Well, if we begin with different assumptions and perhaps a slower rate of development, the years between Pech de l'Azé and Le Moustier could be longer. Just how many could it be? Just suppose, and it is a very likely assumption, that the six-year molar didn't always develop on time and erupt around the sixth year. Suppose all the teeth were delayed in development and eruption dates in relation to modern children. This would really change the age calculations in the above tables. None of the given ages would be valid. I believe this is what almost all of the evolutionist paleontologists fear the most. I think that's why the four Neanderthal children in this book that I report on have been reconstructed or misinterpreted.

What if this were really so? If they really were slow, it would only point in one direction — the Bible!! Have problems with slow and fast rates ever shown up in studies of recent populations?

TOOTH DEVELOPMENT CHARTS

Many dentists in America have some sort of dental development chart hanging on the wall in his or her office. B. Holly Smith of the University of Michigan Museum of Anthropology has made some very detailed studies on the history of tooth development charts.[16] Smith opened up a can of worms when she specified some major and minor differences in tooth formation charts originating from what used to be thought of as very reliable sources. She identified many studies in her article, but I'd like to compare two well-known studies on primary teeth from 1939 and 1963.[17] She reported that the 1939 study always gave dates that are "relatively late" in comparison to the 1963 figures. She also added that they were still in the 95% confidence limits of the 1963 authors.[18] But she meant to cast doubt on these older figures. The figures showed that the 1939 kids had slower development and thus later dates for tooth development. I believe that she didn't like this implication. When she said, "relatively late," she meant too long a time period for these teeth to develop compared to our kids today. In one of her figures she showed three dental developmental charts, from 1883, 1884, and 1936. These charts make very plain that the rates of development from the 1880s were slower than the rates of today.

Let me emphasize that these charts were not fabricated by obscure people. One of these (1883) is taken from the work of the "father of dentistry," G.V. Black. He was a man held in high esteem by many of my professors at the University of Pennsylvania School of Dentistry in the 1960s. Smith called these charts, including Black's, "quite inaccurate"[19] as compared to modern studies. That's one way around the problem. Just call everything in the past that disagrees with your evolutionary views, inaccurate. That solves everything! She does have more accurate methods of measurement today than Black had, but to discount their knowledge altogether, especially when it calls into question the prevailing assumptions of today, is acting like our modern historians who put a "spin on history" according to their own belief system.

Now, what happens when somebody comes along 100 years from now (if the world lasts that long) when the 6-year molar is erupting at 3-4 years old and developing early, and calls Smith's charts inaccurate because they are "too late"?

I can almost hear them now . . . the year is 2100. Doctor's Clark and Jones in a huge HMO clinic are examining a seven-year-old female patient and her dental x-rays:

"Look at this Dr. Jones. This old dental chart of B.H. Smith's from the

1990s is really far off. By her calculations the age of our patient Molly, here, is nine years old."

"Give me her chart, Dr. Clark. Ah, yes, you're 100% right. It says here that she was born in the year 2093. That makes her seven years old."

"I thought so, Dr. Jones!"

"That's progress, Dr. Clark, that's progress. We're much more accurate today. That B.H. Smith . . . she probably even drove a gasoline car."

UNIVERSITY OF MICHIGAN AND CASE WESTERN RESERVE (BOLTON) DATA [20] THE ANGLE AT THE BACK OF LOWER JAW (SEE FIGURE 32A)

As I first noticed when examining the Pech de l'Azé child's cephalometric radiograph, the face was very small and seemed wound-up in a clockwise direction ready to unwind in future rotational counter-clockwise growth. Now I am aware that our orthodontic facial growth expert Dr. Enlow calls "downward and forward growth" a "cliché" because of the complex nature of facial development.[21] I understand that. However, for our purposes in this book I am going to refer to it in as simple terms as I can for the purpose of being understood. I even apologize at this point for the complicated terminology of the subject that is to follow.[22]

This unwinding mechanism of facial growth utilized some parts of the facial bones more than others. All parts move and adjust to each other's move-

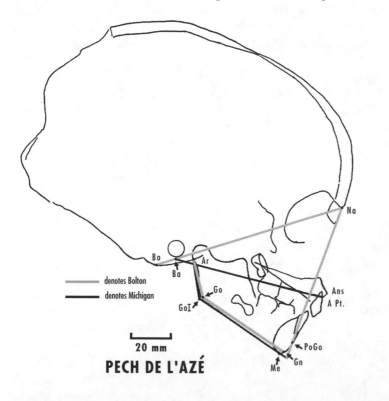

Figure 32a. Lateral cephalometric x-ray tracing of Pech de l'Azé.

denotes Bolton
denotes Michigan

20 mm

PECH DE L'AZÉ

ments. They change in their shape and they move in space. Some change more, some less. All children's faces unwind in growth in relation to the head. It's the size of the face that makes infants all look so cute. When we become adolescents and adults, we don't look that cute anymore. It's then that we have bigger faces. This Pech Neanderthal child had a really tiny face which the evolutionists didn't want anyone to know about. So, they put the lower jaw in a very awkward forward position outside of its natural limits as shown earlier in this book (see figure 2). Tiny faces are not supposed to belong to Neanderthal children.

Obviously, as the unwinding motion relative to the head proceeds, it starts in the back of the face and goes downward and forward. You would expect that the parts of the face that had to move the most to accomplish this unwinding motion would have to move faster than the other parts of the face that were slower. This is true. Some parts of the face, as they remodel, do move faster than others in the same face. This is what is known as allometric growth. Knowing this, can we then compare the faster parts and slower parts between modern and ancient children? We're not going to compare the slower and faster ones in the same face. What if we find rates for the fast parts which exceed those of modern children' s fast parts? Conversely, slower parts that exceed modern slower parts?

Now some researchers would say that our cephalometric measurements don't exactly correspond to "real anatomical parts." For instance, my ramus measurement uses the same points as the Michigan and Bolton methods but does not measure all the way to the top of the condyle. This is customary in orthodontic analysis. This is how Michigan, Case Western, and Loyola of Chicago graduate orthodontic departments (where I did my graduate work) measured this part of the jaw. So, while this is true, they are just measurements on a radiograph, they are as close as anyone can come to the actual parts with this radiographic technique. Moreover, we are mainly concerned with "relationships" between the same measurements, carried out with standardized procedures and technically excellent equipment, between modern children and Neanderthals. So, artificial or not, they still represent "the exact same thing" in two different groups, the "same measurements." That is fair, that is a comparative analysis.

This may be difficult to understand but it's essential. In 1974 four scientists from the University of Michigan Center for Human Growth and Development harvested a multitude of data and produced a monograph on the growth of 83 school children from the ages of 6 to 16.[23] This study had begun in 1930 and continued on through the 1970s. Forty-seven boys and 36 girls were the subjects of this longitudinal (same children) research that had many more children over the 44 years. Obviously they weren't children when they finished. One of their charts from 6 to 16 years listed the mean values in the same jaw angle (gonial) as seen in tables A and B, but this time for modern children.[24] To repeat, the gonial angles are treated as one image in the cephalometric radiograph as long as the head is not tilted in or out, up or down. This is what the cephalostat does, holds the head in a standardized position. For future reference, you should know that all the bi-lateral structures in the cranium and mandible (skull proper and lower jaw) are treated as one image on the radiograph.

In ten years the Michigan boys' average rate of decline for the gonial angle was 0.85 degrees per year. The two angles of their jaws became smaller as the boys became older. Let's compare these boys' 0.85°/year rate to the two male Neanderthals in the above chart who happened to live less than 20 miles away from each other (as the crow flies) in southern France, Pech de l'Azé of Carsac, and Le Moustier of Peyzac. [25]

Using the average modern boys' rate of 0.85 degrees per year for the 23 degrees of Neanderthal change (Pech to Le Moustier), a total of 27 years between those two Neanderthals is calculated. Simple calculation! If they grew like modern boys, it would take 27 years for Pech to become a Moustier.

Next, the Bolton study from Case Western Reserve University has a data base of over 5,000 children and also has charted this back of the jaw angle change for modern boys with optimal faces.[26] Michigan's boys were just average boys, but the Case Western boys were supposed to be really nice-looking kids. "Optimum condition," as they termed it.[27] Beauty is in the eye of the beholder! But let's move on through these statistics. They began with the one-year-old child and proceeded to the 18 year old, so it exceeded the Michigan study in its age range and produced an average rate of change of this angle for 16 years of 0 .57° per year. It was partly longitudinal.

Watch this, because it is tricky. The Broadbents of the Bolton study measured their angle a little differently than the Michigan folks, as I said before. Doing it their way, I came up with only a 15-degree change between these two Neanderthal neighbors. For the Neanderthals, 15 degrees of change at 0.57 degrees per year would require Pech 26 years to become a Le Moustier. This is quite different than what you have heard and read in the newspapers and magazines about Neanderthal children. Some of you are going to start wondering now when you begin to recognize that I am treating the two Neanderthal children as if they were simply two stages of growth of "the same Neanderthal child." Well, I am doing this for two reasons. First, you cannot find a skull of a child when he was young and one when he was older. Second, I agree that this is a very abbreviated cross-sectional study. I would love to have more subjects, but first I have to be sure they were genetically close as the classic Neanderthals of France were, and second, I would need access to more skulls which I have tried to obtain in Spain but it has been in . . . you guessed it . . . vain. The Spanish Neanderthals should be pretty close to the French. My pediatrician daughter-in-law, Lilia, even wrote the letter for me in Spanish. Doors shut pretty quickly for us looking for truth buried alive.

ALLOMETRIC GROWTH

We have already seen the choice we had to make between the 1.7°/yr to 1.4°/yr supposed Neanderthal rates and 0.85°/yr modern Michigan boys' rate for the gonial angle change. We have also seen the 1.1°/year to 0.94°/yr. supposed Neanderthal rates and 0.57°/yr modern Bolton boys' rate for gonial angle. Both Neanderthal rates would exceed the modern rates of decline.

Allometric growth is a reality and some parts of the facial bones actually move faster than others when you consider the same face. This is what allometric means: relative growth of a part in relation to the entire organism or skull. But when you compare Neanderthals rates of growth of identical parts of the face with mean population rates of humans, as I have done, and find discrepancies like this, something is wrong. (Certainly there will be some discrepancies, but these are large.) Perhaps it could be the basic assumptions.

COUNTERCLOCKWISE ROTATION OF JAWS

One of the slower-moving parts of the face that should also be moving in tune with the counterclockwise rotational direction of growth is the height of the vertical part of the mandible or lower jaw, the ramus (see figure 32a). The Michigan data previously mentioned produced an average rate for the mean male ramus growth over a 10 year period from 6 to 16 of 1.2 mm per year.[28] Using this value with the number of millimeters of change (30.6 mm between Pech and Moustier rami) (Pech 18 mm and Le Moustier 48.6 mm) yields 26 years that it would take for Pech's ramus to grow into Moustier's.[29]

The Bolton ramus study measures the distance between the same points.[30] They also found the average boys' rate of ramus growth between the modern 2-year-old mean and the modern 18-year-old mean to be also 1.2 mm per year (30.4mm-49 mm/16). Using this now with the 30.6 mm (48.6 mm - 18 mm) of Neanderthal change, we find again a total of 26 years that it would take for Pech's ramus to grow into Moustier's.

Let's look at the minimum and maximum growth of this ramus in the Bolton study compared to the Pech ramus. The smallest 2-year-old ramus that they measured in the 5000 children study was 26.5mm.[31] Compare that to the 18mm size of Pech's ramus. Pech's ramus height is 8.5mm less than the smallest 2-year-old boy's ramus of the entire 5000 Bolton study. One SD from the mean for two-year-old boys is 3.12 mm. Pech is more than twice this amount below the smallest boy among all the two year olds. *Pech is also four standard deviations below the mean*. The important fact to remember here is that the deviation from the normal and the smallest jaws of modern two year olds is in a non-ape direction, meaning smaller not larger than the average two year old. If it were less evolved than our children, I would not expect the size of this measurement to be almost four standard deviations (on the minus side) below the mean. If the Bolton mean falls in the center of a normal distribution curve, and there is no indication that it doesn't, it signifies that approximately 100% of all the measurements for this bony area should be within three standard deviations on either side of the mean. Our little Neanderthal is outside of that distribution curve on the minus side by a good amount.

Now some may say this is not a significant measurement by which to determine skeletal maturation. *Think of this, significant or not, it is so far and away from our modern children that either we have to think of these children as different species or that they were extremely slow developers.* If someone can come up with a verified, two year old, non-birth-defected, normal, modern male child four standard deviations smaller from the Bolton two-year male mean ramus, without any significant habits like tongue-thrusting and thumbsucking (no open bite) and a 14 degree (downward anteriorly) tilt of the palatal plane to the eye-ear plane (Frankfort Horizontal), I will say that I am wrong. There may be many skeletal open bite kids close to this ramus height, but that is not the condition that I am describing.

This is not good news for the British Museum people who would like the Neanderthals to be advanced, age for age, and larger, age for age, in comparison to their modern counterparts. It is also not good for any Christians who want to say Neanderthals are perfectly normal humans like us. Their posterior faces are so much smaller, tucked in and wound-up than us when they are two years old that it really shows what biblical immaturity in humans was all about. We must be careful when we say perfectly normal humans like us.

BAD NEWS FOR THE BRITISH MUSEUM

More bad news for the British museum people comes in the length of ramus of the so-called rapidly developing Gibraltar II child, a new age of 3.1 years (see chapter 17, "What about this tooth enamel?") See figure 33.

Here in figure 33, using the Bolton-Michigan standard measurement technique, I measured the ramus height (Ar-Go) of the Gib II mandible at 28.3 mm for the Ar-Go height.[32] Now, the Bolton male mean one year old is 28.4 mm, the two year old is 30.4mm, and the three year old is 32.1mm. The mean female measurements for any skeptics out there: one year old, 27.9mm; two year old, 30; and three year old, 31.2mm.

Age for age, Chris Stringer and many other evolutionary workers think

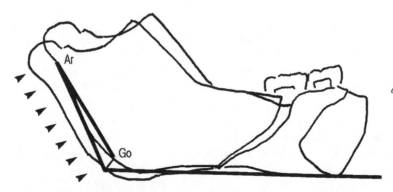

Figure 33. Side view of x-ray tracing of Gibraltar II showing forward rotation of back piece.

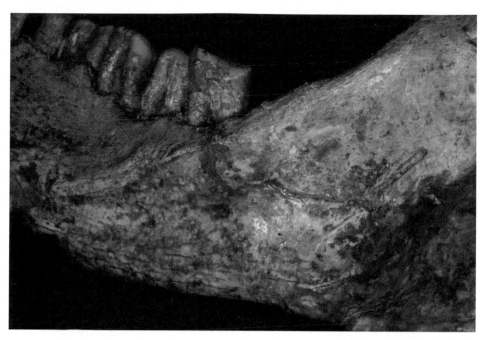

Figure 20. La Ferrassie I inside lower jaw, red ochre between roots of teeth.

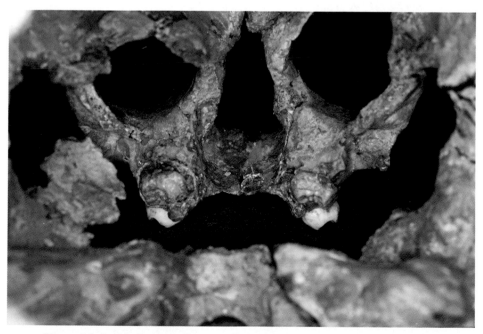

Figure 21. Inside Pech de l'Azé skull, looking out, with traces of red ochre.

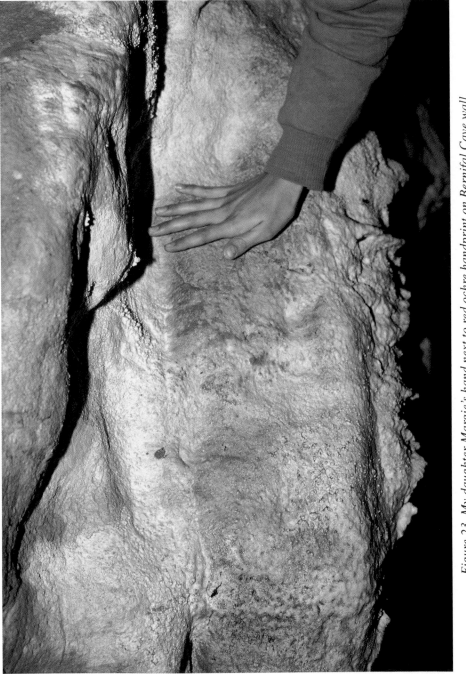

Figure 23. My daughter Margie's hand next to red ochre handprint on Bernifal Cave wall.

Figure 25. Red mammoth on wall of Bernifal Cave, carved mammoth head below.

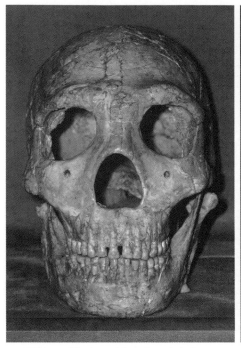

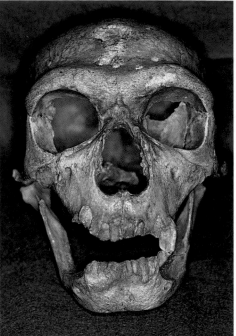

Figure 70. Amud I male adult from Israel. Notice small nasal opening. Almost the entire nasomaxillary complex is reconstructed of artificial material. Is this correct?

Figure 70a. La Chapelle-aux-Saints. Contrast the vertical size of this actual nasal opening and slope of nasal bones to Amud I.

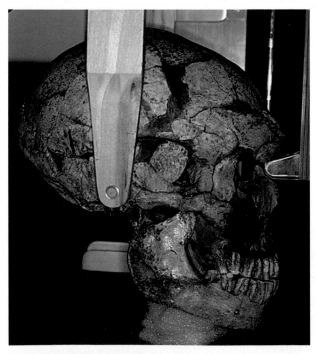

Figure 70b. La Ferrassie I in head holder. His nasal complex is partially reconstructed, but closer to La Chapelle in form.

Neanderthals had bigger faces. He has said, "Further application of these methods to the study of the Neanderthal children will teach us more about their biology, but it is already evident that at any given age they were likely to have been more robust, lower-skulled, larger faced, and as large or perhaps larger-brained than comparable modern children."[33] This man is the top paleoanthropologist in England. One of the greatest in the world, saying that their faces were bigger age for age. I hope you caught that larger-faced part. If not, read it again.

The conclusion I must make here is that Dorothy Garrod, an older paleoanthropologist in British history, was partly right when she called the jaws small, and the present British Museum people are partly wrong.[34] Obviously, she meant this part was small, the back of the lower jaw, because the horizontal part of the mandible, the body, is approximately 57 -58 mm (altered by the break).[35] This length is in the vicinity of the Bolton five year old. The fact that the back of the mandible is smaller than the modern two-year-old boy or girl means in modern times usually signifies that the face is slowly unwinding, tucked in, and that the facial appearance was not prognathic or protruded or projected as was shown in the *National Geographic* article of 1996.[36] Even if this body of the mandible was long, if the ramus were tiny as it is, the whole lower jaw would be tipped downward from the face and the lower jaw would look small. Why do I say this? Well, consider the tilt of the palate of the Pech child at 14 degrees. The modern two-year-old child has a zero degree tilt (in relation to the eye-ear plane) to the palate or perhaps a few more degrees of angulation, but not 14 degrees. Couple this tilt with the small ramus and any orthodontist can tell you what you would have. If the palate weren't tilted so much you would have an extremely open bite in the front of the mouth. The upper and lower teeth would be widely separated like those of a thumb sucker unless there was an extremely long anterior alveolar process (no evidence of this in Neanderthal children). Based on these observations it is possible to say that Neanderthal kids did not have big projecting faces until they became older, no matter how many plastic, resin, or fiberglass skulls they make. Projecting the jaws in their hypothetical reconstructions makes the children look almost like the adults. Of course, this is the whole plan.

ALL IS NOT WELL

All is not well for the advanced 3.1-year-old theory built on perikymata and the reproduction skulls of Gib II and La Ferrassie I in *National Geographic*. These reproductions, done with high tech equipment, were sitting on desktops with their faces protruding upward rather than as they would appear when sitting on someone's shoulders (eye-ear plane parallel to ground). Another trick is just showing us the frontal view with this plane of Gib II anatomically correct and not being able to see any retrusion of the jaws.[37] It is true, Gib II child was building surface bone on the outside of his upper jaw for a much longer time than modern children, but this is not the same as the whole upper jaw jutting forward in a skeletal procumbency.[38] Somehow, paleoanthropologists are becoming confused as to the difference between a true skeletal protrusion (basal bones jutting forward) in relation to the skull and merely a dentoalveolar protrusion (bone surrounding the teeth).

WORLD RECORD GROWTH OR LONGER CHILDHOOD?

Also, think about the difference between Pech's ramus 18mm at 2 to 2.5 years old and the Gibraltar child's ramus at 28.3 mm at 3.1 years old. This represents 10.3 mm of growth in less than a year, if we are to take them as a typical Neanderthal 2 year old, and a typical Neanderthal 3 year old. The average growth for modern males between 2 and 3 years is approximately 2 mm (actually 1.7mm). *This Neanderthal difference would be five times greater than the modern child's growth, be it boy or girl.* Are we prepared to believe in this high-speed growth process and different species category or do we think of more time in between these stages of development? I am giving you facts to digest, but I can't form your assumptions for you.

THE MAXI AND MINI BOLTON RAMI

The fastest rates that I could produce for modern boys from 2 years to 18 years for the ramus growth from Bolton figures was 1.7 mm/year. The maximum size that they found for the 18 year old is 53.6mm. This is larger than Moustier's ramus. The smallest two year old is 26.5. Therefore, 53.6-26.5 = 27.1 mm/16 years. The average rate this gives us for ramus growth is 1.7 mm/year. The Neanderthal average rate for 13.5 years with 30.6 mm of change is 2.3 mm per year or 1.9mm/year if you divide by 16 years. If we believe the evolutionary story we are going to have to accept these exceptionally fast rates of growth. These are faster than the smallest Bolton 2 year old growing into the largest Bolton 18 year old in 16 years. This is as far as one can go with these statistics.

At the risk of sounding redundant let me reiterate that these latter figures represent two opposite growth patterns in a heterogeneous Cleveland population. It represents two very different Caucasian children. In another way of describing this reasoning, it's like comparing former NBA players big 6'11" Darryl Dawkins' lower jaw while he was growing up and little 5'7" Spud Webb's lower jaw while he was growing up. I know little children can have growth spurts and become pretty big, but that's not what I mean here. Just two very different growth patterns are being compared. I knew Darryl personally when I was the chaplain for the New Jersey Nets NBA basketball team for five years. He was a huge person with a big heart and a big lower jaw. I even looked in his mouth one night before a game when he was having wisdom teeth problems. These Neanderthals had more in common than Darryl and Spud. They were from a small isolated homogeneous population in southwestern France living less than 20 miles from each other. Gibraltar II was from the island of Gibraltar but he is thought to be very typical of the group of Neanderthal children.

THE FRONT OF THE FACE

Let's go to the front of the face. The front of the face is going to move forward slowly as the back rotates out from under the cranium (skull) so it seems justified to look at an angular measurement for this forward movement from Case Western Reserve's Bolton Study.[39] This angle is measured from the base of the brain to the point where the nasal bones meet the forehead and down to the chin point (see figures 32a and 42).[40] The Bolton study rate or velocity of change in boys from 2 to 18 is 0.32° per year. This means the face goes forward at that pace from 2 to 18 years in boys. This was measured by those three points on the cephalometric radiograph. I must add the fact that growth spurts are built into all these rates in case you didn't read that in the beginning of this discussion. Pech's angle for this facial growth is 53° while Moustier is 71°. The difference here is 18°. Pech's face has to grow forward 18° to be a Moustier face. How long did this take? Using the rate of change 0.32mm per year we arrive at a total of 56 years. Before anyone laughs at this number think for a moment that the evolutionists are willing to say that Pech would have reached Moustier in 13.5 to 16 years, which would have required astronomical rates of 1.1 to 1.3 degrees per year. This would be more than three times faster than the mean modern boys.

There is no question Neanderthal children were slightly faster than modern children in this category (allometric growth allows different rates in the same face), but I would cast doubt on the fact that the Neanderthals were three times faster than modern children, seeing the results of the other measurements. Once more, let's take the smallest 2-year-old modern boy in the Bolton study (57.2°) and the largest 18-year-old boy (67.8°). Our two Neanderthal facial angles are outside of them. Pech is minus 2.9 SD away from the smallest 2-year-old face in the Bolton study, not the mean. He is minus 4.9 SD away from the mean of 60 degrees in a non-ape direction.

Moustier is 71° and the largest 18-year-old boy in the Bolton analysis is 67.8° (SD 2.01). He is plus 1.6 SD from the largest face for modern 18 year olds and plus 2.9 SD away from the mean 18 year old. He is at the very edge of a standard distribution curve but still within 3 SD of the mean. We expect that 95% of all the Bolton measurements for this angle to be within ±2 standard deviations from the mean. Moustier is outside of that in the 5% area. To obtain the fastest human rate that the Bolton study can give us we'll use two heterogeneous boys again, like Darryl when he was 18 and Spud when he was 2, and see what we get. The largest 18-year-old boy and the smallest 2-year-old boy are 67.8° and 57.2°. Their difference is 10.6°. The 10.6° divided by the 16 years that separated the two kids equals a rate of 0.66°/year. Now, we have artificially manufactured the highest possible human rate from the Bolton data. This is probably one of the highest human rates that could exist. Notice it is not greater than the one degree per year that we would be forced to use if we accepted the ages of 2 and 18 as real chronological ages for the Neanderthals, or if we accepted 2.5 and 16 as genuine and divided 18 degrees by 13.5 years. This equals a 1.3 degree per year rate. Using this higher rate, 0.66°/year, the Neanderthal change of 18° would take 27 years for Pech to become Moustier. This 0.66°/year is more reasonable. The rate is not the modern 0.32°/year and not super-fast 1.1° to 1.3° per year some would have us accept.

Another slow factor to be considered in the unwinding of the facial complex is the pure forward linear growth of the upper jaw as it relates to the posterior base of the skull.[41] The tip of the posterior base is called basion and from that point the University of Michigan researchers measured the distance to the front of the upper jaw, called A point. It's on the depressed part of your upper jaw right under your nose. You can see these points on the diagrams of Pech (figure 32a) and Moustier (figure 42). I estimated the basion point of Moustier because the foramen magnum is absent.[42]

The average rate from age 6 to 16 in males was 1.3 mm per year. The Pech measurement from the base of the skull to the front of the upper jaw is 75.2 mm and Moustier's is 113 mm. This is a difference of 37.8 mm. Using the modern average 1.3 mm/year rate creates a total of 29 years for the pure linear measurement of the Pech face to reach the young Neanderthal adult Moustier face. If we were to go along with the evolutionist's ages of death for the Neanderthal children's face to grow forward 37.8 mm it would require a super rate of growth of 2.8mm per year for 13.5 years and 2.4mm per year for 16 years. These are close to double the modern rate. You can believe this or reject it, but if you keep reading it's going to become harder and harder to hold to ape-like growth rates. There is only one way to reach a rate such as this with the linear measurement. It is necessary to calculate two SDs below the youngest male mean and two SDs above the oldest male mean, which would produce a very divergent person if such a person is possible.

THE LOWER JAW MEASUREMENT

One of the faster rates in facial growth is the forward growth of the lower jaw.[43] I'm sure all the skeptics have been waiting for this one. The rate is 1.8 mm per year. This distance extends from the basion point to the front of the lower jaw, a point called B point. With Pech at 70.2mm and Moustier at 116.6 mm (the modern rate of the boys from Michigan is at 1.8mm per year), it would take Pech 26 (25.8) years to acquire Moustier's lower jaw length. I'll wager there are some who thought it would take less time than that.

Therefore, because of all the aforementioned data, it seems justified to use Le Moustier as a baseline for adult growth changes. Now we can move forward to the Neanderthal adults from the same area of southwestern France, staying within the homogeneity of the group, and find out how long it would take Le Moustier to become a La Ferrassie I or a La Chapelle-aux-Saints. Also, examine the medio-lateral width (thickness) of Moustier's gonial angle before we begin to see how thick and firm it was even though there is some post-mortem damage (figure 58). Keep this in mind when examining this same area, which is paper thin, in the section Lumps of Bone and Potato Chip Gonial Angles of the oldest Neanderthals in figures 54, 55, 56, and 59.

CONCLUSIONS

After examining the above data for the seven measurements (3 angular and 4 linear measurements) it seems justified to state that there are now just two choices for the scientific world to make once confronted with these facts. Either the Neanderthal face unwound like the cartoon character called the Tasmanian Devil at breakneck speed, or it really did grow downward and forward like the Bible implies in a much longer time period than we have ever seen in our modern world. Keep in mind that the British Museum people do not even think in world-record terms. They said this, "Unlike earlier Plio-Pleistocene Hominids for which there is good evidence for a 'great ape-like' developmental growth period, the developing dentition of the Gibraltar child falls much closer to, or at the lower end of, the expected range of values known for modern *Homo sapiens* and as such must be considered to show an accelerated but essentially human pattern of development."[44] They did not think this for the head. They believed it to be precocious.

Keep in mind that my use of today's mean rates, with the exception of one front of the face angulation, are probably still a bit too fast but that is all we can do at the present. We have nothing but present rates to use. Does this make me a uniformitarian? Not if I assume that the uniform rates that I used to calculate age could have been different in the past. Nevertheless, I did use uniform standard rates to age the Neanderthals. Again, I must add that I do not accept these as "true rates" but useful rates in calculations. The problem is that we have seen the rates necessary for Pech to become Le Moustier in the modern amount of time are much higher than the modern rates in every angle and distance measured.

We are called upon to make an interpretation of this data. I used the uniform rates of today's boys. I came up with data that would change the age of Moustier. Eventually, if accepted, it would cast doubt on the age of Pech, also. If Moustier was slow, would not Pech be slow also?

You must understand this. If you accept Moustier's final age as either 16 or 18, you immediately superimpose another uniform assumption on the results. You may not realize that you are doing this but no one knows the actual chronological age of Le Moustier. There was no tombstone or any other marking for this young man. This may not have been the case for all Neanderthals. Wait until you've read to the end of this book.

Therefore, you and I must make a clear choice in the results. We must believe Moustier was 16-18 years old or not. Notice I said "believe," because here is where the assumptions come in. You can interpret the results either of two ways. Accept or reject the final age of Moustier as 16-18. If you accept, you are accepting non-uniform high rates in the result based on uniform modern standards in the initial calculation (he was 16-18 because of tooth levels, etc.). No human grows like that today. You couldn't calculate the high rates without these uniform ages.

On the other hand, my calculations produce a result that questions the final age of Moustier as 16 or 18. However, I also use something from modern boys. They are uniform modern standard rates of growth and my outcome is a non-uniform "long ages" result. Now we are at the place where you must make an assumption and more observations to accept either "result," since one calls into question the set ages of development in the past (mine) while theirs would call into question the rates in the past. They are non-uniform in rates. I am non-uniform in ages of development. This can be called the "ape-like" versus the "slow human" argument. Now assumptions are called upon to help in that decision, after one more set of facts. Besides our belief systems, we must use some other objective criteria like the morphological characters in the skulls and jaws to see more clearly.

If you think my assumption is wrong, why have the facts that I revealed about small faces in the young Neanderthal children been so suppressed? Why have the evolutionists gone to such lengths to cover up any characters of immaturity in the Neanderthal children's heads and faces? Just check out what they did to promote the speedy rate hypothesis in the four Neanderthal children. Read Fraipont's statement regarding Engis II from Belgium, "Because a delay in secondary or permanent teeth (development) for this species or kind would be a flagrant contradiction with all that we know about his development and his anthropoid characters." What anthropoid characters? Try the 14-degree angulation of Pech's hard palate on an anthropoid and see how it fits. Take a look at the reproduction in the Berlin museum of Moustier and compare it to my radiographs of the skull. What anthropoid characters? Think about the fact that they insist on big faces to go with the big heads of these kids. Contemplate what Fraipont did to make Engis II appear to have a bigger head so he could call the head accelerated rather than the jaws retarded. Think about what we discovered concerning the difficulties in counting perikymata and also the similarity of modern man's total to the Gib II total by Mann and colleagues. Consider the size of the Gib II ramus, its muscularity, large cranium, worn primary teeth, and the very juvenile tympanic bones of Gib II and Engis II. How about Pech being four standard deviations below the modern male two-year-old ramus (vertical part of the lower jaw)? Also, ponder the increasing rapidity of tooth eruption and development as humans progress or should I say digress down through the years. Consider also the protracted eruption schedule in Engis II, and also wait for what is to come for evidence of devolution and then decide which interpretation is correct.

OPENING UP A RUSTY GAS CAN

Tooth and jaw use is an important factor in this section of my research. This is why I made several trips to the Smithsonian Institution in the 1980s to examine, measure, and photograph Eskimo remains. I was told by an anthropologist at the Smithsonian that a strong Eskimo from Kodiak Island could unscrew a gas cap from a rusty gasoline can with his teeth. Wow! That's a pretty huge feat. Glad I never had one of those guys in my dental chair. They could take off your finger with one bite. They had extremely strong chewing muscles.

Thankfully, the jaws I held in my hands were dead. They consisted of skulls of adults and children that lived on Kodiak Island before a real diet change had occurred. Later on, their descendants went from raw meat to the softer food of Western civilization. Ales Hrdlicka, head curator of the anthropology department, cited previously for adult growth work, had collected these in the 1920s. The jaws visible in this section should also be compared to the ancient jaws in chapter 32 for lumps of bone and thickness.

One notable factor to be observed in the adult Koniag Eskimos is the robustness or strength of the bone of the jaws. Their coarse diet caused increased work for the jaw muscles. The foundation of their teeth, like ours, in the lower jaw is the alveolar bone. The heavy forces placed on these during chewing (mastication) were transmitted to the surrounding bones. Some of the first effects of this prolonged and heavy chewing on tough or fibrous foods were lumps of bone that built up under the lower molar teeth as reinforcement against these excess pressures. These lumps are called tori (plural for torus) or exostoses of new bone. It is actually a reaction of the bone itself

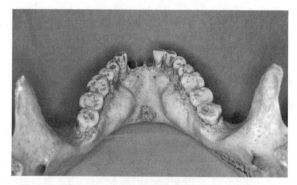

Figure 34. Large bony build-up on the inside of an Eskimo lower jaw in response to heavy chewing.

to heavy stresses placed upon it in accordance with Wolff's law. This is an adaptive response. It produces a firmer foundation for teeth that are heavily burdened. It also reinforces bone in areas of highest tension or stress. See figures 34 and 35 for these exostoses.

These lumps of bone should not be confused with the typical mandibular

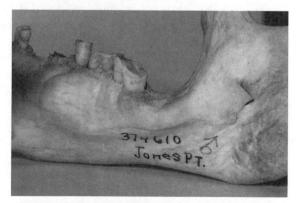

Figure 35. Great lump of bone in reaction to heavy chewing in an Eskimo lower jaw.

tori or mid-palatal tori in the mouth that are of genetic origin. These tori develop in many people and I see them quite often in my practice of orthodontics. They are not a reaction to heavy chewing forces at all. I had a patient once who thought she had a tumor in the roof of her mouth and it was one of the genetic tori.

The children's lower jaws do not show this type of reaction. The Eskimo starts out as a child with no signs of bony torus but when he or she reaches adulthood the signs of a rugged diet have become obvious. Also examine the width of the bone of the gonial angle of the Eskimo (figure 60). It is thick and roughened with several heavy ridges for stronger muscle attachments. It is thicker than Le Moustier's medio-lateral (side-to side) (lower jaw) gonial angle thickness (see figure 58).

A recent article by Frohlich and Pederson on the jaws of four homogeneous populations from Greenland, Alaska, and the Aleutian Islands confirms the fact that these tori were not genetic (inherited). They found that the large mandibular outcropping of bone (tori) were "primarily induced by functional factors, masticatory stress, changes in diet," while loss of molar teeth in adulthood would produce a lack of these features. Masticatory stress means heavy chewing on tough foods.[45] At the University of Chicago, William Hylander came to similar conclusions after studying pre-contact Eskimos whose diet was mainly sea mammals. He showed photographs of these huge lumps of bone. Hylander did mention a report concerning the Eskimo women who chewed on their husband's frozen seal-skin boots in the morning to soften them up before the husband put them on.[46] I'm sure there were some who would have liked to chew on their husband's foot.

There may be many who still think that the chart of Neanderthal gonial angles should be compared to a heavier chewing population than modern children from Michigan and Cleveland's Western Reserve. For them and for the sake of completeness of data, Table I in the notes is from Robert Cedarquist's work at the University of Chicago.[47] It was compiled from a series of cephalometric x-rays taken in Wainwright, Alaska, on 188 native Eskimos who resided there in 1968. Their diet, while not primitive, required stronger chewing forces. According to Cedarquist, their meat was usually boiled; however, a large amount of raw and dried meat, especially caribou, was eaten.

My calculation (from group 1 to 3) from Cedarquist's male Eskimo data shows the rate to be 0.34°/year for (jaw) gonial angle change and a female rate of .42°/yr (from group 1 to 3). This is extremely slow and would equate to over 67 years (.34°/year) between Pech and Moustier for 23 degrees over 54 years using the female .42°/year.[48]

These numbers of years cannot be correct. Neanderthals weren't genetic Eskimos. The male Eskimo data presented much greater years. This male figure cannot be equated with the 0.85° Michigan modern male rate. Stronger chewing forces may mean lower rates of decline. Experimental studies have demonstrated the close relationship between functional and structural components of the facial region.[49] The Michigan study also did not indicate any significant boy-girl factors (dimorphism) in this jaw angle decline.

The Neanderthal males that we are considering were probably somewhere between the rates of 0.85° and 0.34° since they didn't have the Eskimo diet but their food wasn't as soft as modern man either. But, again, the Wainwright Eskimo is an Eskimo, although not entirely. There was some gene flow in this area in the 1800s.[50]

The main point is: who can conceive of faster rates than one degree per year? We know that can't be right. What was the Neanderthal rate? It can only remain tentative for now; however, we can put limits on it. It wasn't super-fast as it appears on the surface or as slow as the Eskimo male.

The following table is a summation of the seven variables used to determine the number of years between Le Moustier and Pech de l'Azé.

Table C
Years Between Pech and Moustier

Linear or Angular Measurement	Avg. Rate/Yr.	Years
1. Michigan Angular Variable 50	0.85°	27
2. Bolton Angular No. 13	0.57°	26
3. Michigan Linear Variable 88	1.2mm	26
4. Bolton Linear No. 5D	1.2mm	26
5. Bolton Angular No. 3.*	0.66°	27
6. Michigan Linear Variable 182	1.3mm	29
7. Michigan Linear Variable 185	1.8mm	26

26.7 ±1
Mean years between
Pech and Moustier

*Uses the maximum 18 year old and the minimum 2 year old, not means.

Pech was at least 2-2.5 years old by modern tooth development charts but could have been as old as 4-5, and there were at least 26-28 years between he and Le Moustier, most likely more because of the speed of modern rates. I am going to tentatively designate Pech 4-5 (4.5) years old and Moustier 32 years old for the sake of discussion and simplicity in the rest of this book. These dates are tentative, but I think closer to reality than 2 and 18. For another aspect of this, figure 36 is the Rocky Mountain Data Systems Forecast to Maturity for 18.5 years taken from the Pech data. The upper and lower jaw result is much smaller than the actual Moustier which is superimposed on the forecast. This should not be at all surprising since it is based upon the rates of growth of modern children.[51]

TOOTH WEAR

By this chapter I am sure those knowledgeable readers will be asking the question: What about tooth wear, does it substantiate these claims? We could

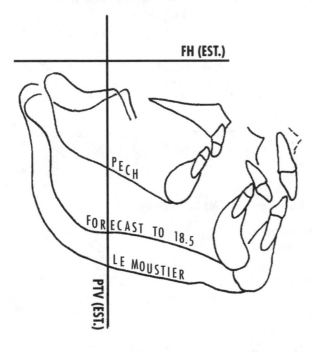

Rocky Mountain Data Systems
Forecast to Maturity for PECH
DE L'AZE to 18.5 Yrs. (Sup. PTV-FH)

Figure 36. How would a Neanderthal child grow from 2 years to 18.5 years if he was a modern male? Le Moustier was much larger than the prediction.

look for the amount of wear on the biting surfaces of the first permanent molars, but once again we can't follow the modern day fact of "no enamel repair." This will be covered later but for now let it be known that checking the amount of occlusal wear on Moustier's molars may not be a really good test of age in Neanderthals for two reasons: one, possible enamel repair; and two, diet. Measurement of enamel heights between Pech and Moustier is a much more objective way to determine enamel loss than subjective wear patterns. Later I will discuss these measurements and probable enamel repair mechanisms which could be more efficient on the occlusal surfaces because of the deep folds which are present in the unworn molars. What was the Neanderthal diet? We'll look at that aspect later. Please see the Research Notes for all the enamel measurements on the first permanent molars of the Neanderthal children. The discussion about them will follow.

THE CLOCK OF THE FACE

For additional assurance that the use of the gonial angle is a genuine clock and is justified in determining time changes and is not only reflecting hereditary differences, we must look at the research of Sheldon Watnick on monozygotic (one egg) and dizygotic (two eggs) twins. He declared, "The findings of this study would seem to indicate that whether heredity or function is the primary determinant of the form and size of the masticatory skeleton depends on what part of the skeleton is under consideration." What he said was that in judging what causes certain bones of our face to be large or small or shaped like they are can be due to either chewing, etc. (function) or inherited factors. Shape and size of bones in the face are determined more by heredity in some and in others more by the way they function.

He further elaborated on the (lower jaw angle) gonial angle area by adding, "This may indicate that functional mechanisms, i.e., environmental factors, have had more influence in these areas than inherited factors."[52] By this he meant that the forces produced by the chewing and other muscles of the face have more to do with the shape and size of our angle of the lower jaw, the gonial angle, than hereditary factors.

This is crucial to my reasoning. Change in the shape and size would be directly proportional to the years of use and forces of that use, i.e., the more years, would equate to more change.[53] Obviously, fetal shape and size are due to heredity, nutrition, and overall health.

Lastly, Thompson and Popovich completed the analysis of gonial angle reliability by stating, "However, unlike many other craniofacial dimensions, the gonial angle size can be estimated with a good degree of accuracy over as much as a thirteen-year interval."[54] It seems, therefore, that we have a very dependable indicator of time by following the decrease in angulation of the gonial angle. Even though they said that the gonial angle is not a good indicator of overall size of the face, one of their conclusions was, "The size of the gonial angle at one age is significantly related to its later size." If you're going to estimate future size of the angle you have to be very confident of a steady rate of decline. Essentially, we now have good evidence that the gonial angle is a real indicator of time, like a clock in the face. Four factors are important: time, function, dimorphism (male or female), and some heredity, assuming good health is a given.

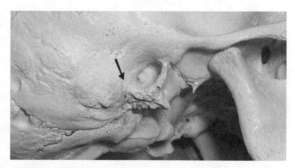

Figure 37. Arrow points to closed (tympanomastoid fissure) separating two parts of temporal bone around a modern child's ear (4-5 years old).

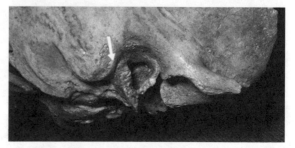

Figure 38. Arrow points to deep open crevice (tympanomastoid fissure) in Engis II, more immature than modern child, age for age.

A WEDGE IN THE EAR

In 1987 I wrote about the Engis II child's fetal ear

formation and how the man who first described it did not consider this structure to be diagnostic of slow cranial development.[55] To be more precise, the external-most bone of the fetal ear is in the form of a partial ring, called the tympanic bone or ring at the early stages. This fetal ring expands to form the tympanic part of the temporal bone as the child grows older. It extends outward and backward to do this. It forms on its posterior surface, some time during the first year, a tight boundary with the mastoid process which it retains throughout adulthood. See figure 37 of 4- to 5-year-old modern child, bony external ear opening. This separation is called the tympanomastoid fissure since it is just a slight crack between these two parts of the temporal bone. It never gets much attention. The floor takes longer to form.

In Engis II Fraipont made special mention of the extremely infantile character of the temporal bone, especially the tympanic ring-like bone (see figure 38). Tillier called Engis II five to six years old and somewhat described this "juvenile character" saying it was the floor of the auditory tube that was incompletely formed.[56] She didn't attach much significance to it either. Fraipont said in reference to this very immature internal ear, "We notice some traces of the human fetus of the modern day child." He didn't assign much significance to this finding which was similar to Garrod's position on the fetal characters of the Gib II, especially the fetal tympanic bone. Remember, Tillier wanted to split the Gib II child into two persons because of the fetal ear that Garrod had also described, and now the same kind of bony ear didn't mean much in Engis II.

Now we arrive at the main point of the ear story. In the following series of figures, I show the Engis II fetal tympanic bone, the modern child (4-5 yrs.) tympanic bone for comparison, and also the Le Moustier's left tympanic bone surrounding the external bony ear opening. I was not allowed to see the Gib II tympanic bone. Notice that what may have been a very wide tympanomastoid fissure like Engis II had is now obliterated by a wedge of bone in Moustier (figure 39). This would have been quite diagnostic of a slow development of the skull, a feature which I believe all Neanderthal children showed (unless tampered with). I do not know who did this, but I suspect that perhaps when this skull fell into Communist hands, since atheism was the official position of the state, a bone got stuck into the tym-

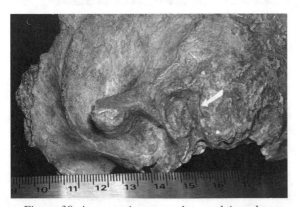

Figure 39. Arrow points to wedge stuck into deep open crevice (tympanomastoid fissue) of Le Moustier to hide less developed fissure.

Figure 40. Arrow points to double external ear opening on right side of La Ferrassie I.

panomastoid fissure so that it didn't look quite so immature and slow developing and biblical.

The last figure (40) in this ear section is a view of the right bony ear opening of La Ferrassie so you may see that the French didn't hide the adult tympanomastoid fissure — but something else is seen here, too. It is an accessory external ear opening. We are going to have to think about this one for a while. It's the only one I've ever seen in Neanderthals.

TWO CHOICES

Therefore, it is easily seen that we are faced with one of two choices as I have said before. Either the Neanderthals had world-record rates of change in the growth of the face or this process took much more time than it does in modern children. Le Moustier was either in his thirties or in his teens. I have presented much scientific evidence that points toward a slower maturing child of the past. One thing you should consider as you mull this over is the lengths the evolutionary paleoanthropologists have gone to in order to convince you that they are right. Consider the four children — Pech de l'Azé, Gibraltar II, Engis II and Le Moustier — and remember that not one was allowed to display the actual anatomy.[57] All were doctored-up one way or another. Please examine the notes for the full reports on these Neanderthals.

Chapter 29

Creation Model Predicts
Downward Path

A ccording to the meeting that Jacob had with Pharaoh in Genesis 47:7-9, there already was a degenerative pattern becoming evident in the lives of the patriarchs.

Professor Edward Wente of the Oriental Institute and Department of Near Eastern Languages and Civilizations at the University of Chicago has studied the royal mummies of the Cairo Museum in Egypt. He wrote about x-ray studies that were conducted on these remains by University of Michigan and Alexandria University research teams.[1] Wente stated in his account, "A comparison of our results in *An X-Ray Atlas of the Royal Mummies,* published by the University of Chicago Press in 1980, reveals that the pharaohs' ages at death as determined by the biologists are generally younger than what the written sources suggested. Part of this disparity may be attributed to a somewhat slower maturation in antiquity — as it is among modern Nubians, who reach puberty two to three years later than modern Americans." My comment on this is simple. Using modern charts, ancient people will give younger ages than the actual ones.

Wyshak and Frisch presented data from 1795 to 1981 in Europe and the USA on the mean ages of girls reaching their first menstrual period during those 186 years.[2] They reviewed 218 reports on the age of menarche in girls from 19 countries covering 220,037 individuals. What they showed is a secular decline, a trend toward lower ages of onset of menarche, over the past two centuries. Their graph is seen in figure 41. They also believed that the trend was leveling off.

According to Wyshak and Frisch, in the days of the very late 1700s and early 1800s, girls were reaching their first menstrual period at approximately 16 to 16.5 years of age. In Europe the rate of decline has been about 2 to 3 months per decade. In The USA it has been about 2 months per decade. Data from my old friend Dr. Wilton Krogman appeared in my *Journal of the New Jersey Dental Association* article.[3] It confirms the data from the Wyshak and Frisch compilation.

Going back to classical Greece, Aristotle (384-322 B.C.) wrote that the "*catamenia*" (Greek for menstrual bleeding) began at "twice seven years old."[4] In another writing, he gives "the 14th year of life as the age of male and female puberty."[5] There could be some doubt about this figure because of the use of the mystical number seven in ancient Greece.[6]

Soranus of Ephesus, in the second half of the first century A.D., claimed "around the 14th year" to be the age at which menstruation began in his day, although that may not be so. The famous Greek physician Galen, who practiced in Rome, wrote, "Some begin puberty at once with the completion of the 14th year, but some begin a year or more after that."[7] There may be some confusion of terms in this case because puberty today is usually meant as the beginning of sexual maturation, with the arrival of menarche some years later. If this is what he meant, menarche would be some time after 14.

As Yen and Jaffe stated, "Moreover, menarche is a late event in the pubertal process and is removed from the factors that affect the time of onset of the hormonal events and the first physical features of sexual maturation."[8] Therefore, the definition of puberty in antiquity may not have been the same as today. It is a time of transition between the juvenile state and adulthood. During this time, secondary sex characteristics appear and mature. Also, a growth spurt takes place and fertility is attained.

The mean age of the first menstrual period was never described as such by

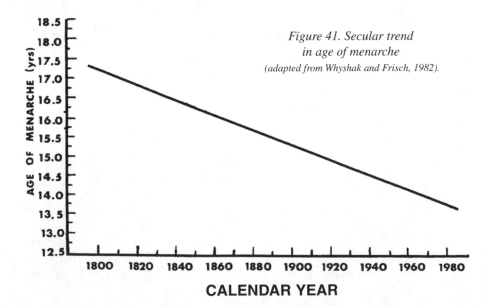

Figure 41. Secular trend in age of menarche
(adapted from Whyshak and Frisch, 1982).

early physicians. However, Oribasius, the personal physician of Roman Emperor Julian the Apostate (A.D. 331/332-363), a nephew of Constantine the Great by a half-brother, said very clearly, "In the majority, the menses begin around the 14th year, in a few around the 13th or 12th, and in many later than 14 years." It is highly probable that in Roman times, more girls were reaching menarche above 14 than below 14. This would probably place the mean age above 14 years. Susruta, the legendary father of Indian medicine (300-200 B.C.) suggested age 16 as the best probable time for conception for girls of his day.[9]

Byzantine sources in the sixth century such as Aëtius, physician to Justinian I, wrote: "The menses appear in women around the 14th year together with puberty and growing of the breasts."[10] This would tend to confirm previous conclusions. A statement, though, from this second-century nun, Hildegard of Bingen, Germany, seems to confuse the issue by describing a time of change and building up. "But little girls are not subject to menstruation and therefore certainly do not conceive offspring, because their members have not yet been completed, just as there is not a condition of completion where only the foundation of a house has been laid and the walls have not yet been raised. When, however, she has reached her 12th year, now her members are in the process of being strengthened, clear up to the 15th year, just as the walls of a house are being completed that are being built above the foundation to the extent of their final height. Now from the 15th year clear up to the 20th the structuring of the members is being wrought to perfection, just as a house that has been completed by the addition of timbers and a roof into which then all furnishings are placed. And so, a woman then, when she has been perfected in her veins and in the structuring of her members, is able to conceive and retain and warm the male semen. But if any woman conceives a child prior to the 20th year of her life, it happens either because of the excessive warmth of her nature and of her husband's or because of much intercourse on their part; but, nevertheless, she produces a child who is weak and frail in some way." It, therefore, seems probable that 12 to 15 was the pubertal time-span and that the menses probably came closer to 15 and perhaps sometimes near to the 20th year. It is also known that in Roman law and canon law of the Catholic Church female puberty was set at the 12th birthday.[11] In this latter instance it may simply demarcate the beginning of maturation, not the menstrual period, for purposes of going on in the teachings and sacraments of the church.

NOT JUST GIRLS

In boys the signs of puberty are not as time specific. Their bodies gradually change but there is no clear-cut line drawn in the sand like the first menstrual period of a girl. However, there is one attribute of males used to demarcate the attainment of adulthood. Besides the bodily gains of hair and sexual characteristics, there is the matter of voice change.

The well-known composer Johann Sebastian Bach had a boys choir in Leipzig, Germany, in the years 1727 to 1749. It has been reported that there were some boys in this choir well into their 16th year who still had voices like little boys.[12] Daw advises us that the average age of voice change in Bach's generation was 17 years.[13] This choir would be impossible today. Presently, the average age of voice change is around 13.5 years. If you gathered a choir of 16-17 year olds in 1998 it would be composed of deep masculine voices. Can this dramatic change be accidental, nutritional, psychological, or is a deeply rooted long-term pattern manifesting itself?

MENARCHEAL TREND BETRAYS UNIFORMITARIANISM

Reproductive endocrinologists tell us that the average age of the onset of puberty demonstrates a secular trend that "cuts across geographic and ethnic lines."[14] Things like this going on in the human body betray any idea that the present is the key to the past. As a matter of fact, what this really does is show up physiologic uniformitarianism for what it really is; a philosophical concept, not a scientific concept. Let us consider the data on this worldwide secular non-uniformitarian trend.

From Japan in 1986 data on the recollected age of menarche of 47,881 women born between 1881 and 1970 were considered in an overall study. "The mean menarcheal age had changed from 15.1 years in those born up to 1900 to 12.5 years in those born during the 1960s." A distinct secular trend was observed in this Asian nation.[15]

Scandinavia plays a considerable role in the enormous amount of literature on the secular trend towards earlier menarche. From Denmark in 1983 the mean age of menarche was examined in two groups. The first group comprised 983 girls from 1965-66 and the second consisted of 1,591 girls from 1982-83. Between those blocks of time the mean age declined from 13.40 to 13.03 years. They concluded, "Comparison with recent data from the other Nordic countries, except Norway, indicates that the age of menarche is close to 13 years, and a halt in the trend towards earlier menarche is not evident."[16] It is extremely interesting that these same authors in Denmark in 1987 re-examined old records and came up with errors made in the 1850 data collection and revised the mean age of menarche in Danish women of 1820 from 16 to 17 years of age.[17]

In 1979 the Norwegian studies began to produce conflicting reports. The bulk of the first modern data is from Oslo considering mean menarcheal ages of the last 140 years.[18] They demonstrated a drop in age from 1860 to 1880 from 15.6 to 14.6 and then a rapid decline in a second group of women from 1905 to 1940 from 14.6 to 13.3 years. Another report said that a plateau has been reached because the age remained the same at "about 13.3" from 1950 to 1985.[19] There is one fact to be noted in this study and that is that they did find a decline amongst the "working class" social group.

The latest news out of Denmark in 1993 asks the question: Is the age of menarche still decreasing in Denmark? This study consisted of 908 girls from 40 schools in Odense. They found the average age of menarche to be 13.27 years, which was consistent with other recent studies in Denmark. They have their doubts about what this means. They said, "These findings suggest a halt in the decline of the average age at the menarche, which may be temporary."[20]

From Finland a nationwide study was completed in 1989 and reported in 1993. Hundreds of girls participated in this throughout the country. It's conclusions were, "At the national level, the secular trend towards an earlier menarche was not observed in the 1980s but the trend was significant among girls living in the North-West and rural areas. Clearly observed regional and urban-rural differences in 1979 disappeared in the 1980s. Social class differences persisted." [21]

From Bologna, Italy, and Iceland communications from 1994 indicate a halt in the secular decline had arrived by 1950-1959 in the former, [22] and 1951-1967 in the latter.[23] There must be an off-again on-again pattern to the worldwide menarcheal decline, as is evident from these two countries, because from Hong Kong the downward spiral is again visible in 1992 through the eyes of researchers at the University of Hong Kong. They stated, "Southern Chinese girls aged 11 years and 9 months to 12 years and 3 months in Hong Kong have a mean menarcheal age of 11.50 years (SD 0.47) using the recollection method. . . . Highly significant differences are found when compared to the 12-year-old girls in Hong Kong studied in the past decades. Therefore a secular trend of earlier menarcheal age is demonstrated."[24] West Bengal also describes in a study of 894 girls that, "Evidence of a steady fall of menarcheal age has been confirmed in the present study."[25]

In Johannesburg, South Africa, in 1996, the University of Witwatersrand Medical School determined the menarcheal age of two generations of South African Indian peoples. There were 146 mother-daughter pairs. The mean maternal age of menarche was 13.20 years while the daughters' mean menarcheal age was 12.40 years. Comparisons were made to similar data from Kark, South Africa, in 1953 and the secular trends for reduced ages were evident by comparison. [26]

CAUSE AND EFFECT

Lastly, in Germany in 1990, University of Bremen researchers reported on the mean age of menarche of Turkish girls living in Bremen. Their menarcheal age was lower than the German girls in the same district. They ruled out nutrition and climatic causes for this early event. They concluded that there is support for a "predominately genetic cause."[27] The early maturers in Hong Kong were taller and heavier than the late maturers from approximately age 11 to 12; however, this would be expected to be associated with early maturers — but is it the cause?

From the University of London we hear that, "Although age at menarche seems to have stabilised and even increased in recent years, the assertion that this is probably a result of dieting and increased levels of exercise is not in accord with recent studies."[28] Another opinion also came from England that changes in body size do not account for menarcheal changes in the current plateau.[29] Further evidence suggests that weight gain goes along with early menarche but is not always a cause. A New Zealand study used the Body Mass Index and concluded, "In general, the results show an association between the menarche and gain in body mass. However, many girls who failed to achieve their expected gain had experienced the menarche (18%), indicating that the relationship between body weight and the menarche may not be causal or is mediated by other factors."[30] On an empirical and personal note, I have seen more early menarche girls (<11 years) in my practice in the past 10 years than in all of my 31 years of practice. Their mothers have reported this fact on my medical history form. This is what first alarmed me and why I wrote the article in 1987 concerning earlier orthodontic treatment.[31] Orthodontic treatment with extensive skeletal movement must be done while there is still sufficient adolescent skeletal and muscular growth remaining. Current menarcheal ages from various countries can be seen in the notes.[32]

Consider the fact that not one of the medieval, or classical, sources ever mentions girls under 10 who have had their first menstrual period. Only two ancient studies mention the age of 10 as a possible figure.[33] In the present studies, there are girls under 10 years old and one as young as 7. The study from Malaga of 777 girls found a mean menarcheal age of 12.4 ± 1.5 years. One standard deviation below this mean is 10.9 years. This may be a small group, but it is still within the 68% level of the group of girls, assuming a normal distribution curve. My point here is that as the mean drops so does the minus side of the mean and these are the ages that have commanded the attention of society and will continue to do so throughout our history.

There are also numerous examples of precocious puberty in our generation. I believe the following findings are what sets our generation apart from the classical or medieval.

PRECOCIOUS PUBERTY (PP)

"Sexual precocity (precocious puberty) is defined as the appearance of any sign of secondary sexual maturation at an age more than 2.5 standard deviations below the mean. In North America, the ages of 8 years in girls and 9 years in boys set these limits." According to some authorities, less than 1% of normal children will develop signs of puberty before 9 years in boys and 8 years in girls.[34]

This statistic does not appear to be true in light of a recent report from Puerto Rico which has found over 3,100 cases of precocious puberty (PP) in the past 19 years. Over 3,100 girls at 8 years and below is a figure unheard of in the past. Fingers have been pointed at estrogens in the meats, possible fungal infections, or some other food contamination as the cause of this extremely high rate. However, this has been treated by modern science as an isolated phenomena.[35]

Premature breast development has been another dilemma in modern girls. In 1994 a German group at the University of Mainz, Children's Clinic, investigated this problem in 39 girls aged 10 months to 7 and 10/12 years.[36] Did you fully comprehend that? Ten months to about 8 years old was the range of ages with premature breast development. Twenty-nine of these girls had precocious puberty while 10 had just premature breast development. Babies with breast development should send strong signals to the evolutionary minded doctors of today that something is seriously wrong.

Precocious puberty is unrelenting. It is being seen in studies all over the world. In 1994, in Rome, Italy, 171 children (135 girls and 36 boys aged 7 ± 1.2 years) with PP were tested. [37] In the same year in the USA, in central Iowa, 26 children with sexual precocity were found.[38] In St. Louis, Missouri, 26 (2 boys, 24 girls) children with Central PP were discovered and their heads were scanned with magnetic resonance imaging (MRI) looking for causes.[39] In Toulouse, France, 13 girls presented idiopathic (unknown) PP in 1995.[40] The condition is being diagnosed but the causes seem to be eluding the medical community.

Experts attempted to play down the magnitude of this enigma at the University of Indiana Medical School in 1995. They said, "The past decade has seen tremendous advances in both the diagnosis and treatment options for children with precocious puberty. Although the precise cause of CPP (Central Precocious Puberty) is still not known, long acting GnRh (Gonadotropin-releasing hormone) analogues provide a safe and effective form of therapy." [41] The message echoed strong and clear: We can control this thing, don't worry.

The issue raised its ugly head again in Ancona, Italy, in 1995 where there were 14 girls aged 5 to 7 with PP.[42] Their ovaries were all larger than similar girls their age. Still no general alarm went out.

This story reminds me of the reports of the incoming Japanese aircraft on December 7, 1941. Apparently, there were advanced warnings that went unheeded even right up to that very infamous day. Then the bombs fell and many American lives were lost.

In 1995 in Helsinki, Finland, pediatricians were confronted by this problem once more.[43] They analyzed the amount of adrenal steroids in 34 children with premature adrenarche (increase in adrenal steroid production). Their conclusion: "Our findings imply that premature adrenarche may start earlier than previously recognized." Scottish doctors in Glasgow in 1995 used pelvic ultrasound on 67 girls with PP and found increased size of ovaries and uterus compared with the normal population of similar age. [44] But still, there did not seem to be any major concern.

From the Middle East, pediatricians in Israel saw 62 children (51 girls, 11 boys) in 1995 with PP.[45] With CT Scan (Computerized Tomography) and/or MRI (magnetic resonance imaging) it was determined that 44 had normal brain findings. There were 18 with intra-cranial (inside the brain) problems. In this case there were 71% of the cases which were supposedly "normal." What was the precise cause? Not one of our evolutionary-minded doctors can give us this answer. To the creation scientist who understands the original perfection of Adam and Eve and their subsequent fall, the increasing PP incidence in our day spells out the overall effect of the downward spiral of mankind.

A very alarming study out of Tubingen, Germany, in 1995 found 55 girls with premature breast development from ages 0.3 to 7 years, and 20 children with Central PP between the ages of 2.1 and 7.7 years.[46] In case these statistics are getting boring so that you might have missed their significance, let me reiterate that the low ends of these groups were 3.6 months and 2.1 years. These are mere babies reaching these stages. I am aware of no historical record of this size to match these findings!

In the Netherlands, 30 more cases (29 girls, 1 boy) of Central PP were discovered of unknown origin reported in 1995. The age range of these 30 children was 1.9 to 11.9 years.[47] Can you believe a 1.9 year old going through sexual changes? This should be a cause for tears for mankind.

How much does it take to see this happening in terms of man's dilemma since the historic time-space fall? The answer to that depends on how sold out we are to evolutionary dogma. There is no place in the evolutionary scenario for a downward spiral of mankind from a perfect beginning. I understand that they would admit to temporary reversals and even extinctions, but that is not what I mean by downward spiral. I am describing the original perfection in creation, a fall from that position, and a subsequent tailspin ever since. There was no accumulation of beneficial mutations coupled with selection which sculpted mankind from the stem primates. After all, the carbon molecule-to-man scenario has been described as a distinct upward trend from simple to complex. Let there be no mistake about that, no matter how much evolutionists may deny the upward trend, it is basic to their system. If this is not so, let someone prove to me that the supposed amino acid (pre-protein) pool was more complex than the supposed final product, man. Stephen J. Gould's bushes may look different from the old phylogenetic trees of the earlier evolutionists but there still is a top and there still is a bottom whether they're skewed from left to right or not.[48]

I have only reported here on most of the 1995 findings of PP and a few earlier. There are more accounts from 1994 and 1993 that could be chronicled but to what purpose? Suffice it to say that these warnings will not go unheeded by the wise. We are experiencing a rapid decline in the maturation rate of mankind, primarily manifested today in females, and, unhappily, it only can get worse as the years proceed. Is the answer in looking for ways to slow this down? Yes, that is desirable and is happening at the present time. More importantly, though, it should really be a directional sign that the Day of the Lord is getting to be very near. How low will God allow this to go before He restores all things?

DON'T WORRY, BE HAPPY – OUR MODEL DOESN'T INCLUDE THAT!

Commenting on an article on the 15-year sex incidence of PP in 197 girls and 16 boys in a London hospital,[49] in the 1995 edition of the *Year Book of Pediatrics*, Thomas Moshang, M.D., Professor of Pediatrics at the University of Pennsylvania Hospital, tried to calm the medical community. After expressing that PP in boys was more serious and often related to organic disease, he said, "The important thing to remember is that for girls seen with precocious puberty, it is unlikely that this is secondary to hidden pathology — including an undiagnosed CS lesion — without symptoms, or any history suggestive of organic pathology." What he seemed to convey here was that the condition of PP in girls was really nothing to be that concerned about. In girls it was not usually accompanied by any form of hidden disease. It is almost normal. To be fair, he does add, that "a very young child needs to be evaluated more extensively."[50]

Don't worry, be happy! I can almost hear the song now. It appears as if this eminent and brilliant doctor has missed seeing the importance of the general trend going on all around him because he, like the rest of the scientific world, has been blinded by the evolutionary glare. It has really hurt science, and good doctors like this do not realize that there is something driving children in this one direction. Since the evolutionary scientific model has no place for this condition, there is no feeling amongst the scientific community that something is going wrong with our children. They are missing the forest because they are only examining the individual trees and they have no scientific model to explain the data. Don't forget, their model does not include any supernatural intervention into the natural cause and effect universe. Theirs is strictly a closed naturalistic cause and effect system.

Recently, a professor at Penn State told my son Joshua's class that during a trip to Africa, he had a mysterious encounter with a witch doctor of a tribe. He watched with horror as this witch doctor put a man into a trance and made the man put his face into burning coals and move them around with his nose on the ground. The man received no burns and wasn't even aware of the sensation of burning his flesh. The professor, being a committed naturalist, had no way to understand this obviously satanic phenomena. His scientific model didn't include any supernatural cause, whether it be godly or satanic. He admitted this fact to the class. He said that he saw what happened, yet he did not believe it, because he couldn't fit it into what he called his scientific model. Could this be the reason that Jesus reported what Abraham said to the rich man who had died and gone to Hades, "If they do not listen to Moses and the Prophets, neither will they be persuaded if someone rises from the dead" (Luke 16:31). If their presuppositions rule out the supernatural, that is that! There is no more. This is a spiritual blindness bolstered by materialistic presuppositions. Unless the Second Law of Thermodynamics is nullified, or the Lord returns, the trend will continue until the numbers grow to larger proportions. The answer, eventually and obviously, will be the latter alternative.

AN EARLY AMERICAN CHILD

In September 1992, after reading a newspaper article, I became aware that there had been an early American grave site discovery from the 1700s in Connecticut. Nicholas Bellantoni, the state archaeologist in charge of the dig, later informed me that the remains of 13 children and a number of adults had been found on the Geer Sand and Gravel Company's land in Griswold, Connecticut, in the 1990 excavations. These skeletal parts were found by accident since this was the location of an active sand and gravel business owned by H. David Geer. It had been in the family for years. While workers were bulldozing a section of the land one day in 1990, a few bones appeared out of the side of a 50-75 foot cliff. All work stopped and archaeologist Nick Bellantoni was called in to supervise the removal of the new discoveries. All of the remains, including the children's bones and teeth, were packed up and shipped to the Armed Forces Institute of Pathology in Washington, D.C., which is located on the grounds of the Walter Reed Army Hospital.

In Building 54, P. Sledzik and A. Wilcox were the resident anthropologists who studied, photographed, and x-rayed this material between 1990 and 1992. I arrived at AFIP on September 30, 1992, with permission to copy all of the dental radiographs, photographs, and written records of the 13 children. All of the remains had been re-buried in Griswold, Connecticut, on September 9, 1992. I first became aware of this discovery upon reading the *New York Times* article on that date.

The most remarkable finding of this entire excavation was a partial coffin with "N.B. age 13" written in brass tacks on its broken cover. This may be the origin of the expression, "getting down to brass tacks."

Inside were the remains of a 13-year-old youth, although when Wilcox had examined the teeth of the lower jaw of this child and had calculated an age based on their crown and root formation, she arrived at an age of 9.5 years if it was a girl and 10.1 years if it were a boy. She had used the standards referred to earlier but did not take any x-rays or photographs of these teeth.[51] Why do you suppose that was? It could have been just overlooked. But my best guess is that these results were so frightening because there was no place in the scientific model held at AFIP for a slowly developing child of yesterday.

It is my opinion that N.B. age 13 was a confirmation of my research. What it means is that it took a child of approximately 250 years ago 13 years to reach the levels that our children reach in 9.5 to 10 years. There was approximately a 3-year gap in the maturation time compared with children of today. Once again, we see the child of today is moving along in his developmental rate much faster than the child of early America or the child of ancient history.

One of America's top dental anthropologists, Robert Corruccini, speaking about the human condition of teeth and jaws, has said, "Human occlusion has changed dramatically in very recent times."[52] By that he meant that the ancestral state of humans as far as their jaws and teeth were concerned was better than ours today. In this he was right. I wrote about this in 1987 citing a number of studies which showed the malocclusion (tooth and jaw alignment problems) rate among our children to be increasing.[53] It is only one more example of the downhill path of modern civilization.[54]

Chapter 30

Neanderthals Were Really Old

With Le Moustier established as the baseline and the downward spiral of mankind understood, it is now possible to attempt to understand the unusual lives of the adult Neanderthals of France. This series of Le Moustier, La Chapelle-aux-Saints, and La Ferrassie I are very closely related. They all were found in the southwestern section of France and are members of the classic Neanderthal group.

While I have also x-rayed other Neanderthal adults such as Gibraltar I, Tabūn C-1, Broken Hill (probable pathology), Amud I, and Skhūl V, (VI, VII fragments), I would like to compare what I consider blood relatives in this matter of adult growth.

LENGTH OF THE HEAD

The first calculation will be the overall head length of the French Classic Neanderthals. In 1863, Parchappe measured 90 French men from 20 to 60 years of age and above.[1]

Parchappe's average maximum length for the 19th century French head, 20-30 year old group, was 185.3mm. (These distances probably included minimal soft tissue.) The average maximum length for the 60-year-and-above group was 187.8mm. This represented a growth in cranial length of 2.5mm in approximately 40 years. This means that the heads grew longer, an average of approximately 0.06mm per year. If you take it to 70 years, the rate is 0.05mm.

In applying this growth rate (0.06mm per year) to the French Neanderthals it must be understood again that the actual rate probably wasn't the same as the 19th century men of France. Therefore, the results that we get won't be exactly correct. I use this rate with caution.[2] It then becomes possible to calculate the approximate years of growth for the Neanderthals using the 19th century figure, but, at the same time, realizing that the Neanderthal rate was surely much slower.

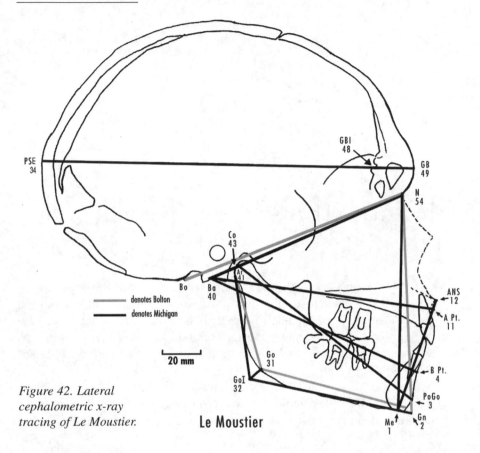

Figure 42. Lateral cephalometric x-ray tracing of Le Moustier.

Le Moustier

So, if anything, then, when we see the ultimate years that Le Moustier would have taken to turn into a La Chapelle, or a La Ferrassie I, we must be careful to remember that these years are less than the actual ones that could have been calculated if we had known the true, slower rate of Neanderthal adult growth.

Table D gives the maximum lengths of the three Neanderthal skulls as measured in the cephalometric lateral x-rays. All have been corrected for magnification. The tracings of these lateral cephalometric radiographs are figure 42, Le Moustier; figure 43, La Chapelle-aux-Saints; and figure 44, La Ferrassie I.

Table D
Max. Cranial length (PSE -GB)[3]

Le Moustier .... 193 mm
La Chapelle-aux-Saints .... 210 mm
La Ferrassie I .... 209 mm [4]

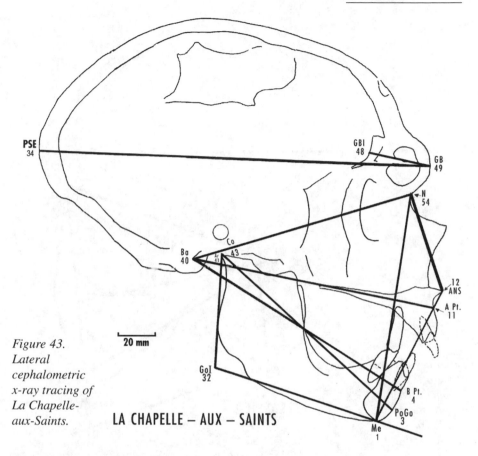

Figure 43. Lateral cephalometric x-ray tracing of La Chapelle-aux-Saints.

LA CHAPELLE – AUX – SAINTS

20 mm

One notices that La Chapelle is 17 mm larger than Le Moustier and La Ferrassie I is 16 mm larger than Le Moustier. Using 0.06mm per year and calculating the number of years it would take Moustier to turn into La Chapelle and La Ferrassie I, we find it would take approximately 283 modern years to reach La Chapelle, which has to translate to over that figure in Neanderthal years since their rate had to be slower, and approximately 267 years to reach La Ferrassie I. Now, with actual growth rates of Neanderthals that were surely slower, the years to accomplish this transformation would be greater. In this case I would estimate we are talking about over 300 years in both cases. If the 0.05 mm/year rate was used it would result in more years.

Certainly these are controversial conclusions in light of the fact that most authorities think the Neanderthals lived only into their forties.[5] Trinkaus and Shipman stated in 1992, ". . . since few Neanderthals lived into their forties and almost none lived beyond the age of fifty."[6]

They base this judgment on bones that have fully matured according to standards that have been developed for modern people. How can they say that we

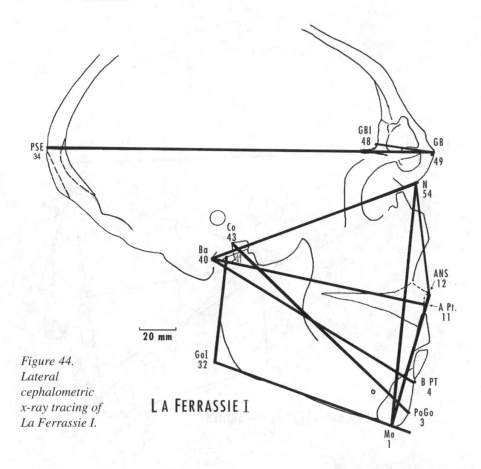

Figure 44.
Lateral
cephalometric
x-ray tracing of
La Ferrassie I.

LA FERRASSIE I

are dealing with bone sutures (joints between flat face and head bones) that have developed on our modern time scale? Bones that develop more slowly will close their sutures on a slower and sometimes proportional schedule. If you use today's bone-closing schedule on a head that has closed at much later dates, the only differences you will find are the ones I am pointing out in this book. Everything else will look similar.

A GOOD EXAMPLE OF SLOW CLOSURE

At this stage we really should see what I saw in my visit to the museum in Paris in 1979. Besides all the concern and fear about seeing problems with the jaws and teeth, I noticed something that made me think back to my embryology[7] days. I looked at the inside of the Pech de l'Azé mandible (lower jaw) in the region below the front teeth (see figure 45). It had three actual primary incisor teeth: left central, right central, and right lateral, besides the rest of the right side teeth. There in the center of this little jaw was an open slot which extended about one-half of the way down from between the two front teeth. This was an open remnant of the original line of fibrocartilage and connective tissue. Wasn't it supposed to be closed by this time (2.5 years)? The editor-in-chief of the *American Journal of Orthodontics and Dentofacial Orthopedics*, Thomas Graber, DDS, MSD, Ph.D, said this in his textbook: "There is a separation between the right and left bodies of the mandible at the mid-line, or symphysis. A

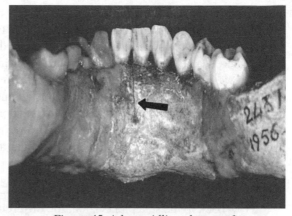

Figure 45. A late midline closure of lower jaw of Pech de l'Azé.

thin line of fibrocartilage and connective tissue exists. Between 4 months of age and the end of the first year, the symphyseal cartilage is replaced by bone." [8] It wasn't supposed to be there at all by this age unless this little child was maturing very, very slowly. So with this example I hope that all of my "suture closure" critics will take heed and read on.

A CONFIRMATION OF SORTS

In consideration of the Le Moustier to La Chapelle-aux-Saints hypothetical transition, please read this statement by the famous anthropologists C. Loring Brace and M.F. Ashley Montagu: "The fact, however, is that at age 16, the Le Moustier youth had relatively little growing left to do, and that in those few remaining years, interrupted by his early death, he could never have acquired the formidable supra-orbital torus or brow ridge so remarkably developed in the remains from Neanderthal, La Chapelle-aux-Saints, and one — not both — of the Spy skeletons."

What they said was that the adult Neanderthals have huge brow ridges over their eyes. How in the world could Le Moustier, a teenager, have developed these huge things over his eyes in what little time he had left to grow? It's very strange that these famous anthropologists could not conceive of a long period of adult growth. They really didn't want to think about it. They continued by stating that, "Because of a variety of circumstances the differences between Le Moustier and the assumed 'typical' Neanderthaler have been generally ignored. As a further and final distressing development in the troubled career of the Le Moustier Neanderthaler, the Museum was the unfortunate target of a bomb during the Second World War and the skeleton is no more." [9] Obviously, the latter part of this statement is false. Part of the skeleton does exist. I saw it in 1991 and you see it as you read this book. What were they talking about?

The story that I heard in the museum in East Berlin where Le Moustier's bones were kept and where I worked on them, was that a bomb in 1945 *was responsible* for the damage and loss of some of the fragments. But some remained which I was allowed to study. Brace and Montagu thought it was completely lost. I think there was a lot of confusion about their whereabouts and condition after 1945. However, in 1955 Herberer and Kurth apparently found some pieces of the skeleton that matched the description of Moustier and in 1977 Dr. Bernd Herrmann published a detailed analysis of some of the long bones.[10] I think the cranial pieces (head) were not "found" until much later. I heard in Berlin that the cranial bones had taken a trip to the Soviet Union after the war and that they came back when the "wall" fell in 1989.

UNUSUAL SHAPE AND SIZE

Now back to the statements about the differences between Le Moustier and the assumed "typical" Neanderthaler. What Brace and Montagu meant by the "typical Neanderthal" phrase was that Le Moustier, if it survived the bomb, would have given them good reasons to believe that Classic Neanderthals were a varied lot; that not all adults had the huge brow-ridges and pulled-forward faces like the majority; that there was at least one semi-adult, if not adult, that could be seen to have more modern morphology (shape) of the head. This could have been their refuge. It still may be, if this book is not widespread and well-read in our generation. If Le Moustier can be considered an adult that was close to the others in age, then classic Neanderthals had a wide range of adult head shapes. I very much doubt that this is true. There had to be sexual differences in head shape and size but that is normal for most humans. This is called dimorphism.

We simply cannot let them get away with sweeping Le Moustier under the table because of the fragmentary nature of the head and face and for reasons as outlined above. He is not a typical old Neanderthal adult. He is a typical young Neanderthal adult who still had a lot of adult growing to do as described in chapter 28. If it weren't for this fossil we would have no idea how the old adults formed their strange-looking features and approximately how long it took them to do it.

DECREASED NUMBERS OF REMODELING CENTERS

According to Herrmann in his 1977 report from Berlin on the compact layer of bone in the femur of Le Moustier, there was very little remodeling going on at the time of his death. While he expressed some caution because of the burnt nature of some of this bone, he did make a rather revealing statement: "I would say that the secondary osteons are so relatively scarce in the compacta of Le Moustier not because they 'disappeared' but because they did not form as 'bone reconstruction' was relatively poor (or 'abnormally' poor taking as normal standard the structure of the majority of present man). Although cases as described by Foote should be rather exceptional in present man — and as a matter of fact I have never found a similar one in over 40 years — it cannot be excluded a priori that they may have been more frequent in prehistoric times, at least in some populations depending on factors on which one could only speculate now (genetic factors, poor feeding conditions, general diseases, troubles of the mineral metabolism?)." Foote was his reference to this condition being found in adults before. This observation is very unusual because normal man should show more packets of new bone formation termed "secondary osteons." There were, however, a few large ones in the outer half or third of the layers, "primary lamellar (periosteal bone) that underwent very little reconstruction,"[11] but not nearly as many as expected and there also were, they believed, some remnants in the inner one-half or two-thirds.

These new bone resorption and formation cylindrical centers in compact bone are now known as part of the Haversian envelope system. Resorption, by means of osteoclasts, always starts out first in little sections of the compact bone making tiny holes with bone eaten away. Next, in that same hole, a new batch of cells, osteoblasts, follow that make bone. Both of these components are part of a BMU (Basic Multicellular Unit). This process goes on for a lifetime. The BMU travels through bone in a controlled direction to its work site. It takes about four months in modern man for these small portions of bone to be replaced in a site. "This new bone remains in place for from one to thirty years (depending on the local remodeling rate) before another turnover 'packet' remodels it out, either wholly or partially."[12] In children the remodeling rate is high and in adults it slows down like everything else. But even in adults there are many more secondary osteons than Moustier had in his outer layer of the femur. Osteomalacia and rickets are ruled out because they are marked by increases in resorption cavities that do not fill up with new bone. Here, in Le Moustier, are lamellae of outer bone unlike that seen today in adults. Besides the burned spots, two factors interfere with a firm diagnosis: first, lytic erosion of the bone and demineralization due to soil microbes; and second, hyper-mineralization of some areas of bony matrix.

If I may offer a tentative hypothesis, it seems that Neanderthals had a difference in osteoclastic and osteoblastic activities which translated into a different kind of remodeling of their compact bone. Today osteoclastic activity and osteoblastic activity occur in equal amounts in normal secondary osteons.[13]

Some claim that "Bone formation takes at least ten times as long as destruction of an equal amount of bone."[14] "Net gains and/or losses of bone become more problems of relative differences in the numbers of osteoclasts and osteoblasts than of individual activities responding to simple biochemical regulation, and so relate primarily to the activities of the mesenchymal cell populations which create them."[15]

A few slow-forming elephantine secondary osteons lumbering along making larger amounts of bone with higher populations of cells relative to the numerous small secondary osteons with fewer bone cells (e.g., compact bone of today) may be part of the slowness factor that was inherent in Neanderthal growth. Could it have taken longer for the big ones to resorb and form large amounts of bone around them (prolonged 2X or 3X) than a multitude of tiny ones all turning over rapidly in four months? There is also the possibility that the larger but fewer secondary osteons worked more efficiently and rapidly than the numerous smaller ones of modern man. However, being very few in number, the overall amount of bone formed per unit of time was less than modern man and henceforth, the growth rate for Neanderthals was slower.

THE STRANGE ADULT HEADS

It has been reported that Neanderthals had more rounded heads when looking at them from the back.[16] The greatest width was lower on the skull and it appeared as if it sagged down on both sides. This is true for the Neanderthal adults. It is not true for the children and young adults. Figure 46 shows a front view of the largest piece of the cranial vault of Le Moustier. It is very evident that the largest width is not low but high up on the skull like modern man. Pech de l'Azé also is built the same way. The width at the bottom stage does not happen until late adulthood. The greatest skull width in modern man is manifested higher up on the skull. Cro-Magnon I man had this width-higher-up skull.

To return to the subject of how long it took the Neanderthal adults to acquire their strange head and facial features, let us now see how different parts of Le Moustier grew at different rates. We have previously considered how Pech could become a Le Moustier but now let's think about how a Moustier could become a La Chapelle or a La Ferrassie I.

The human head is divided, conveniently, into segments for the sake of description which I believe has some basis in fact. They are the head and the face. We do know the head and face are separated by a base upon which sits the brain. This base is called the cranial base and it is treated separately from the bones around the sides and top of the brain and the facial bones.

In the lower jaw, which may be treated as one unit, there are many measurements seen on the cephalometric radiograph. You have already read about a number of these in the account about the Neanderthal children. One of these we already have analyzed is the gonial angle.

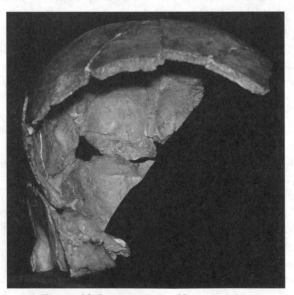

Figure 46. Largest piece of bony cranium of Le Moustier, front view.

You already know that Le Moustier had a gonial angle of 110°. What you don't know is that La Chapelle had one of 105° and La Ferrassie I, 104°. The rate at which this angle changes in the male child to the teenager we have seen to be from 0.85 degrees per year to 0.57 degrees per year for the Michigan and Bolton studies and 0.34 degrees per year for the Eskimo study.

In Behrents' studies we observe an even a slower rate of decline per year for male adults.[17] We know in male adults adolescent active growth is completed and adult or slower, steadier growth begins with no spurts as in children. Male adults also chew with more force than male children. Bony changes would be reflected by proportional amounts of bone remodeling with respect to time, functional forces, and adult nutrition. Behrents' slower adult rate gives us an approximate total number of years for Le Moustier's gonial angle to change into one like La Chapelle as 192 years and to be like La Ferrassie I as 231 years. But, once again, remember that the rate must have been slower and the years greater. Also, it is not my desire to pinpoint Neanderthal ages specifically. I want to unfold another side of the Neanderthal story that has never been allowed — their old ages in general.

La Chapelle's gonial angle must have stopped decreasing some years before the head finished growing in length, because the estimate for final head length is approximately 283 years after the age of Le Moustier. The jaw angle most likely just shut off at an earlier age because of the loss of almost all of the teeth.

Harry Sicher, my professor of anatomy from Loyola of Chicago, wrote, "After the loss of all the teeth, especially if no denture is worn, the condylar angle widens again. This change is often referred to as a senile change. It is, however, not the age of the individual but the loss of function which plays the decisive role; in other words, the change is to be defined as disuse atrophy." Ultimately, said Sicher, this leads to a "radical change of the bony outline and thus to a change of the gonial angle."[18] The loss of La Chapelle's teeth could thus have led to the atrophy of the angle and subsequent loss of bone. Frost wrote in 1994, "Decreased mechanical usage and acute disuse result in loss of bone next to marrow."[19] This means that normal adult growth can cease and bone loss can occur when conditions of mechanical use are altered. Other authors have confirmed the fact that mechanical usage is a key factor to the accumulation or loss of bone. Goodman and Aspenberg have written, "Research has shown that mechanical stimulation can have a profound effect on the differentiation and development of mesenchymal tissues. It would appear that a 'window' of mechanical strain exists which may facilitate or discourage the accretion of bone."[20]

BRAIN BASE

We have seen the length of the head which is a good indicator of bone expansion and brain expansion. Now let's observe another important measurement which involves the base of the brain.

All human brain bases are flexed or bent to a certain degree; however, none of the three classic Neanderthals from southern France have complete brain bases. The bending should usually include the pituitary fossa (pit) to be totally accurate. Although some try to reconstruct the base by estimates, I'd prefer to limit the estimates to only the essentials which can be constructed as accurately as possible from the remaining anatomy.

The base of the brain expands at its extreme ends (points) with time in adulthood. The posterior (farthest back) point called basion is on the front edge of the foramen magnum (the hole in the base of the skull for the spinal connections). The anterior (farthest forward) point is called nasion (the middle of the growth line between the two nasal bones and the frontal bone). Concerning the growth of the cranial base, Behrents said, "However, it is difficult to say what is actually occurring — anterior movement at nasion or posterior movement of basion and Bolton point. . . . A combination of movements is most likely."[21]

Regardless of what is actually happening, Behrents charted a change of 1.5mm for the basion-nasion (base of the brain) distance in the 26.8 years between his male initial and final measurements. This change represents a 1.4% increase from the initial measurement of 106.5mm.

From LeMoustier(108.5 mm) to La Chapelle (123.3mm), the growth of this very same cranial base displayed a 13.6% increase.[22] From Le Moustier to La Ferrassie I (120mm), it was a 10.6% increase. Admittedly, this is over seven times as much an increase as seen in modern man, and for both adults it would require more than 200 modern years to accomplish. Neanderthal would take longer because of the slower than modern rate. But, once again, it is useful to point out the differences between modern man and Neanderthal in terms of adult growth.

The French anthropologist Jean-Louis Heim changed the brain base of La Chapelle in 1983, four years after I x-rayed it. The reason that was given by Erik Trinkaus and Pat Shipman is, "A horrified graduate student examining the La Chapelle-aux-Saints skull found that Boule's old glue joints came apart in her hands." Marcelin Boule was the first anthropologist to put together this skeleton in a very ape-like fashion. The result of this accidental breakage of the entire skull base was a reconstruction to a more modern, less flat, and shorter brain base.[23] It is funny how this accident happened a few years after I had worked with this skull. Now, I'm sure it doesn't look like it would take over 200 years to accomplish the cranial base growth. The glue joints felt pretty secure to me in 1979.

THE BRITISH MUSEUM GIVES US A CLUE

There are a few more pieces of information that you should know about before I close this section. The first is established on the principle that continuous tooth eruption and bone addition proceeds throughout life. This was covered in detail in chapter 27. Part of the notes are highlighted here to emphasize the growth rate that Whittaker, Griffiths, and ultimately Theya Molleson of the British Museum, gave as a figure for the increase of bone and tooth height that led to an increase in facial height in the Spitalfields adults "throughout life."[24]

I highlight Theya Molleson here because she is an integral part in the workings of the British Museum anthropology group headed by Chris Stringer. In this case they studied skulls from an excavation of an 18th century church gravesite in Spitalfields, England, mentioned earlier.

Whittaker, Griffiths, et al., along with Molleson, studied 89 skulls with essentially minor wear from Spitalfields, all of which had exact dates of birth and death accompanying them. Their most important discovery was "that continuing eruption will occur in the absence of attrition." Therefore, their conclusion was that "in the absence of attrition facial height will increase."[25] They also gave some significant figures.

"Our study also indicates an addition of bone to the lower border of the mandible in the molar region of about 1.4mm throughout life, so that the total increase in facial height would be expected to be around 7mm between the age of 20 and 60 years, an increase of 0.18mm per year."[26]

Please, mark this well in your mind because I am not citing my figure or Dr. Behrents' figure for a growth rate. It is the British Museum scientists who are giving us theirs. Facial height increases by 0.18mm per year from 20 to 60 years of age. Now let us examine the three facial heights from Le Moustier, who even they would admit was at least 16-18 years of age, to La Chapelle and La Ferrassie I.

Table E[27]
Facial Height (Nasion to Menton) (From Ceph Radiographs)

Neanderthal	Height (mm.)	Increase (mm.)	Yrs. at 0.18mm/yr.
Le Moustier	110.3	0	0
La Chapelle-aux-Saints	124	13.7	76
La Ferrassie I	135	24.7	137

Using their growth rate of adult facial height (0.18mm/yr), and remembering that there was much attrition (wear) of the biting surfaces of these teeth into adulthood, we get at least 137 years for a Le Moustier to turn into a La Ferrassie I and at least 76 years between Le Moustier and La Chapelle.

An important fact to consider here is that the 0.18mm per year rate was calculated on skulls with teeth which had very little tooth wear. If you have tooth attrition then the rate has to be sped up past 0.18mm/yr. because facial height must build up quicker than the loss of tooth height in the same amount of time to reach the same facial height or you will lose height. But can it be accelerated? If there was a slower rate it would mean more years to achieve increased facial height. Unless you accelerate the facial bone build-up and passive tooth eruption to keep up with the occlusal or surface wear on the teeth, which seems unlikely, there had to be at least 137 years between Le Moustier and La Ferrassie. Most likely the rate was slower and the years greater. This year figure then is a minimal one based on British Museum calculations from skulls of the 18th century.

Behrents' rate for facial height is calculated for the 26.8 year time frame for modern day men.[28] It is 0.101mm per year; a much slower pace. This will produce over 245 years from Le Moustier to La Ferrassie I.[29] Again, their real rate had to be slower so we're probably in the region of 275 years. If you think I've made an error here, remember the Eskimo data where Neanderthal can be compared to modern man when it comes to diet and not the pre-contact Eskimo. If the speed of eruption of the teeth is not fast enough and bone build-up slow, the facial height will actually decrease as the tooth biting surfaces wear down.[30] Of course, this did not happen in the case of the Neanderthals from southern France. The facial height increased considerably, even in La Chapelle. You even would be hard-pressed to find an evolutionist to admit to 76 years between Le Moustier and La Chapelle-aux-Saints, which would put La Chapelle close to 100 even by their standards.

IOWA CONFIRMATION

In chapter 27, I quoted Bishara, Treder, and Jacobsen from the University of Iowa in their cephalometric x-ray study of male adults from 25 to 45 years. Let us apply their male measurements for facial height to the three Neanderthals. I spoke to Dr. Bishara on the phone on 2/1/96 and he told me not to correct for magnification, that all his measurements were exact. The male mean (Na-Me) facial heights are 121.91mm at 25 and 123.91 at 45 from his Table V. The difference is 2mm in 20.32 ±1.23 years.[31] This produces a growth velocity or rate of 0.098mm/year. This is less than the British figure and slightly less than Behrents' rate (0.101). It calculates for 13.7mm at 140 years and for 24.7mm to 252 years. And we know that these rates are all probably too fast. Here, then, is confirmation from Iowa for Behrents' data.

PASSIVE TOOTH ERUPTION AND LOWER FACIAL GROWTH

As stated previously, all of the teeth keep erupting throughout life (passive eruption).[32] Bone is also added on the lower border of the body of the mandible and also to the alveolar margins which surround the teeth. This continuous passive eruption of teeth compensates for the continuous wear or attrition on the biting surfaces. This process attempts to maintain or increase the height of the lower face throughout modern man's life, or in some instances, with excessive attrition as in Australian aborigines, it does not quite keep up with that wear on the teeth and lower facial height is lost.[33]

When this eruption process lags behind that of the surface wear on the teeth the distance between the anterior nasal spine (tip of the median, sharp bony process of the maxilla at the lower margin of the anterior nasal opening) and menton (point-bottom of bony chin) decreases. If this passive eruption process is faster than the occlusal or surface wear over a long period of time, this distance will increase. This is what happens in modern man. There is a rapid increase of lower facial height (LFH) and not much wear on the biting surfaces of the teeth because of our soft diet.

What happens when there is extensive wear of all the biting surfaces of the teeth and the facial height still increases well into adulthood? Would it mean faster tooth wear and faster rate of passive eruption with very rapid bone build-up on the bottom of the lower jaw? Murphy found out in his studies of Australian aborigines that passive really does mean passive. Among modern *Homo sapiens,* Australian aborigines wear down their teeth on the biting surfaces as much and as fast as any group. Murphy measured Australian aborigines' tooth wear on the biting surfaces and the compensating passive tooth eruption and lower jaw bony build-up. He measured anthropometrically (physical measurement) lower facial height of 337 skulls with different levels of tooth attrition. Murphy concluded, "In the Australian aborigines attrition, by its rate and degree, overshoots the anticipated mark. Compensation is not fully adequate and the net result is a decrease in facial height."[34] Aborigines, therefore, lost lower facial height because they wore down their teeth too fast. No amount of passive eruption or bone growth could keep up with it.

Did Neanderthals, who had equally extreme or more tooth wear than aborigines, have faster passive eruption, so that their lower facial height from young adulthood to late adulthood increased?

Figure 47 shows the disarticulated tooth-bearing portion of the maxilla (upper jaw) in optimal occlusion (best bite) with the lower jaw of Le Moustier. I have tentatively calculated his age at 32 years. As you know, Brace and Montagu have called him 16, others 18. The Neanderthal adults, La Ferrassie I and La Chapelle-aux-Saints, have been aged at 40 to 45 years by standard methods.

Let us now use the paleoanthropologist's ages of 16 years and 40-45 years for the lower facial height increase found between Le Moustier's radiograph (figure 48) and La Chapelle-aux-Saints' radiograph (figure 49) and the La Ferrassie I radiograph (figure 50). See Table F. We can compare the difference of Lower Facial Height (LFH) to those of the Behrents' study of modern males in Table G.

These LFH calculations are very firmly based on well-known phenomena. I do not think that they will be overturned unless somebody adjusts the fossils.

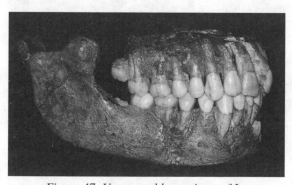

Figure 47. Upper and lower jaws of Le Moustier in maximum bite (occlusion).

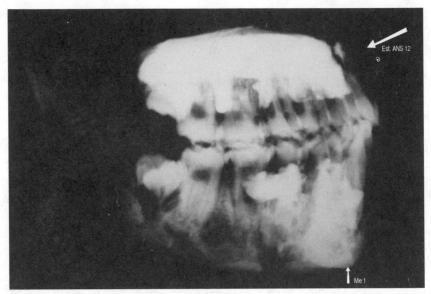

Figure 48. X-ray of upper and lower jaws of Le Moustier.
Arrows on points for age estimates (ANS est. and Me).

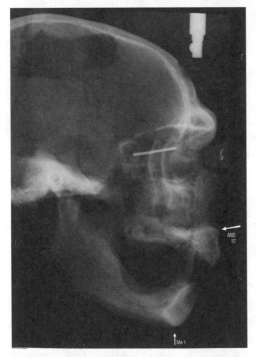

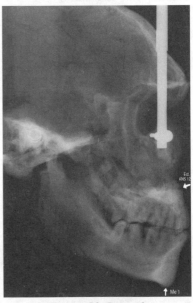

Figure 49. Lateral cephalometric x-ray of
La Chapelle-aux-Saints, arrows on points
for age estimates (ANS-Me).

Figure 50. Lateral
cephalometric x-ray of La
Ferrassie I, arrows on points
for age estimates (ANS est.-Me).

TABLE F
LFH Measurements Made From Cephalometric Radiographs

Neanderthals	Years of Age	Lower Facial Height (mm)(ANS-Me)	Diff. mm	Rates mm/yr.
La Ferrassie I	40-45	75.8 (estimated ANS)	17.5	0.73-0.60
La Chapelle-aux-Saints	40-45	78.7 (actual ANS)	20.4	0.85-0.70
Le Moustier	16	58.3 (estimated ANS)		
	24 -29			
	years			
	difference			

TABLE G
University of Michigan Data Calculation 200, LFH Modern Males

Years of Age		Mean Low Facial Height (mm) (ANS-Me)	Diff. (mm)	Rate mm/yr.
Final	46.6	68.7		
Initial	19.8	67.0	1.7	0.063
	26.8			
	years			
	difference			

The modern rate of 0.063mm per year for LFH increase with practically no wear on the teeth contrasts sharply with the rate of 0.85 to 0.70 mm/year from Le Moustier to La Chapelle or the 0.73 to 0.60 to La Ferrassie with enormous tooth attrition. Now, let us even assume that Le Moustier had 5 more years of active youthful growth remaining until the age of 21. The average growth for modern males from 16 to 18 is 1.98 mm.[35] The Bolton standards do not go any further than that. Let us allow Le Moustier up until 21 years of age to cease his active or youthful growth period. If we do so at a generous youthful rate of 1.0 mm per year for 5 more years, his lower facial height would be 5.0mm+ 58.3mm= 63.3 mm. For Le Moustier to become La Chapelle he would have to advance his LFH to 78.7 during the onslaught of extreme molar occlusal attrition. This is an increase of 15.4 mm. Starting with this maximum level of attained growth as a young person, he would enter the adult growth stage at that point and have to attain an adult rate of change of 15.4/19 = 0.81mm/year to arrive at 40 years or 15.4/24 = 0.64mm/year to be 45. This would be over 12-1/2 times to 10 times faster than the rate of modern man (0.063). To become La Ferrassie it would be 0.66mm/year to 0.52mm/year or from over 8 to over 10 times faster than modern man. From what is known about attrition and severe attrition, the rate of LFH increase would slow down and not speed up.

Because of the extremely fast growth rates necessary for Neanderthals to acquire adult characteristics, it seems that the physiologic process of a Le Moustier growing into a La Ferrassie or a La Chapelle is better explained by longevity than increased rates of growth. At the modern rate of growth for LFH it would take Le Moustier 324 years to achieve the La Chapelle LFH, and 278 years to achieve the La Ferrassie LFH. Just as a point of information, apes only grow and develop twice as fast as humans. Is anyone willing to concede Neanderthal growth at 8 to 12 times as fast as modern man?

CHEWING YOUR WINDOWS SHUT

One of the first to designate the eyes as "windows" was Solomon (Eccles. 12:3). William Shakespeare also called them "windows," while William Blake and John Greenleaf Whittier described them as "windows of the soul." [36] I had never heard this concept before I went on to post-grad education. It was then that I heard my professor at Loyola, Harry Sicher, say that if we didn't have certain pillars of bone and buttresses in our heads, we would chew these "windows" shut. Sounds strange doesn't it? Some people have argued with me over this point, but I believe it is true.

The forces of chewing would actually be detrimental to the eyeball over a long span of time by putting too much pressure on the eye socket. When the teeth are used for chewing, forces are transmitted to the underlying bone and certain parts of the face and head. As discussed previously, the absorption of these forces in the lower jaw is the task of the bone in which the teeth are housed. If these forces become strong enough in the lower jaw, the underlying bone requires some shoring-up and is reinforced by big lumps of bone (tori) as seen in the Eskimo. These are not to be confused with hereditary tori.

However, in the upper jaw, it's a different story. The forces in the upper jaw are not only transmitted to the immediate underlying bone but also to the bones of the upper part of the head so they may be spread out and absorbed. This is why Sicher said the pillars and buttressing elements are important to shunt or transfer these pressures around the eye into the forehead or backwards toward the ear. The eyeball in the socket never feels the pressure of chewing when this system is working normally. The nasal cavity is also spared in this process since the forces are conveyed around it as well. The cheekbone can be visualized as one large "flying buttress," very similar to the ones supporting the roofs of the mighty cathedrals of Europe.

The introduction of "flying buttresses" around A.D. 1180 made possible the addition of huge stained glass windows in the great cathedrals of Europe. Previous to this invention, huge windows in cathedrals were impossible, because glass doesn't hold up a heavy roof very well. Such buttresses can be found supporting the roof of Notre Dame Cathedral in Paris, whose stained glass windows include the three Rose Windows. Without the aid of flying buttresses, most of these windows would come crashing down, being unable to support the very large and heavy roofs. The flying buttresses also reduced the amount of stone necessary in the walls by relieving them of their duty of structural support of the roof. The forces of weight generated by the massive roof were transferred or shunted into the ground. This was the hallmark of Gothic construction which emphasized light and soaring spaces.

THE PRICE OF PROTECTION

Just like these buttresses absorb the forces of the roofs, so the flying buttresses of the face and head absorb the forces of chewing. But, what if someone were to live a very long life and have their face grow forward and also chewed moderate to heavy foods? What effect would it have upon the bones moving forward that absorbed hundreds of years of intermittent forces? This is the price of protection. See figure 51. Typical of men and women of very old age were large brow ridges over the eyes. Sicher said that this build-up of bone over the eye sockets must be interpreted as "a forward shift of the masticatory anchorage in response to the pronounced facial prognathism in primitive human races."[37] Masticatory anchorage means bone supporting the chewing forces. Facial prognathism means the forward position of the face in the head.

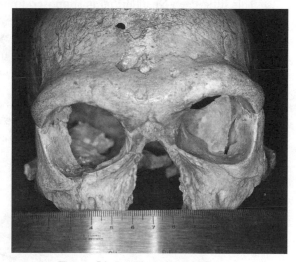

Figure 51. La Chapelle-aux-Saints enormous brow ridges.

At Tokyo University, B. Endo has shown with biomechanical models that strong forces from the chewing muscles working through the teeth generates intensive concentration of compression in the nasal and forehead region. He established that strong bending moments of force due to tooth pressures are produced in the region over the nose and between the eyes. This is termed the "glabellar area." A skull with a vertical forehead can resist these pressures with its entire height. A skull with a sloping forehead, such as the Neanderthal acquired as his face moved forward during the aging process, can resist these pressures only at its base, in the eyebrow ridge or brow ridge. Endo concluded that a sloping forehead compensated for these forces by its outer layer of bone drifting forward through a remodeling process, i.e., a bigger brow ridge.[38]

Both lateral cephalometric x-rays of La Chapelle and La Ferrassie I show a thickened pillar of bone which travels up from the cuspid area of the upper jaw to the brow ridge. La Ferrassie only shows it beneath the eye since much of the intervening bone has been lost. This is the result of hundreds of years of chewing.

A ROTATION OF THE ROOF OF THE MOUTH

Before closing this section on age estimates for the adult Neanderthals let us examine one more fact. It was produced by Rocky Mountain Data Systems of Calabasas, California.[39] They did an independent study on my cephalometric x-rays for my use. They had a data base in 1980 of approximately 100,000 children and adults with which to compare the Neanderthals. Figure 52 shows the upper jaw (hard palate) (roof of the mouth) of Pech de l'Azé in a side view tracing. It is superimposed over the Rocky Mountain Data Systems average 5-year-old upper jaw. It was their youngest normal age at the time.

This little Pech Neanderthal is supposed to be about 2.5 years of age. The Rocky Mountain Data Systems' normal 5 year old has a hard palate that is parallel to a line going through the bottom of the orbit (eye socket) to the top of the ear rod in the external auditory meatus (ear hole). This anatomically correct but imaginary line is called the Frankfort Horizontal Plane and is used by many researchers who study cephalometrics.

The hard palate of 5-year-old norm is closer to parallel to the Frankfort Plane at zero degrees or perhaps minus one to three degrees at most. As I told you earlier, Rocky Mountain measured Pech de l'Azé as having a minus 14° angula-

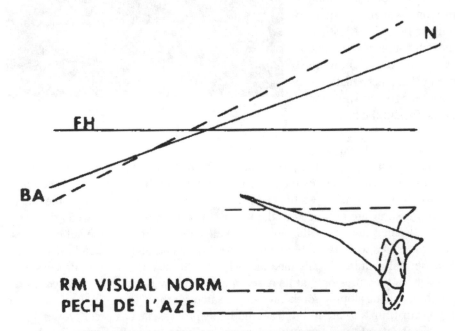

Figure 52. Angulation of Pech de l'Azé' roof of mouth, and modern standard.

tion from this horizontal eye-ear plane.[40] In my own measurements I found the angle to be minus 17°. No normal modern child has a similar angulation at this age. This is the angulation of an approximately 9- to 12-week-old human embryo. The amazing thing is this — no embryologist or anthropologist can tell us how a palate can start out like this at minus 14° or 17° in childhood with all the primary teeth present and end up in adulthood at a level of plus 3.6° in La Chapelle or plus 1° in La Ferrassie in a normal lifetime of 40 to 45 years. This represents a counterclockwise rotation of the maxilla of around 15 to 20 degrees. This is spectacular. This does not happen in man today. This fact alone should be enough to convince most paleoanthropologists that there is something very different about these people. Now Le Moustier measured somewhere between minus 9-11° (lack of complete bony orbit, or eye socket) in this angle. Apparently the hard palate had not rotated to its old-adult stage yet, which also confirms another fact about adult aging in Neanderthals. Most of this spectacular rotation takes place after the adult stage of growth has been reached. This fact cannot be ignored by evolutionists or creationists. The former wish to create another species while the latter wish to place Neanderthal in another "race" category, but otherwise maintain that the Neanderthals were humans just like us.

Chapter 31

How Could Teeth Last That Long?

My first attempt to write a research paper for the *American Journal of Orthodontics and Dentofacial Orthopedics* lasted five years, from 1982 to 1987. I was rejected numerous times because of evolutionary concepts which permeated my orthodontic colleagues as deeply as they did the paleoanthropologists. On one occasion one of my critics wrote: "The figures explain virtually nothing. Figure 9 shows not a stage of maturation but a certain orientation in certain structures. Neanderthal age-at-death is also calibrated by dental attrition, which certainly must not have been significantly slower than their growth as these authors imply. Attrition supports the age estimates as traditionally given."[1]

To refute this statement, first let me say that bones in growth always show stages of maturation. I fully realize that craniofacial cephalometric radiographic standards were not established to determine levels of skeletal age (SA) or maturity. There are better ways to do this in living children with wrist and hand radiographs.[2] No hand or wrist bones were recovered for Pech de l'Azé and what little there was for Le Moustier was destroyed during the war (from what I gathered in Berlin). Therefore, you must use what you have, and we do have fine craniofacial radiographs that are taken with a standardized technique. This enables us to compare them with the standards I have already cited. Valid information regarding bony stages of development related to dental development can be gained, and comparisons can be made to modern populations. Rothenberg et al. said, "The skeletal age appears to be a better indicator of physical maturation than does the chronological age of the individual."[3]

A 1995 study on twin girls and their genetic relationships also called this critic to task. "A genetic system controlling skeletal maturity was identified as the only genetic determinant of menarcheal age, independent of those systems of the two remaining physical measures."[4] What he meant was that there exists a genetic system in our DNA which controls skeletal growth and maturation and the menarcheal age which have nothing to do with the height and weight of the individual girls in this case. The other two measures were height and weight of the 86 sets of twins and these factors didn't count. Therefore, my critic was incorrect in disassociating sexual maturation and bony or skeletal maturation and calling a stage of development not a stage. It also is possible to determine rates of growth of facial components from cephalometric radiographs.[5]

His next criticism concerned dental wear. A slower rate of dental wear on the teeth would mean a softer diet, harder enamel, more enamel per square millimeter of biting surface of the tooth, or another mechanism. Which was it? Softer diets can not be postulated for peoples living in such difficult conditions. Harder enamel would be a good thought, if it could be proved. I have no evidence to support harder enamel.

There are several factors. To begin, it was most likely that the surface topography of the Neanderthal primary and permanent molars was different. There seemed to be more enamel folds per unit area than a modern molar. Using an analogy from geography, it is like comparing two coastlines: one that has more harbors, and one with less. The one with more harbors has an overall length of shoreline when stretched out that would be longer than the smoother, less-indented coast. In the same way, unfolding a Neanderthal molar would reveal more surface area than a modern *Homo sapiens* molar (see figure 53).

But what does this increased surface area mean in terms of enamel protection? There is a membrane mechanism on the surface of all tooth enamel that is referred to by Job in the Book of Job. He called it "the skin of my teeth" (Job 19:20). This mechanism could have been a very important factor in the renewal of tooth enamel surface scratches in early people. Today this membrane is called by various names but we will refer to it as the enamel pellicle.

In 1961, Schlatter et al. at the University of Zurich made scratch marks on human upper incisor teeth in 34 students with a diamond point; very small ones, 5.07-5.34 microns deep.[6] They made replicas of the teeth. The surprise came when they were able to detect some type of crude repair mechanism six weeks later (average depth: 4.57-4.77 microns). Most of the scratch marks had

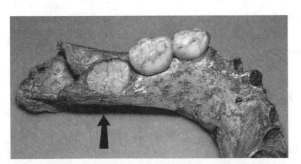

Figure 53. Gibraltar II unerupted permanent first molar (arrow) with extensive enamel wrinkling.

started to fill in with deposits from this pellicle, or "skin," of the tooth. The pellicle, in turn, is supported by the proteins and calcium and other minerals from the saliva.

Japanese scientists at Kyushu University looked at a small enamel crack in an extracted human molar tooth with an electron microscope. The inside of the crack was filled with an "irregularly oriented layer of plate-like crystals" of minerals. These crystals were similar in shape and size to the original enamel crystals that make up the whole outside of the tooth crown (hydroxyapatite). Another mineral, whitlockite, was part of the fine crystals which they thought was being transformed into the plate crystals. They said that these fine crystals were "newly formed mineral deposits" which they believed originated in the saliva.[7] It is now known that there are certain proteins in the saliva which mediate the orderly crystallization process of re-mineralization of the enamel but prevent the over-deposition of minerals on enamel when the saliva is supersaturated with them. This protein is called statherin. Raj et al. said it was "partly responsible for the protection and re-calcification of tooth enamel." It has also been suggested that this molecule's activity on hydroxyapatites of enamel is mediated by its "negative charge density, sequence, and helical conformation at the N-terminal region."[8]

Jenson et al. found that certain phosphoproteins as well as some histatins "selectively absorb to hydroxyapatite."[9] Since salivary statherin is such a powerful lubricant and inhibitor of over-calcification one can only imagine that this inhibitory molecule would have to be inactivated or removed in our past. They "probably became incorporated into the mineral-inducing system, where they assumed a regulatory role in fine-tuning crystal growth."[10] This quote was meant to convey an evolutionary perspective in its original context, but it fit so well in this context that it could be a logical conclusion to this unique viewpoint as well.

These biologic processes of today are probably a mere shadow of what once was an elaborate system of enamel repair from the saliva in our earliest ancestors. In order to assume this, we must once again think in terms of more viable mechanisms in earlier peoples rather than less efficient ones. This, again, is devolutionary thinking, not evolutionary.

I also referred to the biting surface of the molars of Neanderthal peoples being less reliable as a monitor of age than other less-folded surfaces. Thus, crystallization may proceed whenever you have a point of nucleation (critical number of nuclei) to precipitate hydroxyapatites in the depths of enamel folds rather than on smooth surfaces.[11] Therefore, if the repair to the enamel is proceeding in the folds of the biting surfaces, comparing these teeth to moderns may be very unreliable. Neanderthal teeth still wore down, but probably with a slow rate at first that increased as these mechanisms started to breakdown in devolution.

Tool use in Neanderthals was one of the functions of their front teeth. They would grip hides and such in their teeth and strip them with flint knives. This would also outstrip the repair mechanisms and produce extreme attrition of the teeth, creating pulpal exposures.

THE SKIN OF MY TEETH

What did Job mean by his statement when he said, "My bone clings to my skin and my flesh, And I have escaped only by the skin of my teeth" (Job 19:20)? This much we know. He was afflicted with a disease which produced skin infections of some type in every part of his body. He was apparently starving also, because of the painfulness of lesions even on the inside of his mouth; he had some canker sores. He asked, "Can something tasteless be eaten without salt, Or is there any taste in the white of an egg? My soul refuses to touch them; they are like loathsome food to me" (Job 6:6-7). Try eating the pure raw white of an egg. In fact, this used to be a way to get children to vomit who had swallowed something they shouldn't have. It feels like you're swallowing nasal mucous.

He couldn't put salt on his food because it would have really irritated the sores in his mouth. Warm salt water rinses in dentistry help a patient with mouth sores only if it is very dilute. Too much salt in a wound is painful. Over the years, numerous patients have come to me with really painful canker sores (mucous membrane ulcers). They have been rinsing with warm strong salt water. You should see how red and inflamed they are. I have always given them a benadryl, 2% viscose xylocaine, and amphogel liquid mixture and healing is usually quite rapid after that.

SATAN UNDERSTOOD SKIN SENSITIVITY

Apparently, the one "skin" of Job's body that wasn't affected by his skin disease was the skin on his teeth because it was so different and also put "out of bounds" by God. This tooth skin was an enamel-repairing mechanism maintained and fed by the saliva, unlike all the rest of the surface skin or mucous-membrane layers in his body. He was affirming that this tooth skin was intact by his famous statement later to be adopted as a only a symbolic expression. I believe that he was declaring it to be crucial in the preservation of his life.

God told Satan, "Behold, he is in your power, only spare his life" (Job 2:6). It was the only skin Satan was not allowed to touch when Satan, "smote Job with sore boils from the sole of his foot to the crown of his head" (Job 2:7). Previously, Satan had answered the Lord: "Skin for skin!" (Job 2:4). Satan understood skin sensitivity very well since the snake he inhabited lost his legs after the curse in the Garden of Eden and had to crawl on the skin of its belly. This was probably very painful until its underside skin toughened up from prolonged rough usage, like calluses on our hands.

We should also learn some information about the biological properties of saliva to understand what might be the meaning of the skin of the tooth which provided Job with a method to preserve his life.

In 1995, researchers at the Semmelweis University Medical School in Budapest, Hungary, concluded that the saliva has certain growth and healing properties that come from the substances secreted from the salivary glands of the mouth. They said in their title, "The fountain of youth resides in us all." They cited 90 reference studies in this review. In speaking about the biologic and physi-ologic factors of saliva, they said that there is a "wide range of growth factors" secreted in saliva. "Animal studies with epidermal growth factor have provided evidence of a role in both oral and systemic health, through promotion of wound healing rates."[12] The Nobel Award Committee in 1986 gave their prize in Medi-cine and Physiology to Levi-Montalcini and Cohen for their identification and characterization of epidermal growth factor from mouse salivary glands in the 1960s. It also has been demonstrated that salivary histatin 5 (a protein of the saliva) has anti-microbial action against such things as Candida Albicans, a type of yeast (fungus).[13] It is candidacidal, meaning it kills them. Other proteins in the saliva are also anti-microbial, such as proline-rich proteins, lysozyme enzymes, and lactoperoxidase enzymes.[14] Let me add that my own opinion is that the quan-tity and potency of these anti-microbials today is probably infinitesimal to what it was in Job's day. But don't forget Satan was really working on Job. As soon as one sore in his mouth would heal over, two or three may have popped up. Even his powerful regenerating mechanisms were fighting for dominance over these evil agents. For those of you who remember Superman, I picture it as a "Super-man saliva" versus the evil "Kryptonite invaders."

JOB SPAT ON HIS WOUNDS

To come back to our modern level of battle against infection, just think of what a dog or cat does when a part of its paw or leg is hurt or cut. They lick it! God has built this response into their instinct system. Therefore, in regard to these growth factors, the Semmelweis researchers said, "Thus, the ability to ma-nipulate their rates of synthesis and absorption from the saliva holds the potential to enhance tissue regeneration and homeostasis" (health). I would add here, yes, if we could magnify them.

Ancient people like Job and the Neanderthals probably had higher rates of saliva secretion in their mouths with very powerful regenerative capacities for teeth and the skin of their own entire bodies. We have remnants today of this very potent system. It doesn't take much to destroy us.

Besides scraping his wounds with a broken clay pot (Job 2:8), Job probably was spitting on his wounds. How do we know this? He said to God during his agony and torment, "How long wilt thou not depart from me, nor let me alone till I swallow down my spittle?" (Job 7:19;KJV). While this could mean: "Won't You leave me alone until I humble myself," it could also mean: "Won't You let me alone (stop allowing Satan to torture me) until I stop spitting on my wounds and swallow my spittle instead."

For Job to stop spitting on his wounds would be a sign of really giving up; complete brokenness and surrender, totally resigned to the will of God and, of course, death. Spitting on his wounds represented his only fractional means of healing. Maybe he did stop shortly before God healed him. Whatever the case, the story ends with God "turning" or "restoring" Job to health. The Hebrew word is "*shub*" which means to come again, to be turned, to be restored. Return again signifies a return to health. But to Job, he had escaped total decimation and his life was spared by the "skin of his teeth." He was expressing the fact that because this tooth skin was intact and it was dependent on the salivary glands for its very existence, then the saliva was still potent for healing purposes. The healing factors present in saliva today in small amounts are epidermal growth factor, transforming growth factors, nerve growth factor, fibroblast growth factor, and insulin-like growth factors.[15] Some other proteins that are in saliva are also bound to the skin of our teeth like anti-microbial histatin 3 and histatin 5.[16] They were probably on Job's tooth surface, too. The growth factors may not be in the skin of the tooth itself, but we don't know for sure.

If the skin of his teeth and saliva weren't spared, I believe Job would have died. Remember, God commanded Satan to spare Job's life and Satan knew what that meant long before the biochemists at Semmelweis did.

I would like to impart a word of caution to my readers. I must say that your saliva will only work, in a limited way, on your own cuts today, not on someone else's. It will produce infection in another person. I know this fact from the many small cuts that I have received in over 30 years in dentistry. The patient's saliva can be the source of a major finger infection in an open cut on the dentist's hand, or if a sharp instrument should penetrate the latex glove. I have had a few. Thank God for powerful anti-microbial soaps and antibiotics in our fallen world. I prefer really strong soaps like Betadine Surgical Scrub as we use in our hospital. I don't spit on my cuts.

It now seems reasonable to conclude, on the basis of the Bible and current research, that the enamel of the teeth at one time did have a powerful means to repair itself via the cuticle or pellicle membrane and the healing mechanism of the saliva which fed this system. This probably was mediated by electrical charges in the mouth and most likely the teeth acted like electrodes in solution when chewing forces were placed upon them due to the piezoelectric nature of the entire tooth, primarily coming from the dentin and cementum crystals, but producing a positive electric charge on the enamel.[17] When piezoelectric crystals deform they give forth electrical charges. Only a remnant of this original system is left in our mouths today.

WHAT DID THEY EAT?

According to Chase, there is not much evidence available for the Middle to Upper Paleolithic peoples' use of plant materials.[18] My own feeling is that I doubt very seriously they ate no vegetation, no herbs, no green, leafy plants, especially when the land could provide it. Again, remember that Noah grew grapes immediately after the flood. The northern ice in Europe could have seriously curtailed the grape industry in present-day France and most other vegetables as well. Were European Neanderthals farmers? I doubt it because it seems that they had a nomadic existence and basically they were hunters.

I'll be quick to say that I have no evidence to prove that they ate much vegetation. My thinking on this subject is based on Genesis 1:31 in the fact that God gave mankind green plants in the beginning as the only food. But in Genesis 9:3, He gave mankind the animals as well. As far as meat eating is concerned, there seems to be plenty of remains of animals from the caves of France that cover this period of time (Middle Paleolithic) documenting this fact. For instance, in the La Chapelle cave, as small as it was, there were some bison bones and some backbones of deer, plus a horn. There were also some charred pieces of various kinds of animal bones and evidence of a hearth where fires had once burned. In one place Bergounoiux specifically described this little fireplace as a ritual fireplace "un petite foyer ritual," perhaps as a ritual altar after burial. He wrote that it was made of "des pierre plates," some flat stones, like plates. He said that someone used it to cook several small game animals for meals.[19] This is evidence enough that Neanderthals cooked their meat and probably burnt the bones to break them more easily to suck out the nourishing marrow. Tooth wear was a factor here. Even though there was repair by the end of their lives the Neanderthals had lost a lot of enamel. The rates of loss therefore were probably just slower. Therefore, our computer diagrams from 100 to 500 (figures 28 and 29) are not accurate from the standpoint of tooth attrition when comparisons are made to ancient people of the Bible or even present-day Third World countries, because grinding stones always leave minute traces of grit in the flour of bread. Humans have been using stones to process food for thousands of years. Stone tools left grit, also. Little pieces of flint would fracture from a flint knife and get into the meat or vegetables. Ancient man's dental wear had to be slightly greater as it was just a few centuries ago. We also know that different populations wear their teeth down at different rates and it is directly related again to diet, enamel amount and repair, and quality and eruption dates of teeth. Even teeth in the same mouth have different rates of enamel wear or occlusal attrition. There is also attrition between the teeth.[20] I have had 12-year-old patients who had worn down whole cusps on the lower first permanent molars on one side or both by bruxism (grinding the teeth).

AN ANCIENT CUSTOM

When I think about La Chapelle and his little fireplace or altar in his cave I am reminded of the first thing that Noah did after coming out of the ark right after the flood. The account in Genesis relates, "Noah built an altar to the Lord, and took of every clean animal and of every clean bird and offered burnt offerings on the altar" (Gen. 8:20). Noah's altar was obviously made of stones. Here in La Chapelle-aux-Saints' burial cave, we find specific evidence of a ritual fireplace made of stones. It is clear that this fireplace was also used for meals. But could the contemporaneous kin of this old man be harkening back to an ancient ritual first learned by his approximately great grandfather Japheth, who watched his father, Noah, conduct this offering after the flood? Some of you may be thinking

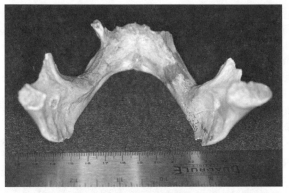

Figure 54. Lack of bony lumps, inside of La Chapelle-aux-Saints' lower jaw.

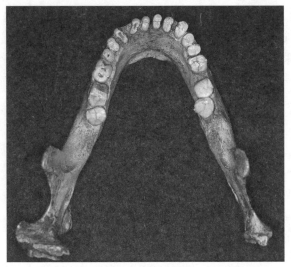

Figure 55. Absence of bony lumps inside of La Ferrassie I lower jaw.

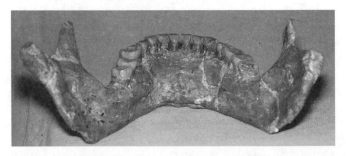

Figure 56. Lack of bony lumps inside of Tabūn C-I lower jaw.

about the smoke in the cave. It was very small with a wide opening at its entrance.

In support of this logic, another piece of the Neanderthal puzzle came together in 1990 and was just disclosed in 1996. As mentioned before, in 1990 a cave in southern France was discovered called Bruniquel. Several hundred meters from the cave's entrance, which is at least three American football fields long, a complex quadrilateral structure was found.[21] It was made of stalagmite and stalactite. A burned piece of bear bone found in the cave was radiocarbon-dated to the Neanderthal period at least 47,600 years ago. While I do take issue with that date based on uniform carbon-14 assumptions, let's accept the fact that this places the cave into Neanderthal times in France.

According to French archaeologists, this represents a real problem because it demonstrates that Neanderthals had a mastery of fire for which they were never credited. But you may say, what about the Bergounioux report to which I just referred? My reply is that if they ignored the jaspers mentioned twice in that report, the fire evidence was ignored, too. Burnt remains of cave bears and other animals were found very deep in the cave. Hélène Valladas believed that because they were found so deep in the cave, there was no question that the burns on these bones were the result of human activity."[22]

The former assistant director of the Musée de l'Homme, Yves Coppens, the man who let me in the first museum, now with the Collège de France in Paris, said, "I think the Neandertal will surprise us, I think he was much more clever than we thought." He also thought that because of the complexity of the artificial structure so far underground, the builders would have had to communicate, implying a much more sophisticated language than previously admitted. [23]

Randall White of NYU in New York City thinks that it would have been impossible for them to have found their way and to have constructed this thing in total darkness. Therefore, he believes, they had some sort of portable light. This advancement was never attributed to Neanderthals. A team now plans on more digging and searching, this time paying special attention to carbon deposits which, according to them, could be the remains of fireplaces.

Based on the aforementioned evidence, it can be confidently said that Neanderthals roasted their meat and bones over fires.

LUMPS OF BONE AND POTATO CHIP JAW ANGLES

The following collection of three Neanderthal lower jaws show conclusive evidence that there were no lumps of bone called exostosis or reinforcement bone due to hard chewing in them, as is present in the pre-contact Eskimos.

They are: La Chapelle-aux-Saints (figure 54), La Ferrassie I (figure 55), and Tabūn C-I (figure 56). Compare these to the pre-contact Eskimos from the Hrdlicka collection of the Smithsonian Institution seen in chapter 28 ("Opening Up A Rusty Gas Can"). You will see in figures 34 and 35 the very lumpy jaws created by the bone's reaction to the extreme forces produced by chewing on tough foods before civilization reached into their igloos and softened their diet.

The bone thickness and roughness of the jaw angles of the lower jaws of Pech de l'Azé (figure 57), Le Moustier (figure 58), and La Ferrassie I (figure 59) are not close to this Eskimo condition. Remember that two of the major chewing muscles attach at the gonial angle. Compare them with the Eskimos' bend in the lower jaw for thickness. You will quickly see that La Ferrassie I and La Chapelle-aux-Saints had potato chip thin jaw angles, and the Eskimos' were very thick and rough for heavy muscle attachment (figure 60). Moreover, the Neanderthal children had thicker angles than the adults. Therefore, the Eskimos were the champs at chewing hard foods. There is no evidence that the Neanderthal diet was as tough and fibrous as that of the early Eskimos although La Ferrassie did use his front teeth to grip objects, from the look of the wear patterns. This is nothing unusual since many modern people hold pens, pencils, needles, pipes, etc., in their front teeth. Lots of my patients break their braces that way.

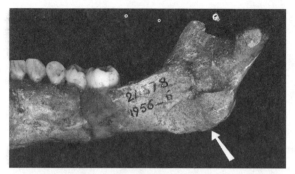

Figure 57. Arrow on thick Pech de l'Azé lower jaw angle.

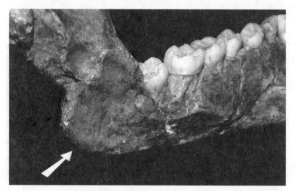

Figure 58. Arrow on thick Le Moustier lower jaw angle.

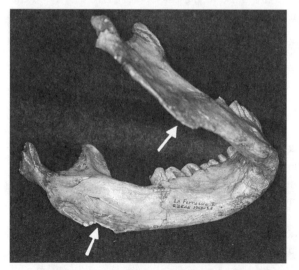

Figure 59. Arrows on La Ferrassie I potato chip lower jaw angles.

There seems to be good evidence here that the muscles didn't even attach at the bend in the jaw in late adulthood, but migrated forward as the teeth moved forward to improve their mechanical advantage, leaving this angle to thin down. Forward positions of the masticatory muscles were found by Carlson and Van Gerven in their study of ancient Nubian skulls, as mentioned earlier in the Research Notes.[24] It is much easier to chew when the muscles are farther away from the fulcrum (the condyle).

This now allows us to look into the wear factor on the teeth, knowing that the Neanderthal's meat was not eaten raw. This is not to say that it was never eaten raw, but in general I think it safe to say that these descendants of Noah did not order their T-bone or porterhouse steaks ultra-rare.

CONFUSING ANALYSES ABOUND

I have made many claims concerning the teeth of Neanderthals. It is now time to report on the examination of the original specimens firsthand. Most creationist efforts in analysis of paleoanthropology, until now, have been merely critical reviews of the work of others, without any original information to back up their critique. It is with this understanding that most of this book was written. I now offer a very crucial section of my research: tooth wear, based on original specimens.

It is totally false and inaccurate to measure teeth that have been extensively worn down on their biting surfaces and on their sides

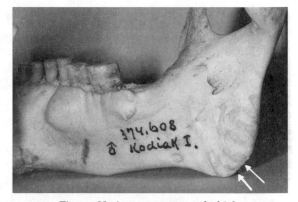

Figure 60. Arrows on rugged, thick Koniag Eskimo lower jaw angle.

and call it a study of the actual size of such teeth. This, unfortunately, has been the practice of various Neanderthal experts for a good many years. One partial exception to this practice has been Erik Trinkaus who studied the Shanidar Neanderthals and described them in great detail. Trinkaus offered a suggestion that his dimensions on the relatively small premolars and molars could be wrong because of interproximal wear (contact wear between teeth in the same row). Having admitted this, he proceeded to treat the tooth dimensions as if they were really accurate and compared them to other studies.[25] Such confusing analysis can be found to abound in the paleoanthropology literature. How can you measure a tooth with such variables as occlusal (biting surface) wear and interproximal wear and use it to compare to teeth that had more or less wear? It tells us little about the original or "real size" of the teeth which can be used for "real comparison purposes." If you ask me, there is too much of this comparing of worn teeth to other worn teeth and then saying that some were smaller than others. It's just another game to confuse the issue. When you want to make a case for big teeth, just look for less interproximal wear.

I discovered that I had placed too much confidence in studies such as these. An important piece of work comparing Neanderthal and early *Homo sapiens'* teeth had attracted my attention in preparation of this book. It had been conducted on the molar teeth of 15 Neanderthal lower jaws in contrast to those of 31 early modern lower jaws, *Homo sapiens sapiens.* From both sides of the lower jaw a total of 90 first and second permanent molars were x-rayed, using ordinary dental x-ray equipment with ordinary dental radiation exposures for each film.[26] This is basically, the same way I x-rayed the Neanderthals, though their x-ray technique sounded strange.[27] Measurements were taken from these radiographs (x-rays) of the internal parts of the tooth — the height of the enamel (outermost layer), width of enamel, etc.[28]

HOW THICK WAS IT WHEN IT WAS NEW?

The problems began when it came time to deal with the crucial factor of tooth function that produced tooth wear and how it affected the thickness or thinness of the outermost coating of the tooth, the enamel.

This represents the most important part of the analysis. You can't talk about the thickness of anything — shoe leather, wood, rubber on a tire, or anything — unless you show how thick it was when it was new. This fact should be elementary. This should not be that tough a question. All one must do is to obtain some unerupted Neanderthal and modern man permanent lower molars and take standardized x-rays of them and measure the enamel. Unerupted teeth have never been used before. Like new shoes in the box or tires on the rack, they're still covered completely by jaw bone and have their original enamel. They will have a completely untouched outer surface, unless they have fallen out of their crypts and laid around for a long time in museum drawers rubbing against other teeth. Fortunately, this is not the case for the precious Neanderthal teeth except for the Gib II lower left second permanent molar. It goes in and out of its crypt. Let us now go back to the experts in the literature and see what they have said about this subject of unworn molars.

In their report, Dr. Zilberman and Dr. Smith said, "Unerupted first permanent mandibular molars were measured for both groups and the results compared with those of erupted first mandibular molars."

What they said was that lower, unused, enamel covered, permanent, unerupted molars from both groups were compared to those that have been chewed on for many years in both groups. In a table they reveal the number of unerupted, unused, unworn Neanderthal teeth to which they compared the 16 erupted, used, and worn-down Neanderthal teeth.

ONE TOOTH

The number of new, unused, unworn Neanderthal lower first permanent molars in this large study is the grand total of one. That's right, one! All of the discriminant analyses, Pearson's correlation coefficient calculations, were based on just one unworn permanent Neanderthal tooth and 16 worn permanent Neanderthal teeth. Based on that tooth, they concluded that enamel height of *Homo sapiens sapiens* was greater than in the Neanderthals.

WELL, I HAVE TWO UNERUPTED NEANDERTHAL PERMANENT TEETH!

This doesn't make me much better than the one tooth scientists, but if they could use one unworn molar, then I could at least make some statements about my two unworn lower first permanent molars.

They gave the mean value of enamel height of 41 erupted, worn lower permanent first molars of *Homo sapiens sapiens (Hss)* as 1.67mm.(SD 0.47). The enamel height for 16 erupted, worn lower permanent first molars of Neanderthals was 1.43mm.(SD 0.34). This represents a difference of 0.24mm between the two sets of worn lower first molars. *Hss* is 0.24 mm thicker in the worn stages of the molar biting surface than Neanderthal. But look at the SDs — they're greater than 0.24mm.

For the four new, unworn, unerupted permanent lower first molars of *Hss* the mean enamel height was given as 2.08mm (SD 0.44). So, 2.08 minus 1.67 equals 0.41mm. That is how much wear there was on the surface of the *Hss* molars over a lifetime. For the one unworn, unerupted, permanent lower first molar of Neanderthal the enamel height was 1.84mm. It was not a mean, since it was only one tooth. So the 1.84 minus 1.43 equals 0.41mm again.

Now the difference from unworn to worn enamel in *Hss* was 0.41mm and the difference from the unworn to the worn enamel in Neanderthals was also 0.41mm. This means that *Homo sapiens sapiens* teeth wore down *exactly the same amount in adulthood* as the Neanderthal molars. This would mean that they had exactly the same sort of diet, living conditions, environment, and enamel composition.

This is a *remarkable result* that no one would have ever believed unless an evolutionist had done the study. I mean Neanderthal teeth wearing at the same rate as early *Hss* teeth. That has important implications. It usually means same type of diet, same tooth mineralization, and same muscle forces. However, does it mean in the same amount of time?

THE SAME TOOTH?

In their list of Neanderthals used in the above mentioned study, the name Gibraltar appears. There is only one Gibraltar child with a mandible that has an unerupted permanent first molar in its lower jaw. It belongs to Gib II. This is probably the unworn, unerupted lower first molar that was used in their study. The tables in the notes supply all the details for two unworn Neanderthal lower unerupted first molars in my studies, plus all of the other molars that I x-rayed.[29] Pech de l'Azé's unerupted lower right first permanent molar is the second unerupted lower permanent first molar.

I wrote to Zilberman concerning this matter and he hasn't answered me in nearly two years, so I assume it was the Gibraltar child's unerupted lower first molar.

We find, when examining my data on this tooth from the Gib II, the lower permanent first molar enamel height is 1.99mm and not 1.84mm. If Zilberman and Smith's *Hss* measurements are correct, it means that modern man is larger by 0.09 mm than the Neanderthal Gib II, not .24mm larger. This is not in itself a big deal. Anyone could be off 0.15 mm. However, when you consider that it was used against a figure for *early Homo sapiens sapiens'* unworn permanent molars of 2.08mm, it is important. First, because since early *Homo sapiens sapiens'* enamel is really thicker by only .09mm instead of .24mm; and second, because the standard deviation for unworn *Hss* enamel height is 0.44mm. The .09mm difference is much closer to the mean than 0.24mm, which was still within one SD. But this makes the difference of little importance. It is well within the one SD of .44mm, almost on the mean.

Using Their Rate of Tooth Enamel Loss*
You Arrive at 125 to 159 years
* Calculated using their dimensions

Their most meaningful measurements concern the amount of wear on the biting surface of the tooth. In their own measurements, to go from Neanderthal unworn to Neanderthal worn, the amount lost is 0.41mm in less than 35 years. Chris Stringer claims less than 10% of Neanderthals were over 35 years of age.[30] The effective wear time would be less than 35 years because you have to allow at least 6 years for the lower first permanent molar to erupt. (This is probably longer than 6 years in Neanderthals.) Twenty-nine years produces an approximate rate of enamel wear of 0.014mm per year.

Now applying this rate of 0.014 mm per year to the amount of surface loss (1.75mm) that I measured from Le Moustier's to La Ferrassie's lower right first permanent molars, produces a total number of years that it would take for this to happen: 125 years. If there was enamel repair it would produce a greater number of years, effectively slowing down the rate of wear. You must remember as you

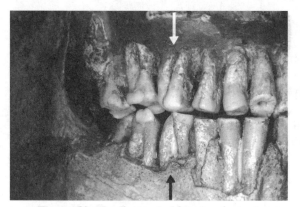

Figure 60a. La Ferrassie I bite (occlusion), displaying lack of enamel on first molars (arrows), worn almost down to roots.

look at figure 60a that there was much more than this biting surface enamel lost in La Ferrassie — the whole crown was gone, which involves dentin and enamel. There is no way of calculating entire crown loss down to the roots, but we are certainly looking at many more years than 125 years of tooth use.

The result is staggering to an evolutionist. It is death to his theory. Now don't forget, I am using the evolutionist's figures for the average Neanderthal life. I do not believe the first permanent molar erupted in the sixth year nor their mean age was 35 years, but for the sake of following their reasoning down a logical course let us assume as they assume.

Let's say LaFerrassie I was one of the older Neanderthals and died at 45 years old. So, 45-6 = 39 years of effective use of that lower first molar. Now with the evolutionists' 0.41 mm loss of enamel in 39 years, the new rate of enamel loss is 0.011mm/year, not .014. This would produce 159 years between Le Moustier and La Ferrassie I.

A Large Difference in Rates

One more fact, please. The Le Moustier unerupted lower third molar on the right side is 13.09mm M-D width. The La Ferrassie I worn lower third molar on the right side is 10.31mm M-D. width. The difference is 2.78 mm. The rate I calculated for Zilberman and Smith's M-D enamel loss rate was 12.30-11.80= 0.5 mm in 17 years (35-18) is 0.03mm/year, or in 22 years (40-18) is 0.02[31] Now I know I can't use lower first molar rates on lower third molars, but let us just compare the two to see if they're close: Moustier to Ferassie in third molar eruption schedule using their logic, 18 years to 35-40 years of age. A 2.78mm/17 years mm loss implies a 0.16 mm/year rate of enamel loss. A 2.78mm/22 years gives us 0.13mm/year. Could the loss of third molar enamel on the front and back of these teeth be five to over six times faster than Zilberman and Smith's Neanderthals? This is one question they really have to answer: the large difference between third molar rates and first molar rates, unless, of course, they are willing to admit to more time. We spoke about high rates of growth versus low rates of growth for Pech to Moustier in head and jaw measurements, and now, using third molar interproximal attrition, we have to decide again on high rates versus low rates. Only this time if you go for the high rates and low ages you are going to have to come up with a good reason for a five to six and one-half times increase in tooth wear rate, from first to third molars, which I think is extremely difficult. The case for older ages is becoming more valid by the minute, or should I say by the millimeter rule.

No More than an Approximation

This 125-159 year figures tell us that even with their estimates of total years of Neanderthal life being used to determine enamel rate loss, it takes more years to loose all the enamel from Moustier to La Ferrassie I than they would accept. However, I do not think that the Neanderthal life was that short; therefore, the enamel loss rate must have been slower. This is where we look again at the statement by one of my *American Journal of Orthodontics* critics when I submitted an article to them.

"Neanderthal age-at-death is also calibrated by dental attrition, which certainly must not have been significantly slower than their growth as these authors imply. Attrition supports the age estimates as traditionally given."[32] But does it?

Whittaker et al. examined 500 Romano-British skulls after using Brothwell's 1963 criteria for aging skulls based on molar wear in pre-Mediaeval British skulls, roughly aligned with age-range given by the pubic symphysis in males. They said this, "It is not possible to assess the age of adults at death with any degree of certainty, especially in the older age groups. Our assignment of ages to each group is therefore no more than an approximation."[33]

"No more than an approximation" at old ages means that the enamel rate of loss could be far off when calculated by means of their standard "age estimates." "No more than approximation" places the entire aging system on sandy soil when delving into the ancient past. There was no greater forensic anthropologist in the world than my old friend Bill Krogman. He is considered the "father" of the science. He said to me one day in his office in Lancaster, "Jack, I think you're on the right track." He took a journal off the shelf behind his desk, where he also kept the Bible that I gave him, and said, "Look at this." He handed me a large yellow journal, the 75th Anniversary Issue of the *American Journal of Roentgenology,* August 1981. He opened it up for me to the Neuhauser Lecture by Dr. Stanley Garn. We looked at a paragraph together entitled, "Continuing Bone Growth Throughout Life." He showed me the paragraph that read, "However, there is good radiographic evidence that such increases in size are real, not illusory, contradicting the notion that bone growth stops as soon as we can legally imbibe."

I asked him, "If people really did live longer in the past, wouldn't we find crania that looked different than ours?" As best as I can remember, he did not reply but just stared at me and said to read the article. I looked at it very quickly but I did notice that Stanley Garn also said this, "Yet many of us have also observed an increase in our hat sizes. If we are political conservatives we blame this on the declining quality of manufactured goods. If we are hypochondriachal, we suspect the onset of Paget disease." [34] We spoke no more of this at the moment because I could see Bill was uncomfortable with this concept, yet he was encouraging me to pursue it.

When you read this section, please try the hat experiment that Garn mentioned, if you are old enough. If not, ask your parents or grandparents about it or just look at some pictures of them when they were in their twenties.

JUST PLAIN BIGGER!

Most scholars will agree that Neanderthal teeth were larger than the teeth of modern people.[35] It is granted that the front to back (MD) and the inside to outside (BL) crown dimensions are not exact representations of cross-sectional areas since crown form is not precisely parallel-sided, but it is what is conventionally used in anthropology.[36] Also, it is a fact that the actual biting surface is smaller than the total cross-sectional area because of the bulging of the borders before interproximal wear reduces them.

Modern children's lower first molars are 112 to 103 square millimeters.[37] Since Gibraltar and Pech and Moustier were in the 150-160 sq.mm range in their lower first molars it means a lot of biting surface on the tooth. Given the amount of enamel folding and the larger-sized biting surfaces, this equates to a lot more total enamel for the Neanderthal child even though it was only very slightly thinner than *Homo sapiens sapiens* but not "statistically significant."[38]

One interesting chart for Neanderthal children's teeth is in an article by A.M. Tillier. She gives the size of the lower left first permanent unerupted molar of Gibraltar II as 11.6mm front to back length and 10.6mm cheek side to tongue side width, which produces a 123 sq. mm cross-sectional area for this tooth.[39] My figure is 152.9 sq. mm.[40]

One more Neanderthal upper molar tooth should be emphasized in this section. It was the one that I found in the small can that was in the cabinet drawer with the La Chapelle-aux-Saints skull in the Musée de l'Homme. I repeat what was written on the top of the little can, "Bouffia de la Chapelle aux Saints." The tooth is very likely an upper permanent first molar but there is a slight possibility it could be an upper second molar. The ruler over the crown is divided into millimeters. The view in figure 61 is one that allows visualization of the buccal and lingual surfaces and the buccal and lingual roots. The lingual root is the shorter one. The enamel is worn heavily on its biting surface and mesial and distal surfaces. The two surfaces you see are curved similar to unworn surfaces right to the edges of the biting surface. This is the bucco-lingual measurement. So, while it is essentially a much-used tooth, this radiograph provides a good view to compare to modern upper molar teeth in this one dimension. It measures 14.53 mm including a 1% reduction for magnification. This was measured by the method described in the notes and not the plastic ruler in the illustration. This is a huge tooth. The modern norm for this B-L width given by the University of Michigan Standards for male upper first molars is 10.88mm, and 9.96mm upper second molar. The standard deviations are .72 mm for first molars and 1.34mm for

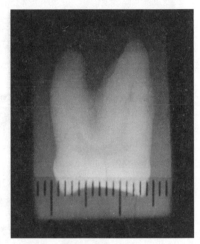

Figure 61. Huge La Chapelle-aux-Saints upper molar found in burial cave.

second molars.[41] This molar is five standard deviations from the modern male first molar norm and almost three and one-half standard deviations from the second molar norm. That's probably why it was in the can. The modern female norms are both smaller.

Trinkaus reports on the Shanidar Neanderthal B-L dimension in first, second, and third upper molar widths as all in the 11.6 -13.4 mm range.[42]

The size reduction that modern humans have experienced represents devolution again and a downward slide, not just a little bend in a branch of the evolutionary bush. Lavelle et al. wrote that there was a strong genetic component in the development of crown size and cusps, and that this magnitude was partly subject to X-linked inheritance.[43] This, again, is typical of reduction and loss, characteristic of the fossil record. This downward trend should provide a new lens with which to view fossils.

BULL-LIKE TEETH

The last consideration in the area of teeth and their longevity should be the strange shape of the permanent and primary molars. In the notes covering the three Neanderthal children I go into some detail about the nature of the primary molars. Undoubtedly they were built to last a long time. In our modern children, primary molars usually are cast aside and out of the mouth by the time the child is 12 years old. Some second primary molars can be retained a few more years but in my experience all of the primary teeth are usually gone in girls by 12 and boys by around 13. Occasionally you will see retained primary teeth where there is no permanent tooth to take its place or if the permanent tooth has taken an inappropriate path of eruption. However, this is not the norm. Some can even last into the late twenties.

In the Neanderthal children that I've seen, there are many evidences for protracted use of the primary teeth and delayed primary dental loss.[44] In the adults there is evidence of protracted use as was seen in the previous discussion on the wear of the enamel.

There is another system in the human tooth which increases the longevity of that tooth or set of teeth. It is the process of laying down reparative or defense dentin.[45] It is also called adventitious secondary dentine.[46] Immediately underneath the enamel layer exists the main substance of the tooth, which is the dentin. It surrounds the pulp or nerve area and adds bulk to the tooth. It is also an insulator for the contents of the pulp. It is this function of pulp protection that I would like to discuss. Dentin, sometimes called dentine, is approximately 65-75% inorganic and 25-35% organic material and water by weight[47]. The inorganic part is the mineral portion. Technically, these are calcium phosphates in a crystalline form called apatites, like enamel but shorter, resembling the crystals of bone.[48]

Contrast this to the enamel which is 96-97% inorganic mineral crystals, 0.4-0.9% organic protein, and 2.1-3.6% water by weight.[49] Obviously, dentin is much softer and filled with tubules that contain fluid and odontoblast processes.[50] This fact is discovered immediately in dental school when you penetrate your first real tooth in someone's mouth with a high-speed, water-spray hand piece and diamond or carbide bur (drill) without local anesthetic. You peel away the enamel carefully with hand and finger pressure. However, when you hit dentin two things happen: one, the sensitivity of the tooth heightens dramatically; and two, you have to let up on the pressure of your touch on the hand piece, otherwise you'll be seeing blood real fast. Which means you hit the pulp, or the "nerve," to the layman. This you don't want to do.

The mediators of the sensitivity in the dentin are tiny tubules thinner in diameter than a red blood cell. When these are cut you feel it because fluid moves inside them (hydrodynamic theory) and communicates with the nerve fibers of the pulp.[51] I'm sure that some of you who are reading this have had a "memorable" experience in the dental chair similar to this and the mere mention of it brings on a cold sweat.

What does all this have to do with Neanderthals' teeth? Well, this cushion-like dentin protects the pulp when the tooth is attacked by wear or decay. It does so by adding more layers of itself on the inside of the pulp wall that corresponds to the side or top of the tooth where the injury occurred. This additional dentin in response to irritation is called reparative dentin. It is laid down mainly over the pulp in molars and in the front teeth it happens on the lingual and labial walls in response to enamel wear.[52] This happens in all healthy teeth. It is a reaction to the injury of the tooth surface in cases of decay or just plain old wear and tear.

For instance, when wear on a molar biting surface removes the overlying enamel and exposes the dentin to the oral environment, some dentinal tubules become exposed that connect right down to the nerves of the tooth. The pulp actually has to retreat a little as cells migrate in from the deep regions of the pulp and the reparative dentin builds up in that space. This happens so the reparative dentin can cover up the exposed tubules, and in itself has very few tubules.

A pulp in a taurodont or bull-like molar can retreat farther than a pulp in a normal modern molar. This fact is caused by the presence of a very large pulp chamber inside the large body (crown) of the molar. Because of the larger body the roots are shorter (see figures 62 and 63). This has nothing to do with molars in bulls. It is called taurodont because it has a large body and short legs and there-fore is bull-like.

If the roots were longer the pulp could not retreat as far because the dividing

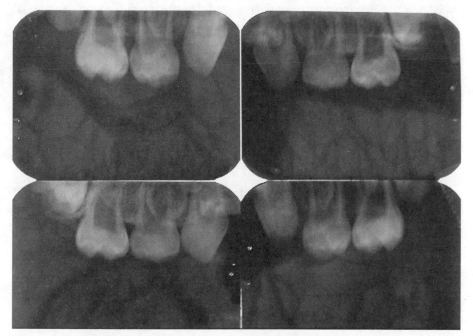

Figure 62. Primary (baby) taurodont molars, Pech de l'Azé.

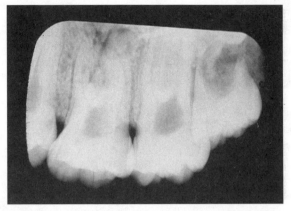

Figure 63. Upper taurodont molars, Le Moustier.

point in the root structure would be closer to the body. Since it is low-down in the lower jaw or high-up in the upper jaw, the pulp can retreat quite far as reparative dentin builds up. This means the taurodont tooth will last longer than the normal "cynodont" tooth which, by the way, means "dog-like."

Hillson said taurodonts were also found in modern man but it was a rare variant. Pinborg found it in less than 0.1% of modern humans.[53] Stringer thought the shape of these roots is produced by "a delayed turning-in of the base of the roots" during their formation. He also thought this feature was related to the extreme wear endured by Neanderthal teeth, because teeth with undivided roots will maintain a whole chewing surface even when worn past the crown into the unseparated root area.[54]

Notice what Stringer thought about the delayed turning in of the roots. Our roots today, for the most part, are not delayed. This also points to a slower dental maturation in line with a slower skeletal one.

Finally, a taurodont molar will resist gum (gingival) recession better than a modern tooth merely because of its size and shape. Since the division between the roots, called the "furcation," is much farther away from cemento-enamel junction (crown-root), and hence the original gingival (gum) margin, it takes longer for gum and bone recession to reach this point. As the Neanderthals aged their gum margins probably receded like ours do now. Although it also was slower than modern gum recession, it also had a longer distance to traverse in order to reach the "furcation." Any periodontist can tell you that once this point is reached, the tooth is quickly doomed to extinction because of food and plaque getting stuck in between the roots and more infection and rapid bone loss from there, if there is no periodontal treatment.

Chapter 32

Good Old Pinocchio

The Italian journalist Carlo Lorenzini (1826-1890), otherwise known as Carlo Collodi, or Disney illustrator Arthur Babbitt (1907-1992) may not have heard of the long-nosed people of antiquity when Pinocchio was created for modern children's pleasure. Nevertheless, we all remember Pinocchio's nose grew longer and longer with every falsehood he told. The idea of a nose growing in response to some moral character flaw was frightening to me as a child and I suppose the same thought went through other children's minds, too. What I didn't know, and I guess most people still don't realize, is that the nose does become longer with age. From the previous aging soft tissue facial growth descriptions it may also be said with confidence that the nose does grow in old age and it has nothing to do with how much a person lies, "a la Pinocchio," but it has everything to do with how long a person lives. From the caves of France comes evidence that ancient men knew this was happening to them and wanted to document it.

From the shelter called "Cave" Taillebourg near the village Angles-sur-l'Anglin, Vienne, France, comes a stone carving from a wall, or perhaps it was found detached, but it now

Figure 64. Long-nosed rock sculpture "Cave"
Taillebourg near the village Angles-sur-l'Anglin,
Vienne, France (Museum of Saint-Germain-en-Laye).

is on exhibit in the Museum of Saint-Germain-en-Laye (figure 64). I saw this carving in August of 1982. It is a carving of a man who has an elongated, up-turned nose and a slightly enlarged brow ridge. The tip of the nose is gone. It appears to have been broken off, either by chance or perhaps in fear that it might create an impression that the museum people did not want to convey. However, the up-turned angle of this man's nose is very similar to the nasal bone angle-forehead angle of La Chapelle-aux-Saints. Of course, due to the standard inter-pretation, the credit for this carving is given to people of the Magdalenian cul-tural stage of development of the Upper Paleolithic (12-17 thousand years ago).[1] This, if true, would illustrate one of the first "portrait sittings" ever recorded in history: a Cro-Magnon sculptor carving a Neanderthal man. This would be very similar to a Cro-Magnon dentist carving the La Chapelle-aux-Saints tooth.

Ann Sieveking said that there was "another portrait from this shelter which has a long, pointed nose." So there are two examples of this nasal phenomena in one place.[2]

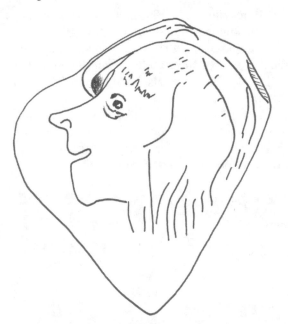

Figure 65. Drawing of a small plaquette from La Marche, Vienne, France (Museum of Saint-Germain-en-Laye). Long nose and brow ridges are emphasized.

A third example of a long-nosed individual is seen in figure 65. I drew this in pen-cil from the original small flat stone engraving in the Mu-seum of Saint-Germain-en-Laye. It represents a man with an up-turned, long, pointed nose which is very similar to the one from the "Cave" Taillebourg at Angles-sur-l'Anglin. This one also comes from a small cave in the same area of France, Vienne. It is from a cave called La Marche on the right bank of a stream near a small mill, Lussac les Châteaux, 35 km. SE of Poitiers. It has been attributed to the Middle Magdalenian stage in the same range as the "man from Angles." Notice that the forehead exhibits a series of elevations. Could these be the way that the artist was portraying future growth of the brow ridges and frontal area?

In the Bernifal cave we saw another long-nosed man. Visible on a wall is the entire left side of this full-sized man who has a Cossack-type hat, a full beard, and a long nose. He is looking down and his left shoulder is outlined very sharply. His hat is reminiscent of the top-knot hats of the Easter Island statues.

There probably are many more long-nosed rock carvings of man that have been placed on remote shelves and in multiple cabinets of the museums of Europe that could testify to this same prolongation of nasal growth. Suffice it to say that if you should ever see one you'll know what it means. Our projections into old age in figure 29 shows that we would have the same elongated noses if we lived beyond 200 years. There may be a difference in the angulation of the nasal bones and cartilage because their noses protruded pretty much straight forward, whereas our projection noses seem to droop downward.

Were these long-nosed peoples Neanderthals? Pat Shipman summarized Erik Trinkaus' thoughts concerning the Neanderthal face: ". . . the overall forward thrust of the middle region of the face — an arrangement described by a later scholar, Erik Trinkaus, as looking as if a modern human face, made of rubber, had been grabbed by the nose and pulled forward."[3] Chris Stringer also thought the Neanderthal nose was long and wide and stuck out nearly horizontally.[4] Both Stringer's and Trinkaus' definition of Neanderthal noses rules out that these long-nosed peoples in the cave portraits were Upper Paleolithic peoples or modern men. They had to be Neanderthals, based on the important fact that modern peoples don't have horizontal noses. I doubt if a Neanderthal sat and had his portrait carved by a Cro-Magnon in France. That would mean he not only had his tooth facets trimmed by the Cro-Magnon dentist but went to their art studios as well. If we keep up this line of thought we could believe in the Wizard of Oz. As long as we're discussing noses, let's look at what falls into our noses when we are really sorrowful.

Figure 66 is a lateral view of La Chapelle-aux-Saints. Look at the angle that those broken nasal bones jut out from his face. He had a really long "schnozzola," as Jimmy Durante used to call it.

REAL PEOPLE, REAL TEARS

It has been brought to my attention that there have been some claims that Neanderthals were not human because they could not cry, because they had no tear ducts.[5] These claims were based on reports by Schwartz and Tattersall in

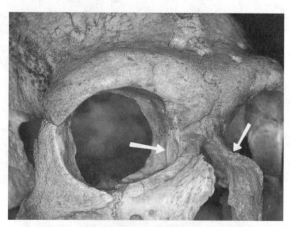

Figure 66. Arrows on ski-jump nose and teardrop-shaped nasolacrimal groove of La Chapelle-aux-Saints.

1996 that there was a "lack of ossified roof over the lacrimal groove."[6] This means that they found no real tear duct canal from the eye to the nose in two Neanderthal children (Engis and Roc de Marsal). The purpose of this paper was to prove that Neanderthals were not real people like us and therefore a different species, *Homo neanderthalensis*.

I also studied and photographed the Engis child in Belgium in 1982 as described earlier. It is my opinion that the uncovered lacrimal duct in the frontal process of the maxilla is incomplete because this section of bone is only a fragment and the rest has been broken off.

Now look at figure 67, the side view of a modern skull. In the anterior or front corner of the right eye socket there is a large groove (nasolacrimal groove, also called the lacrimal groove). It is a vertical depression in the inside wall of the socket which is bounded by a front and back crest. This is the place where the lacrimal sac sits in the eye socket. Here is where the ducts from the lacrimal gland drain. It is almost "tear-shaped."

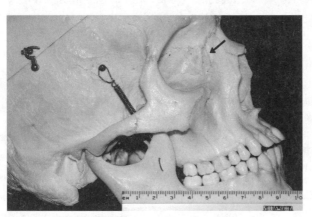

Figure 67. Arrows on teardrop-shaped nasolacrimal groove in modern male skull.

Tears originate higher up in the eye. The lacrimal or tear gland "lies under the shelter of the bone forming the upper and outer part of the wall of the eye socket. The tears, after flowing over the surface of the eye, are drained from it's inner angle into the nose by these small tubes, the lacrimal ducts."[7] The lacrimal sac sits in this large groove with a hole at the bottom of it and opens into the nasolacrimal duct that sends tears into your nose via the membranous duct in this bony canal. That is why we usually have to blow our nose after we cry.

Figure 66 is a side view of the right eye socket, brow ridges and nose of La Chapelle-aux-Saints. You have already examined this photo for angle of the nasal bones; now look at where the other arrow is pointing. It is a nasolacrimal groove. It was verified by an ophthalmologist, Joseph Calkins M.D., a friend of mine from Pennsylvania. It means La Chapelle cried.

There is no reason for all those dire conclusions by Ross about no tears and Neanderthals being another species.[8]

From this firm data it has to be concluded that Neanderthals were not only human and cried, but uniquely slow-developing and long-lived humans.

WORRIED AND WRESTLING AT THAT AGE?

Did you ever wonder why Abraham lied about his relationship to his wife to the King of Gerar? It was definitely because of her beauty. Her beauty? Wasn't she supposed to be a really old woman? Backtrack a little now to recall the earlier words of Abraham when he first took her to Egypt and asked her to lie to Pharaoh about their relationship.

Abram said to his wife in Egypt, "I know what a beautiful woman you are. When the Egyptians see you, they will say, 'This is his wife.' Then they will kill me but will let you live. Say you are my sister" (Gen. 12:11-13). So she did that and eventually Pharaoh found out the truth through the plagues God produced. He finally had to let her go. However, it is noteworthy here to see Sarai through the eyes of the Egyptians: "The Egyptians saw that she was a very beautiful woman" (Gen. 12:14). Therefore, it wasn't only Abraham's opinion expressed in this scene but also that of the Egyptians.

Did the fact ever strike you as strange that a husband would have to worry about someone killing him for his wife's beauty when she was 90 years old? Her age is revealed in Genesis 17 after God gave Sarai the name "Sarah" and Abram, "Abraham," God declared that He would give her a son and that she would be blessed. "Abraham fell face down; he laughed and said to himself, "Will a son be born to a man a hundred years old? Will Sarah bear a child at the age of ninety?" (Gen. 17:17). Later on in Genesis 20, Abraham and Sarah played the same brother-sister role before the King of Gerar after the destruction of Sodom and Gommorah and just before the birth of Isaac.

Now this is not a modern, wealthy woman or movie star who has had numerous face-lifts, tummy-tucks, and breast implants to spruce her up a bit. She had no sun-blocker cream, or cool "shades." This is a 90-year-old wife of a desert nomad, who had been exposed to the harsh winds, blowing sand, and blistering sun of the wilderness.

Abraham was a wealthy patriarch and a man of God to be true, but there were no advanced medical treatments available for Sarah to be transformed into a "beautiful woman" at that time in history. We are not discussing "inner beauty" either. Abraham's concern was genuine because Sarah probably looked like a modern woman in her fifties or even early sixties. You might ask why? After reading this whole book it should be evident that she probably looked much younger than her 90 years because she was aging slower than the 90 year old of modern day.

Sarah died at the age of 127 (Gen. 23:1). At the time of the angelic visitation near the great trees of Mamre, Sarah also laughed about having a baby because she was past the age of childbearing (Gen. 18:12). This stage of life, the menopause, usually comes to women in our day at 48-59 years of age, with the average age being 53.2 years.[9] Whatever the menopausal age was in ancient Palestine, we can be sure it was a bit later than it is today. Sarah laughed because she was past that age. We have no idea of what that age could have been, but an average estimate of perhaps 65-70 years could be close.

A recent study in the Department of Obstetrics and Gynecology, Brigham and Women's Hospital in Boston, Massachusetts, identified 344 women who had their last menstrual period and had experienced early menopause at the average age of 42.2 years. They matched them up with 344 women who went through menopause later than 46 years and tried to find the cause of "early menopause." Their conclusion was, "Although preferential recall of family history by women with early menopause could contribute to the association between family history and early menopause observed in this study, a genetic factor is also plausible including partial deletions of the X chromosome compatible with the deficiency of male siblings in cases with family history of early menopause." [10] In another study of the same 344 woman it was found that they were more likely to have had menarche at or before age 11.[11] In South Carolina, Schwartz et al. found 131 women who were called "fragile X carriers." They identified a strong genetic factor in early menopause.[12]

Abraham did one other feat of strength after he had passed his one-hundredth birthday that was very unusual for a man of his age. Isaac was a grown boy when he took him to the mountain for the sacrifice. Abraham wrestled a ram with long curly horns out of a thicket after God told him not to harm his son Isaac (Gen. 22:13). This is a rather remarkable feat for a man over 100. He untangled this ram, which was probably not too happy to be caught in such circumstances, and threw him down like a rodeo cowboy on top of a pile of wood to kill and offer as a burnt sacrifice. How many 100-plus men do you know that can do this?

A very sad day came for Abraham when he buried this beautiful woman who had been his dear wife for many years. The account in Genesis tells us that he purchased a cave, the cave of Machpelah in Hebron to bury Sarah (Gen. 23:19). We also know that Abraham, Isaac and Rebekah, Jacob and Leah, were all buried in the same cave (Gen. 49:31; 50:13). This obviously was a custom of the early peoples of this land, the patriarchs. Here in the cave of Macpelah six people were buried — Abraham, age 175 (Gen. 25:7); Isaac, age 180 (Gen. 35:28); and Jacob (Israel), age 147 (Gen. 47:28). This was the usual custom.

THE BIG FOREHEADS OF SHINAR

As was previously discussed, the area between the Tigris and Euphrates Rivers was settled immediately post-flood (Tower of Babel period), supposedly around 3000 B.C. by a group of people known to archaeologists as the "Sumerians." They are also known in the Bible as the people of the land of "Shinar" (Gen. 10:10).

Samuel Noah Kramer, former University of Pennsylvania Cuneiform Scholar, has written about tablets dating from the first half of the second millennium B.C. which deal directly with the Sumerian school system. He wrote, "As already noted, we have at our disposal quite a number of essays relating to education which the ancient schoolmen themselves prepared for the edification of their students, and these give a graphic and vivid picture of various aspects of school life, including the inter-relationships between faculty, students, parents, and undergraduates." He described these essays. They are essays one through four and are as follows.

In the first essay a teacher speaks to his student. "Thus, when you put a kindly hand on the . . . of the teacher, (and) on the forehead of the "big brother," then(?) your young comrades will show you favor." Therefore, big brothers seem to be teachers.

In the fourth essay, which is an argument between two older men, one a scribe and the other an "ugula" which is like a superintendent of a large estate, they are speaking about their old school days. This paragraph is found in the series of fragments from a dozen tablets. "Attend him (therefore) before the sun rises (and) before the night cools; do not turn back the pleasure of being by the side of the "big brother"; having come close to the "big foreheads," your words will be honored." It seems from this piece that the big brothers have big foreheads that distinguish them from others.

Also from essay four is: "He (the "big brother") vaunted not his knowledge, his words are restrained — had he vaunted his knowledge, eyes would pop." The big brothers are also full of wisdom and knowledge. In the same essay is, "He (the "big brother") did not turn back a second time . . . the fastened eyes . . . he bound about your neck a garland (?) of man's courtesy and respect(?)" He was one who gave rewards for good work.

Finally, in essay three, we find a father exhorting his son to go to school and take advantage of the benefits there. The father said, "You who wander about in the public square, would you achieve success? Then seek out the first generations. Go to school, it will be of benefit to you. My son, seek out the first generations, inquire of them."[13]

Our conclusion as to the identity of the big brothers must necessarily be that they had big foreheads, wisdom, and were the first generations. Samuel Noah Kramer never came to this conclusion, but having the anatomical knowledge of the ancient peoples of Genesis 10 and 11, we have new information that makes his work on these early tablets more understandable.

CAVE DISCOVERIES IN ISRAEL

The caves in Mt. Carmel have yielded a large group of human remains from the so-called Paleolithic age. The B levels of the cave of the kids, Mugharet es-Skhūl, and the C level of the larger "oven" cave, Mugharet et-Tabūn, yielded the principle finds. They were excavated between 1929-1934 by a team led by D.A.E. Garrod of the British School of Archaeology in Jerusalem and T. McCown of the American School. The fauna (animal bones) recovered in the Skhūl cave deposit at the B levels were almost identical to those recovered in Level C of the Tabūn cave. The stone tools were almost indistinguishable in their workmanship.[14] These discoveries led the original researchers to believe the two levels were contemporaneous. Since this time there has been much dispute on the subject because the Skhūl remains are essentially modern while the Tabūn remains are very archaic and Neanderthal-like. In western Europe Neanderthals always preceded modern humans, but not here. They were either contemporary or Tabūn came second.

THE B LEVEL

From the B (B1 and B2) level of es-Skhūl, most important of all the levels, they uncovered the remains of at least ten men, women, and children. The skeletal remains at Skhūl were numbered by Roman numerals I through X and some are very fragmentary. The following were studied and x-rayed by me in the Rockefeller Museum (Jerusalem) and the Peabody Museum (Harvard University): Skhūl I, II, V, VI, VII, VIII.

The partial lower jaw of Skhūl I came from a child, because of the absence of erupted permanent teeth. It has been reconstructed with artificial material in the area of the chin and lower front teeth. Tillier reported that the bone of this lower jaw was more robust (stronger, thicker) than the modern child's lower jaw at the same age (approximately four years) and that the unerupted permanent first molar has the heavy enamel folding pattern of Neanderthals.[15] I disagree on the jaw, and describe this lower jaw as essentially modern except for the permanent first molar crown form.

We have spent most of this entire book discussing why modern children are aging much faster than children of just a few hundred years ago.[16] Therefore, we must be aware that the first molar which erupts in modern children around the age of six years could not possibly have done so in ancient children. It is, therefore, reasonable to assume that Skhūl I, like Pech and Le Moustier, was older than the age of four assigned by Tillier and the discoverers McCown and Keith.[17]

I believe that this child was not a Neanderthal but most likely in the group devolved from Neanderthals called modern man *(Homo sapiens)* on the basis of the form (cynodont) of its primary second molar. Since all Neanderthal children had taurodont primary molars that did not exfoliate (fall out) until their late twenties and early thirties, this primary molar does not qualify as Neanderthal, although the heavy folding of the biting surface enamel of the lower permanent first molar does appear to be a characteristic similar to all Neanderthal adult molars. This combination presents a seemingly inexplicable problem. However, it does have a solution when you view it from a biblical perspective and not an evolutionary one.

Skhūl I child was on the way towards an earlier maturation than his parents had experienced. He or she showed this devolved trait by the shape of the baby molar tooth and roots. However, since he or she still bore the Neanderthal permanent molar folded enamel, the specimen represents a mosaic of ancient and modern traits. Its skull was immature in development and had a modern shape, also. There was no brow ridge development or sinus enlargement between the eyes at

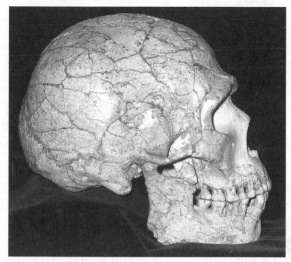

Figure 68. Skhūl V adult male from
Mt. Carmel, Israel.

the root of the nose.

The B level yielded another important discovery, an adult male — the Skhūl V remains (see figure 68). The skull and lower jaw had some long bones and ribs from the rest of the skeleton associated with it, but it is the skull which is the most important part. It is mostly complete with the exception of the bones of the nose and cheeks and some of the upper jaw. This has all been filled in with an artificial plastic-like material. The shape of the skull (cranium) is modern in most parts with the exception of a slightly elevated brow ridge, which in this case could be exaggerated. It has a chin on its lower jaw. All its teeth are worn down but have modern root-form. The general shape of the crowns of the teeth is the same as modern man with the exception of the upper third molars. These teeth have not lost their fourth cusp (hypocone) as have the majority of modern man's upper third molars.[18] So, in this instance, they are not as devolved as modern man. The upper permanent incisors have lost their accessory ridges for strength and durability and the lower molars have lost their taurodont (bull-like) form of the Neanderthal type. The Skhūl V upper molars show some elongation of the crowns. This analysis of Skhūl V again presents a mosaic of traits that reveal a man who was buried in a cave in Palestine supposedly 80,000-100,000 years ago, according to the latest determination.[19] However, an earlier study had placed Level B at a dating range of 33,000 to 55,000 years BP.[20]

The Skhūl V cranium shows traces of red ochre on it. It also appears as if an attempt was made to minimize this effect because the filling material used to cement and build up the missing portions has been flecked with a rust-brownish red dye. Red ochre, as you know, is an iron oxide called hematite and is mainly known from the Mesopotamian civilizations allegedly 2000-4000 B.C.[21] No record of it has been reported from a burial professedly this old. In European caves it has been found on the walls and in handprints on those walls. Remember, I mentioned before that I found this red ochre power on the lower jaw of La Ferrassie I, a Neanderthal adult from France, but I didn't tell you that he was buried in a nearly identical pose as the Skhūl V skeleton. He was on his back, head turned to the left (Skhūl V head more upright and chin on chest), legs tightly flexed, La

Ferrassie's knees not as high up as Skhūl V but both had their knees pointing to the right.[22] Similar burial customs could mean tribal relationships.

In the arms of Skhūl V was found a large jaw bone of a wild boar.[23] We remember that Samson used a jaw bone of a donkey as a lethal weapon to fight against the Philistines in this same land (Judg. 15:15-16). Could this wild boar jaw bone have been used in the same way during the life of Skhūl V, and buried with him as a remembrance of his fighting skill?

THE OLD NEANDERTHAL WOMAN

From the "cave of the oven" a skeleton of an old Neanderthal woman was recovered from the C layer. It is called Tabūn C-I (see figure 69). I studied the

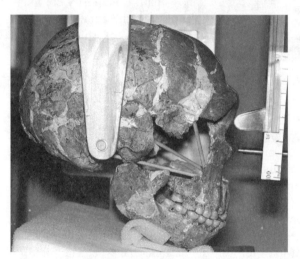

skull and lower jaw of this woman in the British Museum in London. I also x-rayed other loose Tabūn teeth from Series III like n-7456 at the Peabody Museum, Harvard University. Tabūn C-I skull and lower jaw had Neanderthal features in the size of the eye sockets, nasal opening, slanted cheek bones, shape of head, taurodont molars, and apparent chinlessness. The size of the head indicated it was a female in that it was smaller than the Neanderthal norm for overall cranial capacity.

Figure 69. Tabūn C-I female adult from Mt. Carmel, Israel.

Level C was dated in 1963 by radiocarbon at 40,900 B.P. ±1,000 years,[24] in 1979 by sediment studies at 51,000 years,[25] by amino acid testing in 1982 at 51 thousand years,[26] and in 1982 again at 50-60 thousand years.[27] Identical stone tools were found in Layer C of Tabūn as were found in Layers B1 and B2 of the Skhūl cave. The faunal (animal) remains were essentially the same.[28] Hippopotamuses were found in both caves.[29] Some have suggested their presence at Lake Kinneret but I would also think that the post-flood period that these layers comprise implies that there may have been marshes closer than 60 km. The conclusion of the 1980s was that these levels B of Skhūl and C of Tabūn were contemporaneous. Now it is thought from new dating techniques which the experts assure us are better (How do they really know?) that Tabūn C level could be as much as 90 to 200 thousand years old.[30]

This new date for Tabūn doesn't mean that they weren't contemporaneous but it does cast cold water on the idea. Why is this a problem for them? Simply because the older evolutionists like McCown and Keith would have liked to see a nice passage of archaic Neanderthal features into a modern *Homo sapiens* to make evolution smooth and have what is now called regional continuity. They believed the Mt. Carmel caves encompassed a single population in the throes of evolutionary change.[31] I emphasize the word "now" because the multi-regional evolution paleoanthropologists are the new version of these older evolutionists. They would expect that this phenomenon happened all over the world with all moderns going through a Neanderthal "phase" although not necessarily at the same time. This change was dependent upon a balance of gene flow between populations, natural selection, and genetic drift.[32]

Opponents of this theory, like Vandermeerch, thought there was too little time available to presume a direct and very fast evolutionary transition from Neanderthal to modern forms in the Middle East.[33] Dobzhansky wrote an addendum to his 1963 article in Washburn's book, "This article was concluded and sent to the publisher before the appearance of *The Origin of Races* by C.S. Coon. Dr. Coon and I are in agreement that the now-living polytypic species, *Homo Sapiens,* is descended from the single polytypic *Homo erectus* of the mid-Pleistocene. Dr. Coon has, however, chosen to believe that *H. erectus* was transformed into *H. Sapiens* not once but five times, and that this transformation occurred much earlier in some places than others. This belief, which has made Dr. Coon's work attractive to racist pamphleteers, is not supported by conclusive evidence nor plausible theoretical grounds."[34]

Of course, Dr. Coon's work became the intellectual basis of some races being "more evolved" than others. Racism is supported by this version of evolution, but man's autonomy from God is intellectually supported by the entire science of evolution. This knowledge does not falsify the bushes or trees of evolution growing like weeds on our earth. However, when society consumed the deadly fruit of its branches, mankind's morality sank deeper because the Bible was mythologized. I must add that F.C. Howell was an early opponent of the Neanderthal phase in 1957.

Because of Neanderthal skulls that were discovered in Israel's caves at much later dates, a general trend away from the multi-regional theory in Israel began and some paleoanthropologists believed that they had to come up with a replacement theory that allowed for abrupt changes in the fossil layers from modern to Neanderthal or vice versa. Replacement theory allowed modern men to migrate into an area and replace Neanderthals without mating or Neanderthals to wander in after moderns had been there for many years and settle at a later date. No major evolution had to take place in the area for this to be true. One population replaces another.

Now, the reason for this strange logic is because two other rather obvious Neanderthal discoveries higher up in the sedimentary levels and more recent in time made it necessary for the them to squirm out from under these uncomfortable facts.

In 1961 a Japanese team digging in a cave in the Wadi Amud about 50 km from Mt. Carmel, near the Sea of Galilee, discovered a shattered Neanderthal adult skeleton so high up in the stratigraphy that it had Upper Paleolithic artifacts and even pottery associated with it.[35] Obviously, Amud I (see figure 70 in color insert section) was a recent Neanderthal. There was no way anyone could admit that Amud I was really associated with pottery and Upper Paleolithic artifacts, so they applied the rule that I described previously. What to do when finding something too archaic, too shallow — just say it came from a lower level, and they did. The oldest dates they could get on this level were approximately 27 to 28 thousand years BP. The youngest were radiocarbon dates of 5,710 years B.P. ±80. Day said this latter date was "too young." He blamed contamination by higher-up, more modern carbon.[36] Amud I was a man of about six feet tall with a cranial capacity (brain size) of 1740 ml/cc in volume,[37] a huge skull by modern standards. Consider that modern men and women average between 1200 and 1500 ml/cc. New dating revisions had to be found for this dilemma and they did come up with a new date: 40-50,000 years B.P. which was taken from ESR (Electron Spin Resonance) on a mammal tooth.[38] I studied and x-rayed this fossil skull and cranium and found it to be very fragmentary and pieced together with great liberty and imagination, although in general the shape and size are almost accurate. Figure 71 presents a cephalometric x-ray of the Amud I skull.[39]

The Kebara II skeleton, also found on Mt. Carmel, presented similar problems with more recent dating than Skhūl and Tabūn. He was a full-fledged Neanderthal found in 1983 with modern stone tools. Kebara II had the

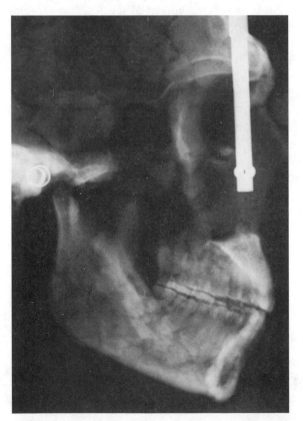

Figure 71. Lateral cephalometric x-ray of Amud I.

only hyoid bone ever found for a Neanderthal and the most complete hip bones.[40] The hyoid bone is a floating bone in the neck connected only by muscles and connective tissues to the lower jaw above and structures below. It is essential for speech and the Kebara hyoid was that of a normal human.

The explanations of regional continuity don't fit the data because the moderns preceded the ancients and it has to be reversed for continuity to be true. The replacement theory merely brings in modern man from Africa at an early date and establishes the presence of two separate species of man in Israel contemporaneously. No mating or genetic mixing of these groups is supposed to have taken place. That is practically impossible. Did they fight? I see no way they could not

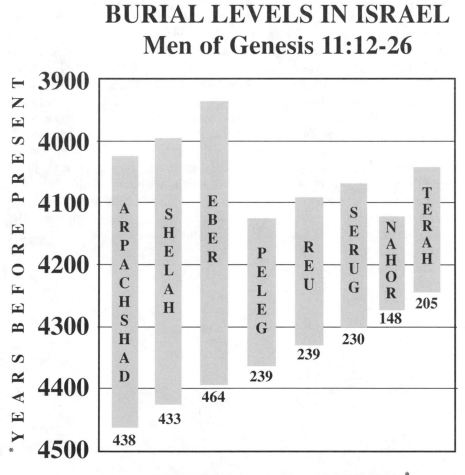

BURIAL LEVELS IN ISRAEL
Men of Genesis 11:12-26

FLOOD circa 4459 BP*
(FLOOD DATE FOR COMPARISON PURPOSES ONLY)

Figure 72.

have fought if this truly is the right theory. Observe the Middle East conflict today.

In conclusion, it should be firmly stated that the Bible gives us the best explanation for the presence of modern skeletons buried beneath more archaic or Neanderthal skeletons. In line with the evidence presented above, the more archaic the skull and lower jaw, the older it is. The more modern-appearing skulls and their jaws are usually younger in age at death. There were also genetic differences. These are a necessary ingredient to the equation since the fall extracted its price. Let me emphasize that the loss of genetic code or the silencing or sequence re-arrangement of the DNA does not mean that Neanderthals like Amud I, Kebara II, and Tabūn C-I were not human. They were more vital humans, they lived longer. The only explanation that makes sense is the following.

The older men of Genesis 11 (over 400 years) — Arpachshad, Shelah, and Eber — should all have been buried at higher levels (more recent) than the younger men (around 200 years) — Peleg, Rue, Serug, and Terah. This burial arrangement would put men with very aged Neanderthal-like features at higher levels and later dates in time than the earlier more modern-appearing men. Figure 72 gives the ages and dates and relative burial levels of these men from Genesis 11 in the line of Shem. As you can see from the chart in figure 72, when the men's lives are plotted from the time of the flood over close to a 600-year period, their birth and death dates produce a high-low bar graph. The flood date given here is only for comparison purposes and is not meant to be exact. The more modern-like men could very well be classified as *Homo sapiens sapiens* (like Skhūl V) while the very aged ones (like Amud and Tabūn, a woman) could be termed Neanderthals. It would appear as if more than one species of man lived at the same period of time, with the modern ones preceding the more archaic ones. The biblical record truly is the best guide for studying the ancient burials of Israel.[41]

Chapter 33

Like a Garment

A ltamira, the closed cave described in chapter 25, had radon levels 40 times the pediatrician's recommendation for action level in a home. When we purchased our first home in 1966 there was not a mention of radon testing by real estate brokers or state agencies. Not so in 1998. You cannot sell your home today without a radon inspection of the basement. In the 1980s, radon awareness began to rise in non-industrial settings. In 1988 J. Lubin of the National Cancer Institute in Bethesda, Maryland, wrote, "Radon-222 is a radio-active decay product of radium-226 and uranium-238, which are found through-out the crust of the earth."[1] Please understand this: radioactive elements exist throughout the crust of the earth . . . some areas more concentrated than others, but essentially worldwide in scope! Earlier I discussed the reasons for this phe-nomena which was global volcanism during the flood of Noah.

Radon has been linked to lung cancer in humans. From the University of New Mexico Medical Center in 1990 came this statement, "Radon, a long-estab lished cause of lung cancer in uranium and other underground miners, has re-cently emerged as a potentially important cause of lung cancer in the general population." This is not meant to frighten you but to emphasize the extent of the problem. They also wrote about the "widespread exposure of the population to radon."[2] As I stated earlier, radon gas has been marked as one of the main causes of myeloid leukemia and other cancers by scientists at the University of Bristol in England. They say, "The international incidence of myeloid leukemia, cancer of the kidney, melanoma, and certain childhood cancers, all show significant corre-lation with radon exposure in the home."[3] Fabricant, from the Donner Laboratory at the University of California in Berkeley, wrote this in 1990: "The evidence compels the conclusion that indoor radon daughter exposure in homes represents a potential life-threatening public hazard, particularly in males, and in cigarette smokers."[4] Radon daughters polonium-210 and lead-210 are both natural components of cigarette smoke.[5] Therefore, no matter whether it is inhaled in the air of your basement or much faster through habitual cigarette smoke, the same radionuclides are absorbed. It's no wonder that Senator John McCain was so concerned about teenage smoking that he introduced pertinent legislation in the senate. It's no wonder non-smokers don't react well to smoke-filled rooms.

The EPA is very concerned about its presence in our drinking water.[6] Public and private wells in 16 counties in Maine were surveyed in 1983 for Rn222, and concentrations in the water ranged from 20 to 180 thousand pico curies per liter. "Granite areas yielded the highest average levels (mean 22,100 pCi/l n=136). Over one hundred wells had 22,100 pCi/l counts.[7] The Altamira cave was only 160 pico curies per liter. These wells were 138 times worse than Altamira cave in Spain. At the Altamira concentration of radon (160pCi/l.) the exposure level for a guide who worked 170 hours each month for 11 months would be 299,200 pCi-hr/l. This is "four times higher than the maximum level established for the protection of uranium miners." The Carlsbad Caverns in New Mexico are not as high as Altamira but the three Mecsek caves in Hungary have similar high counts. My guess is that if they tested radon in all the tourist caves in the world, eyes would pop, as the Sumerians would say. In contrast to these reports, the average radiation from terrestrial sources including what you eat and drink is given as approximately 78-267 millirems per year in the USA for the annual dose.[8] A very tiny amount — less than one dental x-ray (250 mrems).

There is no question that we have only now become aware of a problem that has been around for quite sometime. Can I build a hypothetical word picture for a moment? Let's imagine we were able to go back into time to join Noah soon after he had landed on the mountain. We would begin by surveying the territory on the mountain where the ark had landed. Let us also suppose we came equipped with a device that could detect terrestrial radioactivity. After 30 days of scouting out the land, we see a cave and go into it with our monitoring device. What does our alpha-radiation detector show? My assumption is that it would reveal a very high radon-222 count. If we had a gamma ray detector I believe it would also register a high mark. I base this hypothesis on all of the preceding information that I have presented and a statement by Dr. J. Selman in his book on x-ray and radium physics. "Since a sealed source of radium reaches a state of equilibrium with its descendants after approximately thirty days (i.e., the same number of atoms of a particular daughter is appearing as is disappearing in a given time interval" and then actually consists of a mixture of these descendants, we speak loosely of radium emitting all three types of radiation. Whether we start with radium or radon gas, there is soon a sufficient accumulation of radium B and C to give appreciable intensities of beta and gamma radiation."[9] Radium A is polonium 218, radium B is lead 214, radium C is bismuth 214, and radium D is lead 210. I believe all of these would be in that cave. It may not have been totally sealed as Dr. Selman's radioactive radium pouch, but in their depths many caves have poor ventilation. Eventually a post-flood cave would be filled with radon-

222 gas which in time would coat the walls of the cave with lead-210 similar to the walls of Mystery Cave.[10] How high was the count? We can only guess.

Noah did not need our 20th century advanced system to warn him about the caves, because we read in Genesis 9:20 that he lived inside a tent, and we assume that God's wisdom had forewarned him. He settled in relatively good land because he became a farmer and grew grapes. However, he could not have escaped the radiation spewed forth from the extensive volcanism and aerosols in the post-flood atmosphere. His grapes had to have been tainted with a good deal of radium-226 and even its potent decay product lead-210. We can assume that the early soil levels were higher, being freshly deposited, than our levels today just from the very low levels of these "natural radionuclides" in our food. In the U. K. a 1984 study showed that radium-226 is contained in beverages, cereals, other vegetables, bread, sugars, and preserves. Lead-210 is in bread, milk, cereals, beverages, other vegetables, sugars and preserves, and meat products.[11] All of Noah's food had to be full of these particles if his generation experienced the predicted volcanic aerosols.

Noah's tent was on soil that obviously had to be contaminated by high levels of uranium-238, radium-226, thorium-232, and decay products such as radon, possibly not as heavily salted as other places, but still contaminated. The ordinary air content of radon had to be slightly higher than it is today and probably some was concentrated in the air in the tent, although air circulated through the tent skins better than in a cave or a sealed home. He and his family were now living in the midst of a hostile environment. But I believe Noah and his family were resistant to these injurious substances to a certain extent. I believe it was a superior immune system and/or a superior DNA repair system. What makes me think that this is so?

Backtrack with me now to Genesis 6, before the great cataclysm. God was very angry at mankind for violence and criminal behavior. The earth was filled with violence when the Lord pronounced, "My Spirit shall not contend with man forever, for he is mortal; his days will be a hundred and twenty years" (Gen. 6:3). Based on this pronouncement and the carcinogenic radioactive environment, Noah, his wife, their three sons, and their wives should have all contracted lung or another form of cancer. But Noah lived another 350 years after the flood and Shem another 502 years. Noah was 600 and Shem was 98 when they disembarked the ark. How could they possibly have achieved this longevity given the new conditions under which they had to live?

Allow me to quickly interpose one thought in this place. Many other and unique conditions have been postulated for the post-flood world including increased cosmic radiation; new flora, and, therefore, less beneficial nutrients in the plants; general dietary changes; hostile climatic conditions and severe weather fluctuations; proximity to growing glaciers; and less atmospheric pressure and reduced partial pressure of oxygen in the atmosphere. While I am in agreement with these environmental changes, a full treatment of them is outside my immediate objectives and the scope of this book. They have been covered many times and can usually be found in other creationist literature.

I return to the Bible for a theory to answer the question of protection from cancer. Sometime before the migration eastward to the land of Shinar and building of the Tower of Babel with heat-hardened mud bricks, Noah settled in a place where he and his wife lived in a tent, not bricks. This is where he also began farming and planting grape vines. The fact is Noah eventually became drunk and took all his clothes off in his tent and went to sleep. Ham saw his father and notified Shem and Japheth. They covered him up with a garment in an unusual way. They walked in backwards with it on their shoulders, and while not looking at him laid the garment over Noah's prostrate and naked body. An act of profound respect, no doubt, but also of embarrassment for the family. Every father's drunkenness is.

The word for this garment in the Hebrew transliteration is *"simlah."* It is not the same word for garment *"beged"* used in Isaiah 51:6 or Psalm 102:26. These verses speak of the earth wearing out like a garment. Like a *beged,* not a *simlah.* Noah's *simlah* is an outer garment, more protective than ordinary linen or woolen garments of the usual *beged* type. This *simlah* type of garment is spoken of in Proverbs 30:4 where it is written, "Who has wrapped the waters in the garment?" This implies a tougher type of garment, since in the previous sentence it makes reference to gathering the wind in his fists. This is *atmospheric control*, plain and simple, by a supernatural God. It is my prayerful opinion that the outer *simlah* of Noah, with which Noah was wrapped, also designates some type of *atmospheric control*. I think it symbolizes the atmospheric control of the carcinogenic effects of radiation for Noah and his family, but this *simlah* wore out eventually like the other garment *beged*, but not as quickly. A hyperactive immune system, more efficient DNA repair mechanisms, less absorption, more excretion, or any of a number of things could have contributed to this temporary defense. Please remember that this is only my interpretation of that scene. It may not be correct, but let us explore a little.

What do we find in the scientific literature and my own findings about cancer in ancient times? Can this interpretation of the covering of Noah be supported with any scientific evidence?

THE IMMUNE SYSTEM MAY HAVE BEEN DIFFERENT

Starting with malignant tumors of bone, osteosarcoma of the long bones occurs in patients under 30 years of age in 80% of the cases. It is the most common bone tumor of the young. To the best of my knowledge, it has never been reported in a Neanderthal. Neither have the remainder of bone malignancies like multiple myeloma, Ewing's sarcoma, and metastatic carcinoma ever been found in Neanderthal bones. The same is true for chondrosarcomas, which have effects on bone. The Kaman lower jaw fragment, not a Neanderthal but supposedly further back in time, has been associated with a bone tumor. More recent opinion, however, suggests that this bone swelling is a callus related to a fracture of the jaw rather than a tumor.[12] The Gibraltar I female adult has a rounded infectious-like lesion in the medial wall of the left orbit. The medial wall of her right orbit is partially broken, but it looks like post-mortem damage. The Trinil I femur from Java has a bone tumor in its upper third. This has been associated with a *Homo erectus* calotte (top of the skull). Day wrote that "doubts have been cast on the provenance of the Trinil I femur following new analytical studies on the Javan Trinil remains." Day also wrote that the gross and microscopic anatomy and radiologic findings do not distinguish any of the femora (femurs) from modern man. Concerning the tumorous femur, he remarked, "The complete femur is remarkable in its general resemblance to modern man."[13] The reason being it probably was modern man.

This covers the field of malignant bone tumors in Neanderthal. The results equal zero. To be perfectly candid, I haven't seen or read about any benign tumors either. Benign tumors could be problematic because I have reported in this book on the probable adenoma of a recent man from Broken Hill and there may be more acromegalic cases in the fossil record. There are always new discoveries and I may have missed one somewhere, but in close to 20 years of study, this is all I have been able to find. Trinkaus has reported on all the traumatic injuries and degenerative disease in the Shanidar Neanderthals, a large group, and there were no reports of bone tumors. Fennell and Trinkaus also reported that La Ferrassie I had a non-invasive femoral and tibial periarticular periostitis, usually due to thoracic infection, sometimes carcinoma. They were indecisive in the diagnosis of the primary cause because periostitis is not bone cancer and there are no signs of it in La Ferrassie I.[14] La Chapelle had trauma to the left hip and a broken rib. He had many arthritic changes in his bones with degenerative disease evident, but no bone tumors. Trinkhaus even mentions four other authors plus himself who agree that the incidence of trauma among the older Neanderthals was quite high compared to those of recent humans.[15] I'm sure they would attribute it to a rougher life and not extended longevity.

Just because I have ruled out hard tissue tumors does not mean we have ruled out soft tissue tumors. This type of identification is impossible with Neanderthals because there has never been any soft tissue recovered. If there was, it would mean mummification, freezing, or some other preservation process such as in the peat bogs of Windover, Florida, in the United States.[16]

The soft tissue findings of tumors in antiquity were excellently summarized by Gerzten and Allison at an international conference, "The total number of documented soft tissue tumors from ancient civilizations is fewer than ten, including the present findings of lipoma and a rhabdosarcoma, with more than a thousand complete autopsies performed in our studies in Peru and Chile of pre-Columbian mummies alone. The most important factors for this low incidence of neoplastic lesions in mummified materials include the fact that almost all of the known carcinogenic agents prevalent in today's world have only recently been brought into contact with humans, and that the immune system of ancient populations may have been different."[17] This paper by these two doctors from the Medical College of Virginia in Richmond was presented at the International Congress of Anthropological and Ethnological Sciences, in Zagreb, Yugoslavia, in July of 1988. The audience reaction was recorded in a short summary: "We do not know when the high incidence of cancer began." It was agreed that the frequency was low in antiquity as far as they can tell for the present. This was the opinion of the majority of this world anthropology conference in 1988. Was it the *simlah* effect wearing out? My son Frank, who is finishing his master's degree in biology, believes that there were better DNA repair mechanisms designed to detect replication or transcription errors that could have malignant results, an excellent idea.

MUTILATED, FOLDED FINGERS, OR RADIATION BURNS?

So you may hear an opposing view to my above theory on radiation protection, four caves do exist that contain no bony evidence of cancer but with many handprints on the walls with incomplete fingers. I am referring to the Gargas and Tibiran Caves in the Pyrenees in Spain; Maltravieso Cave in Spain; and the Cosquer Cave in the Mediterranean Sea near Marseilles, on the southern coast of France. Sieveking wrote of interpretations of the hands of Gargas Cave as being ritually mutilated or ravaged by leprosy.[18] There has been much speculation about these. There are 114 hands with one or more shortened fingers in Gargas according to Clottes and Courtin.[19] In their major work on the underwater cave of Cosquer, Clottes and Courtin described 25 handprints with "folded fingers." This cave has a 260-foot entrance tunnel into the first gallery. The entrance hole is 100 feet out from the cliff and 120 feet underwater. There is no other entrance to the cave, meaning that it once was accessible from dry land and therefore not underwater in the time of its use. It has numerous animal paintings and carvings. The water level in the main galleries is low enough to see many of these with modern lighting equipment. Three men were drowned in a crude attempt to enter this cave without the proper equipment.

I wonder if these fingers represent a similar condition to the roentgen-ray dermatosis that I was warned about in my radiology course in dental school. We were told never to hold a radiograph in a patient's mouth because of the accumulation of the undesirable x-rays in the tissues of our hands over a long period of time. We were also shown numerous examples of this radiation-caused skin disease that burned the skin and caused ulcers to form carcinomas which resulted in loss of some fingers. The median time from first exposure to malignancy was nine years, some cases as short as four years.[20] What kind of a sequence of events can be postulated for this type of disease?

Remember radium-D or lead-210 that was found on the rock walls of Mystery Cave in Minnesota? Lively and Ney in 1987 compared the lead-210 on those walls to that of a basement in a house in Minneapolis and found the lead-210 alpha activity in the cave to be 100 times greater.[21] However, remember that the greatest risk from lead-210 is the gamma radiation.[22] Dr. Eva Callery reported on gold rings with embedded radon gas seeds which gave off gamma rays and beta rays. They were made when radioactive gold was incorporated into jewelry by accident or somebody bought some gold at a very low price and it wasn't accidental at all. In any event, the ring bearers eventually contracted squamous cell carcinoma of the fingers. One of the rings gave off the equivalent of 240 seconds of dental x-rays per year.[23]

If the rocks of some of the Paleolithic caves were heavily contaminated with lead-210, it could have affected their hands as well as the meat that they cut with the sharpened edges of the flint rock. Little flecks of stone and radioactive particles could easily have combined with the meat. Let me emphasize that no tumors of finger bones have ever been found of Neanderthals or so-called Upper Paleolithic peoples. But then again, would they tell us if they did?

Theya Molleson did tell us in her article on the accumulation of trace metals in fossils, that uranium in a bone is sure evidence that the bone has been buried. Flourine and uranium are two elements freely accumulated in bone buried in the ground with ground water percolating through it. However, if the conditions in the soil are oxidating rather than reducing, no uranium will be absorbed, or if a change from reducing to oxidating occurs while the bone is buried, leaching of the uranium from the bones will take place. They will lose uranium and their daughter products.[24]

IMMATURITY WEARS OUT, TOO

The problems begin when we observe how low the radiation levels have become and how much cancer has increased. Obviously the slack created by the mild doses of radiation in the present (excepting man-made) is being taken up by an abundance of carcinogens and a decline in our immune systems or genetic control mechanisms. Just to understand how everything is wearing out like a *beged,* let us examine just four years of data from the United Kingdom. According to data from 1984 to 1988 in England, the National Radiological Protection Board of the United Kingdom reported on average modern radiation exposure. They reported on terrestrial radiation from gamma rays declining from 0.40mSv to 0.35mSv. Radon from earth materials went up from 0.7mSv. to 1.2mSv. from 1984 to 1988, but this increase was due to increased surveillance. Ingested radionuclides went down from 0.37 to 0.30mSv.[25] In the USA in 1987, the exposure to gamma rays from the earth was slightly lower at .28mSv.[26] Even though these figures look high they do not amount to a great deal of exposure in terms of damage to the human body. This is good news unless you have high counts of radon in your home. Therefore, the amounts of natural radiation figures seem to be decreasing as the earth wears down. The general sense of the Second Law would seem to point backward in this regard to a time when the natural radiation counts were higher (Isa. 51:6). Of course, this will always be confounded by man-made radiation which is on the increase with events like the Chernobyl and the Pakistani and Indian renewed underground atomic testing. But, hopefully, this will remain under control in the future.

Some major questions arise as we turn the last corner in this book. We know that some cells are particularly hypersensitive to radiation. Also, we know that there is a scale of tissue hypersensitivity to radiation in the body. The most rapidly dividing cells are at the top of the sensitivity list while those that are the slowest are at the bottom. Mitotic activity, periods of increased metabolism, and embryonic or immature cells seem to render a cell hypersensitive.[27] It has been a rule in my office not to take any dental x-rays on a pregnant woman in her first trimester because of the potential damage to the embryo or fetus even with a lead apron. This requires a questionnaire to be filled out prior to any examination. We know immature cells are very radiosensitive and I have concluded that Neanderthal children were immature relative to modern day children. Background radiation is very minor now with the exception of caves, radon-filled homes, and Chernobyl-type places.

Bone remodeling rates seemed slower in Neanderthals but brain growth seemed larger than normal. The Pech cranial base was larger than a modern three year old but his face was more posterior than a modern one year old. The tremendous angle of the roof of Pech's mouth, his palate, was a prime indicator that the face was slow and the cranium not accelerated. This was a fetal angulation, and he showed no signs of cleft or malformation of the palate; therefore, I found no congenital abnormality. The long time span between Pech and Moustier, based on growth of the face and also shown in tooth attrition, all testify to a slower mechanism involved in growth. Then we must think of the Neanderthal fetal ear and all the futile attempts to cover up many evidences of immaturity. Now we must approach the loss of this immaturity based on some mechanism concerning the breakdown and decay which is emphasized by Paul in his letter to the Romans (Rom. 8:20).

The first point is that early maturity must be related to the process of loss of longevity. Loss of longevity is evidence of the "creation was subjected to futility" principle. Then in a logical syllogistic progression, loss of immaturity must be part of the degeneration of mankind.

In 1994 a report was released from the Christie Hospital and Holt Radium Institute in Manchester, England, on the relationship between cranial irradiation and early puberty. In essence, what it said was that high doses of cranial irradiation for children with brain tumors caused a more rapid onset of puberty. It had already been known that low doses in girls for leukemia caused a downward shift in menarcheal ages. However, they were able to show that the brain tumor itself had nothing to do with the rapid maturation levels. They studied 30 boys younger than 9.14 years and 16 girls younger than 8.65 years. The brain tumor, as stated before, did not include the pituitary or hypothalamus which are the centers for maturity changes in the brain. They stated, "There was a significant linear association between age at irradiation and age at onset of puberty. They did not analyze girls for menarche, just pubertal changes were measured for both sexes. The onset of puberty occurred at an early age in both sexes, (mean 8.51 yr. in girls and 9.21 yr. in boys plus 0.29 yr. for every year of age at irradiation). For example, the estimated age at the onset of puberty in a boy irradiated at 2 years of age would be 9.79 yr, and that for a boy irradiated at 9 years of age would be 11.82 yr. . . . A similar trend was seen for bone age, which was abnormally early at the time of pubertal onset." They concluded, "The mechanism for early puberty after irradiation is likely to be related to disinhibition of cortical influences on the hypothalamus. Puberty then proceeds through the increased frequency and amplitude of GnRH pulsatile secretion[28] by the hypothalamus."[29] GnRH is secreted and sent by portal vessels to the anterior pituitary gland where FSH and LH are stimulated[30] and sent into the blood plasma. The child is now transformed into an adult.

The disinhibition of the hypothalamus could be carried out in two ways, one would be as they propose from mechanisms within the brain itself.[31] The brain inhibitor or brake (as in car) (Intrinsic CNS Inhibitory Mechanism) would thus be released and the hypothalamus (car) would go speeding off and send GnRH to the pituitary, resulting in sexual changes. The other inhibitor or brake is the circulating sex hormones or sex steroids (small amounts of testosterone in boys and estrogen in girls). There are also small quantities of FSH and LH that are at very low circulating levels from their early secretion by the pituitary in the fetal stages of that child. These are a brake on the hypothalamus (car) and do not allow GnRH to be secreted either. Otherwise, this GnRH would shoot up to the pituitary and boom, off go more FSH and more LH, resulting in sexual maturity. Somehow, in either one of these mechanisms the "set point" of the hypothalamus is gradually raised so that the low concentrations of sex steroids are no longer capable of braking the hypothalamic (car) and off it goes secreting GnRH to the pituitary, which in turn sends out much LH and FSH, resulting in sexual maturity.

Allow this analogy, please. If your car was running and it was in gear in drive and your foot was on the brake pedal, as long as your foot was healthy you could keep the car from moving. If you had gradual increasing pain in your foot from arthritis or something, as the pain increased each day the less pressure you could exert on the pedal, until one day you had to let go and the car would speed off with no brake. This is an overly simplified but close analogy to our sexual maturity system. Down through the thousands of years that separate us from Neanderthals something has gradually let up on that brake pedal and now our kids are speeding off. This is a big unanswered question because it is multi-factorial, and radiation today is inconsequential. Cooper et al. in the Southampton Hospital in the UK concluded in 1996 that in 1,471 girls of Scotland, England, and Wales the menarcheal age was linked to "programmed patterns of gonadotropin release established in utero, when the fetal hypothalamus is imprinted, and is subsequently modified by weight gain in childhood."[32] The girls who were heavier at birth had menarche at a later age. What imprints the hypothalamus in utero?

WALDEYER'S HYPOTHESIS

A 19th-century embryologist by the name of W. Waldeyer said that every female mammal is born with a finite number of egg cells, otherwise called oocytes for reproduction purposes. He believed that there was a finite stock of "germ cells" inside of each female mammal, human or non-human. Each female uses these germ cells up in the course of her reproductive life and she develops no more. Many are purely lost in her menstrual periods. Unlike the males among mammals who continue to manufacture sperm cells all the time, the female has a set number and once they are used up, he said, she was out of them.[33] Evans and Allen, in the early 1900s, took issue with this view and changed the scientific thinking about oogenesis "egg-making" and regeneration.[34] Zuckerman found the numbers of oocytes decreasing with age as did Arai in 1920.[35] By 1951 he was convinced that there was a limited supply. A number of researchers working on this subject since then have confirmed this. Beaumont, Ioannou, and Baker discovered that Waldeyer was right in the first place.[36]

At this point the work of these men touches on the place where we've come to in my research. Zuckerman stated, "About the same time as we started to worry about the question of the relationship of fertility to the numbers of oocytes in the ovary, we embarked upon a quantitative microscopic study of the germ cells in the fetal ovary. Had this work been performed in 1947, part of our early labors might have proved unnecessary. This work provided ample evidence that in the rat, guinea pig, monkey, chick, and man, the maximum number of germ cells occurs before birth, and that up to sixty percent of the peak stock degenerates by the time the infant is born (or hatched). The human female is born with a stock of about two million oocytes, of which about half are degenerating. The peak oocyte population in the human ovary, seven million, occurs at the fifth month of gestation."[37] This is 4 months before birth. This means that the human baby girl today is so advanced in her development and maturation that before she is even born, while she is still in the uterus, years before the rest of the system is capable of supporting a fetus, she's done making eggs. This is especially unusual since the male can produce more sperm after birth but all female egg production and its peak are terminated before birth. Even then, half of her precious cargo is lost to degeneration.

M. Warren from the Obstetrics and Gynecology Department of Columbia University College of Medicine said, "All females are born with ovaries filled with primary follicles that contain eggs (oogonia) in an arrested phase of development (one egg for each follicle). Thus, a girl is born with all the follicles she will ever have, a quantity estimated at 400,000. However, only a limited number will ever develop; during the entire reproductive years only 400-500 oogonia will be used in the ovulatory process while the majority undergo atresia (involution) after a period of aborted growth."[38] This supply has to last all her reproductive lifetime. Two million or 400,000 down to 400-500 is a dramatic decline. This seems to be another evidence of the Second Law working its way out in females.

When God said to Eve, "I will greatly multiply thy sorrow and thy conception" (Gen. 3:16;KJV), was this the beginning of the loss of the follicles and eggs?[39] This may mean more than just the pain of the actual childbirth, although that increased, too. Will Eve and her children be sorrowful over the increasing loss of fertility, the rapid maturation, and shorter childhood as time marches on? The answer to these questions seems to be yes.

Evidence for this concern over fertility loss is expressed in all the post-flood art work labeled Upper Paleolithic. Numerous examples from all over the continent of Europe have been found of so-called fertility goddesses.[40] Much has been made of the superstitions of the ancient peoples regarding these matters but evolution has little to say about the reasons for these superstitions. Could they be based on the rapid decline in longevity, fertility, and maturation after the flood?

Was there ever a time in history when egg production proceeded through the adolescent years? If it is true that girls are sexually maturing earlier and earlier as we go down through history, can we hypothesize a time when the egg production was not "so early" and may have continued to a later date? It might even have terminated during infancy or adolescence. Humans, then, may be becoming more precocious even in egg production.

Another important factor besides the lack of eggs is poor egg quality. Poor oocyte (egg) quality has been cited as a reason for declining female fertility as women grow older.[41] Apparently the eggs experience some process of degeneration with age. This is not unlike the spoilage that takes place in milk or eggs in the refrigerator. When you bring home your bag of groceries from the supermarket, you start out with a date on the milk or eggs which says "use by 11/10/98," for example. The modern female's human eggs start out with a date, too. The only problem is that hardly anyone knows about it.

The modern uterus, if healthy, can sustain a good egg through the fifth decade of life.[42] Therefore, the real problem lies in the egg spoilage. It is not too hard to realize that changing the date on these eggs and decreasing the time they take to spoil could eventually force people to have children at younger ages. How that can be balanced with increasing levels of graduate education and financial insecurity in our age is a tough question.

POST-FLOOD MATURATION

We are not sure of post-flood maturational decline of years between Shem and his son because it is probable that Shem was sexually mature many years before his wife gave birth to Arpachshad when he was 100 years old. Mahalalel and Enoch are the lowest two maturational ages that we have in the pre-flood men. Both were 65 years when Jared and Methuselah were born (Gen. 5:15-21). You really should subtract 9-10 months from all of these ages to allow for the approximate time of gestation in the womb, or as you may suspect, about 18 months for a longer gestation period. But I am going to use the ages given in the Bible for the sake of simplicity.

It is likely that Shem was close to the age of Mahalalel and Enoch when he experienced pubertal changes. Arpachshad reached sexual maturity at 35, then in six generations from Shelah to Nahor the average age of maturation hovered around 30, with Eber at 34 and Nahor at 29. This appears to be a post-flood plateau, similar to the findings in some countries today.

In chapter 29 you have seen that the average age of voice change in modern males is around 13.5 years and this pubertal change corresponds to what Demir et al. found in Finland in 1995. By testing for hormones in the urine, this group from University Hospital in Helsinki discovered a 5-fold increase in FSH and a 50-fold increase in LH in boys starting at the age of 12. Girls also showed dramatic urinary hormone increases after 10 years of age.[43] Could Shem, Ham, and Japheth have had this urinary increase of FSH and LH at age 12? Could La Ferrassie I, La Chapelle-aux-Saints, or Amud I have had similar urinary hormone output at 12 or did they all have their peak urinary hormone output at later ages? Delay usually means delay, but for them it was not like our modern constitutional delayed puberty, which results in decreased bone mineral density in adulthood.

Doctors at Massachusetts General Hospital wrote, "Adult men with a history of constitutionally delayed puberty have decreased radial and spinal bone mineral density. These findings suggest that timing of puberty is an important determinant of peak bone density in men. Because the peak bone mineral density achieved during young adulthood is a major determinant of bone density in later life, men in whom puberty was delayed may be at increased risk for osteoporotic fractures when they are older."[44]

If there is one thing Neanderthals did not have, it was decreased bone density. It was not thin osteoporotic bone as in rickets and osteomalacia. Their compact bone was dense. Ancient men of early post-flood times most likely had a late onset of puberty with their peak bone mineral density merely accomplished at a later date. When today's late developers miss the crucial pubertal peak stage which begins at 10 in girls and 12 in boys, it affects their bone density. They still seem to be bound to a restricted time frame for bone accretion by modern day mechanisms even when they are delayed in puberty. It seems that Neanderthals had no such restrictions.

Remember what I said about bone growth being slower in Le Moustier because of the fewer and larger secondary osteons compared to modern man in his compact bone. Hypothetically now, let us suppose that for every 5 secondary osteons of Neanderthal, modern man had 10. Imagine also that each one of Neanderthal's osteons had an efficiency of bone production of 3 units a day. Imagine modern man's osteons had an efficiency of 2 units a day. Modern man would make 20 units a day and Neanderthal just 15. The overall growth rate for Neanderthal would be slower, even though each individual bone unit was faster. This could be a mechanism for slow overall growth, with less but more efficient bone units.

PATRIARCHAL GESTATION

Arpachshad's embryological period in his mother's uterus was undoubtedly post-flood. He was born two years after the flood and we do not know how long his mother carried him. Was it for our approximately nine-month gestation period or was it longer? Does "two years" have more than one meaning?

It had been suggested that Neanderthals carried their children for longer gestation periods based on the very large pubic rami (part of the human pelvic bones) of La Ferrassie I, Krapina, and Tabūn C-1.[45] But this was subsequently questioned when the male Kebara pelvis was discovered in 1983 and shown to be only wider than modern humans in the front. The pubic bones were longer and thinner but the idea of longer gestation was very distasteful to most evolutionists. They would rather attribute the strange pelvic anatomy to a different way of walking[46] than anything so biblical as: "I will greatly multiply thy sorrow and thy conception" (Gen. 3:16). Smaller pelvises would mean more pain in childbirth.

Personally, I think this Kebara pelvis may have been a mosaic in the throes of devolution as so much of the Israel material demonstrates. Most likely men and women were created with larger pelvises and they became smaller by the same process by which the serpent lost his legs.

A TOMBSTONE?

A final word on a Neanderthal grave is in order. In the La Ferrassie group of six graves, number six belonged to a small child of approximately three years old according to Day[47] and Oakley et al.[48] I never saw this skeleton in France. The grave of this little child had a triangular slab of stone over it, like a big patio slate. I do not know what kind of rock it was but it is described by Mellars in his new book[49] and by Bergounioux as having "cupules" on its inner side.[50] Both sources make reference to a group of artificial "cup" depressions on the under-surface of this slab. They look as if they were ground into the stone. If you can imagine taking a small rubber ball and sinking it half-way down into wet concrete and then taking it out as the cement was drying, you would see a similar cup-like depression. Their were five pairs of "petite cupules" (small cups) around a "une plus grande" (larger one) with a line cut across the center of the larger hemisphere. Three pairs on one side and two pairs on the other. Could this be a tombstone engraving of the child's age? Could this be signifying 10 years of age? This would even be a slower growing child than my estimates.

ANCIENT ENZYMES

My son John now has his Ph.D in molecular biology and has collected this information on devolution that adds some mechanisms to our knowledge. It concerns enzymes, which is his area of expertise. Reconstructing ancient mammalian enzymes has given us some clues as to how the molecular systems worked in antiquity.

It has recently been found that the turnover value or rate for a reconstructed ancient chymase molecule was five times faster than modern man's chymase and 80 times faster than the modern angiotensin I converting enzyme.[51] Therefore, the early state of the chymases was more efficient than the present-day state and some loss occurred during devolution.[52]

Also, recently, 13 ancient ribonucleases (enzymes) have been constructed from the mammal order of artiodactyls. This order includes sheep, camels, pigs, deer, and ox. The authors stated, "Going back in time, a significant change in behaviour, namely a fivefold increase in catalytic activity against double-stranded RNA, appears in the RNase reconstructed for the founding ancestor of the artiodactyl lineage, which lived about 40 million years ago."[53] More efficient enzymatic activity is seen once again in this research concerning the past. This is another interesting example of devolution.

The following is a list of advantages to the cells and their systems if they possessed faster and more efficient enzymes. These were suggested by my son John. They are hypothetical, of course, and we have no way of knowing whether the ancients had these, but let us examine what might have been. The main point is that having better parts in any system contributes to the longevity of that system.

1. Faster defense enzymes to protect from free radicals.

2. A longer half-life for the structural enzymes of a cell would be an improvement.

3. Faster DNA repair enzymes to repair damage.

4. Quality control enzymes involved in the cell or in folding of other proteins that are secreted from the cell could be improved by allowing them to interact with more substrates at faster rates.

FINAL ADVICE

Ultimately, it appears as if man is headed for younger ages of maturation. We were truly fearfully and wonderfully made, but the Fall made a major difference. This is exactly the opposite message to evolution where the biological world becomes more complex, not less efficient, less vital. The good news is that we can still adapt and we can still find more scientific breakthroughs.

Jesus Christ proclaimed the word of God to be "Truth." I found this to be true in all of my research. I therefore urge all the readers of this book to consider the facts that I have presented which uphold the scientific and historical accuracy of the Scriptures. The Bible is not just another finite book. It is the infinite Word of God. My research is finite and I do not for one minute equate it with the Bible. Jesus said, "Heaven and earth will pass away but my words will never pass away" (Matt. 24:35; Mark 13:31; Luke 21:33).

My words are part of the passing away of the earth but maybe just for a little while they could stimulate some to advance these concepts by doing research in these areas. This would mean new paths have to be blazed through the maze of evolutionary science. This type of work would in no way stunt science or stop advancement. It would create new avenues of approach. Remember, the Bible does not give us exhaustive knowledge about man and the universe, just "true truth" as Dr. Schaeffer would say. What is stunting science now is the prohibition of a freedom of expression into research that is Bible-based. That's no freedom of choice like all the "choice people" in our generation desire for themselves. This is the dichotomy of our time — scientists who claim to be liberal restricting the freedom of their opponents.

If used properly, ideas such as I have put forth could lead us in a new direction if they are allowed to. They could lead towards a new paradigm of perfection and devolution and not evolution from primitive forms. This would be a breakthrough.

One final word on the use of this book. I realize that many will be angry at the colossal twisting of facts to suit the needs of evolution. To many I believe they thought it to be their duty, even thinking that the only interpretation is an evolutionary one and a biblical interpretation was invalid. To them and to all of my readers, I say this: Don't beat people over the head with this book. My purpose is not to stir up anger but love. I urge my readers to change the course of history by working within the system so that biblical principles are incorporated once again into science. If a man like Robert Boyle, the father of chemistry, were to come back from the dead he would not be hired by a major university if his biblical position was known. This should not be.

Let us strive together in a peaceful way to open up the pathways of research so they can carry young minds toward the mind of God, not away from Him. Foundations can do this with monetary prizes for college and grad students each year for research along these lines. But let us begin, and never see the truth "Buried Alive" again.

Research Notes

Chapter 2, Research Note 1. Initially, one of my basic problems was the acceptance of Jesus' raising people instantaneously from the dead in the New Testament and the triune God using the long process of evolution and death to create man in the beginning. This seemed to me a contradiction. The dead son at Nain sat up immediately when Jesus spoke the word. Lazarus came forth immediately after Jesus called him. How could God not raise Adam immediately from the dust in the beginning? Did God have to obey a scale of miracles rated by degree of difficulty? Besides all of this, Jesus didn't seem to like death at all, which is an integral part of evolution. He cried in front of Lazarus' tomb. How could He have called the earth "very good" in the beginning when it was full of dead bones and blood?

Could I find any facts that could help me understand this dilemma? I knew teeth and I knew craniofacial bones. In addition to this, I had a young family with five small children. So, we had to do this together. Through the inspiration of several people my interest in biblical paleoanthropology grew. Dr. Francis Schaeffer encouraged me in 1977. Listening to him lecture and reading his works started my thoughts along devolutionary lines. Dr. Henry Morris and Dr. Wayne Frair were both inspirational in my understanding of Genesis. Of course there was Dr. Bill Krogman, my professor at Penn, and for many years thereafter a real blessing. These men and my questions led to a process which began a series of adventures that you will read about in this book. To me this meant loving God with my whole mind. We started to collect information in the laboratories of museums and universities in April 1976. My last trip was in 1995.

Chapter 3, Research Note 1. *Cephalo* comes from the Greek word for "head," and metric conveys the meaning of "measurement"; therefore, a head-measuring machine. The cephalometric radiograph is an 8 x 10 inch film that is taken in a standardized manner so as to be reproducible in any orthodontic office. It can also be compared with other standardized studies as I have done in this work. The advantage of a cephalometric radiograph is that it is taken with the central beam of the x-rays perpendicular to the mid-sagittal plane of the skull. Any right-left asymmetry found in the radiograph is therefore due to true asymmetry of the specimen and not horizontal rotation of the skull. This portable machine was similar to all the machines in orthodontic offices in the world. However, it was divided into many precision-fitting parts to enable maximum portability in two large, strong metal cases to any research location with a level floor and electricity. It also had a transformer for 220 volt current. It employed the standard 60 inch tube (target) to mid-sagittal plane of specimen distance. The headholder was a (W- 109 M) Wehmer cephalostat. It was coupled with a General Electric 1000 x-ray unit. The skull series were usually shot at 90 KVP and 15 MA with exposure times of 1.5 to 1.75 seconds on the average. Broken Hill radiographs were taken at 10 seconds each because of the zinc and lead from the Zambia mine in which it was found. All the radiographic cassettes were donated by the B.F. Wehmer Co., Franklin Park, Illinois. All service to the x-ray head and master control system was donated by the General Electric Company (now Gendex), Milwaukee, Wisconsin.

Chapter 4, Research Note 1. In 1977, Dr. Krogman had written to me concerning his reception of the Lord Jesus Christ as his Saviour:
"He has been good to me and to mine, I bow my head, offer my heart."
Bill 2/16/77 4 p.m.

Chapter 9, Research Note 1. Since Neanderthal adults had very protruding faces and jaws it was believed that the children's faces were similarly protruded. Howell[1] thought that the distinctive shape of the head and face of the classic Neanderthal group of which Pech was a member began at an early age and was the result of a special pattern of growth and development. Many human paleontologists thought it was natural for Neanderthal children to have miniature adult faces.

Chapter 9, Research Note 2. I examined the original Neanderthal fossil, the Pech de l'Azé child, at the Musée de l'Homme in Paris, France, and found, to my surprise, that there was no protrusion (forward position) of the lower jaw and that it fit perfectly into the TM (glenoid) fossae[2] with the teeth fitting exactly together. I tried several different times to produce Patte's position but I couldn't do it. See figure 1 in text. The left side of the lower jaw also fit perfectly into the (TM or glenoid) fossa on the left side of the cranium.

The cephalometric radiographs which were taken of Pech showed the facial structures of this supposedly two to two-and-one-half-year-old child were retruded (backward positioned) and not protruded in relation to a plane of reference in the head called the Bolton Plane[3] (see figure 73). When comparisons are made to modern day children in the previous figure it is seen that the lower face of Pech is less forward than even the modern 1 year old. This facial retrusion for a Neanderthal child does not fit the facial reduction theory. The only accurate measurement of the length of the head (cranium) of this child (because the back of the head was broken) is a line drawn from nasion (point between nose and forehead) to basion (point on base of skull, ant. margin of foramen magnum) in the cephalometric radiograph. It measured 85.42 mm. The modern three year old is 82.47mm. The base of the Pech skull is larger than a modern three year old. Another significant finding was the steep (14°) angulation of the hard palate of the upper jaw to a straight line drawn from below the eye to the external opening of the ear canal. It was a wide, flat palate but very tilted. By the time a modern child has reached two years of age his or her hard palate is parallel with this eye-ear plane (Frankfort Horizontal Plane). The impression one gets from looking at this little child is that

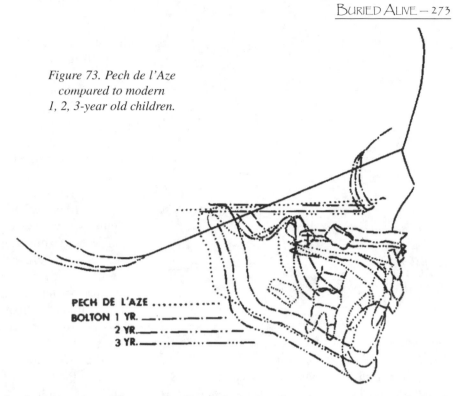

*Figure 73. Pech de l'Aze
compared to modern
1, 2, 3-year old children.*

PECH DE L'AZE ....
BOLTON 1 YR. —.—.—.—.
       2 YR.—— .. —— . ——. —
       3 YR.—— ... ——— ... —— ... —

the face is extremely wound-up in a clockwise direction ready to unwind in a long growth period. At what level of maturity did this child die? One clue comes from a comparison of Pech to the modern 9-12 week old human embryo which shows a very similar angulation of the hard palate structures.[4] Since there is a conflict between the size of head and face, the question now becomes: Are the face and teeth delayed in growth in relation to the head? The cranial base from nasion to basion measures 85.42mm[5] and the Bolton study four year old is only 85.23 mm for the Na-Ba measurement.[6] Therefore, I am assuming the child's cranium had already gone through at least four years or more of growth. This is assuming a growth rate that is equal to the modern day child. I really believe it was slower, but for now let us stay with uniform logic, not ape-heritage logic for a faster growth rate at this age. His primary anterior teeth show excessive incisal wear for only two and one-half years of age. I do not postulate enamel repair for primary incisors. So I have designated him at least four to five years of age.

Chapter 9, Research Note 3. The lateral view of La Chapelle-aux-Saints[7] in the 1st edition has the lower jaw in a forward position. This edition, and all of them up to the 4th, had an ape-like position for the lower jaw which was corrected only in the 4th edition in only the frontal view of the skull. Day's new lateral view in the 4th edition[8] shows the skull and lower jaw turned around from the original position, now facing to the right, with the jaw still forward (ape-like) and the area of the two teeth so dark that you can't see how they occlude because they are on

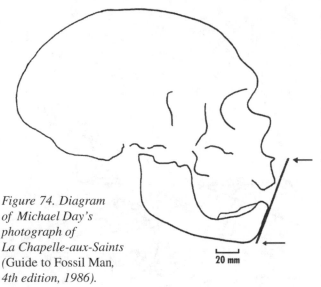

Figure 74. Diagram of Michael Day's photograph of La Chapelle-aux-Saints (Guide to Fossil Man, 4th edition, 1986).

20 mm

the left side and the right side faces the camera. The La Chapelle tracing in figure 43 is the true relationship of the jaws based on the occlusion of the two opposing bicuspids.

M. Day's 1986 lateral view, redrawn by me (figure 74), has a black line drawn along the anterior bony outline of the chin. Notice how far forward of the actual jaw position the mandible protrudes (figure 43) so they can maintain the prognathic mandibular hypothesis.

The frontal view x-ray and photograph that I took in 1979 of La Chapelle are identical to Tappen's frontal view seen in the 1985 version, when they came up with this official reappraisal and Day's frontal view of the skull in the 1986 *Guide to Fossil Man.*

Chapter 15, Research Note 1. It soon became obvious that a definite pattern was developing as I traveled from one collection to the next. It appeared as if the paleoanthropologists had made a concerted effort to adhere to a uniformitarian-evolutionary viewpoint in relation to the growth, maturation, and aging process in ancient populations, no matter what the evidence showed. The two assumptions that undergird this position is that the present is the key to the past, but there are also many ape-like characters in our past. In the study of children of ancient history, this axiom requires that their rates of growth and development be equal to or faster than modern children. Equal to, because of the present-to-past assumption, and faster because of the supposed primitive ape-like heritage. Never could it be presumed that children developed slower in ancient times because that would point to a non-ape or biblical position for early man.

However, there is another key assumption, the facial reduction theory, that says, "Almost all alterations of the dentition in the course of the phylogenetic evolution of man can be regarded as a consequence of the reduction of the face and its adaptation to the upright position."[9] This was stated by Franz Weidenreich in 1949.[10] Weiss and Mann, in 1985, echo the same sentiments. "Two of the major changes in human evolution are the reduction of the face and teeth and the enlargement of the braincase. Both have contributed to the differences in the jaws of modern humans and apes."

Man has a tendency towards orthognathism (straight face) while the ape is prognathic (protruding face). Many humans have prognathic faces. None, however, are as prognathic as the chimpanzee, orangutan, gorilla, or gibbon. These two basic false assumptions, plus creative imagination, I believe, have been the source of all the problems in the reconstruction of fossil men and fossil apes.

This leaves only three possible positions for the craniofacial growth of early man. Fast development like the apes, equal rates of development like us now, or slower rates of development like the ancient people described in the Bible.

Chapter 16, Research Note 1. Is disease the cause of Neanderthal form?

The Neanderthal facial and skeletal form have been attributed to pathological and nutritional phenomena for years. This represents an attempt to classify them as non-evolutionary features and put them on the "shelf," thereby closing the issue.

There are three major categories of causation that have been referred to in the literature: arthritis deformans, syphilis, and rickets. Arthritis deformans is an old name for rheumatoid arthritis, which has multiple causes and mainly affects the joints and post-cranial bones. Polymyalgia rheumatica is a rheumatic inflammation affecting shoulder and hip girdle muscles often associated with giant cell or temporal arteritis (artery inflammation). With any kind of arthritis, very little bony change is seen in the head except for the arthritic changes one would expect to see in old age, if one suffered from arthritis, in the jaw joint (TMJ). La Chapelle-aux-Saints had TMJ arthritic erosion and in the spine, also. It would be impossible for rheumatoid arthritis to cause the adult Neanderthal cranial features such as large brow ridges, facial protrusion, dolichocephalic skull, forward cheekbones, large noses, etc. Arthritis does not create Neanderthals from modern people who have the disease. It is a nasty disease that destroys bone of the joint surfaces (erosion). There is also much soft tissue inflammation. I am not saying that Neanderthals did not have arthritic joint changes in many places, I am just saying that the very pronounced cranial form minus the TMJ is not due to arthritis.

Lubenow mentions in his book that J. Lawrence Angel of the Smithsonian Institution wrote about the bones of the pelvis and base of the skull being deformed by vitamin D deficiency, otherwise known as rickets, also by a protein deficiency.[11]

In Newton and Potts text, *Radiology of the Skull and Brain*, they list the following aspects of skull pathology found in rickets.[12]

> 1. Craniotabes, (presence of areas of thinning and softening of the skull especially the posterior parietal bones).
> 2. Bossing or box-like skull look due to protuberance of bony lumps, front and side of skull.
> 3. Base of the skull flattening or invagination, but not the top or roof of the skull.

4. High arched and narrow hard bony palate of the upper jaw.

5. Delayed eruption of the teeth, not delayed development of the jaws and teeth in a forward direction.

6. Craniosynostosis or premature closure of the skull sutures resulting in a "locked-in brain" inside a skull unable to expand properly in growth.

Of all of these features, the Neanderthals showed only some flattening of the base of the skull, but not a great deal. I have had patients who were perfectly human and had flattening of the cranial base, the saddle angle from Nasion-Sella-Articular (norm around 123°) in the high 130's with no rickets. None of the other features were present.

Gibraltar I (adult) has an intact sella turcica and the saddle angle measures approximately 140° because there is no mandible.

Two examples of Neanderthal children's hard palates, Pech de l'Azé and Gibraltar II, display flatter and wider palates than many modern normal children. I have had hundreds of high-arched palates in 31 years, many with bilateral crossbites, none of them with rickets, either; not angulated like Pech but high in relation to the occlusal plane.

The Neanderthal brains were large, but the braincases not "box-like." If anything, they are the most un-boxlike crania I have seen.

Figure 46 is the right side of the Le Moustier cranium, parietal, temporal, and occipital fragments pieced together. Notice how the temporal is depressed like a modern skull.

The Neanderthal adult cranial bones were very thick and not thin and soft in spots like a bone with rickets pathology.

J. Eideiken lists one more feature found in rickets in his text on *Roentgen Diagnosis of Diseases of Bone,* and that is extensive caries.[13] None of the Neanderthal children I examined had any caries at all, and that includes Le Moustier. Of the adults, only La Ferrassie I had periapical abscess formation on many teeth due to the extensive attrition or wear and the exposure of the pulps of those teeth and possible periodontal disease. The only extensive decay I saw was in Broken Hill Man and that could be attributable to normal decay-causing processes and not systemic disease — don't forget to read my explanation of his strange skull features and recent existence.

Lubenow also quotes Ivanhoe's article in *Nature* about rickets being the reason for the Neanderthals' strange features.[14] Ivanhoe was following the early diagnosis of the famous German pathologist, Rudolf Virchow, the father of pathology.[15] We must remember that Francis Ivanhoe is the man who said that Pech de l'Azé's teeth were "grossly maloccluded with numerous enamel irregularities and crown anomalies." Ivanhoe also said, "It has long been held that the Neanderthal child is a small replica of the adult." As I pointed out in my explanation in these notes, Ivanhoe only copied Patte's mistakes and was wrong, and probably never saw the real skull. Rickets does not create Neanderthals, either.

I do not blame Lubenow because he had no way of knowing that what Ivanhoe said was totally fabricated. I would have never known if the Lord didn't open doors for me in these museums. I have made my share of errors in my day and none of us can claim perfection. This only points out the need for Christians to do more original research. I hold myself accountable to this challenge, too, because on numerous occasions I have reported on the work of others, and do so extensively in this book. However, we as creationists are in a tough position. No one is *ever sure* that the paleoanthropologists are telling the truth about fossils unless they see the bones themselves. I have tried to do research in Kenya since 1989 and still can't get in to see anything in Nairobi, thanks to the Leakey family monopoly. Dr. Alan Walker, who works with Richard, had no objection to my research. Let me say he is one of the more open-minded of the paleoanthropologists and a true scholar. He treated my son Joshua like a prince at Penn State. I can't say enough good things about him. He has told my son's anthropology class that there are such things as "political reconstructions" of fossils. This is very true.[16] Fixing fossils to fit ideas is common and the world should know.

Lubenow also relates that D.J.M. Wright examined certain skulls at the British Museum and concluded the Neanderthal man had congenital syphilis.[17] Lubenow lists the skulls at the British Museum that Wright says he examined. In fact, Wright claims this fact also in his 1971 letter to *Nature*.[18] They are:

1. The first recognized Neanderthal skull cap ever found, in 1856. The original "Neandertal" is actually in the Rheinisches Landesmuseum in Bonn, Germany. It is not in the British Museum. Many museums have casts of originals.

2. Gibraltar II original, this is in the British Museum. I studied it, x-rayed it, and found no evidence of congenital syphilis.

3. Starosel'e — the original is actually in Moscow State University, Museum of Anthropology, in Russia. It is not in the British Museum.

4. Pech de l'Azé, — original fossil is in the Museé de l'Homme in Paris and not in the British Museum. I know of no casts of Pech de l'Azé, although I may be wrong.

Tooth signs of congenital syphilis are:

1. Mulberry molars showing very little enamel
2. First molars very small and second molars larger than first molars
3. Notched permanent incisor crowns on the incisal edge, upper and lower (Hutchinson teeth)
4. Barrel-shaped lower permanent incisors[19]

None of the Neanderthals had any of these. Some have thought that the extensive molar enamel wrinkling was due to congenital syphilis, but Dahlberg commented on this phenomena in many so-called "hominid" teeth, that there were many cases that have been designated as systemic effects of congenital syphilis "without sufficient substantiation."[20]

Late skull manifestations of congenital syphilis are:

1. frontal bossing of Parrott
2. short maxilla
3. high palatal arch
4. saddle nose
5. relative protuberance of mandible
6. perforation of the hard palate
7. Hutchinson teeth
8. syphilitic osteomyelitis[21]

Again I saw none of these in Neanderthal except in the relative protuberance of the mandible, which was fabricated most of the time. None of the Neanderthals was what we call in orthodontics a Class III malocclusion. If Neanderthals look Class III'ish it is because of tooth drifting or the condyles are out of the TM sockets. La Chapelle does not have a saddle nose which would be a depression of the bridge and nasal bones not due to a huge frontal sinus expansion. The British Museum people insisted I take my ceph radiographs of Tabūn C-1 in what they called attritional occlusion, which meant protruding the mandible out of the socket by a large amount.

Vitamin D is actually Vit D2 and D3. Ultraviolet light (UV-B) (280-320 nanometers wave length) from the sun converts (photobiogenesis) (at 282 nm UV-B) 7-dehydrocholesterol in the human skin to Pre-Vitamin D3 and to Vitamin D3 and subsequently transports to the liver where it forms 25-OH-D3 which is the major circulating form of Vit D in the blood. This then goes to the kidney to form 1,25-(OH)2D3. D2 is thought to follow a similar pathway to the liver to form 1,25 or 25-(OH)-D2. The 1,25-(OH)2D3 is the major calcium-regulating hormone. Lack of this Vit D brings about calcium deficiency in bones because it is essential for calcium absorption, and adequate calcium in the plasma for other functions. It activates the transport of calcium and phosphorus in the intestine, improves renal re-absorption of calcium, and the mobilization of calcium from the bone fluid compartment, essential for bone formation and remodeling.[22]

A supposed Vit D deficiency in Neanderthals and immediate post-flood people has been attributed to the lack of UV light from all the aerosols or dust in the atmosphere from the volcanic eruptions of the flood.

There are three points here: (1) There must have been a lot of dust, but (2) there was a rainbow after the flood. That required sunlight from a horizon position unless it was a miracle since it was a sign of a covenant. (3) "It has been estimated that approximately 10 to 15 minutes of summer sun exposure of the hands and face will produce 10µg of Vitamin D3, sufficient to meet the recommended daily allowance."[23] Pigmented skin will take longer. Tanning reduces the efficiency. (4) There was also vegetation immediately after the flood. The dove Noah sent out came back with a leaf in its beak. Also, Noah grew grapevines and made juice from grapes immediately post-flood. Visible light (400-750 nm. wave length) (red and blue violet parts) is necessary for photosynthesis by the chlorophyll molecules in those leaves. This is longer in wave length than UV light, which has a short wave length and is very penetrating. Even though most of the UV light is absorbed today by the ozone layer, sufficient amounts get through. I assume that the long wave visible light came through the immediate post-flood atmosphere for the chlorophyll in the grape leaves to produce oxygen, glucose, and hydrogen from carbon dioxide — then the shorter more powerful UV B light also came through to be absorbed by Noah and his family to prevent Vit D deficiency. There would be no sugar in Noah's grapes without the visible light spectrum. Another practical observation is that you can get sunburned on a cloudy day. UV light gets through.

I sincerely hope that these outlined diagnostic signs for rheumatoid arthritis, rickets, and congenital syphilis will finally put to rest the speculation of all those who have tried to explain away the Neanderthal features using these diseases. By the end of this book I think you will have sufficient evidence for the real cause of this phenomena.

Chapter 16, Research Note 2. The diagnosis of acromegaly or excess secretion of growth hormone (GH) in *Homo sapiens rhodesiensis* for the Rhodesian or Broken Hill cranium or Kabwe cranium (all the same skull) is made using the following criteria:

> 1. A straightened dorsum sellae (most of it missing) seen in the lateral cephalometric radiograph, which is seen often in adenoma of the pituitary gland, formerly classified according to the type of cells inside the tumor (eosinophilic chomophil cells of the anterior pituitary) but now classified as a macroform adenoma if equal to or greater than 11 mm in length.[24] For the following criteria see figures 7 through 14.
>
> 2. Absence of the posterior clinoid processes.
>
> 3. No broken appearance of the dorsum sellae, thin anteriorly, but well-formed lamina dura.
>
> 4. Enlargement of sella turcica in general (12.95mm from tip of dorsum sellae to tip of anterior clinoid processes).
>
> 5. The anterior clinoid processes are undercut, and they are longer bony processes above the sella turcica as compared to the radiograph by R. Singer from 1958. In Singer's radiographic lateral view there is no prominent bony projection in this area (see figure 13). The radiograph by Singer is in the negative form where all bone appears black and all empty spaces are white. The bullet hole does not appear in Singer's x-ray either.

6. The frontal sinuses are extremely enlarged and widespread in the A-P x-ray view.

7. The paranasal sinuses are multiple and appear to invade many bones of the upper face (maxilla, nasal, zygomatic, ethmoid, vomer, lacrimal).

8. The maxillary sinuses are extremely large.

9. There is almost a 2mm space, or anterior diastema, between the upper central incisors (anterior teeth) in the actual skull and the fossil replica that I purchased from Carolina Biological Supply with an official British Museum seal on its base. The two upper central incisors have been joined together by 2mm of plastic that is dark on the front side and light on the back to mask this space in the replica. There is another space 1+ mm between the left central and left lateral incisor.

10. The mastoid process on the left side appears to have been broken or chopped or sawed off, this could be a deliberate attempt to mask the hypertrophied process. The other side is absent.

11. The maxilla is extremely elongated in an inferior direction.

12. The mandible is missing that could have been definitive in the diagnosis.

13. The thickness of the whole cranial vault is excessive. Example: occipital bone thickness at Lambda is 13.8mm from the lateral cephalometric x-ray. The norm from Todd (1924) is 6mm. Some leeway could be allowed here because Todd's measurements came from male Caucasians. This skull is from Africa.

14. A large part of the external occipital protuberance is broken off where the superior nuchal line rises up high too early to be normal to join the protuberance. What little is left of the protuberance appears to be sanded down. The missing occipital fragment that broke off at this place under the protuberance was like a triangular wedge-shaped slice that thins out as it proceeds anteriorly towards the foramen magnum that preserves most of the inner bone at a 1-2mm thickness. I think it was supposed to have broken off this way when most of the right side was lost. In essence, the temporal bone is gone on the right side, so no mastoid is there, and the only other one is broken off. This is extremely suspicious in that most of the signs to diagnose acromegaly have disappeared or have been altered.

Other post-cranial bones have been found at the site; however, they are thought to belong to two or three more individuals. Day reports that the "limb bones are stout and long."[25] This could put them in the *Homo sapiens* range.

Stringer and Gamble claim that the Broken Hill remains are 200,000 years old or more. They classify him outside the limits of Neanderthals because the long bones found near the skull were strong but close to modern humans in certain respects.[26] On the jacket cover of Mellars and Stringers' book *The Human Revolution*, there is a drawing of Broken Hill, also known as Kabwe or Rhodesian man. There is a darkish spot on the side of the skull, not at all round and looks like a little bug on the temporal bone. This is the bullet hole.[27] They wish it were a bug.

Chapter 16, Research Note 3. The child Gibraltar II, from Devil's Tower on the Island of Gibraltar, was described by Dorothy Garrod in 1928. She says, "When the fragments were originally found we had only portions of the skull-cap on which to base our estimate of age. Since that time the discovery of the jaws, *whose evidence is somewhat conflicting when compared with the skull-cap,* has made a fairly exact estimate possible" (italics mine). She goes on to specify, "The most important evidence is necessarily provided by the teeth. It may be accepted as a good rule that the first permanent molars erupt in the sixth year."[28]

Garrod was applying the rigid uniform assumption that the modern day eruption time of the first permanent molars has *always been the same throughout history.* It has always been in the sixth year. Is this true? According to Garrod this fact made the Gibraltar child five years old.

Chapter 16, Research Note 4. Uniformitarianism: The idea of history or something else being the same yesterday, today, and tomorrow is basically a biblical concept. It just has been applied to God's creation instead of God himself. The writer of the Book of Hebrews speaks of Jesus Christ being "the same yesterday, today, yes and forever" (Heb. 13:8). Therefore, to apply this principle (universal, absolute) to nature is to exchange the "truth of God for a lie, and worshiped and served the creature rather than the Creator" (Rom. 1:25).

Chapter 16, Research Note 5. I examined the Gibraltar II child's upper and lower jaws in the British Museum in London, England. For some unexplained reason I was not allowed to see the skull-cap, or the bones of the ear. However, in the lower jaw I was able to discover an error in reconstruction that would have made a difference in the determination of its age *if tooth levels* were not allowed to dictate the conclusion. In figure 75 the lower jaw shows two primary molars and one unerupted permanent first molar on the left side. These teeth are absent on the right side. The radiographs show no permanent teeth on the right side. On the right side, an artificial tooth has been put in place of the first permanent molar. There has been a break through the jaw on the right side, in the socket of the second primary molar (small arrows, figure 76). We know this socket has been compressed because the socket for the first primary molar (a smaller tooth) has a larger socket. The back piece of bone (ramus) has been rotated outward so that the artificial tooth (first permanent molar) has its top surface facing straight up. Notice the wide whitish outer edge of the compressed socket (figure 75). That's the leading edge of the rotated back piece. The broken piece (ramus) has been pushed out about 10 mm and probably rotated forward 7-8 degrees. This anterior

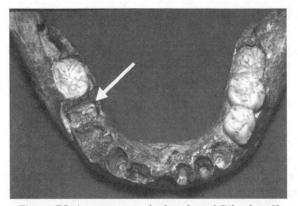

Figure 75. Arrow on crushed socket of Gibraltar II lower jaw in misconstruction of size and jaw angle.

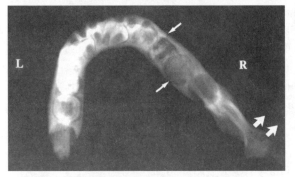

Figure 76. Arrows show direction of outward misconstruction of lower jaw of Gibraltar II.

rotation is seen in the side diagram, figure 33. The arrows point to the way the ramus and part of the body were rotated forward to decrease the gonial angle.

Most physical anthropologists know that a very young lower jaw shows a tipping in (toward the midline) and a tipping back of the condyle and upper part of the ramus. This imaginative adjustment in reconstructing the fossil jaw made it appear older.

If you look at the January 1996 issue of the *National Geographic Society,* the cover story is on Neanderthals.[29] Check out the photograph on page 17. It shows the actual Gibraltar child's skull bones, one of which is the mandible. The broken piece has been adjusted to conform to my criticism of it. No longer are the edges of the alveolar sockets uneven in the vicinity of the right missing lower primary second molar. The edges are now even and the permanent molar is tipped inwards in its socket. The Carolina Biological replica has been changed, too — it now conforms to almost the normal anatomy.

Garrod finally admitted that "the jaws are both absolutely and relatively small and the brain case large." She adds, "The massive size of the cranium seems at first sight to be rather remarkable in one so young." Garrod goes on to describe the following features which should have convinced her to abandon her uniform tooth eruption position but didn't. They are: very infantile inferior temporal bone (ear area), remarkable jaw muscle development, slow sutural growth on the side of cranium, infantile character of frontal bone (upright forehead, no supra-orbital brow ridges), rounded front surface of the upper jaw (very fetus-like), almost no chin development, very small mastoid process (lump of bone behind ear), and the absence of many small foramena (holes in bone) for blood vessels in mastoid area. In addition to these, the two primary molars are taurodont teeth (bull-like).

They are capable of much greater and longer wear than modern children's teeth. She saw these teeth and remarked, "The crowns of the teeth are very much worn, to an unusual degree for temporary teeth." Lastly, she came close to questioning her own presuppositions when she considered the growth of the side of the head. She said, "Although the breadth of the parietal is unusually large, it is possible that it may be within the normal limits of variation, although here also, unless we presume a slower rate of growth in this region than modern man, we are certainly dealing with an unusual specimen." She almost came to the conclusion that more than five years were necessary for the brain case to grow this large, even though the teeth only appear five years old. She almost broke away from the uniform tooth eruption schedule and followed the evidence. However, I think she knew that the evidence was leading to a child who had lived longer, had more tooth wear than five years, and was maturing and growing very slowly.[30]

Chapter 17, Research Note 1. Even though Dean, Stringer, and Bromage (1986) use a 7-day period for the formation of one layer of enamel between two perikymata, this period has been reported by Lavelle, Shellis, and Poole as an 8 to 10-day period. Lavelle et al. said that the daily incremental markings of the enamel prisms are 24-hour intervals, but that there could be 8 to 10 days involved from one line of Retzius (inside enamel) to another or from one perikymata (enamel surface) to another. What if in each 24-hour day only 1/2 or 1/3 of our modern daily increment were to be formed? Did a full increment always take just 24 hours? This would have caused the tooth in question to have formed in twice or three times the amount of time. The time between perikymata may have been 14 or 21 days. Evolutionary scientists are depending on the axiom here that the present is key to the past. If this is true, they are correct, but if it isn't, they are wrong. Also, more incremental days could have been involved within each stria of Retzius, which could only be determined by sectioning the tooth.

The root cone angles that are mentioned by Dean, Stringer, and Bromage are what you might expect from taurodont teeth, but not from rapidly developing teeth.[31] They said, "Several other points are also worth noting. One is that the developing root cone angles for the first permanent molars of the Gibraltar specimen fall below the values given for modern *Homo sapiens* by Dean (1985) by more than 10 degrees. This may simply reflect the taurodont morphology of the growing root, and there is as yet no comparative data about the way taurodont roots grow."

Chapter 19, Research Note 1. At the University of Liège in Belgium I studied the Engis II child. This fossil was discovered in Belgium in 1830. There is a loose upper jaw that was found with the skull. Most of the face is missing. This upper jaw contains four primary teeth and two empty sockets. From the length of the primary left lateral incisor the age looks to be about five to six years (modern standards).[32]

Charles Fraipont determined the age at death of this child as six to seven years from the teeth and skull.[33] Figure 17 shows four loose primary molars and two first permanent molars that belonged to the Engis II child. The length of the first primary molar roots and their root tips, which show some resorption (erosion) from this view, make it very difficult to age this child any older than five. Some contradictory evidence against Fraipont's estimate of age comes from a 1963 study by Moorrees et al.[34] Figure 17 also shows that the Engis II lower first permanent molar had just initiated its root formation at the time of this child's death. According to Moorrees et al., modern children achieve this stage of lower first molar development between 3.1 years in the female and 3.2 years in the male. Today, the root is half completed by 5.4 to 5.5 years. (These stages represent midpoints, not ages of attainment.) Therefore, according to recent standards, this child could be as young as three. However, Fraipont did not have these modern standards and he was distracted by the forehead.

"Le bourrelet supra-orbitaire de l'adulte se montre deja" means "the supra-orbital torus of the adult is already showing itself."[35] There is some small supra-orbital ridge formation and slight swelling between the ridges. When faced with this mature and older look of the frontal bone and youthfulness in tooth age, he was faced with a dilemma. It seems he knew that he had to call the head accelerated, rather than the teeth delayed based on his uniformitarian ideas of tooth eruption schedules, but he knew he couldn't call the head accelerated unless it were longer; henceforth, he took the actual 164mm length as seen in figure 18 and inflated it to 188mm. It is not 188mm, regardless of how you measure the length, even if the broken piece is repaired in the furthest back area (occipital bun). My measurement may be off by 1-2 mm, but not by 24mm. His figure could not have been obtained by measurement. He then states, "L'Enfant néanderthalien présente une accélération dans le dévelopment du squelette cranien." Translation: "The neandertal infant presents an acceleration in the development of the cranial skeleton." But why did he do this? Loyalty to the ape and uniformitarian causes demands statements like this.

In order to arrive at his conclusions he also had to ignore some immature features which should have showed him signs of a slowly growing skull. He made special mention of the extremely infantile character of the temporal bone, especially the tympanic ring. He said in reference to this very immature internal ear, "We notice some traces of the human fetus of the modern day child." He didn't attach much significance to this finding which was similar to Garrod's position on the fetal characters of the Gibraltar II child. Instead, he stood by the teeth which he called, "semblable à celui de l'enfant actuel." Translation: Similar to that of today's child.

The ape-like proposition is once again brought forth in one of Fraipont's conclusions. After the above quotation about the accelerated skull he went on to add, "Ce phénomène, qoique visible encore dans les races inférieures actuelles, est, chez elles, très atténué; au contraire, il est fortement accentué chez les grands Singes." Translation: "This phenomena, although still visible in today's inferior races, is, in their case or kind, very diminished, but in the opposite way, it is strongly pronounced in the kingdom of the great Apes." Therefore, great apes have accelerated skulls and, since he thought man was related to them, so must Neanderthals.

Notice the tone of racism in his statement. This is a huge problem with evolution which they think was cast aside with the "Out of Africa" theories. It just created the same problem in reverse. As soon as you make any race superior because of it being first or last you will have problems. Try the Noah theory for racial harmony where everyone comes from three sons in the same family. It's the only base to build on.

If Fraipont allowed the other facts to figure into the age equation, it might mean that the teeth were delayed in eruption and this would have been unforgivable in the world of anthropology. He adds, "Car un retard dans le seconde dentition chez cette espece serait en contradiction flagrante avec tout ce que nous savons de son développement et de ses caractères anthropoïdiques." Translation: A delay in secondary or permanent teeth (development) for this species or kind would be a flagrant contradiction with all that we know about his development and his anthropoid characters. Once again, this changing of facts (because of assumptions) is not science. It mandates acceleration of the head even if it means adding 24 mm and flies in the face of a thoughtful assessment of all the evidence.

Anne-Marie Tillier wrote an article on Le Crâne d'enfant d'Engis II: "Un exemple de distribution des charactères juvéniles, primitifs et néanderthaliens." On page 53, tableau 1 it gives the length of the cranium of the Engis child as being 176mm — exactly 12mm less than Fraipont's 188mm and 12mm more than the real value of 164mm.[36] She got it half right!

Chapter 19, Research Note 2. A most remarkable fact is gleaned from a new book on Neanderthals. In it there is a photograph from an original page of Charles Lyell's book *Antiquity of Man*, published in 1863. It shows a lateral view of the left side of the cranium of the Engis child, with a short description at the bottom of the page. The sentence, reads, "The extreme length of the skull is 7.7 inches, and as its extreme breadth is not more than 5.25, its form is decidedly dolicephalic."[37] These may be the words of P.C. Schmerling, the discoverer of the skull, because there are quotation marks at the beginning of the sentence, but it is in Lyell's book. *Antiquity of Man* is a crucial book in the history of man and the geologic record. It was Lyell who convinced Charles Darwin about the long gradual geologic ages. This 7.7 inches equates to 195.58mm. This is over 31mm off (see side view of Engis). This is a total fabrication on an original page from the father of modern geology. Much of modern geologic history rests on his words.

Chapter 20, Research Note 1. To quote the reference abstract from Trinkaus and Villeuremeur: "More importantly, the relative shortness of the Neanderthal proximal pollical phalanges (nearest bone of the thumb to the hand) and the relative lengthening of their distal pollical phalanges (end bone of the thumb) was confirmed, and it was determined that, despite some minor differences in articular (size of joint of thumb bones) dimensions between Neanderthal and recent humans, these pollical phalangeal length contrasts (difference in length in the two bones) translated into significant differences in mechanical advantages for the flexor muscles across the MCP and IP articulations."[38] MCP = metacarpophalangeal joint, IP = interphalangeal joint, flexor muscles = those muscles that are used in grasping objects with the thumb and fingers.

What he is saying here is that in comparison to modern man's thumb, the end bone of the Neanderthal thumb is longer and the next bone of the Neanderthal thumb is shorter; therefore, the muscles were at a disadvantage in the thumb grip or flexion on an object. This means that the muscles had to work harder to do the same task modern man's thumb does with less energy. The big question here is: Even if the muscles had to work harder to accomplish this precision grip does that mean Neanderthal never used a precision grip? My old bike did not have the gears to go up hills like my new bike does. Does that mean I never went up hills? I just pumped harder and went up hills and when I got the new bike it was easier.

I wrote an article in 1991 on the mechanical advantage problem one of my patients was having in her chewing mechanism (her jaws).[39] She was 50 years old and was experiencing a great deal of muscle pain in her right Temporalis M. with severe headaches which would start on the side of her head. Her right side was a normal Class I occlusion and her left a Class II or abnormal occlusion. The mechanical advantage of the muscles of chewing (mastication) was greater on the right than on the left, because of the position of the teeth and their distance from the fulcrum or condyle; they were closer. The mandible is a Class III lever, like an upside-down wheelbarrow, the wheel is the fulcrum or the condyle. She chewed on the right because it was easier, but in the long run experienced pain because the muscles were overused and traumatically inflamed. She almost never chewed on her left because it required more energy. She was completely able to chew on the left side, and with some adjustment of the teeth and an appliance it became easier. The whole point of this is simple: the necessity for more muscle activity doesn't equate to impossible movement, just more energy required in that movement. The Neanderthals were strong people.

If you examine M. Day's picture of the La Ferrassie I hand in his book, you will see a large lump of bone on the inside or ventral surface (gripping surface of the thumb) in the middle of the distal pollical phalange or end of the thumb bone.[40] If you look at Gray's anatomy you will see a depression for that insertion — the flexor pollicus longus muscle right next to the IP joint. Gray describes it as arising from the grooved anterior or volar surface of the body of the radius (a bone of the lower arm) and some other areas and inserts into the base of the distal bone of the thumb. It is essentially a large lower arm muscle. So modern man's insertion of this large arm muscle on the inside surface of the last bone of the thumb is closer to the IP joint than the Neanderthal. The Neanderthal's is farther away on the elevation (due to muscle forces on that small surface of thumb bone). Trinkaus even says in his book, "Interestingly, the Shanidar 3, 4, 5, and 6 pollical phalanges all have extremely large insertions for the M. flexor pollicis longus tendons, as do those of other Neandertals." This implies an exceptional development of this muscle, which may be a partial compensation for the elongation of their distal phalanges."[41]

The mechanical advantage of a muscle is directly proportional to distance from the insertion point to the joint upon which the muscle works. Therefore, the farther away from the joint the insertion point is, the more the mechanical advantage. The more pull or force it can exert with the exact same expenditure of energy. The closer the insertion point is to the joint, the harder the muscle has to work to produce the same force or pull; i.e., less mechanical advantage. If you could move the insertion area of your biceps muscle farther down towards your hand you could do curls with barbells like Superman, providing the rest of your body could take the strain. This conclusion by Trinkaus and Villeuremure looks to be extremely flawed.

Chapter 20, Research Note 2. Upper first molars of Le Moustier show much interproximal wear on the mesial surface and the lower left first permanent molar shows almost identical interproximal wear as the right.

Chapter 20, Research Note 3. The Hublin et al. article, which is mentioned later in the main text, shows that Neanderthals did small decorative work with their hands, but did they give them credit for the advance? No. They said the advanced carved articles found were indicative of a Châtelperronian culture associated with a Neanderthal fossil (juvenile temporal bone) from Arcy-sur-Cure, but basically used it to support long-term co-existence of the two species, meaning that modern humans shared tech-cultural information with Neanderthals. They dated it to about 34,000 years ago. The Châtelperronian culture was supposed to be an outgrowth of the Mousterian culture. The Mousterian tools are supposed to be cruder in style than the later Châtelperronian or Aurignacian tools.[42]

Chapter 20, Research Note 4. In chapter 36 of Numbers, we find Moses commanding the daughters of Zelophehad to marry their first cousins so that their inheritance will not be removed from the tribe of their fathers. They were of the tribe of Joseph. This command, which came directly from God to Moses, would have resulted in what is termed "consanguineous marriages" today.[43] This term means "same blood" marriages and is generally condemned in the modern world, although still practiced in many Third World countries and religious sects. It is also called "inbreeding." The reason this practice is discouraged is that the rate of birth defects produced from consanguineous marriages is very high. This is due to the union of a male and a female who are carrying similar "recessive genes." The union of two similar recessive genes results in the child of the union actually manifesting a full-blown physical birth disorder or defect. This is due to the similar genetic make-up of relatives and the fact that blood relatives usually carry many of the same recessive genes. This passage in the Book of Numbers implies that these recessive genes were not present in the daughters of Zelophehad, or present to a very small degree. This, therefore, implies more genetic breakdown in modern man (harmful mutations) and a less genetic breakdown (harmful mutations) in the daughters of Zelophehad and their cousins.

Chapter 24, Research Note 1. The "old man" Cro-Magnon skull (Magnon pronounced almost like mignon in filet mignon) was in one of the bottom drawers of the cabinet in the lab of the Musée de l'Homme in Paris. His cranium (approximately 200 mm) was not nearly as long as La Chapelle and La Ferrassie and his cranium was higher and more modern-appearing. I thought the cranial capacity of 1600 cc was greatly exaggerated. The surface of the facial bones had the look of a sponge. I didn't x-ray it or even take any photos because it looked eroded by disease, worms, or insects. It was a small face and it was ugly. I didn't see the other two partial crania that were supposed to be there in any of the drawers. I may have missed them, but I looked carefully. In any event, 5 Cro-Magnons were supposed to have been found at this rock shelter near the station in Les Ezyies de Tayac. [44]

Chapter 24, Research Note 2. The first true serpent, according to Alfred Roemer in *Vertebrate Paleontology,* was one called "Hylonomous." It was a four-legged serpent found in the Coal Measures of Nova Scotia, the Carboniferous period of the Paleozoic era.[45] Snakes without legs did not appear until the Cretaceous layers which are supposedly dated almost 200 million years later. Another four legged-reptile was recently found in Scotland.[46] The curse of Genesis 3:14 is the only real explanation why the first reptiles lost their legs and later became snakes.

Chapter 24, Research Note 3. Just what ecological niches could mean in a pre-flood canopy-covered world is difficult to define. It may have had different types of plants and perhaps different types of water locations, lakes, rivers, brooks, etc. Terrain and lithographic features could also be different. It might help to imagine the different settings in a modern zoo like Brookfield Zoo in Illinois (the Chicago area), except that they'd be separated by hundreds of miles, and there wouldn't have been rain.

Chapter 24, Research Note 4. The Geologic Time Scale as outlined by Romer indicates that the Cretaceous Period started at 130 million years ago and lasted 68 million years and ending at about 62 million years before the present (BP).[47] The Tertiary Period started at 62 million years BP running up to the 2 million or 1.6 million years BP mark. Therefore, between the beginning of the Cretaceous Period and the beginning of the Tertiary Period there are approximately 68 million years. Man wasn't supposed to have made an appearance before a few hundred-thousand years, and those who could draw within approximately 20,000 years. Even if dinosaurs survived right up to the Cretaceous-Tertiary border at 62 million years ago, man could never have actually seen a live one, according to their scheme. But this could be very wrong because of the Bernifal Cave evidence.

Chapter 25, Research Note 1. God said to Adam and Eve in Genesis 1:29-30, " 'Behold, I have given you every plant yielding seed that is on the surface of all the earth, and every tree which has fruit yielding seed; it shall be food for you. And to every beast of the earth and to every bird of the sky and to everything that moves on the earth which has life, I have given every green plant for food,' and it was so." All trees and fruit with seed were given to man, all plants to birds, beasts, and everything else on the earth. Therefore, birds had to eat plants. They probably required teeth in order to do this, which they do not have today. They only have embryonic teeth in some species that do not develop into real teeth (chickens). However, the most important part of this is God later put a prohibition on one fruit tree (Gen 2:16-17) in the garden after he had said they could eat from "every tree which has fruit." Did he go back on his word? Well, if we believed the Bible could be wrong in some parts we might say there was a mistake in the translation somewhere, instead of looking any further. But, since we know the Bible to be historically and scientifically accurate, we press on to find the meaning of "every tree which has fruit," and not this one. Remember what "every tree" specifically was in Genesis 1:29. It was a tree with fruit yielding seed, not just fruit. What is the difference? The tree of the knowledge of good and evil must not have had any seed for further propagation of the species. It is my opinion that it was only for a season. The temptation was only going to last as long as the tree lasted, whose life span we don't know. However, we do know Adam lived past 900 years and perhaps the tree of knowledge of good and evil had a much shorter existence. Temptation, therefore, was a test for only a certain period of time — to test their love, based on free will. Although it was temporary, they still failed.

Plant death obviously was a reality from the beginning, because when eaten, it died. It is not the same kind of death as human and animal death. It involves no blood. Tree sap and plant fluids are not the same as blood. Therefore, I believe that when Adam and Eve ate fruit from the trees and plants that the plants were digested with some of the biochemical reactions that are present today. The trees probably had a limited life span also. Does this mean that the Second Law existed before the fall? All that I can say is that those processes necessary for biological and botanical life were active. After man fell, these processes were included in the Second Law and were potentiated in their harmfulness.

Chapter 27, Research Note 1. Jarcho's three groups from Russia, Kirghiz, and Uzbekistan followed the same pattern, with the height gain for Russians, .5mm; the Kirghiz, .5mm; and the Uzbeks, .1mm, when the lengths were increasing nearly 3-4mm. The lengths were expanding close to seven times more than the height.[48]

Chapter 27, Research Note 2. Parchappe studied the five age categories, 20-30, 30-40, 40-50, 50-60, and 60 and over, and from his measurements the cephalic index (width/length x 100) can be calculated. It went from 77.0 to 74.7 from the first, youngest group to the last, oldest group among men. He also found that the cephalic index went from 76.9 to 75.8 from the first to last groups among women. Overall, then, his study showed that the head of the French in 1836 gained more in length than in width as it aged, with the men more than the women. It can be said there was a tendency for these heads to move in the direction of a "doli-chocephalic" skull with age. Parchappe's conclusion was, "Augmentation in volume does not appear to cease at the time assigned as the end of growth in general, but seems, on the contrary to continue gradually up to 60 years."[49]

Chapter 27, Research Note 3. Hrdlicka also measured the heads of adult Indians of the Southwest and Northern Mexico other than Pueblos.[50] They ranged from below 28 years to 28 through 50 years and 50 and above. The groups were divided into these three levels which again displayed the same direction in the reduction of the cephalic index. The first group was calculated at 80.6 and the last, or 50 and over group, at 79. Again a trend was observed towards more lengthening than widening. Hrdlicka's laboratory skulls had a cephalic index of 78.4 for the 20-29 year group and a 78 for the 50-59 year group. The heights decreased by 1.5mm. The Pueblo Indians showed equal increases in width with lengths almost stable.

Chapter 27, Research Note 4. The Pueblo Indians from 28-50 years had a different response. The females displayed a 3.3mm increase in height and the males 1.7mm while the lengths were stable in males and increased in females slightly, and the widths increased in both sexes. All the other Indians Hrdlicka studied showed 2 to 1 increases in length to height among men and women. Hrdlicka stated, "In the Pueblo males, and especially in the other-than-Pueblo females, the youngest adults show a tendency toward a higher cephalic index than that of the older ages, or at least that of the 20-50 year groups."[51]

Chapter 27, Research Note 5. Nasjletti and Kowalski in 1975 looked for proportional changes over time with aging in the vertical dimensions of the front of the face.[52] They found by examining 510 whites (20-86 years of age) that all the ages exhibited increases in total facial height and that these were always in constant proportions. The upper face was always very close to the same proportion of the entire face throughout the entire aging process.

Chapter 27, Research Note 6. Kowalski and Nasjletti conducted a similar facial height study on a group of Black American males in 1976, and found the facial proportions to be very close to constant in all ages even though there was growth occurring as with the white American group.[53]

Chapter 27, Research Note 7. Israel took 26 females and 26 males aged 24.9 to 78.8 years. He demonstrated that differential growth had taken place in separate areas and this proved that his radiographic technique did not simply display a "uniform enlargement " of the skull.[54]

Chapter 27, Research Note 8, Dr. Behrents' Study.[55] The following diagram, figure 77, is a typical cephalometric tracing taken from Dr. Behrents' work and is basically as standard as there is in orthodontics. All x-rays were taken according to the original standards of the Broadbent-Bolton study (1975).[56] The magnification factor varied for some x-rays, but Dr. Behrents corrected them all to a standardized

Figure 77.

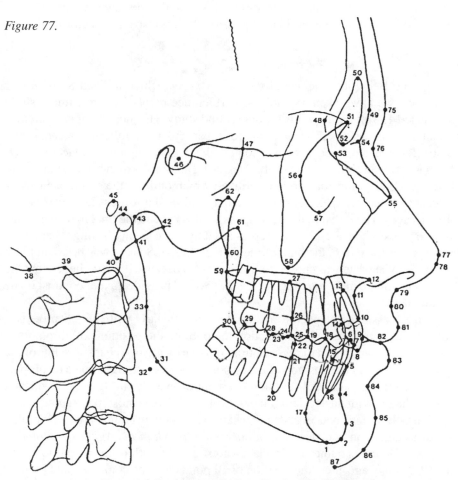

<u>Essential Cephalometric Landmarks For This Study</u>

1. ME (Menton)	32.GOI (Gonial Intersection)	45. APO (Anatomic Porion)
2. GN (Gnathion)	33. PB (Posterior Border Ramus)	46. S (Sella Turcica)
3. PO (Pogonion)	34. PSE (Posterior Skull External)	47. SE (Ethmoid Reg.Point)
4. B (B Point)	39. BP (Bolton Point)	48. GBI (Glabella Internal)
11. A (A Point)	40. BA (Basion)	49. GB (Glabella)
12. ANS (Anterior Nasal Spine)	41. AR (Articulare)	50. FSS (Frontal Sinus Sup.)
30. AB (Anterior Border Ramus)	43. CO (Condylion)	52. FSI (Frontal Sinus Inf.)
31. GO (Gonion)	44. PO (Porion)	54. Na (Nasion)
		57. OR (Orbitale)

6% enlargement factor for uniformity. Therefore, all of the radial distance measurements for comparison purposes taken from the original data have been reduced by 6%. None of the angles have been reduced since they are not effected by magnification.

The lateral cephalograms were digitized to be reduced to x-y coordinate data and superimposition was accomplished using a sella registration and a sella-nasion orientation on the participant's previous data from his lateral cephalometric x-ray. The points are located at various bony landmarks and these are used by orthodontists all over the world to chart growth. It is also a key factor in diagnosis.

PLOTTING CRANIOFACIAL POINTS

From Behrents' tracings of the lateral x-rays which utilized 87 points of reference, we have taken 58 hard tissue reference points for our primary study and added 13 soft tissue points for our second study. The location of each craniofacial point is described by Behrents for a particular age in terms of radial distance (R) from a defined reference point (sella) and an angular displacement (Ø) from a defined reference line (Sella-Nasion). Behrents provides (R,Ø) information for all the points that we have utilized which outlines the craniofacial skeleton at two distinct ages and the points that outline the soft tissue profile at two distinct ages. The initial male mean age is 19.8 years and the final male mean age is 46.6 years. There are 79 males represented by these means. Though there were males older than 46.6, the bulk of the data during 26.8 years was between these two ages. Male data was chosen for this research because it was believed that the robustness of the male osteological features would provide greater contrast in the extrapolations.

If we assume that each R and each Ø vary linearly with age, then the two sets of (R,Ø) give enough information to compute the positions of all points at any age. Following from the assumption of linearity are two characteristics of the diagram plots: (1) the position of every point follows a straight line as a proportional function of age, and (2) the movement of every point follows a constant rate of change with no deceleration or cessation. There is most likely some deceleration as Behrents' data outside the means does show in certain areas. However, as far as cessation is concerned, in his book *Growth in the Aging Craniofacial Skeleton,* Behrents quotes D. Sinclair who stated, "Death is but an end to growing."[57] For any age, then, the position of all points may be computed and plotted, and the corresponding points connected with straight lines to reveal the outlined shape of the craniofacial units.

The outlines of seven of the major morphologic units of the craniofacial complex are computed and plotted in this study. These units are as follows: 1. Anterior cranial base 2. Posterior cranial Base 3. Fronto-nasal 4. Orbital 5. Zygomatic 6. Maxillary 7. Mandibular.

CONNECTING POINTS WITH SPLINES

It is not necessary to use only straight lines to connect plotted points. In fact, a more realistic image may be obtained by using curved lines. The use of curved lines in no way sacrifices the legitimacy of the original data as it can be guaranteed that the curved lines pass directly through the plotted points. Thus, the appearance of the image is merely enhanced without altering the original and governing shape of the image.

There are many well-known methods for mathematically expressing a free-flowing curved line. The method used in this study involves expressing both the horizontal (x) and vertical (y) coordinates of the line as cubic polynomials of the form.

$$x(t) = A_x t^3 + B_x t^2 + C_x t + D_x \qquad\qquad y(t) = A_y t^3 + B_y t^2 + C_y t + D_y$$

where A_x, B_x, C_x, D_x, A_y, B_y, C_y and D_y are arbitrary constants which describe the position and shape of the line, and t is a running variable conveniently chosen to range between zero and one. Thus, the curved line is plotted in the (x,y) plane as a function of

$$t (0 \le t \le 1).$$

The eight arbitrary constants leave eight degrees-of-freedom for choosing the specific position and shape the line is to take. The following eight characteristics were selected to describe each line and determine what each constant should be:

1. starting position (t=0) in horizontal (x) direction.
2. starting position (t=0) in vertical (y) direction.
3. starting position (t=1) in horizontal (x) direction.
4. starting position (t=1) in vertical (y) direction.
5. starting angle with respect to horizontal.
6. ending angle with respect to horizontal.
7. starting curvature (speed of departure from starting angle).
8. ending curvature (speed of departure from ending angle).

Characteristics (1) through (4) are chosen to coincide with the positions of the two craniofacial points the line is to link. Characteristics (5) through (8) describe the shape the line is to take between the two points and are chosen to render a visually appealing image. To insure that consecutive lines (linking a series of craniofacial points) maintain a smooth shape, the starting angle of each line is chosen to equal the ending angle of the previous line. Thus, the craniofacial shape is outlined by a series of SPLIced liNES.

By utilizing the above methods, we have extrapolated Behrents' mean data to outline the craniofacial skeleton for a male at the following ages: 20 (19.8), 100, 200, 300, 400, 500. I am only showing the 100 through 500, lest the 19.8 clutter up the diagram with unneeded lines.

Since none of the three Classic Neanderthals from southern France (Le Moustier, La Ferrassie I, or La Chapelle-aux-Saints) has an intact anterior cranial base from sella to nasion, it was impossible to make direct comparisons with each of the above extrapolations of Behrents' research. Only shape and relative comparisons were possible. However, since Behrents gave calculations from other points that did not include sella turcica (the turkish saddle, or otherwise known as the pituitary fossa), it was possible to make direct comparisons on the basis of those measurements of the cranio-facial complex.

Please note that there is also no measurement for the inside anterior border of the frontal sinus so the age projections only show the glabella external moving forward and down, but the sinus is shown only moving superiorly and not forward or anteriorly.

Chapter 27, Research Note 9. Calculation 146 [58] (width of the ramus) in Behrents' study shows that while some loss of bone is experienced in the course of aging on this frontal border of the vertical part (ramus) of the lower jaw, overall it becomes wider at the angle by 0.19mm in 26.8 years. Therefore, the addition of bone on the backside of the angle must be greater than the reduction on the front side. Calculation 30 is the angle from the SN line to the anterior border of the ramus point. Calculation 30 makes the ramus look as if it's getting narrower when in reality calculation 146 says it gets wider. Calculation 145, a measurement higher up the ramus, shows that reduction takes place on the front border at this level which makes the body of the mandible longer.

The curious thing about the mandible is that while the ramus and body elongate, the center of the anterior border of the ramus resorbs during aging. When using Behrents' final angle for the anterior border of the ramus, we discover that the projection from 200 to 500 shows this area to have resorbed (figure 28, dashed line). When using Behrents' angle for the 31 to 50 years we note there is bony deposition there (figure 28, solid line). In figure 26, this border did not decrease. Perhaps there are male and female differences. However, Behrents' direct measurement across the ramus at this point to the gonial angle showed a 0.19mm increase in males and a 0.19mm increase in females. Therefore, both projections are correct because they display the inner and outer ramal changes. In modern man's lifetime, resorption does proceed at the center of the anterior border and proceeds up the medial side of the ramus onto the coronoid process. The coronoid process elongated at first under 100, but after that became shorter because of this resorption pattern. A large section of the ramus resorbed as shown in figure 28 (dashed line). If the masseter and internal pterygoid muscles (sling muscles of mastication) did not maintain strength and position into old age perhaps both the inner and outer border would resorb. Behrents thought that the coronoid is responsive to increased or decreased biomecranical demands placed on it with age.

Chapter 27, Research Note 10. Our program had no way to determine muscle strength or positioning of the sling muscles in old age. Therefore resorption should overwhelm this anterior border and coronoid process if the sling muscles did not retain their insertion base across the lateral and medial sides of the ramus. Or perhaps the forward movement of the teeth initiated some forward movement of the muscles to increase their mechanical advantage. Anterior muscle positioning has been found in Nubian jaws and skulls by Carlson and Van Gerven in their oldest skulls with more forward facial positions allegedly 12,000 years BP. They found posterior mastication muscle positions in later skulls.[59] Therefore, it is my opinion that the solid line represents the lateral edge of the anterior ramus border that flows into the oblique line, but that immediately medial to that edge the ramus is resorbed and appears scooped out. Both representations are correct. The temporomandibular joint or glenoid fossa became wider and the condyle on the end of the ramus became thicker. As is visible in the 500-year-old male, the teeth moved so far forward that the chin began to look flat. This was the result of the mandibular front teeth and alveolar process tipping back as all the lower teeth slid forward over the chin. A train car analogy can be made here. It is like a moving passenger train car where the car or mandible is moving, but the passengers or teeth are also moving to seats closer to the front. To make it more accurate, the people in the front are reclining in their seats while the people in the back have their seats in the upright position. The maxillary teeth moved forward also, but less than the lowers. The lower teeth moved through all the ages. The chin appeared to become smaller because of the amount of forward movement of the teeth and alveolar bone, but it is not being resorbed. There is just a filling in of bone above the chin.

Chapter 27, Research Note 11. Harry Sicher was my anatomy professor in postgraduate school at Loyola of Chicago. He wrote concerning the continuous eruption of the teeth. He stressed the importance of understanding the whole process. He made the following points for ideal conditions: 1. Attrition on both the occlusal surfaces and the incisal edges progresses at an even rate of speed. 2. The active eruption of a tooth is, under ideal conditions and after facial growth has ceased, equal to the loss of substance on its occlusal surface; thus the facial height is kept constant. 3. The active eruption is achieved by apposition of cementum at the root apices and in the furcations and apposition of bone at the alveolar fundus and at the crests of interradicular septa. 4. Apposition of bone at the free borders of the alveolar process is active even in older persons. The amount of bone formed at the alveolar crest seems to be smaller than that at the alveolar fundus (bottom of the socket).

I am omitting references to the soft tissue attachments as irrelevant to our discussion. Sicher goes on to state that he does not assume that ideal conditions exist in the "normal" conditions. Although he does add, "In spite of the fact that even in 'normal' jaws ideal conditions of the human masticatory apparatus are rarely realized, their analysis seems indispensable for a true understanding and evaluation of this complex system of tissues and organs." He refers to the cementum of the teeth, like bone, aging and degenerating. Instead of cementum replacement like bone replacement, there is a new layer of cementum to cover the old layer which adds to the length of the root while the crown is being worn away.[60]

Murphy agrees with Sicher in his study of Australian aborigine skulls, but does not agree that tooth eruption in adult life is directly related to the amount of wear, attrition or function. He found that tooth eruption varied in adult life with the skeletal growth pattern, and only was indirectly related to tooth attrition. He did see continuous tooth eruption in his study of 337 skulls. While there was some loss of facial height due to tooth attrition and loss of vertical dimension, it was not as great as expected or in saying it another way, it was not a loss to the same extent as the loss of tooth surface structure. Eruption was partially compensating for this loss. Of this eruption, about two-thirds was accounted for by bone growth in and around the socket of the alveolus and the other one-third by the cementum apposition on the root making it longer.[61]

Chapter 28, Research Note 1. I also studied and measured craniometrically the following three Neanderthal children's casts in the Smithsonian Institution: La Quina XVIII (cranium only), Staroselje (cranium and mandible), and Teschik-Tasch (cranium and mandible). I could not include these measurements with the cephalometric measurements of the other Neanderthals for two reasons: 1. Many measurements are incompatible because of the points involved. 2. La Quina XVIII did not have a mandible.

Chapter 28, Research Note 2. The Neanderthal gonial angles in Table A are measured by the Michigan Method with the following cephalometric points: Articulare-Gonial Intersection-Menton (black lines in tracings of Neanderthal children — some black lines in Le Moustier are Behrents' lines).

The Neanderthal gonial angles measured in Table B are measured by the Bolton Method with the following cephalometric points: Articulare-Gonion-Gnathion (gray lines in tracings of Pech and Moustier).

Chapter 28, Research Note 3. I am speaking of the average of the overall rates of craniofacial growth of a child. Everyone knows children have growth spurts, but it doesn't mean they don't have a beginning and an end. I want to know the average rate over the entire growth period to maturation when adult growth begins in the facial area. We know the neurocranium behaves differently, being developed quite early with faster early rates than the facial complex. Its rates slow down much earlier and total "adolescent growth is complete probably between 18 and 25 years of age."[62]

Björk and Helm, 1967, outlined the rates of general body growth.[63] They also looked into maximum puberal growth in the midst of adolescence, upper face, mandible, and body height. These rate curves showed similarity in that they peaked and dipped at close to the same ages. Rates are also dimorphic, so this is a very complex subject. Therefore, I am singling out the maxillo-mandibular complex to focus on, and in particular the measurements most sensitive to the counterclockwise growth of these parts.

Chapter 28, Research Note 4. I went over the records and saw this being done in the Armed Forces Institute of Pathology, Washington, D.C. Children's remains from the period of 1700 to the 1800s were being aged with modern dental means. (See "An Early American Child" in chapter 31.)

Chapter 28, Research Note 5. The Spitalfields' study is very interesting because it and Stringer, Bromage, and Deans' work on Gibraltar II child were supposed to put to rest any claims for slower development in the past. This study of the 0 to 5.4 year old children by direct measurement (no x-ray) finds everything in the 1729-1859 period pretty close to today, except for one thing: the complete crown formation time for the upper permanent central incisor tooth. They didn't find one totally complete.[64] Why? Since by 1935 and 1944 standards it is 4-5 years old.[65] So, up to this 5.4 year age and no full upper central crown yet would be a slower development. However, I think this is integrated with their study on the Gibraltar II child's (Devil's Tower child) age at death and soothed their consciences. Gib II looked extremely advanced in relation to us and to these kids of Spitalfield's. He had a complete crown at supposedly 3.1 years, and remember they used that one upper central incisor for their perikymata count. Now in relation to these 1700-1800 kids, Gib II was much further back in time. Further back in time to an evolutionist always means faster in development. Therefore, they reported accurately on one fact — the 5.4 age limit. I have no proof of the other Spitafield's facts being false, but I have great suspicion based upon all that I've seen. Remember Gib II in *National Geographic*.[66] He appeared without the split alveolar process and the mis-aligned parts were aligned. No article that I know of ever appeared about how they "fixed it" after 1994 (my *CEN Tech Journal* article)[67] which exposed it, except the *Nature* letter which showed it fixed.[68]

Chapter 28, Research Note 6. Pierce, in 1884, described the upper first molar at six years of age as having a root development only up to the bifurcation of the three roots. G.V. Black's chart was similar in 1883.

Chapter 28, Research Note 7. In 1944, Schour and Massler described the upper first molar at the sixth year as having at least one-third of the roots formed above the bifurcation area.

Chapter 28, Research Note 8. In this section I will compare bony measurements from two sets of data from the University of Michigan and Case Western Reserve. These bony measurements have chronological ages which correspond with each measurement, be it angle or distance. I will use these chronological ages of modern male children to set tentative ages for the Neanderthal children. Neither the Michigan nor Bolton researchers give actual growth rates, just the raw data from which these rates can be calculated.

The Bolton data have some longitudinal records and some cross-sectional in their measurements. The Michigan data is all longitudinal.

All Bolton and Michigan distances, not angles, have been reduced according to their magnification specifications.

Chapter 28, Research Note 9. This note is for orthodontists and growth experts. Dr. Enlow gives a definition of facial growth that I basically agree with. It is this: "Growth is a multifactorial cumulative composite of changes in many regions of the head, the summation of which produces the 'forward and downward' expansion seen in the overlay."[69] In this definition he described a simplistic view of two overlays, one "before" and one "after" cephalometric radiographs. One could falsely conclude that it was a straight expansion from one stage to the other. As he pointed out, this naive concept is wrong and most workers know this by 1998. I also agree with him that growth by deposition and resorption and displacement are not distinguishable.

Chapter 28, Research Note 10. I am not writing about comparing a skeletal open bite rami to a closed-bite rami, or open-bite gonial angles to closed-bite gonial angles like Class II Div II patients. The rates are obviously quite different. The open bite has probably a much slower rate and shorter height; the closed-bite ramus, a faster rate and greater height. These are mean normal skeletal range growth rami, 95% within ±two standard deviations of the mean. The Bolton data would reflect this better since their "Bolton faces" were selected as being "aesthetically favorable."[70] I am assuming the two Neanderthal children were also alike in their growth patterns because of their homogenecity. They were probably reproductively isolated also because of the glaciers in the more northern regions of the land and the basic agreement of the anthropological world on classical Neanderthals being a distinctive grouping.

Chapter 28, Research Note 11. Actually the number of two-year-old radiographs was approximately 1,000. The total number of children that were in the study at one time or another was 5,000.

Chapter 28, Research Note 12. The Gib II ramus from Articulare to Gonion was 30.8 mm with a .92 magnification factor .

Chapter 28, Research Note 13. "Procumbency" means protrusion or jutting forward of something, either the entire jaw (as in a skeletal procumbency) or just the teeth and surrounding alveolar bone (as in a dento-alveolar procumbency). You can have a dento-alveolar procumbency without having a skeletal procumbency. As the Neanderthal children aged they deposited bone on the anterior surface of the maxilla when modern children were undergoing resorption. Enlow wrote about this being a depository surface in the fetal period and a few years beyond.[71] It is my observation that in the Gib II maxilla and in the Engis child this deposition was still in progress and at a late date. This is the reason for the bulbous appearance of the maxillary anterior and alveolar surfaces. The right side anterior surface of the zygomatic process of the maxilla of Gib II does show some hollowing-out (resorption), even though most of the labial surfaces are depositing. This is quite unlike the same surface in the Gibraltar I adult which is smooth with no hollowing.

Chapter 28, Research Note 14. Note basion was estimated for Le Moustier with assistance from the following structures: the petrous portion of the temporal bone, tympanomastoid fissure, external auditory meatus and auditory canal, and a small part of the basilar part of the occipital bone and the positions of basion in La Ferrassie I and La Chapelle-aux-Saints.

Chapter 28, Research Note 15.

Table I
Gonial Angles of Wainwright Eskimos[72]

From Cedarquist's Tables 16-22 of Measurement 35 for the angle (ar-tgo-gn) (articulare-tangent gonial angle-gnathion) for seven age groupings, in degrees:

Age Range	Female Mean	S.D.	Male Mean	S.D.	Combined	S.D.
5 yrs- 9yrs/11 mos.	134.3	7.7	133.3	5.9	133.8	6.9
10 yrs-16 yrs/11 mos.	130.7	6.2	131.6	5.7	131.0	6.0
17 yrs-21 yrs/11 mos.	129.3	4.9	129.2	6.9	129.2	6.0
22 yrs-29 yrs/11 mos.	130.1	3.8	127.4	5.4	128.7	4.7
30 yrs-39 yrs/11 mos.	124.1	5.3	129.2	9.2	127.4	8.2
40 yrs-49 yrs/11 mos.	117.8	2.2	127.3	7.9	125.2	8.0
50 yrs-74/11/mos.	120.3	2.8	124.6	5.6	123.3	5.3
Change from 1-7	14°		8.7°			

Cedarquist calculated Gonial Angle just like Michigan Method except he used Gnathion as forward point. Using this method, Le Moustier's gonial angle was 110° again.

Chapter 28, Research Note 16. Figure 36 is a "Forecast to Maturity" by Rocky Mountain Data Systems, Inc. of Calabassas, California. It displays what Pech's bony outline of the maxilla and mandible would have grown to if Pech had lived to 18.5 yrs and matured like a modern day child. It is superimposed on an estimated PTV and on the actual Frankfort Horizontal (Pech) by RM Data Systems. I estimated a PTV and FH for Le Moustier and superimposed it upon the RM predication to see how close it came. It is quite obvious that the forecast is not quite accurate because the Neanderthals grew to much greater sizes. The question becomes: Did they get this much larger by a faster rate of growth (different species argument) or did they get this way by a longer time period of growth?

This RM forecast tells us that if the rate and ages were the same as modern man, then all that would be accomplished would be the forecast size. Lengthen the time and you have greater size, or speed up the rate and the same thing happens.

Chapter 28, Research Note 17. "Indeed, both the masseter and internal muscles insert in the area of the gonial angle. Possibly even more important, the gonial angle and the antegonial notch profiles have been reported to be dependent on the strength of mastication during childhood as well as on the amount of tooth wear."[73]

Chapter 28, Research Note 18. Gonial Angle Changes

There have been other recent studies on gonial angle change. Chang et al. explored facial changes in 80 children and 80 young adults and have found the gonial angle to be "age related." They also have said, "The decrease in size of the gonial angle might contribute mainly to the flattening tendency of the mandibular growth coincident with general growth." [74] Muretic and Rak in 1991 studied the mandibular or gonial angle with a large group of lateral head radiographs of children to adults age groups. "For each age group, three roentgenocephalometric variables were statistically processed. Results, presented numerically and graphically, led to a conclusion that the size of the mandibular angle and its superior segment decreased considerably in a defined period of time. A decrease in the values of all variables was clearly seen in both adolescence and post-adolescence."[75]

Foley and Mamandras found the mandibular plane angle, which is closely related to the gonial angle, to decrease among 14- 20-year-old girls by 1.1 degrees in 6 years from 14 to 20 years of age.[76] From this research a rate of 0.18 degrees per year is obtained. This is much slower than the gonial angle rate of 0.85° or 0.57° per year of the Michigan and Bolton studies, but this is only a 6-year study so is very limited.

Chapter 28, Research Note 19. The fourth Neanderthal child is the older youth or young adult from Le Moustier. I examined and x-rayed this fossil in Berlin, Germany, in the Museum für Vor-Und Frühgeschichte. Le Moustier has been designated as a male between the ages of 16 and 18 years. The skull and facial bones have been broken and separated by a bomb explosion in the museum during WW II. I have recently made my radiographs available to the present museum anthropologists at their request in an attempt to put the skull and face together properly. It is to their credit that they are now trying to put it together correctly.

The original construction was by Klaatsch and Hauser from their article in 1909.[77] Figure 42 is the reconstruction based on my radiographs. This is comprised of the combined radiographs of the frontal bone and the occipital, parietal, temporal complex. Compare the museum exhibit (flat top of cranium and ape-like forehead) to this. Look at the jaws in the drawing of the souvenir museum slide. Both upper and lower jaws are very forward of the modern human range of normal. Carefully examining the position of the lower jaw, it is seen that the condyle or knob at the end of the lower jaw which fits into the fossa of the skull (arrow) is not sitting in the fossa (cup-like indentation), but is about 30 mm forward in the temple or infra-temporal area. The lower jaw would be dislocated if this were its normal position. It is so far out of the joint area that the ligaments which attach it to the back of the fossa would be stretched beyond their elastic limit.

Having the two jaws in this position gives this version a decidedly ape-like appearance and also makes the jaws somewhat similar to the adults. The Le Moustier chin has been crushed. It has been reconstructed as being flat with no curvature or elevation of the modern chin. This fits the chinless assumption taken from the ape heritage assumption, but is it correct? In the study of the other three children, their relative chinlessness could very well be due to infantile characteristics and small jaws. By the time a Neanderthal youth like Le Moustier should have acquired a chin, all that can be found is a broken one. Figure 78 on the following page shows the two facial profiles of Pech de l'Aze and Le Moustier superimposed as the younger face would have rotated counterclockwise into the older one.

ORTHODONTIC CASE REPORT ON LE MOUSTIER

Le Moustier's two lower third molars (wisdom teeth) appeared to be on an impacted pathway. The right is vertical to slightly mesio-angular while the left is disto-angular. But in examining the radiograph of the more vertical right third molar it is evident that there is a small amount of body space behind it. The left side is half in the ramus. But considering the fact that there were no impacted third molars in all the adults that I examined, it becomes evident that the process of delayed maturation which was shut off at this point in Le Moustier's life had not created the ramal-body resorption and growth yet for this to happen. Think also of the long "adult growth" and the ramal resorption on the inside border, and the attrition of the teeth over a few hundred years. There are no impacted third molars in adult Neanderthals that I am aware of. Most of them have large retro-molar gaps behind the wisdom teeth.

Le Moustier did have a lower left impacted cuspid that failed to erupt and had a retained deciduous cuspid tooth that lasted until he died. This was probably the earliest impacted tooth recorded, but not unusual since the effects of the fall were rapidly advancing in immediate post-flood times. Since my specialty is orthodontics I took great delight in diagnosing this problem. This is the kind of patient I see quite regularly.

The key to this is understanding arch length. The impacted cuspid is 8.03 mm wide (M-D). Therefore, in order for this tooth to erupt properly into the arch it would need that much space. There is enough space for the mandibular right permanent cuspid in the alveolar arch and it is 8.00 mm (M-D) in width. There is

Figure 78.

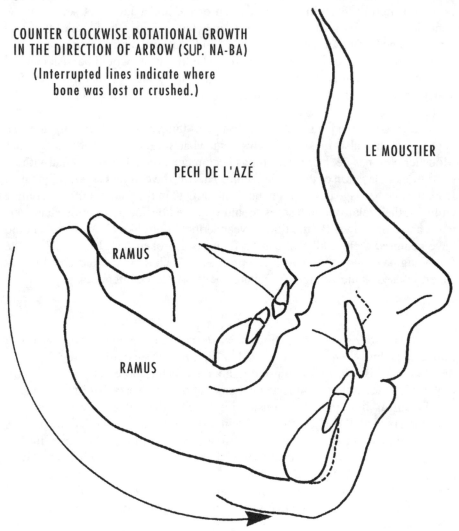

**COUNTER CLOCKWISE ROTATIONAL GROWTH
IN THE DIRECTION OF ARROW (SUP. NA-BA)**

(Interrupted lines indicate where
bone was lost or crushed.)

LE MOUSTIER

PECH DE L'AZÉ

RAMUS

RAMUS

a one-half millimeter space distal to the mandibular right cuspid, and between the first and second bicuspids on the right is a one millimeter space. The primary cuspid on the mandibular left side is 6.0 mm (M-D) with a 0.5mm bit of glue between it and the first bicuspid on the left. Between the first and second bicuspids is one millimeter of space on the mandibular left side with the second bicuspid leaning in a mesial direction. There is a piece of glue of 0.5mm behind the second bicuspid holding it to the first molar. There is mesial attrition on that molar.

The midlines of the lower and upper don't match. There is no contact between the upper right and lower right cuspids. The upper right cuspid occludes with the lower left first bicuspid and has worn a large facet onto the buccal cusp of that tooth. This means all the lower anterior teeth have shifted slightly to the left about a millimeter or more (ruler shows approximately 1mm) when the lower left cuspid did not erupt and the primary cuspid did not exfoliate.

The permanent left impacted cuspid has its root apex closed so it lost all its eruption power before Le Moustier died. If he were alive today it would have to be brought into the arch with fixed orthodontic mechanics. This would not be too hard to do. I will explain this to prove that if the tooth was not genetically predisposed to erupt at a 40° angle on the buccal surface of the mandibular body there would have been enough room for this tooth in the arch. Neanderthals didn't lack space in their dental arches. They had plenty of time to increase the size of their jaws.

Orthodontically, I would recreate what should have happened if the eruption path were not so far off. There *was* enough space, and to prove it we can move this tooth into proper position, hypothetically, without trimming a tooth or extracting another except the primary cuspid. He would need a full bonding of orthodontic brackets on bases to accomplish this task.

I would start by taking advantage of all the spaces and the midline shift. First, I would put the upper right cuspid in occlusion with the lower right by moving the lower first bicuspid and cuspid distally. This would place the upper right cuspid in the embrasure between the lower cuspid and bicuspid and take it off the buccal surface of the bicuspid. It would put the mesio-lingual surface of the upper cuspid in contact with the disto-buccal surface of the lower cuspid. While this may appear to be already the case from the figure in chapter 30 for the Lower Facial Height (LFH), there is actually no contact between the #3's. This move of lower right #3, #4 distally would produce 1.5mm, and by shifting the four mandibular anteriors over to the right we can transfer that space into our 6mm space in the vacated spot of primary left #c. We can have another 1mm if I can move the lower left first bicuspid distally into the space posterior to it without disturbing the occlusion of the upper bicuspid. By intruding the upper bicuspid this would give us vertical room to distal drive the bicuspid (intrusion is a very tough movement). We now have 6mm+ 1.5 mm+ 1mm which equals 8.5mm. Enough to place the 8.03mm cuspid in the arch. These movements prove that there was enough space in the arch before all the compensating movements of teeth took place to produce a functioning occlusion in spite of the imbalance produced by the impacted cuspid.

Chapter 29, Research Note 1.

Table II

Menarcheal Age

Country	(yr)(ref)	Age*	(SD)	Sample	Earliest Age
Spain	1993[78]	12.75	±0.04	894	11.5
Spain	1995[79]	12.4	±1.5	777	9.58
					(group P$_3$)
Hungary	1993[80]	12.9		1494	
Italy	1992[81]	12.2	±1.2		
Nigeria	1992[82]	13.98	±1.30		
USA (Texas)	1994[83]	13.8	±1.5	109	athletes
Bulgaria	1994[84]	12.09	±0.16	91	left-handed 8
South Africa	1995[85]	12.61	±1.25	857	11
New Zealand	1994[86]	12.9		415	59 girls < 12
Ireland	1993[87]	13.13		303	with scoliosis
Sweden	1991[88]	11.6		107	Indian 7.3
China	1991[89]	12.88		937	
USA	1991[90]	12.8			
Fiji	1989[91]	11.80•		216	
Germany	1990[92]	12.90	±1.21	494	Turkish 10

* mean age

• median age

Chapter 30, Research Note 1. In my research, the cranial length measurement is the maximum length of the cranium taken from a lateral cephalometric radiograph. It is measured from Behrents (PSE) or posterior skull, external height of the contour of the occipital bone in the sagittal plane on the back of the skull, to glabella external (GB) height of the contour of the frontal bone over the frontal sinus. Parchappe (1836) did it differently. He measured maximum skull length and used a craniometric measuring device such as calipers, which gives a slightly different measurement than a cephalometric measurement. However, craniometrics can be used to obtain overall growth velocity or rates, but not for one-to-one comparisons with cephalometric measurements.

Chapter 30, Research Note 2. The correction factor for linear magnification is .925 La Ferrassie I and La Chapelle-aux-Saints. All adult Neanderthal measurements in mm were multiplied by this factor. This represents a 7.5% reduction of all the above linear measurements. For example, a 100 mm measurement on the radiograph would actually be 92.5mm. Of course, angles are not magnified.

The magnification factors for Le Moustier are divided into three parts for the three radiographs used to measure the bones. They are as follows: 1. Max.-

Mand. factor = .912 or an 8.8% reduction. 2. Frontal bone factor: .939 or 6.1% reduction. 3. The parietal-occipital-temporal bone factor: .933 or 6.7% reduction. Because of these three separate magnification factors on three radiographs utilizing the cephalometric technique, I have retraced the Moustier composite which is slightly different from the one in the *CEN Tech Journal* where only one average magnification factor was used.[93] In the tracing for Moustier in this book I placed a scale for 20mm. It is an average of the three magnifications, and only good as a rough scale. But all the measurements in the text and notes are exact. All cephalometric measurements in millimeters were made with a 150 mm sliding vernier caliper (micrometer, with dial, accurate to .01 mm, divisions at .02mm) made by the LS Starrett Co., Athol, Massachusetts. All angles made with an 180° protractor, No. 376, with .5 degree divisions, made by C.Thru Ruler Co., Hartford, Conn.

Chapter 30, Research Note 3. Using Behrents' 19.6 and 26.8 male measurements in millimeters with a 6% reduction for enlargement (Behrents' personal instructions, February 1, 1996), I determined the rate of growth of 7 linear segments and one angular segment. I choose these segments because they best represented the craniofacial complex for the areas of intact or partially intact anatomy that were present in the three Neanderthal craniofacial remains. Even so, some estimates had to be made.

I used the individual modern rates from each of these segments and chose the corresponding segment of Le Moustier as the starting point in Neanderthal growth. Then I measured the same segment in the two Neanderthal adults and calculated how long it would take that particular segment in Le Moustier to reach the final adult length or angle of La Ferrassie I and La Chapelle-aux-Saints.

These projections came out to different time spans for each segment. This is not unexpected because Behrents' rates for much of the segments vary in modern humans. This is variable or allometric growth: different segments have different rates or velocities of growth. For instance, in Behrents' discussion of mandibular growth he said, "Using these measurements, males show a significant increase in angulation, implying that the chin continues to come forward at a rate faster than the growth of the midface."

What we are looking for here is not an exact age for the adult Neanderthals but a range of time which would be more accurate than the previous evolutionary estimates based on ape heritage and uniform assumptions of maximum attainable ages. My aim is to discover the approximate length of time it would take Le Moustier, if he had lived longer, to grow into an adult Neanderthal at modern rates. Now since I am not a uniformitarian scientist, I know that these rates are too fast because humans developed slower in the past and are becoming more precocious as man descends through history. It is not my desire to pinpoint the ages of Neanderthal down to the exact number of years, months, and days that they lived, but only to give other assumptions a chance to operate on the data and to see what this new "surgery" will produce.

The following chart covers 8 cephalometric bony segments. The rate for each segment is Behrents' modern rate. Since the rate assumption is probably too fast, the actual total years would be greater using just this assumption. However, there is probably some deceleration of velocity or rate in the later years so that could modify the overall age in the other direction. Therefore, what we understand from this linear adult growth model is (1) that it was highly likely the Neanderthals lived much longer life spans than evolutionary scientists would allow, and (2) that the Neanderthals lived longer than modern man.

Table III
Behrents' Calculations, Neanderthal Measurements, Modern Rates/Velocities, and Extrapolations of Neanderthal Years for Le Moustier to Become La Chapelle or La Ferrassie I

Calc.	Pts. mm/deg.	LM	LF	LC	Rate mm/°/yr.	Yrs. LF	Yrs. LC
252	(41-32-1)°	110	104	105	0.026	231	192
193	(40-11)mm	113.0	119.3	132.0	0.052	121	365
192	(40-54)mm	108.5	120.0	123.3	0.056	205	264
209	(48-49)mm	20.7	32.3	34.2	0.060	193	225
200	(12-1)mm	58.3	75.8	78.7	0.063	278	324
194	(40-4)mm	116.3	131.3	132.3	0.071	211	225
201	(54-1)mm	110.3	135.0	124.0	0.101	245	136
140	(43-3) mm	112.2	135.2	125.0	0.112	205	114

University of Iowa Study [94]

Iowa	(54-1)mm	110.3	135	124	0.098	252	140

Legend for Table
LM = Le Moustier
LF= La Ferrassie I
LC = La Chapelle-aux-Saints
Calc. is Behrents' number, Pts.mm/° are Behrents' landmarks and distance or degrees between them. Rate is mm or degrees/year calculated by me from Behrents' study. Ages are calculated by dividing the linear distance or angular degrees from LM to LF or LC by the modern rate. Rates are arranged from above in increasing order.

252 Gonial Angle (Michigan method) (Loss of Posterior teeth-LC)
193 Length from Basion to A Point on Maxilla (affected by LF use of upper teeth as tools)
192 Length of Entire Cranial Base from Nasion to Basion
209 Width of Frontal Sinus
200 Lower Facial Height
194 Distance from Basion to B Point on Mandible
201 Entire Facial Height (affected by LC Thumb habit?)
140 Mandibular length (affected by LC Condylar erosion)

A NOTE FOR SKEPTICS

I have put this note in for skeptics. In the methods of all orthodontic cepha-lometric studies there is usually a way to check for errors in measurements. I have checked these as thoroughly as I can numerous times; however, that still does not satisfy the requirements of the university studies where many workers go over all of the measurements. In particular, I refer to the University of Michigan studies and the Bolton studies. They say that they verify and check the accuracy of the data. I have done that too, but it might not be good enough to satisfy my critics, so I have worked up a hypothetical problem. Assuming the method is accepted, the worst objection that I can anticipate would be: His figures must not be right. Therefore, I have set up a hypothetical scenario where I calculate the Neanderthal adult ages from Le Moustier and add 5% to the measurements of Moustier to make it larger and take away 5% of the adult measurements to make them smaller. I'm only doing this for Calculation 200 of Behrents' research. I invite you to do it with any others. The outcome is essentially the same; more years than anyone ever thought possible.

Five Percent Changes of Measurements to Calculate Years for Le Moustier to Become La Chappelle or La Ferrassie I

Lower Facial Height

	LM	LF	LC	Rate mm/yr.	Yrs.	Yrs.
200 (12-1)	61.2mm	72mm	74.8mm	0.063	171	216

Conclusion: The primary cause of Neanderthalization of the adult skull is age and function within a superior genome capable of extended longevity; a genome closer to Adam and Eve, therefore less deteriorated. While I would only be speculating at this point, I am willing to suggest that besides the mitochondrial DNA differences, the Neanderthal nuclear DNA differences were significant in the area of repetitive DNA. I suggest that our longevity is hidden in that large fraction of our total DNA.

Chapter 30, Research Note 4. Le Moustier did not have intact anatomy around the foramen magnum; therefore, an estimated basion based on actual La Chapelle and La Ferrassie I basion points was made plus anatomy of Le Moustier described in note 14 of chapter 28.

Chapter 30, Research Note 5. Whittaker, Molleson, et al., studied 500 skulls with intact mandibles from the Poundbury (Dorset) Romano-British cemetery site which dates from A.D. 200-400. They found that with radiographs they were able to measure the distance from the root apices and cemento-enamel junction of the premolars and molars to a fixed line in the mandible, the (IAC) inferior alveolar canal. They stated, "Confirmatory evidence from measurements of IAC to apex showed that continuing eruption was, in fact occurring up to the oldest ages studied."[95] They believed that this phenomena was a mechanism to make up for the loss of tooth structure due to occlusal wear. Whittaker, Griffiths, et al. studied skulls with essentially minor wear from Spitalfields, many of whom had exact dates of birth and death accompanying them.[96] Their study revealed an addition of bone to the lower border of the mandible in the molar region of about 1.4mm throughout life, and an increase in vertical dimension (extrusion of teeth and alveolar bone of more than 5mm). Therefore, the total increase in facial height would be expected to be around 7mm between the age of 20 and 60 years. This increase calculated out to a rate of 0.18mm per year. They said, "In the absence of attrition, facial height will increase." The Neanderthals exhibited facial increase in the presence of attrition.

I would add to this description of tooth wear and increasing Neanderthal facial height that it seems impossible to gain height by means of passive eruption in the presence of severe occlusal tooth attrition, although there is always some additional bone added at the lower border of the mandible. According to Whittaker et al. this lower border addition is less than the amount gained by tooth eruption and bone addition on the alveolar margins.[97]

You can maintain height by compensating mechanisms described by Whittaker et al. and you can lose height of the face as described by Murphy,[98] but to gain height with severe occlusal attrition there must be enamel repair and tooth eruption with alveolar bone growth or excessive bone apposition at the lower border of the mandible. It is likely that we can rule out excessive bone growth at the lower border based on previous findings but just to check that factor, I did the following:

To be perfectly accurate about dividing growth amounts between the alveolar process-CEJ distance and the lower border of the mandible there really should be a wire in the inferior alveolar canal. I have done this for Le Moustier and the wire shows the canal to be slightly slanted. I do not have a wire in the adults. However, La Ferrassie I has a very well-marked mental foramen in the cephalometric radiograph. I measured from the inferior alveolar canal superiorly and inferiorly and found 11.3 mm of passive eruption between Le Moustier and La Ferrassie I. I found 3.9 mm of lower border addition. This is almost a 3:1 ratio. The ratio given by Whittaker et al. is 2.8mm (passive tooth) to 1.4mm (lower border) or 2:1 for 20-60 or 40 years.[99] Using 40 years, I found their rate of 0.07mm per year of passive tooth eruption. I applied this rate to the mandibular first molars of the Neanderthals. This would equal approximately 161 years of passive tooth eruption. This measurement mandates enamel repair with additional amounts slowing down the process of eruption. The rate of lower border apposition is 1.4mm for an approximate 40-year life. This is 0.04mm/per year. Taking the 3.9mm of lower border addition from LM to LF, it would take at the 0.04mm rate 98 years to attain this amount. If other Neanderthals can be tested for this physiologic process of passive eruption it would be valuable to determine the amounts of movement and growth.

If Moustier were only 16-18 years and La Ferrassie 40-45 years, the rate of passive eruption would have to be 11.3mm/22 years = 0.51mm/yr or 0.39mm/yr for 29 years. This would be five and one-half to seven times faster passive eruption than the Spitalfields study. This is like saying a sheep could run as fast as a cheetah or a bee as fast as a thoroughbred race horse.

My conclusion is: If there were no world-record rates of passive tooth eruption to increase the facial height in the face of severe attrition, then the rates had to be slower, growth longer, and the tooth had to have some way to repair itself, inside and out, and in the end the Neanderthal just chewed on roots, some of which had pulpal exposures and pathologic changes.

Chapter 31, Research 1. I would like to introduce the concept of a piezoelectric tooth system of enamel repair. Athenstadt found enamel not to be piezoelectric but it did carry a plus charge. Teeth behave like electrodes in solution.[100] Crystallization can occur with the right ingredients whenever you have a point of nucleation (critical number of nuclei).[101] Precipitated calcium hydroxyapatites in a heavily folded charged enamel of a tooth surface or at the base of any fold under the proper conditions can build up (like a scratch on the inside wall of a test-tube).

Chapter 31, Research Note 2. Robert Corruccini has written extensively and comprehensively on the etiology of malocclusion, or as he likes to call it, "occlusal variation."[102] He correctly has said that we must look back into our "ancestral" state to understand what it means to be well-occluded. He has pointed out that among non-technologic human societies there is a tendency towards nearly ideal occlusion in all individuals.

Krogman found this true in Tepe Hissar, Iran, from an early population of children there.[103] Only 8.8% of the Tepe Hissar children showed any malocclusion. We have today anywhere from 40-60%[104] to 79%[105] (between 14-18), and greater.[106]

Corrucinni wrote, "Malocclusion is a malady of 'civilized' humans." He also thought that while there is much evidence that disuse of our modern jaws (because of soft diets) is an important factor, it is not the only factor involved in the size of our tooth-bearing bony arches (alveolar processes). Disuse of a part of a body does cause a shrinkage of tissues, etc. (broken arm in a cast), and lack of exercise has been shown to be a factor in osteoporosis of bone. But these are not the only factors. Corruccini concluded, "Human occlusion has changed dramatically in very recent evolutionary times. Cross-cultural surveys therefore are of key importance to solving this mystery, for the western world has finished crossing the development transition through which this change occurred." He thinks we crossed the bridge of breakdown and now we're in a static pattern.

The main question that evolution must answer is: If reduction of permanent tooth size and facial size from the early hominids to early men and then to modern man came from natural selection, then the fossil record should show many dead youthful hominids and early children with severe malocclusions that died from feeding problems, infection, or mating selection problems before reproductive age. If evolution is a "numbers game," as many have said it is, then children with genetic smaller teeth and jaws should have survived to be able to reproduce themselves. Henceforth, us!

We do have smaller permanent teeth and smaller jaws. Is that really how we came about? If this is a true hypothesis there must be many dead mixed dentition children in the early agricultural samples with large teeth and malocclusions that never had a chance to procreate. Guess what? That's not true. The further back you go, the less malocclusions you find in the mixed dentition stage or any stage. The overwhelming numbers of dead children with mixed dentition large permanent teeth malocclusions are just not there. Look at Krogman's 8.8% malocclusion (3) in his entire 34 children from 3 years to 18 years with just one at 20 years. His words were "three instances of slight malocclusion."[107] They all came from about 2000-3000 B.C. Krogman said they were of "diverse racial groups."

Chapter 31, Research Note 3. Zilberman and Smith said that they used the parallel technique but described the bisecting technique. I'm not sure which one they used.

The technique that I used in the maxillary and mandibular periapical radiographs is the bisecting technique from Ennis and Berry, my dental school textbook. Dr. Berry was my professor in roentgenology. It involves having a short-cone and a central ray directed perpendicular to the bisecting plane between the mean plane of the tooth and the mean plane of the film through the apex of the tooth. This should produce a one-to-one image of the tooth on the radiograph with no distortion.

According to Ennis and Berry the angulation of the vertical movement of the tube for the lower molar region was 90° to the sagittal plane (SP) of the skull or jaw or zero degrees to the sagittal plane perpendicular through the apices of the teeth (SPP), for lower premolars minus 5°-10° to the SPP.

The horizontal movement for lower molars was 80°-90° to the SP, for lower premolars 70°-80° to the SP. For upper molars the angulation of the vertical movement of the tube was 25° -30° to SPP and upper premolars was 35°-40° to SPP. The rest of the radiographs also followed their rules. However, as they said, "No set of predetermined angles can be used since dental arches vary from on person to another," but the bisecting method was adhered to.[108] Therefore, some personal judgment was used in each case as to exact angulation. Then to be absolutely sure of no error on the side of increasing these dimensions I have reduced all the pa's by 1%, since the previously recorded Neanderthal molar dimensions are smaller than my measurements in the radiographs and photographs with rulers, and also because the short cone technique can produce more enlargement of periapicals.[109]

I have also reduced the occlusal radiographs by 1% even though the occlusal surfaces of the teeth were in close contact with the film for the same reasons. Therefore, my measurements are all reduced for magnification. I realize it is also possible to foreshorten radiographic images, and I am positive I did not do that. The 8x10 radiographs had measuring scales and a metal orbital marker in one. Ear rings in cephs are 9.55mm outside diameter.

Chapter 31, Research Note 4.

Figure 79. (Measurement Diagram for Lower Molars)

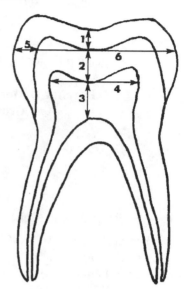

Mesio-Distal and Superior-Inferior Measurement of Lower Molars
(Redrawn from Zilberman and Smith)[110]

1. Enamel Height
2. Dentin Height
3. Pulp Height
4. Pulp Width
5. Enamel Width
6. Crown Length (M-D)

Chapter 31, Research Note 5. Method of measuring radiographs: These radiographs have been measured with a 150mm sliding vernier caliper (micrometer with dial, accurate to .01mm with divisions of .02mm) made by the L.S. Starrette Co., Athol, Massachusetts, and a Bausch and Lomb 5X magnifying glass. Most dentists just refer to radiographs as x-rays, therefore you shouldn't be confused if you speak to your dentist about this study. I call them x-rays in my office, too.

Table IV
Gibraltar II

Mandibular Left 1st Permanent Molar (Unerupted)

Dimension	Measurement (mm)	Radiograph View
Crown Length (M-D)	12.67	Lateral *
Crown Length (M-D)	12.62	Occlusal **
Crown Width (B-L)	12.09	Occlusal **
Enamel Height	1.99	Lateral *
Enamel Width	1.95	Lateral *

* Magnification Factor Lateral 8x10 Radiograph = .93
** Magnification Factor Occlusal 8x10 (with scale) Radiograph = .98

Gibraltar II Mandibular Left 1st Permanent Molar
(M-D) Crown Length Mean

Crown Length (M-D)	12.67	Lateral *
Crown Length (M-D)	12.62	Occlusal **
	12.65mm mean	

* Magnification Factor Lateral 8x10 Radiograph = .93
** Magnification Factor Occlusal 8x10 (with scale) Radiograph = .98

Gibraltar II Mandibular 1st Permanent Molar
Cross-Sectional Area

M-D	B-L Cr.-Sect.	Area
12.65mm	12.09mm	152.9 sq.mm

Table V
Pech de l'Azé
Mandibular Right 1st Permanent Molar (Unerupted)

Dimension	Measurement (mm)	Radiograph View
Crown Length (M-D)	12.97	P.A.
Crown Length (M-D)	12.97	Occlusal **
Crown Width (B-L)	12.08	Occlusal **
Enamel Height	2.01	P.A. *
Enamel Width	1.67	P.A. *

* Magnification Factor periapical radiograph = .99
** Magnification Factor occlusal radiograph = .99

Pech de l'Azé
Mandibular Right 1st Permanent Molar
(M-D) Crown Length Mean

(M-D)	12.97	P.A. *
(M-D)	12.97	Occlusal **
	12.97mm	
	Mean (M-D) Crown Length	

* Magnification Factor periapical radiograph = .99
** Magnification Factor occlusal radiograph = .99

Pech de l'Azé Mandibular Right 1st Permanent Molar
Corss-Sectional Area

M-D	B-L	Cr.-Sect.Area
12.97 mm	12.08 mm =	156.68 sq.mm

Pech de l'Azé Maxillary 1st Permanent Molars
Cross-Sectional Area

	M-D	B-L	Cr.-Sect. Area
Left	12.25	12.43	152.27 sq.mm
Right	12.39	12.77	<u>158.22</u> sq.mm
			155.25 sq.mm
			mean Cr. Sect. Area

Pech de l'Azé Maxillary 1st Permanent Molars
Enamel Height

Left	2.05mm
Right	<u>2.03</u>mm
	2.04mm Mean Enamel Height

Magnification factors same as for mandibular molars: .99

Table VI
Le Moustier and La Ferrassie I
Mandibular 1st Permanent Molar (Erupted)

Specimen	Dimension	Measurement (mm)	Radiograph View
Le Moustier (L)	Crown Length (M-D)	12.81	P.A.
Le Moustier (L)	Crown Width (B-L)	12.71	Occlusal
Le Moustier (R)	Enamel Height	1.75	Lateral pa*
Le Moustier (R)	Enamel Width	1.49	Lateral pa*
La Ferrassie I (R)	Crown Length (M-D)	7.80	Lat.Ceph**& Photo
La Ferrassie I (R)	Enamel Height	0	Lat Ceph** &Photo
La Ferrassie I (R)	Enamel Width	0	Lat Ceph** & Photo

* Magnification Factor for Le Moustier pa radiographs: .99
** Magnification Factor for La Ferrassie Ceph radiograph: .925

Le Moustier Mandibular Left 1st Permanent Molar
Cross-Sectional Area

M-D	B-L	Cr.-Sect. Area
12.81mm	12.71mm	162.81 sq.mm

Le Moustier Maxillary Left 1st Permanent Molar
Cross-Sectional Area

M-D	B-L	Cr.-Sect.Area	Radiograph
12.51mm	13.11mm	164.00 sq.mm	Occlusal

**Le Moustier Maxillary 1st Permanent Molars
Enamel Height**

Left	1.75mm
Right	<u>1.73mm</u>
	1.74 mm Mean Enamel Height

Magnification factors same as for mandibular molars: .99

Chapter 31, Research Note 6.

Table VII
Modern Children
Mandibular 1st Permanent Molar Mean/mm

	M-D	S.D.	B-L	S.D.	Cr.-Sect. Area
Male	10.71	.60	10.46	.53	112.03 sq.mm
Female	10.29	.74	10.04	.57	103.31 sq.mm

Maxillary 1st Permanent Molar Mean/mm

	M-D	S.D.	B-L	S.D.	Cr.-Sect. Area
Male	10.58	.56	10.88	.72	115.11 sq.mm
Female	10.18	.58	10.44	.60	106.28 sq.mm

Adapted from University of Michigan Center for Human Growth and Development (1976) [111]

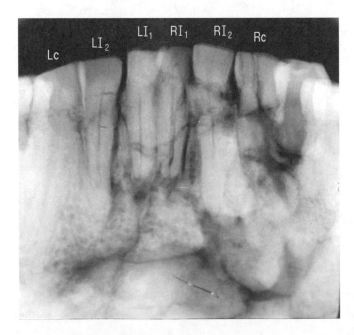

Chapter 32, Research Note 1. To be complete, please examine the only anterior discrepancy (crowding of teeth, artificially) I ever saw in Neanderthals. Figure 80 shows that the lower mandibular anterior teeth of

Figure 80. X-ray of lower front teeth, Amud I.

Amud I of Israel have been artificially crowded together in dental arch by those who reconstructed it. The radiograph in figure 80 displays what they did.

From right to left on the radiograph: R^C, the right cuspid has no root; RI^2, the right lateral incisor, looks like a lightening bolt in the sky. It is three pieces. There is such a thing as bent roots, curved roots, or dilacerated roots, but this is like none of those. There is a separate crown sitting on top. The next piece down is the upper part of the root and it is pushed mesially out of alignment with the crown by 2mm and out of alignment with the piece below it by 2mm in the other direction. The last bottom piece is disconnected totally and tilted distally. This misconstruction takes up an extra 2mm on the mesial side of the tooth and 2mm on the distal side of the tooth. It reminds me of some of the teeth I saw resulting from bar fights when I was a dentist in the navy.

RI^1, the right central incisor, has a complete but cracked root with a diagonal split in the crown and something glued on the lingual (back) of the crown that doesn't appear to be part of the tooth. It looks like a little chip of bone that has been flattened on the top or incisal edge and also carved to look like a tooth crown. The only problem is that it has *no enamel* in the radiograph. Funny thing about bone chips — they don't look much like enamel. Forgive the humor. LI^1, the left central incisor, is a tooth with a tilted crown that is leaning on the right central partial crown partial bone chip. Now there is a one millimeter space between the tilted crown and the left lateral incisor, LI^2. LI^2 is the whole tooth correctly positioned next to L^C, the left cuspid, which appears to be whole also. I believe Amud I would have well-aligned anterior teeth without all this imaginative dental magic.

Chapter 32, Research Note 2. I have no ages on Skhūl V or Amud I or Tabūn C-1 because I do not have a cephalometric radiograph of a young adult like Le Moustier from the Middle East by which to date them.

Chapter 33, Research Note 1. Besides the maturational drop between Shem and Arpachshad and his other children, there probably was the same type of rapid decline between Japheth and his children and Ham and his children. We are told in Genesis 11 that there was a great division between these families because God had separated them according to different languages that He had supernaturally produced. Obviously, this would introduce more genetic variability, but ultimately all races of mankind today can be traced back to Noah and his wife. The genetic potential of this couple and the process of devolution was enough to produce mankind as we know it today.

I certainly do not pretend to know all the ramifications of genetic devolution and adaptation to new environments based on that devolution; however, it could be a field of rich study if science were allowed to go in that direction.

Chapter 33, Research Note 2. Following up on the research just cited, the title and subject is "Angiotensin II-forming activity in a reconstructed ancestral chymase."[112] Angiotensin II is a blood pressure regulator. The authors have assembled an ancestral chymase gene based on parsimony analysis of a number of mammalian sequences (human, baboon, dog, rat, and mouse). The first sentence of the abstract is, "The current model of serine protease diversity theorizes that the earliest protease molecules were simply digestive enzymes that gained complex regulatory functions and restricted substrate specificities through evolution."[113] Interestingly, the ancestral molecule appears to have unique specificity for cleaving the bond that generates angiotensin II from angiotensin I. Also the kcat, or turnover value for the ancestral enzyme is close to 700 per second or fivefold more than human chymase and 80 times more than angiotensin I converting enzyme. The authors stated, "Indeed it is one of the highest turnover numbers reported for any protease. . . . Thus, angiotensin II-forming activity is the more primitive state for chymases, and the loss of such activity occurred later in evolution of some of the serine proteases."

If I were to re-word the latter sentence I would substitute for "primitive" the word "earlier," and for "evolution" the word "devolution." This would give a clearer picture of what actually happened. Earlier enzymes were more efficient. Also, angiotensin II is a potent stimulator for the release of prolactin in the body. Prolactin is the pituitary hormone that stimulates milk production in the nursing mother.[114]

Notes

Chapter 2

1. See Research Note 1, Chapter 2.
2. A radiograph is also called in layman's terms, an x-ray film. There are many sizes. The machine produces x-rays but the picture is called the radiograph or x-ray film. Hitler's were periapical radiographs, which is the typical dental radiograph and showed the whole tooth root.
3. A number of Mt. Carmel original remains are at Harvard's Peabody Museum. There were apparently some Shanidar human remains at the University of New Mexico with Erik Trinkaus, now at Washington University in St. Louis.

Chapter 3

1. Dr. Brown is a ficticious name.
2. See Research Note 1, Chapter 3.
3. Their name is intentionally not mentioned to protect them.

Chapter 4

1. See Research Note 1, Chapter 4.

Chapter 5

1. Pronounced almost like "Mignon" in filet mignon.
2. The study of ancient fossil man.
3. Chapter 24 explains our exploration of the abandoned cave (Bernifal).

Chapter 6

1. This statement is attributed to Aristotle by Will Durant, *The Story of Philosophy* (New York: Simon and Schuster, 1953), p. 49.

Chapter 7

1. P. Appleman, editor, *Darwin*, "Scientific Creationism — A New Inquisition Brewing?" by P. Cloud (New York: W.W. Norton Co., 1970), p. 368-382.
2. Appleman, *Darwin*, "On the Relations of Man to the Lower Animals" by T.H. Huxley (1863), p. 231-241.

Chapter 9

1. I prefer using the word Neanderthal rather than Neandertal. In this I am following the example of Dr. Krogman, Dr. Chris Stringer, and Dr Ian Tattersall.
2. See Research Note 1, Chapter 9.
3. K. Oakely, B. Campbell, and T. Molleson, *Catalogue of Fossil Hominids, Part II, Europe* (London: Trustees of the British Museum of Natural History, 1971).
4. G.H.R. Von Koenigswald, editor, *The Neanderthal Centenary*, "L'enfant du Pech de l'Azé," by E. Patte (Utrecht, Netherlands: Wenner-Gren Foundation, 1958), p. 270-276.
5. See Research Note 2, Chapter 9.
6. Francis Ivanhoe, "Was Virchow Right about Neandertal?" *Nature*, 1970:227, p. 577-579.
7. Michael Day, *Guide to Fossil Man*, 1st edition (Cleveland, OH: World Publishing Co., 1965), p. 37-42.
8. See Research Note 3, Chapter 9.
9. Michael Day, *Guide to Fossil Man*, 4th edition (Chicago, IL: University of Chicago Press, 1986), p. 31-36.

Notes — Chapter 9, Contd.

10. N.C. Tappen, "The Dentition of the 'Old Man' of La Chapelle-aux-Saints and Inferences Concerning Neandertal Behaviour," *American Journal of Physical Anthropology*, 1985:67, p. 43-50.
11. Von Koenigswald, *The Neanderthal Centenary*, plate V and plate XIII, by L. Pales (ch. 9, note 4).

Chapter 15

1. E. Trinkaus and W.W. Howells, "The Neanderthals," *Scientific American*, 241:December 1979, Vol. 241, no. 6, p. 118-133.
2. P. Mellars and C. Stringer, *The Human Revolution* (Princeton, NJ: Princeton University Press, 1989).
3. Harry S. Barrer, *Orthodontics: State of the Art* (Philadelphia, PA: University of Pennsylvania Press, 1981).
4. See Research Note 1, Chapter 15.

Chapter 16

1. See Research Note 1, Chapter 16, concerning disease among Neanderthals.
2. D.R. Brothwell, *Digging Up Bones*, 3rd ed., British Museum (Oxford: Oxford University Press, 1981), p. 119.
3. W.R. Maples and M. Browning, *Dead Men Do Tell Tales* (New York: Doubleday, 1994), p. 116-117.
4. Von Koenigswald, *The Neanderthal Centenary*, "The Dating of Broken Hill," by P. Oakley, p. 265-266 (ch. 9, note 4).
5. F.C. Howell, editor, *African Ecology and Human Evolution,*"Pleistocene Mammal Faunas of Africa, with Particular Reference to South Africa," by H.B.S. Cooke (Bourlière, London: Methuen and Co. Ltd., 1964), p. 65-116.
6. R. Noorbergen, *Secrets of the Lost Races* (Indianapolis/New York: Bobbs-Merrill, Inc., 1977), p. 174.
7. Day, *Guide to Fossil Man*, 4th edition, p. 271 (ch. 9, note 9).
8. S.L. Washburn, editor, *Classification and Human Evolution,*"Quantitative Taxonomy and Human Evolution," by B. Campbell (Chicago, IL: Aldine Pub. Co., 1963), p. 50-74.
9. T.W. Todd, "Thickness of the Male White Cranium," *The Anatomical Record*, 27 (5), 1924, p. 245-256.
10. H. Minagi, *Radiology of the Skull and Brain,* "Skull Changes in Endocrine Diseases" (St. Louis, MO: Newton & Potts, CV Mosby Co., 1971), p. 665-673.
    See Research Note 2, Chapter 16.
11. Von Koenigswald, *The Neanderthal Centenary,* "The Rhodesian, Florisbad and Saldanha Skulls," by R. Singer, p. 52-62, plate XXI (ch. 9, note 4).
12. C. Stringer and C. Gamble, *In Search of the Neanderthals* (New York: Thames and Hudson, 1993), p. 124.
13. John W. Cuozzo, "Neanderthal Children's Fossils," *Bible Science News*, Vol. 33:2, March 1995, p. 1-7.
14. W.M. Krogman, "Dental Arch Form and Facial Growth Pattern in Healthy Children from Prehistoric Populations," *Jour. ADA & Dental Cosmos.*, Vol. 25, 1938, p. 1278-1289.
15. M.C. Dean, C.B. Stringer, and T.G. Bromage, " Age at Death of the Neanderthal Child from Devils Tower, Gibraltar and the Implications for Studies of General Growth and Development in Neanderthals," *American Journal of Physical Anthropology*, 70:1986, p. 301-309.

16. D.A.E. Garrod, L.H.D. Buxton, G. Elliot Smith, and D.M.A. Bate, "Excavation of a Mousterian Rock-Shelter at Devils's Tower, Gibraltar," *Journal of the Royal Anthrolpological Institute of Great Britain and Ireland,* Vol. 58,1928, p. 33-91.
17. See Research Note 3, Chapter 16.
18. See Research Note 4, Chapter 16.
19. See Research Note 5, Chapter 16.
20. Garrod et al., "Excavation of a Mousterian Rock-Shelter at Devils's Tower, Gibraltar" (ch. 16, note 16).
21. Gibraltar II child's remains will be referred to as Gib II.
22. This is also called dentine.

Chapter 17

1. C.L.B. Lavelle, R.P. Shellis, and D.F.G. Poole, *Evolutionary Changes to The Primate Skull and Dentition* (Springfield, IL: Charles Thomas Pub., 1977), p. 198-222.
2. Dean et al., "Age at Death of the Neanderthal Child . . ." (ch. 16, note 15).
3. S. Hillson, *Teeth* (Cambridge, England: Cambridge University Press, 1986), p.121.
4. Striae of Retzius
5. Lavelle et al., *Evolutionary Changes to The Primate Skull,* p.199 (ch. 17, note 1).
6. Hillson, *Teeth,* p 123 (ch. 17, note 3).
7. Dean et al., "Age at Death of the Neanderthal Child" (ch. 17, note 2).
8. See Research Note 1, Chapter 17.
9. John W. Cuozzo, "Neanderthal Children's Fossils: Reconstruction and Interpretation Distorted by Assumptions," *Creation Ex Nihilo Tech Journal,* 8:(part 2) 1994, p. 166-178.
10. Personal communication to Dr. Koepp.
11. A. Mann, J. Monge, and M. Lampl, "Dental Caution," Scientific Correspondence, *Nature,* Vol. 348, November 1990, p.202.
12. T.G. Bromage and M.C. Dean, "Re-evaluation of the Age of Death of Immature Fossil Hominids," *Nature,* Letter, 317:1985, p. 525-527.
13. Tappen, "The Dentition of the 'Old Man' " (ch. 9, note 10).
14. Kenya National Museums — East Rudolf, plus number of the fossil (designation by the museum for identification purposes).

Chapter 19

1. Charles Lyell, *Principles of Geology,* 1830-1833.
2. Francis Darwin, *The Autobiography of Charles Darwin and Selected Letters* (New York: Dover Publications Inc., 1958), p. 61-64.
3. See Research Note 1, Chapter 19.
4. Charles Fraipont, "Les Hommes Fossiles D'Engis," Archives De L'Institut De Paléontologie Humaine, Memoire 16, Masson et Cie Editeurs, Paris, June 1936.
5. Ibid.
6. Ann Marie Tillier, "Le crâne d'enfant d'Engis 2: un exemple de distribution des caracterès juvéniles, primitifs et néanderthaliens," Bulletin, Soc. Roy. Belge Anthrop et de Préhist., 94: Bruxelles, 1983, p. 51-75.
7. See Research Note 2, Chapter 19.
8. R. Joffroy, *Les antiquités préhistoriques,* 4th ed. (Paris: Ed Des Musées Nationaux, 4th Ed., 1976), p. 11-33.
9. Stringer and Gamble, *In Search of the Neanderthals,* p.143 (ch. 16, note 12).

Chapter 20

1. Naturalism: a philosophy which completely rules out anything supernatural.
2. Alexander Marshak, *The Roots of Civilization* (Mt. Kisco, NY: Moyer Bell Limited, 1991), p. 110.

Notes — Chapter 20, Contd.

3. E. Trinkaus and I. Villemeur, "Mechanical Advantages of the Neanderthal Thumb in Flexion: a Test of an Hypothesis," *American Journal of Physical Anthropology*, 84(3), March 1991, p. 249-260.
   See Research Note 1, Chapter 20.
4. *Homo neanderthalensis* (species) *Homo sapiens neanderthalensis* (sub-species).
   M. Krings, A. Stone, R. Schmitz, H. Krainitzki, M. Stoneking, and S. Pääbo, "Neandertal DNA Sequences and the Origin of Modern Humans," *Cell*, 90:1997, p. 19-30.
5. Dr A. Walker, taped lecture, Penn State University.
6. See Research Note 2, Chapter 20.
7. Marshak, *The Roots of Civilization*, p. 57 (ch. 20, note 2).
8. See Research Note 3, Chapter 20.
9. Philip E.L. Smith, "The Solutrean Culture," *Scientific American*, Vol. 211, August 1964, p. 86-94.
10. The term "Mousterian" stands for a type of tool made of flint stones found in the Le Moustier cave. This word is also seen on the sign over the Bouffia Bonneval Cave of La Chapelle-aux-Saints: "UN HOMME MOUSTERIEN."
11. D.W. Frayer and M.D. Russel, "Artificial Grooves on the Krapina Neanderthal Teeth," *American Journal of Physical Anthropology*, 74 (3), 1987, p. 393-405.
12. J.J. Hublin, F. Spoor, M. Braun, F. Zonneveld, and S. Condemi, "A Late Neanderthal Associated with Upper Paleolithic Artifacts," *Nature*, (381) May 16, 1996, p. 224-226.
13. Aurignacian refers to the Cro-Magnon tools, etc.
14. P. Mellars, *The Neanderthal Legacy* (Princeton, NJ: Princeton University Press, 1996), p. 405.
15. Mellars and Stringer, *The Human Revolution,* "Mousterian, Châtelperronian and Early Aurignacian in Western Europe: Continuity or Discontinuity?" by F. Harrold, p. 705 (ch. 15, note 2).
16. J. Shreeve, "The Neanderthal Peace," *Discover*, September 1995, p. 70-81.
17. A more complete explanation of Neanderthals in Israel is in chapter 32.
18. Marshak, *The Roots of Civilization*, p. 25 (ch. 20, note 2).
19. Shreeve, "The Neanderthal Peace," p. 71-81 (ch. 20, note 16).
20. Stringer and Gamble, *In Search of the Neanderthals*, p. 147 (ch. 16, note 12).
21. C.M. Goss, *Anatomy of the Human Body*, Henry G. Gray, ed. (Philadelphia, PA: Lea & Febiger, 1959), p. 133.
22. E. Trinkaus and P. Shipman, *The Neanderthals* (New York, NY: Alfred A. Knopf, 1993, p. 47.
23. See Research Note 4, Chapter 20.

Chapter 21

1. Termed "pre-history" because there are no written records as we know them. This is not to say there are no inscribed records at all. See Marchak, *The Roots of Civilization* (ch. 20, note 2).
2. Joffroy, *Les antiquités préhistoriques* (ch. 19, note 8).
3. Stringer and Gamble, *In Search of the Neanderthals*, p. 143 (ch. 16, note 12).
4. J. Wymer, *The Palaeolithic Age* (New York: St. Martins Press, 1982), p.117.
5. Oakley et al., *Catalogue of Fossil Hominids*, p. 20 (ch. 9, note 3).
6. Stringer and Gamble, *In Search of the Neanderthals* , p. 15 (ch. 16, note 12).
7. Trinkaus and Shipman, *The Neanderthals*, p. 414-415 (ch. 20, note 22).
8. Stringer and Gamble, *In Search of the Neanderthals*, p. 73 (ch. 16, note 12).

9. P. Appleman, *Darwin*, 2nd edition, "On the Relation of Man to the Lower Animals" by T. Huxley (1863) (New York: W.W. Norton & Co., 1979), p. 231-240.
10. P. Miller, "Jane Goodall," *National Geographic*, 188(6), 1995, p. 102-128.
11. Francis Schaeffer, personal communication, L'Abri, Huemoz, Switzerland, Summer, 1977.
12. Wymer, *The Palaeolithic Age*, p. 177 (ch. 21, note 4).
13. Stringer and Gamble, *In Search of the Neanderthals*, p. 55 (ch. 16, note 12).
14. Wymer, *The Palaeolithic Age*, p. 135-136 (ch. 21, note 4).
15. Oakely et al., *Catalogue of Fossil Hominids*, p.142-143 (ch. 9, note 3).
16. Von Koenigswald, *The Neanderthal Centenary*, "Les Néanderthaliens en France," by L. Pales, p. 32-37 (ch. 9, note 4).
17. Oakely et al., *Catalogue of Fossil Hominids*, p. 161-163 (ch. 9, note 3).
    Von Koenigswald, *The Neanderthal Centenary*, "Les Néanderthaliens en France," Pales, p. 32-37 (ch. 9, note 4).
18. Wymer, *The Palaeolithic Age*, p. 144 (ch. 21, note 4).
19. Stringer and Gamble, *In Search of the Neanderthals*, p. 221-225 (ch. 16, note 12).
20. Wymer, *The Palaeolithic Age* (ch. 21, note 4).
21. Stringer and Gamble, *In Search of the Neanderthals*, p. 40 (ch. 16, note 12).
22. Wymer, *The Palaeolithic Age*, p. 17 (ch. 21, note 4).
23. M. Oard, *An Ice Age Caused by the Genesis Flood* (San Diego, CA: ICR, 1990).
24. E. Ericson, "Air-Ocean-Icecap Interactions in Relation to Climatic Fluctuations and Glaciation Cycles in Causes of Climatic Change," J.M. Mitchell Jr., ed. *Meteorological Monographs*, 8, (30), American Meteorological Society, Boston, MA, 1968, p. 68-92.
25. Oard, *An Ice Age Caused by the Genesis Flood* (ch. 21, note 23).

Chapter 22

1. James Hutton (1726-1797), Charles Lyell (1797-1875).
2. W. Kenneth Hamblin, *The Earth's Dynamic Systems*, 5th ed. (New York: Macmillan Co., 1989), p. 130.
3 Stanley Malamed, "Medical Emergencies," Continuing Education Course, Western Essex Dental Association, May 15, 1996, West Orange, NJ.
4. Hamblin, *The Earth's Dynamic Systems*, p. 131 (ch. 22, note 2).
5. Douglas Futuyma, *Evolutionary Biology*, 2nd. ed. (Sunderland, MA: Sinauer Assoc. Inc., 1986), p. 2.
6. Phillip E. Johnson, *Darwin on Trial* (Washington, DC: Regnery,Gateway, 1991), p. 28.
7. Norman Geisler, *The Creator in the Courtroom, Scopes II* (Milford, MI: Mott Media, 1982), p. 91.
8. J. Buell and V. Hearn, eds., *Darwinism, Science or Philosophy*, "Radical Intersubjectivity," by Frederick Grinnell (Richardson, TX: Foundation for Thought and Ethics, 1994), p. 99-106.
9. Darwin, *The Autobiography of Charles Darwin and Selected Letters*, p.61 (ch. 19, note 2).
10. Giesler, *The Creator in the Courtroom, Scopes II*, p. 70 (ch. 22, note 7).
11. R. Grizzle, Book Review, *Darwin, Darwinism, and Religion of Darwinian Paradigm: Essays on Its History, Philosophy and Religious Implications* by M. Ruse, Routledge, NY, 1993, *Bioscience* (44) 8, September 1994, p. 560-562.
12. Stratification is the geological concept that the oldest layers will be deposited first, on the bottom, and the younger on top of that. A synonym for older is earlier; for younger is later or recent.
13. Wymer, *The Palaeolithic Age*, p. 16-17 (ch. 21, note 4).
14. John Gowlett, *Ascent to Civilization* (New York: A. Knopf, Inc., 1984), p. 115.
15. H. Breuil and R. Lantier, *The Men of the Old Stone Age* (London: Harrap & Co. Ltd., 1965), p. 96-98.

Chapter 23

1. I. Tattersall, *The Last Neanderthal* (New York: Simon & Schuster, Macmillan Co., 1995), p. 90.
2. Trinkaus and Shipman, *The Neanderthals*, p. 414-415 (ch. 20, note 22).
3. Day, *Guide to Fossil Man*, 4th edition, p. 56-58 (ch. 9, note 9).
4. Mellars and Stringer, *The Human Revolution*, "Mousterian, Châtelperronian and Early Aurignacian. . ." by F.B. Harrold, p. 677-706 (ch. 15, note 2).
5. Stringer and Gamble, *In Search of the Neanderthals*, p.166 (ch. 16, note 12).
6. Tattersall, *The Last Neanderthal*, Plate 1 Frontispiece (ch. 23, note 1).
7. Ibid., p.90 (ch. 23, note 1).
   Stringer and Gamble, *In Search of the Neanderthals*, p.137 (ch. 16, note 12).
   Mellars, *The Neanderthal Legacy*, p. 404 (ch. 20, note 14).
8. Trinkaus and Shipman, *The Neanderthals*, p.186 (ch. 20, note 22).
9. Ibid.
10. Von Koenigswald, *The Neanderthal Centenary*, " 'Spiritualité' de l'Homme de Néandertal," by F.M. Bergounioux , p. 154 (ch. 9, note 4).
11. Mellars, *The Neanderthal Legacy,* p. 376 (ch. 20, note 14).
12. Von Koenigswald, *The Neanderthal Centenary*, " 'Spiritualité' de l'Homme de Néandertal," by Bergounioux, p. 154 (ch. 9, note 4).
13. Trinkaus and Shipman, *The Neanderthals,* p.186 (ch. 20, note 22).
14. John Pfeiffer, *The Emergence of Man* (New York: Harper and Row, 1972), p. 250.
    John Gowlett, *Ascent to Civilization* (New York: A. Knopf, 1984), p. 126-127.
    Hublin et al., *Nature* (381) May 16, 1996, p. 224-226 (ch. 20, note 12).
15. Mellars and Stringer, *The Human Revolution*, "Production Complexity and Standardization in Early Aurignacian Bead and Pendant Manufacture: Evolutionary Implications" by R. White, p. 366-390 (ch. 15, note 2).
16. Stringer and Gamble, *In Search of the Neanderthals,* p. 18 (ch. 16, note 12).
17. P.E. Smith, "The Solutrean Culture," *Scientific American*, Vol. 211, 1964, p. 86-94.
18. Cornelius S. Hurlbut, *Minerals and Man* (New York: Random House, 1970), p. 245.
19. Stringer and Gamble, *In Search of the Neanderthals*, p. 158-159 (ch. 16, note 12).
    Wymer, *The Palaeolithic Age*, p. 250 (ch. ch. 21, note 4).
20. Lloyd Seton, *The Archaeology of Mesopotamia* (London: Thames and Hudson, 1984), p. 46.
21. Jackson J. Spielvogel, *Western Civilization,* Vol. 1 (St. Paul, MN: West Pub. Co. 1991), p. 4-5.
22. Ibid.
23. Samuel Noah Kramer, *The Sumerians* (Chicago, IL: University of Chicago Press, 1963), p. 100.
24. Hurlbut, *Minerals and Man*, p. 228 (ch. 23, note 18).

Chapter 24

1. D. Vialou, *Guide Des Grottes Ornées Paléolithiques ouvertes au Public,* Masson, Paris, 1976, p. 75.
2. Ann Sieveking, *The Cave Artists* (London: Thames and Hudson, 1979), p. 104-106.
3. Number 75, Bordeaux-Tulle.
4. Marshak, *The Roots of Civilization*, p. 209 (ch. 20, note 2).
5. A period of time in the Upper Paleolithic in France supposedly about 10,000 years ago. It came after the Solutrean we discussed earlier.
6. See Research Note 1, Chapter 24.
7. Called a bâton in French meaning stick, staff, or rod.
8. See Research Note 2, Chapter 24.
9. Oakley et al., *Catalogue of Fossil Hominids* (ch. 9, note 3).

10. Sieveking, *The Cave Artists*, p. 43 (ch. 24, note 2).
11. Vialou, *Guide Des Grottes Ornées Paléolithiques ouvertes au Public* (ch. 24, note 1).
12. Seiveking, *The Cave Artists*, p.106 (ch. 24, note 2).
13. Ibid., p. 204.
14. Alfred Roemer, *Vertebrate Paleontology*, 3rd edition (Chicago, IL: University of Chicago Press, 1966), p. 312.
15. See Research Note 3, Chapter 24.
16. See Research Note 4, Chapter 24.
17. Sieveking, *The Cave Artists*, p. 103 (ch. 24, note 2).
18. Ibid., p. 103.
19. Gowlett, *Ascent to Civilization*, p. 130 (ch. 23, note 14).
20. Seiveking, *The Cave Artists*, p. 102 (ch. 24, note 2).
21. Louis-René Nougier, *Rouffignac, La Grotte Aux Cent Mammoths*, 2nd. Ed. Les éditions du périgord noir, "Mémoires de l'Académe" Tome XLIV Imprimerie Nationale-Paris, 1958; after p. 66 no page designation for English translation of this guide book.
22. Michael Balter, Archeology, Research News, "Cave Structure Boosts Neanderthal Image," *Science,* (271), January 26, 1996, p. 449.

Chapter 25

1. F. Schaeffer, personal communication.
2. Exceptions to the curse of physical death have been men such as Elijah (2 Kings 2:11) and Enoch (Gen. 5:24), and Paul's description of the final rapture in 1 Corinthians 15:51.
3. This is now the work of my son John.
4. Specific Gravity of Diamond (3.52).
5. Diamonds are 10 on the Mohs scale.
6. Lead (Pb) has a high specific gravity but is not a rare metal 11.34 at 20° C.
7. See Research Note 1, Chapter 25.
8. All Specific gravities are at 20°C.
9. R.J. Jackson, J.H. DiLiberti, P.J. Landrigan, G. Nathanson, and H.L. Needleman, "Radon Exposure:A Hazard to Children," *Pediatrics*, 83(5) 1989, p. 799-902.
10. D. Henshaw, J. Eatough, and R. Richardson, "Radon as a Causative Factor in Induction of Myeloid Leukaemia and other Cancers," *Lancet*, 335(8696):1008-12, April 28, 1990.
11. Edward Lurie, *Louis Agassiz, A Life in Science* (Chicago, IL: Phoenix Books, University of Chicago Press, 1960).
12. Oard, *An Ice Age Caused by the Genesis Flood*, p. 33 (ch. 21, note 23).
13. Khris Olsen and Jonathan Fruchter, "Identification of the Physical and Chemical Characteristics of Volcanic Hazards," chapter 5, *American Journal of Public Health*, Supp. Vol.76, (3), March 1986, p. 50.
14. Ibid.
15. M. Camiel and D. Thompson, "Delayed Hazards of Radon Irradiation," *Journal of the American Medical Association*, 1/17/92 (219) No. 3., p. 384.
16. J. Selman, *The Fundamentals of X-ray and Radium Physics* (Springfield, IL: Charles C. Thomas Pub.), p. 175.
17. Olsen and Fruchter, "Identification of the Physical and Chemical Characteristics of Volcanic Hazards" (ch. 25, note 13).
18. S. Schneider, "The World's Crazy Weather," *1984 Britannica Book of the Year* (Chicago, IL: Encyclopedia Britannica, 1984), p. 307-309.
19. J.E. Moore, Earth Sciences, Geophysics, *1984 Britannica Book of the Year* (Chicago, IL: Encylopedia Britannica, 1986), p. 198-199.

Notes — Chapter 25, Contd.

20. L. Kownacka, Z. Jaworowski, and M. Suplinska, "Vertical Distribution and Flows of Lead and Natural Radionuclides in the Atmosphere," *Science of the Total Environment, 91*, 1990, p. 199-221.
21. P.L. Fernandez , L.S. Quindós, J. Soto, and E. Villar, "Radiation Exposure Levels in Altamira Cave," *Health Physics*, Vol. 46 (2), February 1984, p. 445-447.
22. N.K. Sandars, *Prehistoric Art in Europe*, 2nd edition (Middlesex, England: Penguin Books Ltd, 1985), p. 25.
23. Fernandez et al., "Radiation Exposure Levels in Altamira Cave" (ch. 25, note 21).
24. Jackson et al., "Radon Exposure: A Hazard to Children" (ch. 25, note 9).
25. Fernandez et al., "Radiation Exposure Levels in Altamira Cave" (ch. 25, note 21).
26. Jackson et al., "Radon Exposure: A Hazard to Children" (ch. 25, note 9).
27. Olsen and Fruchter, "Identification of the Physical and Chemical Characteristics of Volcanic Hazards" (ch. 25, note 13).
28. Jackson et al., "Radon Exposure: A Hazard to Children" (ch. 25, note 9).
29. R.S. Lively and E.P. Ney, "Surface Radioactivity Resulting from the Deposition of 222 Rn Daughter Products," *Health Physics*, 1987 52 (4), p. 411-415.

Chapter 26

1. Leonard Hayflick, *How and Why We Age* (New York: Random House, 1994), p. 15.
2. S. Olshansky, B. Carnes, and C. Cassel, "In Search of Methuselah: Estimating the Upper Limits to Human Longevity," *Science* (250) November 2, 1990, p. 634-40.
3. Ibid.
4. Alex Comfort, *The Biology of Senescence,* 3rd edition (New York: Elsevier, 1979), p. 5.
5. Thomas Perls, "The Oldest Old," *Scientific American*, January 1995, p. 70-75.
6. Olshansky et al., "In Search of Methuselah: Estimating the Upper Limits to Human Longevity" (ch. 26, note 2).
7. Hayflick, *How and Why We Age* (ch. 26, note 1).
8. Comfort, *The Biology of Senescence*, p. 5-6 (ch. 26, note 4).
9. Perls, "The Oldest Old," p. 75 (ch. 26, note 5).
10. William Arnet, "Growing Old in the Cradle: Old Age and Immortality Among the Kings of Ancient Assyria," *Int. J. Aging and Human Development*, Vol. 32 (2) 1991, p. 135-141.
11. AAO anonymous critic or referee for a paper submitted to that publication in 1985, 6, 7.
12. Merrill Unger, *Archaeology and the Old Testament* (Grand Rapids, MI: Zondervan Publishing House, 1954), p. 134.

Chapter 27

1. S.E. Bishara, J.E. Treder, and J.R. Jacobsen, "Facial And Dental Changes in Adulthood," *American Journal of Orthodontics and Dentofacial Orthopedics*, 106 (2), August 1994, p. 175-186.
2. Longitudinal means using the same people for the study, following them over a long period of time. Cross-sectional studies use different people.
3. Ales Hrdlicka, "Growth During Adult Life," *Proceedings of the American Philosophical Society,* 76:847-897, 1936.
4. Parchappe, "Reserches sur l'encéphale," Vol. I, Du volume de la tête et de l'encéphale chez l'homme, Paris, 1836, cited from Ales Hrdlicka, "Growth During Adult Life" (ch. 27, note 3).
5. W. Pfitzner, "Der Einfluss des Lebensalters auf die anthropologischen Charactere," *Zeitschriftver Morphologie und Anthropologie,* I 1899, p. 325-377.

6. A. Jarcho, "Die Altersveranderungen der Rassenmerkmale bei den Erwachsenen," *Anthropologischer Anzeiger,* 12: Hft. 2, p. 173-179, 1935.

7. Cephalic index is arrived at by dividing the maximum head width by the maximum head length and multiplying by 100. 80 to 84.9 is brachycephalic, 75 to 79.9 is mesocephalic, and less than 75 is dolichocephalic.

8. See Research Note 1, Chapter 27.

9. Parchappe, "Reserches sur l'encéphale" (ch. 27, note 4). See Research Note 2, Chapter 27.

10. Pfitzner, "Der Einfluss des Lebensalters auf die anthropologischen Charactere" (ch. 27, note 5).

11. See Research Notes 3 and 4, Chapter 27.

12. T.W. Todd, *The Anatomical Record* (Philadelphia, PA: W.B. Saunders Co., 1924), "Thickness of the Male White Cranium," p. 245-256.

13. J.A. Campbell, "Roentgen Aspects of Cranial Configurations," Radiologic Clinics of North America, 4:11-31, Vol. 4, 1966, p. 11-31.

14. A. Tallgren, "Changes in the Adult Face Height Due to Aging, Wear, and Loss of Teeth and Prosthetic Treatment," Acta Odont. Scandinavica 15: suppl. 24, 1957.

15. Milo Hellman, "Changes in the Human Face Brought about by Development," *International Journal of Orthodontia, Oral Surgery — Radiography* (13), 1927, p. 475-516.

16. Pfitzner, "Der Einfluss des Lebensalters auf die anthropologischen Charactere" (ch. 27, note 5).

17. Hrdlicka, "Growth During Adult Life" (ch. 27, note 3).

18. E. Hooten and C. Dupertuis, "Age Changes and Selective Survival in Irish Males, Studies on Physical Anthropology," American Association of Physical Anthropology and Wenner-Gren Foundation, 2, 1951, p. 1-130.

19. G. Lasker, "The Age Factor in Bodily Measurements of Adult Male and Female Mexicans, *Human Biology,* Vol. 25:1, February 1953, p. 50-63.

20. K. Sarnas, "Growth Changes in Skulls of Ancient Man in North America," Acta Odont. Scandinavica, Vol. 15:1957, p. 213-271.

21. C.B. Ruff, "Age Differences in Craniofacial Dimensions Among Adults from Indian Knoll, Kentucky," Am. J. Phys. Anthrop, 53: p. 101-108, 1980.

22. See Research Notes 5 and 6, Chapter 27.

23. E.C. Buchi, "Anderung der Korperform bein erwachsenen Menschen, eine Untersuchung nach der Individual-Methode," Anthropolgische Forschungen (Anthrop. Gesellsch, in Wein), Hft. 1 p. 1-44, 1950.

24. J.I. Thompson and G.S. Kendrick, "Changes in the Vertical Dimensions of the Human Male Skull During the Third and Fourth Decades of Life," Anat. Rec. 150:209-214, 1964.

25. G.S. Kendrick and H.L. Risinger, "Changes in the Anteroposterior Dimensions of the Human Male Skull During the Third and Fourth Decades of Life," Anat. Rec. 159:77-81, 1967.

26. H. Israel, "The Dichotomous Pattern of Craniofacial Expansion During Aging," Am. J. Phys. Anthrop. 47:47-52, 1977. See Research Note 7, Chapter 27.

27. C. Susanne, "Individual Age Changes of the Morphological Characteristics," J. Human Evolution, 6:181-189, 1977.

28. R. Behrents, "Growth in the Aging Craniofacial Skeleton," Monograph 17, Craniofacial Growth Series, Center for Human Growth and Development, University of Michigan, Ann Arbor, 1985.

29. R. Behrents, "An Atlas of Growth in the Aging Craniofacial Skeleton," Monograph 18, Craniofacial Growth Series, Center for Human Growth and Development, University of Michigan, Ann Arbor, 1985.

Notes — Chapter 27, Contd.

30. See Research Note 8, Chapter 27.
31. Presently chairman of Department of Orthodontics, Baylor College of Dentistry.
32. Behrents, "Growth in the Aging Craniofacial Skeleton," p. 102 (ch. 27, note 28).
33. See Research Note 9, Chapter 27.
34. See Research Note 10, Chapter 27.
35. See Research Note 11, Chapter 27.
36. Trinkaus and Shipman, *The Neanderthals*, p. 340 (ch. 20, note 22).
37. Stringer and Gamble, *In Search of the Neanderthals*, p. 88 (ch. 16, note 12).

Chapter 28

1. C.L. Brace and M.F.A. Montagu, *Man's Evolution, An Introduction To Physical Anthropology* (Toronto, Canada: McMillan Co., 1965), p. 156-158.
   Oakely, et al., *Catalogue of Fossil Hominids*, p. 150 (ch. 9, note 3).
2. See Research Note 19, chapter 28.
3. Dean et al., "Age at Death of the Neanderthal Child . . ." p. 301-309 (ch. 16, note 15).
   A.M. Tillier, "Les enfants néanderthaliens de Devils Tower (Gibraltar)," Zeitschriftuer Morphologie und Anthropologie, 73: 1982, p. 125-148.
4. Dean et al., "Age at Death of the Neanderthal Child . . ." p. 301-309 (ch. 16, note 15).
5. Mellars and Stringer, *The Human Revolution*, "The Evolution of Modern Humans: Evidence from Young Mousterian Individuals," by A.M. Tillier, p. 286-297 (ch. 15, note 2).
6. See Research Note 1, Chapter 28.
7. C.F.A. Moorrees, E.A. Fanning, and E.E. Hunt, "Age Variation of Formation Stages for Ten Permanent Teeth," *Journal of Dental Research*, 1963, Vol. 42:1490-1502.
8. See Research Note 2, Chapter 28.
9. See Research Note 3, Chapter 28.
10. L. Graber, editor, *Orthodontics, State of the Art, Essence of the Science,* "Structural and Functional 'Balance' During Craniofacial Growth," by D. Enlow (St. Louis, MO: CV Mosby Co, 1986), p. 15-20.
    D. Enlow, *Handbook of Facial Growth* (Philadelphia, PA: W.B. Saunders Co. 1975), p. 82-101, 132.
11. Moorrees et al., "Age Variation of Formation Stages for Ten Permanent Teeth" (ch. 28, note 7).
 I. Schour and M. Massler, *Development of the Human Dentition Chart*, 2nd edition (Chicago, IL: American Dental Association, 1944).
12. See Research Note 4, Chapter 28.
13. H.M. Liversidge, M.C. Dean, and T.I. Molleson, "Increasing Human Tooth Length Between Birth and 5.4 Years," Am. Jour. Phys. Anthrop. 1993, 90: p. 307-313.
14. Theya Molleson, personal communication, November 9, 1993.
15. See Research Note 5, Chapter 28.
16. Marc A. Kelley and Clark S. Larsen, editors, *Advances in Dental Anthropology,* "Standards of Human Tooth Formation and Dental Age Assessment," by B. Holly Smith (New York: Wiley-Liss, Inc., 1991), p. 143-168.
17. Ibid.
    R. Kronfield and I. Schour, "Neonatal Dental Hypoplasia, J. Am. Dent. Assoc. 26: 1939, p. 18-32.
    C.F.A. Moorrees, E.A. Fanning, and E.E. Hunt, "Formation and Resorption of Three Deciduous Teeth in Children," Am. Journ. Phys. Anthropol. 21: 1963, p. 205-213.
    See Research Notes 6 and 7, Chapter 28.

18. Kelley and Larsen, *Advances in Dental Anthropology,* p.157 (ch. 28, note 16).
19. Kelley and Larsen, *Advances in Dental Anthropology,* p.146 illustration caption (ch. 28, note 16).
20. See Research Note 8, Chapter 28.
21. Enlow, *Handbook of Facial Growth,* p. 43-44 (ch. 28, note 10).
22. See Research Note 9, Chapter 28.
23. M. Riolo, R. Moyers, J.A. McNamara, and W.S. Hunter, *An Atlas of Craniofacial Growth* (Ann Arbor, MI: Center for Human Growth and Development, University of Michigan, Ann Arbor, 1974).
24. Ibid., Angular measurement variable 50, p. 74.
25. See Research Note 10, Chapter 28.
26. B.H. Broadbent Sr., B.H. Broadbent Jr., and W. Golden *Bolton Standards of Dentofacial Developmental Growth* (St. Louis, MO: The C.V. Mosby Co., 1975), Angular measurement #13.
27. See Research Note 10, Chapter 28.
28. Riolo et al., *An Atlas of Craniofacial Growth,* Linear measurement variable #88, p.116 (ch. 28, note 23).
29. Both methods measure the ramus height the same way, same points.
30. Broadbent et al., *Bolton Standards of Dentofacial Developmental Growth,* Linear measurement #5D (ch. 28, note 26).
31. See Research Note 11, Chapter 28.
32. See Research Note 12, Chapter 28.
33. Stringer and Gamble, *In Search of the Neanderthals,* p. 86 (ch. 16, note 12).
34. Garrod et al., "Excavation of a Mousterian Rock-Shelter. . ." (ch. 16, note 16).
35. See Research Note 5, Chapter 17.
36. R. Gore, "Neanderthals," *National Geographic,* Vol. 189, No. 1, January 1996, p. 2-35.
37. Ibid., p. 15-17.
    C.P.E. Zollikofer, M.S. Ponce de Léon, R.D. Martin, P. Stuckl, et al., "Neanderthal Computer Skulls," cover, and Scientific Correspondence, *Nature* (cover), Vol. 375:6529, 1995, p. 283-285.
38. See Research Note 13, Chapter 28.
39. Broadbent et al., *Bolton Standards of Dentofacial Developmental Growth,* Angular measurement #3 (ch. 28, note 6).
40. Bo Na-Pogo.
41. Riolo et al., *An Atlas of Craniofacial Growth,* Linear measurement variable # 182 (ch. 28, note 23).
42. See Research Note 14, Chapter 28.
43. Riolo et al., *An Atlas of Craniofacial Growth,* Linear variable #185 (ch. 28, note 23).
44. Dean et al., "Age at Death of the Neanderthal Child. . ." (ch. 16, note 15).
45. B. Frohlich and P.O. Pederson, "Secular Changes Within Arctic and Sub-Arctic Populations: A Study of 632 Human Mandibles from the Aleutian Islands, Alaska, and Greenland," *Arctic Medical Research,* 1992, 51(4), p. 173-188.
46. W.L. Hylander, "The Adaptive Significance of Eskimo Craniofacial Morphology," Dissertation for Ph.D., University of Chicago, Dept. of Anthropology, Chicago, Illinois, 1972, p. 156 -166.
47. Robert Cedarquist, "Craniofacial Description of Wainwright Alaskan Eskimos," Unpublished masters thesis, Dept. of Anthropology, University of Chicago, 1975.
48. See Research Note 15, Chapter 28.
49. D.S. Carlson, *Craniofacial Biology,* "Functional Determinants of Craniofacial Size and Shape," by J.A. McNamara, Center for Human Growth and Development, Mono. 10, Craniofacial Growth Series, University of Michigan, 1981, p.181-221.

Notes — Chapter 28, Contd.

50. Cedarquist, "Craniofacial Description of Wainwright Alaskan Eskimos" (ch. 28, note 47).
51. I. Schour and M. Massler, *Development of the Human Dentition Chart*, 2nd edition (Chicago, IL: American Dental Association, 1944.
52. Sheldon Watnick, "Inheritance of Craniofacial Morphology," *Angle Orthodontist*, Vol. 42(4), 1972, p. 339-351.
53. See Research Notes 17 and 18, Chapter 28.
54. G.W. Thompson and F. Popovich, "Static and Dynamic Analysis of Gonial Angle Size," *Angle Orthodontist,* (44)3:1974, p. 227-234.
55. John W. Cuozzo "Earlier Orthodontic Intervention: A View from Prehistory," *Journal of the NJ Dental Association*, Vol. 58, No.4., Autumn 1987, p. 33-40.
56. A.M. Tillier, "Le crâne d'enfant d'Engis 2: un exemple de distribution des caractèrs juvéniles, primitifs et néanderthaliens," Bull. Soc. Roy. Belge Anthrop. Préhist., 1983, 94: p. 51-75.
57. See Research Note 19, Chapter 28.

Chapter 29

1. E.F. Wente, "Who Was Who Among the Royal Mummies," *Oriental Institute News and Notes*, (144), Winter 1995.
2. G. Wyshak and R.E. Frisch, "Evidence for a Secular Trend in the Age of Menarche," *New England Journal of Medicine,* April 29, 1982, p. 1033-35.
3. Cuozzo, "Earlier Orthodontic Intervention: A View from Prehistory" (ch. 28, note 55).
4. B. Datta and D. Gupta, "The Age at Menarche in Classical India," *Annuals of Human Biology*, Vol. 8 (4), 1981, p. 351-359.
5. D.W. Amundsen and C.J. Diers, "The Age of Menarche in Medieval Europe," *Human Biology*, 45 (3), 1973, p. 363-369.
6. Ibid.
   D.W. Amundsen and C.J. Diers, "The Age of Menarche in Classical Greece and Rome," *Human Biology,* 41, p. 125-132.
7. Datta and Gupta, "The Age at Menarche in Classical India," p. 351-359 (ch. 29, note 4).
8. Samuel S.C. Yen and Robert B. Jaffe, *Reproductive Endocrinology* (Philadelphia, PA: W.B. Saunders Co., 1986), p. 329.
9. Datta and Gupta, "The Age at Menarche in Classical India," p. 351-359 (ch. 29, note 4).
10. Amundsen and Diers, "The Age of Menarche in Classical Greece and Rome," p. 125-132 (ch. 29, note 6).
11. Ibid.
12. Yen and Jaffe, *Reproductive Endocrinology,* p. 314 (ch. 29, note 8).
13. S.F. Daw, "Age of Boys' Puberty in Leipzig, 1727-49, as Indicated by Voicebreaking in J.S. Bach's Choir Members," *Human Biology*, Vol.42 (1), 1970, p. 87-89.
14. Yen and Jaffe, *Reproductive Endocrinology,* p. 314 (ch. 29, note 8).
15. I. Nakamura, M. Shimura, K. Nonaka, T. Miura, "Changes of Recollected Menarcheal Age and Month among Women in Toyoko Over a Period of 90 Years," *Annals of Human Biology*, 1986, Vol. 13(6), p. 547-554.
16. P. Helm and S. Helm, "Decrease in Menarcheal Age from 1966 to 1983 in Denmark," Acta. Obstet. Gynecol. Scand. 63, 1984, p. 633-635.
17. P. Helm and S. Helm, "Uncertanties in Designation of Age at Menarche in the Nineteenth Century: Revised Mean for Denmark, 1835," *Annals of Human Bioligy*, Vol. 14 (4), 1987, p. 371-374.
18. J.E. Brudevoll, K. Liestol, and L. Walloe, "Menarcheal Age in Oslo During the Last 140 Years," *Annals of Human Biology*, Vol. 6 (5), 1979, p. 407-16.

19. K. Liestol and M. Rosenberg, "Height, Weight, and Menarcheal Age of Schoolgirls in Oslo — an Update" *Annals of Human Biology*, 22 (3), 1995, p. 199-205.

20. J.L. Boldsen, B. Jeune, K.L. Bach-Rasmussen, M. Sevelsted, and E. Vinther, "Age at Menarche Among Schoolgirls in Odense — Is Age at Menarche Still Decreasing in Denmark?" *Ugeskrift for Lager,* 155 (7), 1993, p. 482-484.

21. A.H. Rimpela and M.K. Rimpela, "Towards an Equal Distribution of Health? Socioeconomic and Regional Difference of the Secular Trend of the Age of Menarche in Finland from 1979 to1980," *Acta Paediatrica,* 82 (1), 1993, p. 87-90.

22. F.M. Veronisi and P. Gueresi, "Trend in Menarcheal Age and Socioeconomic Influence in Bologna, Northern Italy," *Annals of Human Biology*, 21 (2), 1994, p. 187-196.

23. L. Tryggvadottir, H. Tulinius, and M. Larusdottir, "A Decline and Halt in Mean Age at Menarche in Iceland," *Annals of Human Biology*, 21 (2), 1994, p. 179-186.

24. L.L. So and P.K. Yen, "Secular Trend of Menarcheal Age in Southern Chinese Girls," *Zeitschrift fur Morphologie und Anthropologie*, 79 (1), 1992, p. 21-24.

25. I. Chakraborti and A.K. Sinha, "Declining Age of Menarche in West Bengal," *Journal of the Indian Medical Association,* 89 (1), 1991, p. 10-13.

26. N. Cameron and I. Nagdee, "Menarcheal Age in Two Generations of South African Indians," *Annals of Human Biology*, 23 (2):113-9, March-April 1996.

27. H. Danker-Hopfe and K. Delibalta, "Menarcheal Age of Turkish Girls in Bremen," *Anthropologischer Anzeiger*, 48 (1), 1990, p. 1-14.

28. A. Baxter-Jones, P. Helms, and M. Preece, "Age at Menarche" (Letter), *Lancet,* 12, Feb. 343: 1994, p. 423.

29. T.C. Dann and D.F. Roberts (Letter), *Lancet,* 12, Feb. 343: 1994, p. 423-424.

30. I.M. St. George, S. Williams, and P.A. Silva, "Body Size and Menarche: The Dunedin Study," *Journal of Adolescent Health*, 15(7), 1994, p. 573-576.

31. Cuozzo, "Earlier Orthodontic Intervention: A View from Prehistory" (ch. 28, note 55).

32. See Research Note 1, Chapter 29.

33. Datta and Gupta, "The Age at Menarche in Classical India," p. 351-359 (ch. 29, note 4).

34. Yen and Jaffe, *Reproductive Endocrinology,* p. 361 (ch. 29, note 8).

35. A. Pérez-Comas, C.A. Saénz de Rodriguez, F. Sánchez Lugo, "Abnormalities of Sexual Development in Puerto Rico: Status Report," *Boletin-Asociacion Medica de Puerto Rico*, 83(7), 1991, p. 306-309.

36. J. Pohlenz, P. Habermehl, H. Wemme, W. Grimm, and W. Schonberger, "The Differentiation Between Premature Thelarche and Pubertas Praecox on the Basis of Clinical, Hormaonal and Radiological Findings," *Deutsche Medizinische Wochenschrift,* 119(39), 1994, p. 1301-1306.

37. R. Balducci, B. Boscherini, A. Mangiantini, M. Morellini, and V. Toscano, "Isolated Precocious Pubarche: An Approach," *Journal of Clinical Endocrinology & Metabolism,* 79(2), 1994, p. 582-589.

38. D.M. Cathro and S.G. Golombek, "Non-classical 3 Beta-hydroxysteroid Dehydrogenase Deficiency in Children in Cental Iowa. Difficulties in Differentiating This Entity from Cases of Precocious Adrenarche without Adrenal Enzyme Effect," *Journal of Pediatric Endocrinology*, 7(1), 1994, p. 19-32.

39. M.J. Sharafuddin, A. Luisiri, L.R. Garibaldi, D.L. Fein, K.N. Gillespie, and E.R. Gravis, "MR Imaging Diagnosis of Central Precocious Puberty: Importance of Changes in the Shape and Size of the Pituitary Gland," *American Journal of Roentgenology*, 162(5), 1994, p. 1167-1173.

40. C. Pienkowski, M.T. Tauber, P. Pigeon, I. Oliver, and P. Rochiccioli, "Precocious Puberty and Polycystic Ovarian Syndrome: Apropos of 13 Cases," *Archves de Pediatrie*, 2(8) 1995, p. 729-734.

Notes — Chapter 29, Contd.

41. R.R. Shankar and O.H. Pescovitz, "Precocious Puberty" [Review], *Advances in Endocrinology & Metabolism,* (6) 1995, p. 55-89.
42. G. Ciotti, O. Gabrielli, I. Carloni, A.M. Gangale, M. Bevilacqua, F. Principi, G.G. Garzetti, and D.L. Giorgi, "Studio ecographico e flussimetrico delle ovaie in bambine con puberta precoce," *Minerva Pediatrica,* 47(4), 1995, p. 107-110.
43. A. Pere, J. Perheentupa, M. Peter, and R. Voutilainen, "Follow-up of Growth and Steroids in Premature Adrenarche," *European Journal of Pediatrics,* 154(5), 1995, p. 346-352.
44. I.J. Griffin, J. Cole, K.A. Duncan, A.S. Hollman, and M.D. Donaldson, "Pelvic Ultrasound Findings in Different Forms of Sexual Precocity," *Acta Paediatrica,* 84(5), 1995, p. 544-549.
45. L. Kornreich, G. Horev, S. Blaser, D. Daneman, R. Kauli, and M. Grunebaum, "Central Precocious Puberty, Evaluation by Neuorimaging," *Pediatric Radiology,* 25(1), 1995, p. 7-11.
46. H.P. Haber, H.A. Wollmann, and M.B. Ranke, "Pelvic Ultrasonography: Early Differentiation Between Isolated Premature Thelarche and Central Precocious Puberty," *European Journal of Pediatrics,* 154(3), 1995, p. 182-186.
47. S.G. Robben and W. Oostdijk, "Idiopathic Isosexual Central Precocious Puberty: Magnetic Resonance Findings in 30 Patients," *British Journal of Radiology,* 68(805), 1995, p. 34-38.
48. S.J. Gould, *Full House* (New York: Crown Publishers, 1996), p. 165, 180.
49. N.A. Bridges et al., "Sexual Precocity: Sex Incidence and Aetiology," Arch. Dis. Child. 70, 1994, p. 116-118.
50. T. Moshang, Comment after article "Sexual Precocity: Sex Incidence and Aetiology," *Year Book of Pediatrics,* Chapter 17, Endocrinology (Chicago, IL: Year Book Medical Publishers Inc., 1995), p. 474-475.
51. Moorrees et al., "Formation and Resorption of Three Deciduous Teeth in Children" (ch. 28, note 17).
52. Kelley and Larsen, *Advances in Dental Anthropology,* "Anthropological Aspects of Orofacial and Occlusal Variations and Anomalies," by R. Corruccini, p. 295-323 (ch. 28, note 16).
53. Cuozzo, "Earlier Orthodontic Intervention: A View from Prehistory" (ch. 28, note 55).
54. See Research Note 19, Chapter 28.

Chapter 30

1. Hrdlicka, "Growth During Adult Life" (ch. 27, note 3).
   See Research Note 2, Chapter 27.
2. Measured craniometrically as opposed to cephalometrically as I have done.
3. See Research Note 1, Chapter 30, for posterior skull external and glabella external measurements.
4. See Research Note 2, Chapter 30.
5. Stringer and Gamble, *In Search of the Neanderthals,* p. 88 (ch. 16, note 12).
6. Trinkaus and Shipman, *The Neanderthals,* p. 340 (ch. 20, note 22).
7. Development of the human embryo.
8. Thomas M. Graber, *Orthodontics, Principles and Practice* (Philadelphia, PA: W.B. Saunders Co., 1961), p. 44.
9. C.L. Brace and M.F.A. Montagu, *Man's Evolution, An Introduction To Physical Anthropology* (Toronto, Canada: McMillan Co., 1965), p. 156-158.
10. Bernd Herrmann, "Uber die Reste des postcranialen Skelettes des Neanderthalers von Le Moustier," Z. Morph. Anthrop., 68, 2, 1977, p. 129-149.
11. Ibid.

12. H.M. Frost, *Bone Remodelling and Its Relationship to Metabolic Bone Diseases*, Orthopaedic Lectures, Vol. 111 (Springfield, IL: Charles C. Thomas Pub., 1973), p. 54.
13. Ibid., p. 15.
14. D.J. Ortner and W.G.J. Putschar, *Identification of Pathological Conditions in Human Skeletal Remains* (Washington, DC: Smithsonian Institution Press, 1985), p. 21.
15. Frost, *Bone Remodelling and Its Relationship to Metabolic Bone Diseases,* p. 145 (ch. 30, note 12).
16. Tattersall, *The Last Neanderthal*, p. 11 (ch. 23, note 1).
17. Behrents, "An Atlas of Growth in the Aging Craniofacial Skeleton," p. 147 (ch. 27, note 29). See Note 3 Chapter 30, Calculation 252.
18. Harry Sicher, *Oral Anatomy,* 3rd edition (St. Louis, MO: C.V. Mosby Co., 1960), p. 123.
19. H.M. Frost, "Wolff's Law and Bone's Structural Adaptations to Mechanical Usage: An Overview for Clinicians," *Angle Orthodontist*, 64(3), 1994, p. 175-188.
20. S. Goodman and P. Aspenberg, "Effects of Mechanical Stimulation on the Differentiation of Hard Tissues, *Biomaterials,* 14(8), 1993, p. 563-569.
21. Behrents, "Growth in the Aging Craniofacial Skeleton," (monograph 17) p. 100 (ch. 27, note 28).
22. See Research Note 4, Chapter 30.
23. Trinkaus and Shipman, *The Neanderthals*, p. 354 (ch. 20, note 22).
24. D.K. Whittaker, S. Griffiths, A. Robson, P. Roger-Davies, G. Thomas, and T. Molleson, "Continuing Tooth Eruption and Alveolar Crest Height in an Eighteenth-Century Population from Spitalfields, East London," *Arch. Oral Biol.* (35),2., 1990, p. 81-85.
25. See Research Note 5, Chapter 30.
26. Whittaker et al., "Continuing Tooth Eruption and Alveolar Crest Height. . ." (ch. 30, note 24).
27. Ibid., p. 84
28. Behrents, "An Atlas of Growth in the Aging Craniofacial Skeleton," Calculation 201 (ch. 27, note 29).
29. See Research Note 3, Chapter 30.
30. A. Ainamo and J. Ainamo, "The Dentition Is Intended to Last a Lifetime," Inter. Dental Journal, 34, 1984, p. 87-92.
31. Bishara et al., "Facial and Dental Changes in Adulthood," p.177 (ch. 27, note 1).
32. Ainamo and Ainamo, "The Dentition Is Intended to Last a Lifetime" (ch. 30, note 30).
   B.C.W. Barker, "Relation of the Alveolus to the Cemtento-enamel Junction Following Attritional Wear in Aboriginal Skulls," *Journal of Periodontology*, 46, (1975), p. 357-363.
   T. Murphy, "Compensatory Mechanisms in Facial Height Adjustment to Functional Tooth Attrition," *Australian Dental Journal,* October 1959, p. 312-319.
33. Murphy, "Compensatory Mechanisms in Facial Height Adjustment. . ." (ch. 30, note 32).
34. Ibid.
35. Broadbent et al., *Bolton Standards of Dentofacial Developmental Growth* (ch. 28, note 26).
36. J. Bartlett, *Familiar Quotations*, 14th edition, E. Beck, editor (Boston, MA: Little Brown Co., 1968), p. 193, (from *King Richard III*).
   Bartlett, *Familiar Quotations,* "The Everlasting Gospel," by W. Blake, c.1818, p. 491a.
   Bartlett, *Familiar Quotations,* "My Psalm," st. 2, by John G. Whittier, c.1870, p. 626 a.
37. Sicher, *Oral Anatomy*, p. 87 (ch. 30, note 18).
38. B. Endo, "Experimental Studies on the Mechanical Significance of the Form of the Human Facial Skeleton," J. Fac. Sci. Univ. Tokyo, Section V Anthrop, 3(1), 1966, p. 1-106.
   B. Endo, "Analysis of Stresses Around the Orbit Due to Masseter and Temporalis Muscles Respectively," J. Anthropol. Soc. Nippon, 78, 1970, p. 251-266.
39. Rocky Mountain Data Systems, 23622 Calabasas Rd., Suite 340, Calabasas, CA 91302.
40. Cuozzo, "Earlier Orthodontic Intervention: A View from Prehistory" (ch. 28, note 55).

Chapter 31

1. Unknown reviewer, *American Journal of Orthodonics*, T.M. Graber, editor-in-chief.
2. W.M. Krogman, "Maturation Age of the Growing Child in Relation to the Timing of Statural and Facial Growth at Puberty," Offprint from *Transactions & Studies of the College of Physicians of Philadelphia,* Vol. 1, No. 1, March 1979, p. 33-42.
3. L.H. Rothenberg, R. Hintz, and M. Van Kamp, "Assessment of Physical Maturation and Somatodin Levels During Puberty," Am. J. Orthod., 71, 1977, p. 666-667.
4. D.Z. Loesch, R. Huggins, E. Rogucka, N.H. Hoang, and J.L. Hopper, "Genetic Correlates of Menarcheal Age: A Multivariate Twin Study," *Annals of Human Biology*, 22(6):470-90, 1995.
5. R.S. Nanda, "The Rates of Growth of Several Facial Components Measured from Serial Cephalometric Roetgenograms," Am J. Orthod., 41, 1955, p. 653-673.
6. P. Schlatter, T.M. Marthaler, and H.R. Muhlemann, "Changes in the Depth of Artificial Marks on Tooth Surfaces After Certain Time Intervals," Helv. Odont. Acta. 5, 1961, p. 43.
7. Y. Hayashi, "High Resolution Electron Microscopy of a Small Crack at the Superficial Layer of Enamel," J. of Electron Microscopy, 43(6): Dec. 1994, p. 398-401.
8. P.A. Raj, M. Johnsson, M.J. Levine, and G.H. Nancollas, "Salivary Statherin. Dependence on Sequence, Charge, Hydrogen Bonding Potency, and Helical Conformation for Adsorption to Hydroxyapatite and Inhibition of Mineralization," Journ. Biological Chem., 267(9), 1992, p. 5968-5976.
9. J.L. Jenson, M.S. Lamkin, and F.G. Oppenheim, "Adsorption of Human Salivary Proteins to Hydroxyapatite: A Comparison Between Whole Saliva and Glandular Salivary Secretions," J. Dent. Research, 71(9), 1992, p. 1569-1576.
10. P. Westbroek and F. Marin, "A Marriage of Bone and Nacre, *Nature*, 392, 1998, p.861-862.
11. Personal communication , Thomas Kotch, Ph.D., Professor of Chemistry, Cedar Crest College.
12. T. Zelles, K.R. Purushotham, S.P. Macauley, G.E. Oxford, and M.G. Humphreys-Beyer, "Saliva and Growth Factors: The Fountain of Youth Resides in Us All," *Journal of Dental Research* 74(12), Dec. 1995, p. 1826-1832.
13. P.A. Raj, S.D. Soni, and M.J. Levine, "Membrane-induced Helical Conformation of an Active Candidacidal Fragment of Salivary Histatins," J. Biol. Chem., 269, (13):1994, p. 9610-9619.
14. Zelles et al., "Saliva and Growth Factors: The Fountain of Youth Resides in Us All" (ch. 31, note 12).
15. Ibid.
16. Jenson et al, "Adsorption of Human Salivary Proteins to Hydroxyapatite. . ." (ch. 31, note 9).
17. H. Athenstaedt, "Pyroelectric and Piezoelectric Behaviour of Human Dental Hard Tissues," Archs. Oral. Biol., 1971:16, p. 495-501.
See Research Note 1, Chapter 31.
18. Mellars and Stringer, *The Human Revolution,* "How Different Was Middle Palaeolithic Subsistence? A Zooarchaeological Perspective on the Middle to Upper Palaeolithic Transition," by Philip Chase, p. 321-337 (ch. 15, note 2).
19. Von Koenigswald, *The Neanderthal Centenary,* " 'Spiritualité' de l'Homme de Néandertal," by Bergounioux, p. 154 and 164 (ch. 9, note 4).
20. See Research Note 2, Chapter 31, for diet and jaw size. Please read this very important note.
21. Michael Balter, "Cave Structure Boosts Neandertal Image," *Science*, Vol. 271, January 26, 1996, p. 449.
22. Ibid.
23. Ibid.

24. D.S. Carlson and D.P. Van Gerven, "Masticatory Function and Post-Pleistocene Evolution in Nubia," *American Journal of Physical Anthropology*, 46:3, (1977), p. 495-506.
25. Erik Trinkaus, *The Shanidar Neanderthals* (New York: Academic Press, 1983), p. 174-175.
26. U. Zilberman and Patricia Smith, "A Comparison of Tooth Structure in Early Neanderthals and Early *Homo sapiens sapiens*: A Radiographic Study," *Journal of Anatomy*, 180, June 1992, p. 387-393.
27. See Research Note 3, Chapter 31.
28. See Research Note 4, Chapter 31.
29. See Research Note 5, Chapter 31.
30. Stringer and Gamble, *In Search of the Neanderthals*, p. 88 (ch. 16, note 12).
31. Zilberman and Smith, "A Comparison of Tooth Structure in Early Neanderthals. . ." (ch. 31, note 26).
32. *American Journal of Orthodonics* anonymous critic or referee for a paper submited to the AJO in 1985, 6, 7.
33. D.K. Whittaker, T. Molleson, A.T. Daniel, J.T. Williams, P. Rose, and R. Resteghini, "Quantitative Assessment of Tooth Wear, Alveolar Crest Height and Continuing Eruption in a Romano-British Population," Arch Oral Biol., 1985, 30:6, p. 493-501.
34. S.M. Garn, "Contributions of the Radiographic Image to our Knowledge of Human Growth," Neuhauser Lecture, *American Journal of Roentgenology*, 137,(2) 1981, p. 231- 239.
35. Stringer and Gamble, *In Search of the Neanderthals,* p.76-77 (ch. 16, note 12).
36. Trinkaus, *The Shanidar Neanderthals*, p. 154-175 (ch. 31, note 25).
37. See Research Note 6, Chapter 31.
38. Zilberman and Smith, "A Comparison of Tooth Structure in Early Neanderthals. . ." (ch. 31, note 26).
39. A.M. Tillier, "L a Dentition de l'Enfant Mousterian Chateauneuf 2 Decouverte a l'Abri de Hauteroche (Charente)," L.Anthropologie (Paris) Tome 83 (1979) no.3, p. 417-438.
40. See Research Note 5, Chapter 31.
41. R.E. Moyers, Frans P.G.M. van der Linden, M.L. Riolo, and J.A. McNamara, JA, "Standards of Occlusal Development," Center for Human Growth and Development, University of Michigan, Ann Arbor, Monograph No. 5, Craniofacial Growth Series, 1976, p. 45.
42. Trinkaus, *The Shanidar Neanderthals*, p. 151-177 (ch. 31, note 25).
43. C.L.B. Lavelle, R.P. Shellis, and D.F.G. Poole, *Evolutionary Changes to the Primate Skull and Dentition* (Springfield, IL: C Thomas Pub., 1977), p. 152.
44. Cuozzo, "Neanderthal Children's Fossils. . ." (ch. 17, note 9).
45. S.N. Bhaskar, *Orbans's Oral Histology and Embryology,* 9th edition (St. Louis, MO: CV Mosby Co., 1980), p. 126.
46. G.N. Jenkins, *The Physiology and Biochemistry of the Mouth,* 4th edition (Oxford, England: Blackwell Scientific Publications, 1978), p. 180.
47. Bhaskar, *Orbans's Oral Histology and Embryology,* p. 107 (ch. 31, note 45). Hillson, *Teeth*, p. 269 (ch. 17, note 3).
48. Bhaskar, *Orbans's Oral Histology and Embryology,* p. 117 (ch. 31, note 45).
49. Hillson, *Teeth*, p. 113 (ch. 17, note 3).
50. Bhaskar, *Orbans's Oral Histology and Embryology,* p. 107-108.
51. Jenkins, *The Physiology and Biochemistry of the Mouth,* p. 567 (ch. 31, note 46). C. Bell, *Heinemann Dental Handbook* (Oxford, England: Heinemann Medical Books, 1990), p. 19.
52. Jenkins, *The Physiology and Biochemistry of the Mouth*, p. 180 (ch. 31, note 46).
53. Hillson, *Teeth*, p. 269(ch. 17, note 3).
54. Stringer and Gamble, *In Search of the Neanderthals*, p. 78 (ch. 16, note 12).

Chapter 32

1. Smith, "The Solutrean Culture" (ch. 20, note 9).
2. Sieveking, *The Cave Artists*, p. 84, figure 52 caption (ch. 24, note 2).
3. Trinkaus and Shipman, *The Neanderthals*, p. 317 (ch. 20, note 22).
4. Stringer and Gamble, *In Search of the Neanderthals*, p. 76 (ch. 16, note 12).
5. H. Ross, "No Tears for Neanderthals," *Facts and Faith*, Vol. 10, No. 4, 1996, p. 11.
6. J.H. Schwartz and I Tattersall, "Significance of Some Previously Unrecognized Apomorphies in the Nasal Region of *Homo neanderthalensis*," Proc. Natl. Acad. Sci., USA, October 1996, Vol. 93, p. 10852-10854.
7. C.H. Best and N.B. Taylor *The Living Body, A Text in Human Pysiology*, 4th edition (New York City, NY: H. Holt & Co., 1958), p. 574.
8. Ross, "No Tears for Neanderthals" (ch. 32, note 5).
9. Menopause is the permanent cessation of the menses or menstrual periods, could be irregular bleeding at first but eventually a total shutdown occurs. Termination of menstrual life.
   H. Kroger, M. Tuppurainen, R. Honkanen, E. Alhava, and S. Saarikoski, "Bone Mineral Density and Risk Factors for Osteoporosis — A Population-Based Study of 1600 Perimenopausal Women," Calcif. Tissue Int., 55(1) July 1994, p. 1-7.
10. D.W. Cramer, H. Xu, and B.L. Harlow, "Family History as a Predictor of Early Menopause," *Fertility & Sterility*, 64(4) October 1995, p. 740-745.
11. D.W. Cramer, H. Xu, and B.L. Harlow, "Does 'Incessant" Ovulation Increase Risk for Early Menopause?" Am. Journ. Obstet.& Gynocol., 172 (2 Pt 1) 1995, p. 568-573.
12. C.E. Schwartz, J. Dean, P.N. Howard-Peebles, M. Bugge, M. Mikkelson, N. Tommerup, C. Hull, R. Hagerman, J.J. Holden, and R.E. Stevenson, "Obstetrical and Gynecological Complications in Fragile X Carriers: A Multicenter Study," Am. Journ. Medical Genetics, 51(4) 1994, p. 400-402.
13. S.N. Kramer, *The Sumerians* (Chicago, IL: University of Chicago Press, 1963), p. 237-247.
14. Day, *Guide to Fossil Man*, 4th edition, p. 107 -119 (ch. 9, note 9).
    Mellars and Stringer, *The Human Revolution,* "The Evolution of Modern Humans: Recent Evidence from Southwest Asia," by B. Vandermeersch, p. 156-164 (ch. 15, note 2).
15. Mellars and Stringer, *The Human Revolution,* "The Evolution of Modern Humans: Recent Evidence from Young Mousterian Individuals," by Anne Marie Tillier, p. 286-97 (ch. 15, note 2).
16. G. Wyshak and R. Frisch, "Evidence for a Secular Trend in the Age of Menarche," *New England Journal of Medicine,* 306(17), 1982, p. 1033-1035.
    J.M. Tanner, "Earlier Maturation in Man" *Scientific American,* 218:21-27, 1968.
17. T.D. McCown and A. Keith, *The Stone Age of Mount Carmel*, Vol. 2, "The Fossil Human Remains from the Levalloiso-Mousterian" (Oxford: Clarendon Press, 1939).
18. Hilson, *Teeth,* p. 263 (ch. 17, note 3).
19. Stringer and Gamble, *In Search of the Neanderthals*, p. 103-104 (ch. 16, note 12).
20. A. Ronen, editor, *The Transition from the Lower to Middle Palaeolithic and the Origin of Modern Man,* "An Amino Acid Racemization Chronology for Tabūn," by P. Masters (Oxford: British Archaeology Reports, International Series, 1982) p. 43-54.
21. Seton Lloyd, *The Archaeology of Mesopotamia* (London: Thames and Hudson, 1984), p. 46-47.
22. Von Koenigswald, *The Neanderthal Centenary*, " 'Spiritualité' de l'Homme de Néandertal," by Bergounioux (ch. 9, note 4).
23. Day, *Guide to Fossil Man*, p. 114 (ch. 9, note 9).
24. J.C. Vogel and H.T. Waterbolk, "Grōningen Radiocarbon Dates," *Radiocarbon*, 5, 1963, p. 172.
25. W.R. Farrand, "Chronology and Paleoenvironment of Levantine Prehistoric Sites as Seen from Sediment Studies," J. Arch. Sci., 6, 1979, p. 369-392.

26. Ronen, *The Transition from the Lower to Middle Palaeolithic and the Origin of Modern Man,* "An Amino Acid Racemization Chronology for Tabūn," by Masters (ch. 32, note 20).

27. J. Jelinek, "The Tabūn Cave and Paleolithic Man in the Levant," *Science,* 216, 1982, p. 1369-1375.

28. Day, *Guide to Fossil Man,* p. 114 (ch. 9, note 9).

29. Baruch Arensburg and Ofer Bar-Yosef, *Eretz-Israel, Moshe Stekalis Memorial Volume,* "Paleo-environment of Pleistocene Man in the Levant," by W. Farrand (Jerusalem: Israel Exploration Society, 1977), p. 1-13.

30. Stringer and Gamble, *In Search of the Neanderthals,* p. 121 (ch. 16, note 12).

31. Von Koenigswald, *The Neanderthal Centenary,* "Upper Pleistocene Men of the Southwest Asian Mousterian," by F.C. Howell, p. 185-198 (ch. 9, note 4).

32. Mellars and Stringer, *The Human Revolution,* "Multiregional Evolution: The Fossil Alternative to Eden," by Milford Wolpoff, p. 62-108 (ch. 15, note 2).

33. Mellars and Stringer, *The Human Revolution,* "The Evolution of Modern Humans: Recent Evidence from Southwest Asia," by B. Vandermeerch, p. 155-171 (ch. 15, note 2).

34. S.L. Washburn, *Classification and Human Evolution* (Chicago, IL: Aldine Pub. Co. 1963), Wenner-Gren Foundation for Anthropological Research, "Genetic Entities in Hominid Evolution," by T. Dobzhansky, p. 361.

35. H. Suzuki and F. Takai, editors, *The Amud Man and His Cave Site* (Tokyo: Keigaku Publishing Co., 1970).
Stringer and Gamble, *In Search of the Neanderthals,* p. 99 (ch. 16, note 12).

36. Day, *Guide to Fossil Man,* p. 128 (ch. 9, note 9).

37. Personal Communication, Joseph Zias, Summer 1983, in Israel.

38. Donald Johanson and Blake Edgar, *From Lucy to Language* (New York: Simon and Schuster, 1996), p. 220.

39. See Research Note 1, Chapter 32.

40. Johanson and Edgar, *From Lucy to Language,* p. 218 (ch. 32, note 38).

41. See Research Note 2, Chapter 32.

Chapter 33

1. J.H. Lubin, "Models for Analysis of Radon-exposed Populations," Yale Journ. Biol. and Med. 61(3): 1988, p. 195-214.

2. J.M. Samet and R.W. Hornung, "Review of Radon and Lung Cancer Risk," *Risk Analysis,* 10(1) 1990, p. 65-75.

3. D. Henshaw, J. Eatough, and R. Richardson, "Radon as a Causative Factor in Induction of Myeloid Leukemia and Other Cancers," *Lancet,* 335(8696):1008-12, April 28, 1990.

4. J.I. Fabricant, "Shelter and Indoor Air in the Twenty-first Century — Radon, Smoking, and Lung Cancer," *Environmental Health Perspectives,* 86, 1990, p. 275- 280.

5. E.P. Radford and E.A. Martell, "Polonium-210: Lead-210 Ratios as an Index of Residence Times of Insoluble Particles from Cigarette Smoke in Bronchial Epithelium," *Inhaled Particles,* 4 Pt. 2, 1975, p. 256-281.

6. D.J. Crawford-Brown, "Age-dependent Lung Doses from Ingested 222Rn in Drinking Water," *Health Physics,* 52(2) 1987, p. 149-156.

7. C.T. Hess, C.V. Weiffenbach, and S.A. Norton, "Environmental Radon and Cancer Correlations in Maine," *Health Physics,* 45(2) 1983, p. 339-348.

8. Selman, *The Fundamentals of X-ray and Radium Physics,* p. 543 (ch. 25, note 16).

9. Ibid., p. 674.

10. Lively and Ney, "Surface Radioactivity Resulting from the Deposition of 222 Rn Daughter Products" (ch. 25, note 29).

Notes — Chapter 33, Contd.

11. J.L. Smith-Briggs and E.J. Bradley, "Measurement of Natural Radionuclides in U.K. Diet, *Science of the Total Environment*, 35(3) 1984, p. 431-440.

12. R.T. Steinbock, *Paleopathological Diagnosis and Interpretation* (Springfield, IL: Charles C. Thomas Pub., 1976), p. 363 and 370.

13. Day, *Guide to Fossil Man*, p. 337-345 (ch. 9, note 9).

14. K.J. Fennell and E. Trinkaus, "Bilaterial Lower Limb Periarticular Periostitis in the La Ferrassie Neanderthal," *American Journal of Physical Anthropology*, Supp. 22., 1996, p. 104.

15. Trinkaus, *The Shanidar Neanderthals*, p. 399-423 (ch. 31, note 25).

16. D.J. Ortner and A.C. Aufderheide, editors, *Human Paleopathology*, "8000-year-old Brain Tissue from the Windover Site: Anatomical, Cellular, and Molecular Analysis," by W.W. Hauswirth, C.D. Dickel, G.H. Doran, P.J. Lapis, and D.N. Dickel (Washington, DC: Smithsonian Institution, 1991), p. 60-72.

17. D.J. Ortner and A.C. Aufderheide, editors, *Human Paleopathology* (Washington, DC: Smithsonian Institution, 1991), "Human Soft Tissue Tumors in Paleopathology," by E. Gertzen and M.J. Allison, p. 257-260.

18. Sieveking, *The Cave Artists*, p. 154 (ch. 24, note 2).

19. J. Clottes and J. Courtin, *The Cave Beneath The Sea* (New York: Harry N. Abrams, Inc., Pub., 1996).

20. L. Ennis and H. Berry, *Dental Roentgenology*, 5th edition (Philadelphia, PA: Lea & Febiger, 1959), p. 28-33.

21. Lively and Ney, "Surface Radioactivity Resulting from the Deposition of 222 Rn Daughter Products" (ch. 25, note 29).

22. Camiel and Thompson, "Delayed Hazards of Radon Irradiation" (ch. 25, note 15).

23. E. Callery, "Cancer Caused by Radioactive Gold Rings," Canadian Med. Assoc. Journ, 141, 1989, p. 507.

24. N.D. Priest and F.L. Van De Vyver, editors, *Trace Metals and Flouride in Bones and Teeth*, "The Accumulation of Trace Metals in Bone During Fossilization," by T. Molleson (Boca Raton, FL: CRC Press, 1990), p. 342-363.

25. R.H. Clarke and T.R.E. Southwood, "Risks from Ionizing Radiation," *Nature*, Vol. 338, March 16, 1989, p. 197-198.

26. 1 Sv = 100 rems, 1 rem = 10^{-2} Sv, 1mSv =.1 rem , 1rem =1 rad, 1gray =100 rads.

27. Ennis and Berry, *Dental Roentgenology*, p. 20 (ch. 33, note 19).

28. GnRH is Gonadotropin-releasing hormone, also called Luteinizing hormone-releasing factor (LRF).

29. A.L. Ogilvy-Stuart, P.E. Clayton, and S.M. Shalet, "Cranial Irradiation and Early Puberty," *Journal of Clinical Endocrinology and Metabolism*, Vol. 78. No.6. 1994, p. 1282-1286.

30. FSH is Follicle Stimulating Hormone and LH is luteinizing hormone

31. Yen and Jaffe, *Reproductive Endocrinology*, p. 330 (ch. 29, note 8).

32. C. Cooper, D. Kuh, P. Egger, M. Wadsworth, and D. Barker, "Childhood Growth and Age at Menarche," *British Journal of Obstetrics and Gynaecology*, 103(8):814-7, August 1996.

33. W. Waldeyer, *Eierstock Und Ei* (Leipzig, Germany: Engelmann, 1870).

34. H.M. Evans and O. Swezy, "Ovogenesis and the Normal Follicular Cycle in Adult Mammalia," Mem. Univ. Calif., 9, 1931, p. 119-224.
    E. Allen, "Ovogenesis During Sexual Maturity," Am. J. Anat., 31, 1923, p. 439-481.

35. S. Zuckerman, *Beyond the Ivory Tower* (New York: Taplinger, 1971), chapter 3, p. 22-34.
    H. Arai, "On the Postnatal Development of the Ovary (Albino Rat) with Especial Reference to the Number of Ova," Am. J. Anat., 27, 1920, p. 405-462.

36. H.M. Beaumont and A.M. Mandl, "A Quantitiative and Cytological Study of Oogonia and Oocytes in the Foetal and Neonatal Rat," Proc. Royal Soc. B., 155, 1962, p. 557-559.

J.M. Ioannou, "Oogenesis in the Guinea Pig," J. Embryl. Exp. Morph., 12, 1964, p. 673-691.

T.G. Baker, "A Quantitative and Cytological Study of Germ Cells in Human Ovaries," Proc. Royal Soc. B., 158, 1963, p. 417-433.

37. Zuckerman, *Beyond the Ivory Tower*, p. 33 (ch. 33, note 34).

38. J. Brooks-Gun and A. Petersen, *Girls at Puberty,* "Physical and Biological Aspects of Puberty," by M. Warren (New York: Plenim Press, 1983), p. 3-28.

Ovulation is the release of an ovum (egg) from the follicle.

39. Hebrew transliteration of the word for sorrow is *Itstsabon.*

40. N.K. Sandars, *Prehistoric Art in Europe*, 2nd edition (Middlesex, England: Penguin Books in Europe, 1985), p. 53-59.

41. D. Navot, P.A. Bergh, M.A. Williams, G.J. Garrisi, I. Guzman, B. Sandler, and L. Grunfeld, "Poor Oocyte Quality Rather Than Implantation Failure as a Cause of Age-related Decline in Female Fertility," *Lancet*, 337(8754):1991, p. 1375-1377.

42. D. Navot, M.R. Drews, P.A. Bergh, I. Guzman, A. Karstaedt, R.T. Scott Jr., G.J. Garrisi, and G.E. Hoffman, "Age-related Decline in Female Fertility Is Not Due to Diminshed Capacity of the Uterus to Sustain Embryo Implantation," *Fertility & Sterility*, 61(1): 1994, p. 97-101.

43. A. Demir, L. Dunkel, U.H. Stenman, and R. Voutilainen, "Age-related Course of Urinary Gonadotropins in Children," *Journal of Clinical Endocrinology & Metabolism*, 80(4):1457-60, 1995.

44. J.S. Finkelstein, R.M. Neer, B.M. Biller, J.D. Crawford, and A. Klibanski, "Osteopenia in Men with a History of Delayed Puberty," *New England Journal of Medicine,* 326(9):600-4, 1992.

45. Trinkaus and Shipman, *The Neanderthals*, p. 382-386 (ch. 20, note 22).

46. Y. Rak, "On the Differences Between the Two Pelvises of Mousterian Context from the Qafzeh and Kebara Caves, Israel," 1990, Am. J. Phys. Anthrop, 81, p. 323-332.

47. Day, *Guide to Fossil Man*, p. 39 (ch. 9, note 9).

48. Oakley et al., *Catalogue of Fossil Hominids*, Part II, Europe, p. 112 (ch. 9, note 3).

49. Mellars, *The Neanderthal Legacy*, p. 377 (ch. 20, note 14).

50. Von Koenigswald, *The Neanderthal Centenary*, p. 151-166 (ch. 9, note 4).

51. U.M. Chandrasekharan, S. Sankar, M.J. Glynias, S.S. Karnik, and A. Husain, "Angiotensin II-forming Activity in a Reconstructed Ancestral Chymase," *Science*, 1996, 271, p. 502-505.

52. See Research Note 2, Chapter 33.

53. T.M. Jerman, J.G. Optiz, J. Stackhouse, and S.A. Benner, "Reconstructing the Evolutionary History of the Artiodactyl Ribonuclease Superfamily, *Nature,* 1995, 374, p. 57-59.

Research Notes

1. F.C. Howell, "The Evolutionary Significance of Variation and Varieties of Neanderthal Man," Quar. Rev. Biol. 32(4):330-347, 1957.

2. Cuozzo, "Earlier Orthodontic Intervention: A View from Prehistory" (ch. 28, note 55).

3. Broadbent et al., *Bolton Standards of Dentofacial Developmental Growth* (ch. 28, note 26).

4. C.E. Corliss, *Patten's, Human Embryology* (New York: McGraw-Hill Book Co., Blakiston Pub., 1976), p. 184.

5. Cuozzo, "Neanderthal Children's Fossils: Reconstruction and Interpretation. . ." (ch. 17, note 9).

6. Measured from Bolton Standard 4 year old tracing with magnification factor of .9470, Broadbent et al., *Bolton Standards of Dentofacial Developmental Growth* (ch. 28, note 26).

Notes — Research Notes, Contd.

7. Day, *Guide to Fossil Man*, 1st edition, p. 37-42 (ch. 9, note 7).
8. Day, *Guide to Fossil Man* , 4th edition, p. 31-36 (ch. 9, note 9).
9. F. Weidenreich, *Trend of Human Evolution* (New York: Washburn and Wolffson, Viking Fund Memorial Volume, 1949), p. 9.
10. M.L. Weiss and A.E. Mann, *Human Biology and Behavior, An Anthropological Perspective*, 4th edition (New York: Little Brown and Company, 1985), p. 313.
11. Marvin Lubenow, *Bones of Contention* (Grand Rapids, MI: Baker Book House, 1992), p. 76-77.
12. T.H. Newton and D.G. Potts, *Radiology of the Skull and Brain*, Vol. 1 Book 2 (St. Louis, MO: C.V. Mosby Co., 1971), p. 680-681.
13. J. Edeiken, *Roentgen Diagnosis of Diseases of Bone*, Vol. II, 3rd edition (Baltimore, MD: Williams and Wilkins, 1981), p. 860-861.
14. Lubenow, *Bones of Contention*, p. 77 (research notes, note 11).
15. Ivanhoe, "Was Virchow Right About Neandertal?" (ch. 9, note 6).
16. A. Walker, tape recording.
17. Lubenow, *Bones of Contention*, p. 77 (research notes, note 11).
18. D.J.M. Wright, "Syphilis and Neanderthal Man," *Nature,* Vol. 229, February 5, 1971, p. 409.
19. Ennis and Berry, *Dental Roentgenology*, p. 166-167 (ch. 33, note 19).
20. D.J. Ortner and A.C. Aufderheide, *Human Paleopathology* (Washington, DC: Smithsonian Institution Press, 1991), "Intrepretations of General Problems in Amelogensis," by A.A. Dahlberg, p. 269-272.
21. R.D. Feigin and J.D. Cherry, *Textbook of Pediatric Infectious Diseases*, 2nd edition (Philadelphia, PA: WB Saunders Co., 1987), p. 612-614.
22. M.E. Shils and V.R. Young, *Modern Nutrition in Health and Disease*, 7th edition (Philadelphia, PA: Lea & Febiger, 1988), p. 313-327.
23. Ibid., p. 315.
24. M.J. Kupersmith, C. Rosenberg, and D. Kleinberg, "Visual Loss in Pregnant Women with Pituitary Adenomas," Ann. Internal Medicine (121)7, October 1994, p. 473-477.
25. Day, *Guide to Fossil Man*, 4th edition, p. 269 (ch. 9, note 9).
26. Stringer and Gamble, *In Search of the Neanderthals*, p. 126 (ch. 16, note 12).
27. Mellars and Stringer, *The Human Revolution,* jacket cover (ch. 15, note 2).
28. Garrod et al., "Excavation of a Mousterian Rock Shelter at Devil's Tower, Gibraltar," p. 33-91 (ch. 16, note 16).
29. Gore, "Neanderthals" (ch. 28, note 36).
30. Most of this paragraph is from Cuozzo, "Neanderthal Children's Fossils: Reconstruction and Interpretation. . . ," p. 166-178 (ch. 17, note 9).
31. Dean, Stringer, and Broomage, "Age at Death of the Neanderthal Child. . ." (ch. 16, note 15).
32. Moorrees et al., "Age Variation of Formation Stages for Ten Permanent Teeth" (ch. 28, note 7).
33. Fraipont, "Les Hommes Fossiles D'Engis" (ch. 19, note 4).
34. Moorrees et al., "Age Variation of Formation Stages for Ten Permanent Teeth" (ch. 28, note 7).
35. Fraipont, "Les Hommes Fossiles D'Engis" (ch. 19, note 4).
36. A.M. Tillier, "Le Crâne d'enfant d'Engis II; Un exemple de distribution des charactères juvéniles, primitifs et néanderthaliens," *Bulletin DeLa Société Royale Belge d'Anthropologie et de Préhistoire*, Tome 94, Bruxelles, 1983, p. 53.
37. Tattersall, *The Last Neanderthal*, p. 79 (ch. 23, note 1).

38. Trinkaus and Villemeur, "Mechanical Advantages of the Neanderthal Thumb. . ." (ch. 20, note 3).

39. John W. Cuozzo, "Asymmetric Adult Growth and Mechanical Advantage in the Etiology of the Myofacial Pain Dysfunction Syndrome: A Case Report," *Journal of the NJ Dental Association,* Autumn 1991, p. 23-31.

40. Day, *Guide to Fossil Man,* 4th edition, p. 40 (ch. 9, note 9).

41. Trinkaus, *The Shanidar Neanderthals,* pg. 272 (ch. 31, note 25).

42. Hublin et al., "A Late Neanderthal Associated with Upper Paleolithic Artifacts" (ch. 20, note 12).

43. R.F. Weaver and P.W. Hedrick, *Genetics* (Dubuque, IA: W.C. Brown Pub., 1989), p. 28-29 and 522-523.

44. Oakley et al., *Catalogue of Fossil Hominids, Part II, Europe,* p. 104 (ch. 9, note 3).

45. Alfred Romer, *Vertebrate Paleontology,* 3rd edition (Chicago, IL: University of Chicago Press, 1966), p. 103.

46. T.R. Smithson, "The Earliest Reptile," *Nature,* Letters to Nature, (342) December 7, 1989, p. 676-677.

47. Romer, *Vertebrate Paleontology,* p. 312 (research notes, note 45).

48. Jarcho, "Die Altersveranderungen der Rassenmerkmale bei den Erwachsenen" (ch. 27, note 6).

49. Parchappe, "Reserches sur l'encéphale" (ch. 27, note 4).

50. Hrdlicka, "Growth During Adult Life" (ch. 27, note 3).

51. Ibid.

52. C.E. Nasjleti and C.J. Kowalski, "Stability of the Upper Face Height — Total Face Height Ratio with Increasing Age," *Journal of Dental Research,* 1975, 54(6), p. 1241.

53. C.J. Kowalski and C.E. Nasjleti, "Upper Face Height — Total Face Height Ratio in Adult American Black Males," *Journal of Dental Research,* 1976, 55(5), p. 913.

54. H. Israel, "The Dichotomous Pattern of Craniofacial Expansion During Aging," Am. J. Phys. Anthrop., 1977, 47(1), p. 47-51.

55. Behrents, "Growth in the Aging Craniofacial Skeleton" (ch. 27, note 28).
Behrents, "An Atlas of Growth in the Aging Craniofacial Skeleton" (ch. 27, note 29).

56. J.T. Cook, editor, *Transactions of the Third International Orthodontic Congress* (St. Louis, MO: C.V. Mosby Co., 1975), "Bolton Standards: Chronological Norms in Clinical Application," by B.H. Broadbent Jr.

57. Behrents, "Growth in the Aging Craniofacial Skeleton," p. 128 (ch. 27, note 28).

58. Behrents, "An Atlas of Growth in the Aging Craniofacial Skeleton," p. 94 (ch. 27, note 29).

59. Carlson and Van Gerven, "Masticatory Function and Post-Pleistocene Evolution in Nubia" (ch. 31, note 24).

60. Sicher, *Oral Anatomy,* p. 284-285 (ch. 30, note 18).

61. Murphy, "Compensatory Mechanisms in Facial Height Adjustment to Functional Tooth Attrition" (ch. 30, note 32).

62. Bishara et al., "Facial and Dental Changes in Adulthood" (ch. 27, note 1).

63. A. Bjork and S. Helm, "Prediction of the Age of Maximum Puberal Growth in Body Height," *Angle Orthodontist,* 1967, 37:2, p. 134-143.

64. Liversidge et al., "Increasing Human Tooth Length Between Birth and 5.4 Years" (ch. 28, note 13).

65. Kelley and Larsen, *Advances in Dental Anthropology,* "Standards of Human Tooth Formation and Dental Age Assessment," by Kronfeld, Table 1, (1935), p. 147 (ch. 28, note 16).
Schour and Massler, *Development of the Human Dentition Chart* (ch. 28, note 11).

66. Gore, "Neanderthals" (ch. 28, note 36).

Notes — Research Notes, Contd.

67. Cuozzo, "Neanderthal Children's Fossils: Reconstruction and Interpretation. . ." (ch. 17, note 9).
68. Zollikofer et al., *Nature,* cover and correspondence (ch. 28, note 37).
69. Enlow, *Handbook of Facial Growth*, p. 44 (ch. 28, note 10).
70. Broadbent et al., *Bolton Standards of Dentofacial Developmental Growth*, p. 65 (ch. 28, note 26).
71. Enlow, *Handbook of Facial Growth* , p. 310 (ch. 28, note 10).
72. Cedarquist, "Craniofacial Description of Wainwright Alaskan Eskimos" (ch. 28, note 47).
73. Watnick, "Inheritance of Craniofacial Morphology" (ch. 28, note 52).
74. H.P. Chang, Z. Kinoshita, and T. Kawamoto, "A Study of the Growth Changes in Facial Configuration," *European Journal of Orthodontics*, 15(6), p. 493-501, December 1993.
75. Z. Muretic and D. Rak, "Changes in the Value of the Mandibular Angle and its Segments During Growth," *Acta Stomatologica Croatica*, 25(4) 1991, p. 219-224.
76. T.F. Foley and A.H. Mamandras, "Facial Growth in Females 14 to 20 Years of Age," Am. Journ. Orthod. & Dento.Fac. Orthoped., 101(3), p. 248-254, March 1992.
77. H. Klaatsch and O. Hauser, "Homo Mousteriensis Hauseri," Archiv fur Anthro. Volkerforshung, und Kobnialen Kulturwandel, 1909, 35, p. 287-297.
78. E. Rebato, J. Rosique, and A. Gonzalez-Apraiz, "Age at Menarche from a Biscayan Coastal Population (Basque Country)," *Annals of Human Biology*, 20(2), 1993, p. 191-3.
79. F.J. Soriguer,S. Gonzalez-Romero, J.A. Esteva, F. Garcia-Arnés, F. Tinahones, M.S. Ruiz De Adana, G. Oliveira, I. Mancha, and F. Vasques, "Does the Intake of Nuts and Seeds Alter the Appearance of Menarche?" Acta, Obstetrica et Gynecologica Scandinavica, 74(6), 1995, p. 455-461.
80. I. Dober and L. Kiralyfalvi, "Pubertal Development in South-Hungarian Boys and Girls," *Annals of Human Biology*, 20(1), 1993, p. 71-74.
81. G. Zoppi, "Physiology of Pubertal Maturation," *Pediatria Medicae Chirurgica*, 14(4),1992, p. 375-379.
82. F.O. Dare, S.O. Ogunniyi, and O.O. Makinde, "Biosocial Factors Affecting Menarche in a Mixed Nigerian Population," *Central African Journal of Medicine*, 38(2), 1992, p. 77-81.
83. R.M. Malina, R.C. Ryan, and C.M. Bonci, "Age at Menarche in Athletes and Their Mothers and Sisters," *Annals of Human Biology*, 21(5) 1994, p. 417-422.
84. P. Nikolova, Z. Stoyanov, and N. Negrev, "Functional Brain Asymmetry, Handedness, and Menarcheal Age," Int. Journal of Psychophysiology, 18(3),1994, p. 213-215.
85. M. Henneberg and G.J. Louw, "Average Menarcheal Age of Higher Socioeconomic Status Urban Cape Coloured Girls Assessed by Means of Status Quo and Recall Methods," *American Journal of Physical Anthropology*, 96(1), 1995, p. 1-5.
86. I.M. St. George, S. Williams, and P.A. Silva, "Body size and Menarche: The Dunedin Study," *Journal of Adolescent Health*, 15(7), 1994, p. 573-576.
87. C.J. Goldberg, F.E. Dowling, and E.E. Fogarty, "Adolescent Idiopathic Scoliosis — Early Menarche, Normal Growth," *Spine*, 18(5), 1993, p. 529-535.
88. L.A. Proos, Y. Hofvander, and T. Tuvemo, "Menarcheal Age and Growth Pattern of Indian Girls Adopted in Sweden, I Menarcheal Age," *Acta Pediatrica Scandanavica,* 80 (8-9), 1991, p. 852-858.
89. J.J. Li, "A Study of Developmental Order of Secondary Sexual Characteristics in Beijing Girls," *Chinese Journal of Preventive Medicine*, 25(1), 1991, p. 23-25.
90. M.D. Wheeler, "Physical Changes of Puberty," *Endocrinology and Metabolism Clinics of North America,* 20(1), 1991, p. 1-14.

91. E.J. Clegg, "The Growth of Melanesian and Indian children in Fiji," *Annals of Human Biology*, 16(6),1989, p. 507-528.

92. H. Danker-Hopfe and K. Delibalta, "Menarcheal Age of Turkish Girls in Bremen," *Anthropologischer Anzeiger*, 48(1), 1990, p. 1-14.

93. Cuozzo, "Neanderthal Children's Fossils: Reconstruction and Interpretation. . ." (ch. 17, note 9).

94. Bishara et al., "Facial and Dental Changes in Adulthood" (ch. 27, note 1).

95. Whittaker et al., "Quantitative Assessment of Tooth Wear, Alveloar Crest. . ." (ch. 31, note 33).

96. Whittaker et al., "Continuing Tooth Eruption and Alveolar Crest Height. . ." (ch. 30, note 24).

97. Ibid.

98. Murphy, "Compensatory Mechanisms in Facial Height Adjustment. . ." (ch. 30, note 32).

99. Whittaker et al., "Continuing Tooth Eruption and Alveolar Crest Height. . ." (ch. 30, note 24).

100. Athenstaedt, "Pyroelectric and Piezoelectric Behaviour of Human Dental Hard Tissues" (ch. 31, note 17).

101. Personal communication, Thomas Kotch, Ph.D, Professor of Inorganic Chemistry, Cedarcrest College, PA.

102. Kelley and Larsen, *Advances in Dental Anthropology*, "Anthropological Aspects of Orofacial and Occlusal Variations and Anomalies," by R.S. Corruccini, p. 295-323 (ch. 28, note 16).

103. Krogman, "Dental Arch Form and Facial Growth Pattern. . . ," p. 1278-1289 (ch. 16, note 14).

104. J.S. Kelly and C.R. Harvey, "An Assessment of the Occlusion of Youths 12-17 Years," *USPHS Vital and Health Statistics*, Ser. 11, 1977, No. 162.

105. M. Massler and J.M. Frankel, "Prevalence of Malocclusion in Children Aged 14-18 Years," Amer. J. Orthod., 1951, 37, p. 751-768.

106. J.L. Ackerman and W.R. Proffit, "Preventive and Interceptive Orthodontics: A Strong Theory Proves Weak in Practice," *Angle Orthod.*, 1980, 50(2), p. 75-87.

107. Krogman, "Dental Arch Form and Facial Growth Pattern. . ." (ch. 16, note 14).

108. Ennis and Berry, *Dental Roentgenology*, p. 67-117 (ch. 33, note 19).

109. Tillier, "Les enfants néanderthaliens de Devil's Tower Gibraltar," p. 125-148 (ch. 28, note 3).
   Tillier, "L a Dentition de l'Enfant Mousterian Chateauneuf 2 Decouverte. . ." (ch. 31, note 39).

110. Zilberman and Smith, "A Comparison of Tooth Structure in Early Neanderthals. . ." (ch. 31, note 26).

111. Moyers et al., "Standards of Occlusal Development," p. 45 (ch. 31, note 41).

112. Chandrasekharan et al., "Angiotensin II-forming Activity in a Reconstructed Ancestral Chymase" (ch. 33, note 50).

113. Ibid.

114. Yen and Jaffe, *Reproductive Endocrinology*, p. 243 (ch. 29, note 8).

Index

About the author

Dr. Jack Cuozzo studied at Georgetown University (biology major, philosophy minor) and obtained degrees from the University of Pennsylvania (D.D.S.) and Loyola University/Chicago Graduate School of Dentistry (M.S., Oral Biology; Certificate of Speciality in Orthodontics). He served as a lieutenant in the U.S. Navy, aboard the USS Enterprise CVAN(65). An orthodontist in the New Jersey area for 31 years, Dr. Cuozzo also served for two years as head of the orthodontic section, and two years as assistant director of the dental department at Mountainside Hospital, in Montclair, New Jersey. He and his wife, Diane, have five grown children and three granddaughters.